WORKBOOK
IN SPANISH TWO YEARS

Second Edition

By **ROBERT J. NASSI**

Former Teacher of Spanish
Los Angeles Valley Junior College, Los Angeles, California

and

BERNARD BERNSTEIN

Former Chairman of the Department of Foreign Languages
Martin Van Buren High School, New York City

When ordering this book, please specify:

either

R 45 W

or

WORKBOOK IN SPANISH TWO YEARS

AMSCO SCHOOL PUBLICATIONS, INC.

315 Hudson Street   New York, N. Y. 10013

ISBN 0-87720-506-X

Copyright 1957, 1969 © by
AMSCO SCHOOL PUBLICATIONS, Inc.

Revised 1993

PRINTED IN THE UNITED STATES OF AMERICA

PREFACE

This *Workbook in Spanish Two Years* is offered with a two-fold purpose: (1) To present in concise form, for review, the topics usually taken in Levels I and II; (2) To provide a variety of effective, workable exercises, to help attain mastery of each specific point reviewed.

It contains all topics prescribed in the New York State and New York City Syllabi for Levels I and II. Additional topics are treated, which are not prescribed in either of these syllabi, but which are included for completeness. These topics are labeled as "Optional."

The book is organized in units: Verbs, Grammatical Structures, Idioms, Vocabulary Building, and Civilization. Each unit is divided into lessons, each of which focuses attention on a specific point to be reviewed. This presentation permits the teacher to assign for review any lesson, without the necessity of considering the position of the topic in the normal sequence of instruction. Many of the exercises are in such form as to permit either oral or written treatment.

The following additional features should be mentioned:

1. A set of Mastery Exercises following each section, to provide a comprehensive review of the complete section. These may be used for testing purposes, either as a class activity, or for self-testing by pupils.

2. Special sections which provide copious practice in auditory and reading comprehension.

3. A section on Directed (Guided) Composition, dealing with topics related to the pupil's experience and daily life. Numerous vocabulary aids are supplied.

4. A chart of irregular verbs, classified according to the type of irregularity.

5. A Spanish-English vocabulary list, which includes all the words used in the exercises; also an English-Spanish vocabulary list, as an aid in working out the English-Spanish exercises.

To maintain student interest and increase insight into the life and ways of the foreign peoples, numerous "cultural bits"—skilfully illustrated—have been interspersed throughout the book. For their kindness in providing our artist with photographs for the making of the illustrations, we are grateful to: Puerto Rico Information Service, Moore-McCormack Lines, Mexican National Tourist Council, Spanish National Tourist Office.

Finally, this workbook offers the advantage of permitting the student to write directly in the spaces provided for answers, thus eliminating the need for a separate notebook; the answers, after correction, will afford a unified review in compact form. Of course, the teacher may, at any time, decide to have the answers written on separate sheets of paper and collect them for grading.

Teachers and students alike, it is hoped, will find this book a helpful supplement to the regular textbook.

—The Authors

CONTENTS

Part I—*Verb*s

Lesson   *Page*

1. PRESENT INDICATIVE OF REGULAR VERBS.............................. 1

Common -*AR* Verbs.. 1
Common -*ER* Verbs.. 2
Common -*IR* Verbs.. 2

2. PRESENT INDICATIVE OF IRREGULAR VERBS........................... 5

3. IDIOMATIC USE OF THE PRESENT INDICATIVE......................... 8

4. PRETERITE OF REGULAR VERBS...................................... 11

Common -*AR* Verbs Regular in the Preterite...................... 11
Common -*ER* Verbs Regular in the Preterite...................... 11
Common -*IR* Verbs Regular in the Preterite...................... 11

5. PRETERITE OF IRREGULAR VERBS.................................... 14

6. IMPERFECT INDICATIVE.. 18

Regular Verbs... 18
Irregular Verbs... 18

7. USES OF THE PRETERITE AND IMPERFECT............................. 21

8. STEM-CHANGING VERBS (CLASS I)................................... 25

Common Stem-Changing Verbs (Class I)............................ 25

9. STEM-CHANGING VERBS (CLASS II).................................. 30

Common Stem-Changing Verbs (Class II)........................... 30

10. STEM-CHANGING VERBS (CLASS III)................................ 34

Common Stem-Changing Verbs (Class III).......................... 34

11. THE FUTURE TENSE... 38

Regular Verbs... 38
Irregular Verbs... 38
Uses of the Future Tense.. 38

12. THE CONDITIONAL.. 42

Regular Verbs... 42
Irregular Verbs... 42
Uses of the Conditional... 42

13. THE PRESENT PARTICIPLE (GERUND)................................ 46

Present Participles of Regular Verbs............................ 46
Present Participles Ending in -*YENDO*.......................... 46
Present Participles of Stem-Changing Verbs...................... 46
Progressive Tenses.. 46

14. THE PAST PARTICIPLE; THE PRESENT PERFECT AND PLUPERFECT
TENSES.. 50

Past Participles of Regular Verbs............................... 50
Past Participles Ending in -*ÍDO*............................... 50
Irregular Past Participles Ending in -*TO*...................... 50
Irregular Past Participles Ending in -*CHO*..................... 50
Present Perfect Tense... 50

Lesson	*Page*
Pluperfect Tense	50
15. THE FUTURE PERFECT AND THE CONDITIONAL PERFECT (OPTIONAL)	55
Future Perfect Tense	55
Conditional Perfect	55
16. *ESTAR* AND *SER*	58
Uses of *ESTAR*	58
Uses of *SER*	58
17. REFLEXIVE VERBS	62
Common Reflexive Verbs	63
18. POLITE COMMANDS WITH *VD.* AND *VDS*	67
19. VERBS ENDING IN *-CAR*, *-GAR*, AND *-ZAR*	70
Common *-CAR* Verbs	70
Common *-GAR* Verbs	70
Common *-ZAR* Verbs	70
20. VERBS ENDING IN *-GER*, *-GIR*, AND *-GUIR*	73
Common *-GER* Verbs	73
Common *-GIR* Verbs	73
Common *-GUIR* Verbs	73
21. VERBS ENDING IN *-CER* AND *-CIR*	76
Common *-CER* Verbs	76
Common *-CIR* Verbs	76
22. VERBS ENDING IN *-IAR*, *-UAR*, AND *-UIR*	79
23. THE PASSIVE EXPRESSED BY A REFLEXIVE CONSTRUCTION; INDEFINITE *SE*	83
24. THE PASSIVE VOICE (OPTIONAL)	86
25. FORMATION OF THE PRESENT SUBJUNCTIVE	89
Regular Verbs	89
Stem-Changing Verbs	89
Consonant-Changing Verbs	90
Irregular Verbs	90
26. FORMATION OF THE IMPERFECT SUBJUNCTIVE (OPTIONAL)	94
Stem-Changing *-IR* Verbs	94
Verbs Irregular in the Preterite	95
27. POLITE AND INDIRECT COMMANDS	97
28. THE SUBJUNCTIVE AFTER CERTAIN VERBS	100
29. SEQUENCE OF TENSES (OPTIONAL)	104
30. THE SUBJUNCTIVE AFTER IMPERSONAL EXPRESSIONS	107
31. THE SUBJUNCTIVE AFTER CERTAIN CONJUNCTIONS (OPTIONAL)	111
32. THE SUBJUNCTIVE AFTER AN INDEFINITE OR NEGATIVE ANTECEDENT (OPTIONAL)	114
33. "IF" CLAUSES (OPTIONAL)	116
34. FAMILIAR COMMANDS	118
Regular Verbs	118
Irregular Verbs	118
35. MASTERY EXERCISES	120

Part II—*Grammatical Structures*

Lesson   *Page*

1. FORMS AND CONTRACTIONS OF THE ARTICLES; POSSESSION.............. 126

   Forms of the Definite and Indefinite Articles........................... 126
   Agreement of Articles.. 126
   Repetition of Articles... 126
   Contractions of the Article *EL*....................................... 126
   Possession.. 127

2. USES OF THE DEFINITE ARTICLE.. 129

3. OMISSION OF THE ARTICLES... 133

   Omission of the Definite Article....................................... 133
   Omission of the Indefinite Article..................................... 133

4. THE NEUTER ARTICLE *LO*... 136

5. NOUNS... 139

   Gender of Nouns... 139
   Plural of Nouns.. 139
   Nouns Describing Materials or Contents................................. 140

6. THE PERSONAL *A*... 142

7. POSITION AND AGREEMENT OF ADJECTIVES........................... 145

   Forms of Adjectives.. 145
   Position of Adjectives... 145
   Agreement of Adjectives.. 145

8. ADVERBS.. 149

9. POSSESSIVE ADJECTIVES... 151

10. POSSESSIVE PRONOUNS.. 154

11. DEMONSTRATIVE ADJECTIVES.. 157

12. DEMONSTRATIVE PRONOUNS.. 159

13. COMPARISON OF ADJECTIVES.. 161

    Translation of *THAN*.. 161
    Adjectives Compared Irregularly...................................... 161

14. EXPRESSIONS OF EQUALITY.. 165

15. THE ABSOLUTE SUPERLATIVE (OPTIONAL)............................... 168

16. SHORTENING OF ADJECTIVES.. 170

17. PERSONAL PRONOUNS AFTER PREPOSITIONS............................ 173

18. SINGLE OBJECT PRONOUNS.. 176

    Direct Object Pronouns... 176
    Indirect Object Pronouns... 176
    Position of Object Pronouns.. 176

19. DOUBLE OBJECT PRONOUNS.. 181

    Position of Double Object Pronouns................................... 181

20. INTERROGATIVE WORDS... 185

21. RELATIVE PRONOUNS AND ADJECTIVES.................................. 188

22. NEGATIVE WORDS.. 191

    Idiomatic Negative Expressions....................................... 191

23. CARDINAL NUMBERS.. 195

    Arithmetic Expressions... 196

Lesson   *Page*

24. ORDINAL NUMBERS... 200
25. DATES... 203
    Months of the Year... 203
26. TIME EXPRESSIONS.. 206
    Other Time Expressions... 206
27. THE USE OF PREPOSITIONS BEFORE INFINITIVES........................... 209
    Verbs Requiring the Preposition *A* Before an Infinitive................. 209
    Verbs Requiring the Preposition *DE* Before an Infinitive............... 209
    Verbs Requiring the Preposition *EN* Before an Infinitive............... 209
    Other Common Prepositions.. 210
    Verbs Requiring No Preposition Before an Infinitive.................... 210
28. *PARA* AND *POR*.. 213
    Uses of *PARA*... 213
    Uses of *POR*.. 213
    ESTAR PARA and *ESTAR POR*... 213
29. MASTERY EXERCISES... 216

Part III—*Idioms*

1. IDIOMS WITH *DAR*.. 221
2. THE VERB *GUSTAR*.. 224
3. IDIOMS WITH *HABER*.. 227
4. IDIOMS WITH *HACER*.. 230
5. IDIOMS WITH *TENER*.. 233
    Idioms in Which *TENER* = To Be...................................... 233
    Other Idioms with *TENER*.. 234
6. MISCELLANEOUS VERBAL IDIOMS—I.. 237
7. MISCELLANEOUS VERBAL IDIOMS—II... 241
8. MISCELLANEOUS VERBAL IDIOMS—III.. 245
9. IDIOMS WITH *A*.. 249
10. IDIOMS WITH *DE*.. 253
11. IDIOMS WITH *EN*.. 256
12. IDIOMS WITH *POR*... 260
13. IDIOMS WITH *VEZ*... 263
14. MISCELLANEOUS IDIOMATIC EXPRESSIONS—I................................. 266
15. MISCELLANEOUS IDIOMATIC EXPRESSIONS—II................................ 270
16. MASTERY EXERCISES... 274

Part IV—*Vocabulary Building*

1. SYNONYMS.. 282
2. ANTONYMS.. 286
3. WORDS FREQUENTLY CONFUSED... 295
4. WORD BUILDING... 298
5. CLASSIFIED VOCABULARY... 302
6. MASTERY EXERCISES... 313

Part V—*Hispanic Civilization*

Lesson   *Page*

1. LA GEOGRAFÍA DE ESPAÑA...... 317
2. LA HISTORIA DE ESPAÑA...... 322
3. LA LITERATURA ESPAÑOLA...... 325
4. ARTE, MÚSICA, Y CIENCIAS...... 327
5. LA VIDA Y LAS COSTUMBRES ESPAÑOLAS...... 330
6. MASTERY EXERCISES ON SPAIN...... 333
7. LA GEOGRAFÍA DE LA AMÉRICA HISPANA...... 336
    México...... 336
    La América Central...... 338
    Las Antillas...... 338
    La América Del Sur...... 340
8. LA HISTORIA DE HISPANOAMÉRICA...... 346
9. LA LITERATURA, EL ARTE, Y LA MÚSICA DE HISPANOAMÉRICA...... 349
10. LA VIDA Y LAS COSTUMBRES DE HISPANOAMÉRICA...... 352
11. MASTERY EXERCISES ON SPANISH AMERICA...... 354

Part VI

Auditory Comprehension...... 357

Part VII

Passages for Reading Comprehension...... 363

Part VIII

Practice in Directed Composition...... 378

Appendix

Irregular Verb Forms...... 384

Spanish-English Vocabulary...... 390

English-Spanish Vocabulary...... 401

Part I—*Verbs*

1. PRESENT INDICATIVE OF REGULAR VERBS

The present indicative of regular verbs is formed by:

1. dropping the infinitive ending **(-ar, -er, -ir).**

2. adding to the stem the following endings:

> **-ar** verbs: *-o, -as, -a, -amos, -áis, -an*
> **-er** verbs: *-o, -es, -e, -emos, -éis, -en*
> **-ir** verbs: *-o, -es, -e, -imos, -ís, -en*

	entrar, to enter	**comer,** to eat	**recibir,** to receive
	I enter, am entering, do enter, etc.	*I eat, am eating, do eat, etc.*	*I receive, am receiving, do receive, etc.*
yo	entr**o**	com**o**	recib**o**
tú	entr**as**	com**es**	recib**es**
Vd., él, ella	entr**a**	com**e**	recib**e**
nosotros, -as	entr**amos**	com**emos**	recib**imos**
vosotros, -as	entr**áis**	com**éis**	recib**ís**
Vds., ellos, -as	entr**an**	com**en**	recib**en**

Note

A. In a statement, the subject usually precedes the verb. In a question, the subject usually follows the verb.

> **Ellos comen** a las doce. They eat at twelve o'clock.
>
> *¿Comen ellos* a las doce? Do they eat at twelve o'clock?

B. Unless required for clarity or for emphasis, the subject pronouns may be omitted.

> Tengo mi lápiz. ¿Tiene Vd. mi libro? I have my pencil. Do you have my book?

COMMON *-AR* VERBS

ayudar, to help
bajar, to go down, to descend
borrar, to erase
buscar, to look for, to seek
caminar, to walk
cantar, to sing
comprar, to buy
contestar, to answer
cultivar, to cultivate
dejar, to let, to allow, to leave
desear, to want, to wish
enseñar, to teach, to show
entrar, to enter

escuchar, to listen (to)
esperar, to wait for, to await, to hope, to expect
estudiar, to study
explicar, to explain
gritar, to shout
hablar, to speak
hallar, to find
invitar, to invite
llenar, to fill
llevar, to carry, to wear
mirar, to look (at)
necesitar, to need

pagar, to pay (for)
pasar, to pass, to spend (time)
patinar, to skate
preguntar, to ask
preparar, to prepare
quitar, to take away
regresar, to return
tomar, to take, to eat, to drink
trabajar, to work
usar, to use
viajar, to travel
visitar, to visit

COMMON -*ER* VERBS

aprender, to learn

beber, to drink

comer, to eat

comprender, to understand

correr, to run

deber, to have to (should, ought), to owe

leer, to read

prometer, to promise

responder, to answer

vender, to sell

COMMON -*IR* VERBS

abrir, to open

asistir, to attend

decidir, to decide

escribir, to write

recibir, to receive

subir, to go up, to ascend, to climb

sufrir, to suffer

vivir, to live

EJERCICIOS

A. Traduzca Vd. al inglés las frases siguientes:

1. Beben chocolate. _____

2. María recibe un libro. _____

3. Abre la ventana. _____

4. Cultivan la tierra. _____

5. Vivo en la calle Alameda. _____

6. Halla diez centavos. _____

7. Borran la pizarra. _____

8. Subimos la escalera. _____

9. Patinan en el invierno. _____

10. Trabajan todos los días. _____

B. Escriba Vd. la forma correcta de los verbos *a*, *b*, y *c* en lugar del verbo en letra cursiva (italics).

Ejemplo: Juan no *trabaja* mucho.   (*a*) comer   (*b*) hablar   (*c*) estudiar

(*a*) _come_   (*b*) _habla_   (*c*) _estudia_

1. Yo *deseo* cantar.   (*a*) necesitar   (*b*) deber   (*c*) aprender a

(*a*) _____   (*b*) _____   (*c*) _____

2. Juan y yo *ayudamos* a la profesora.   (*a*) contestar   (*b*) escribir   (*c*) escuchar

(*a*) _____   (*b*) _____   (*c*) _____

3. Las alumnas *caminan* a la escuela.   (*a*) correr   (*b*) asistir   (*c*) regresar

(*a*) _____   (*b*) _____   (*c*) _____

4. Tú no *estudias* la lección.   (*a*) leer   (*b*) enseñar   (*c*) preparar

(*a*) _____   (*b*) _____   (*c*) _____

5. Pedro *decide* comprar un auto.   (*a*) prometer   (*b*) esperar   (*c*) desear

(*a*) _____   (*b*) _____   (*c*) _____

6. ¿Quién *necesita* tinta?   (*a*) usar   (*b*) vender   (*c*) comprar

(*a*) _____   (*b*) _____   (*c*) _____

7. ¿*Gritan* Vds. a sus vecinos?   (*a*) hablar   (*b*) mirar   (*c*) comprender

(*a*) _____   (*b*) _____   (*c*) _____

8. Nosotros *debemos* trabajar.   (*a*) desear   (*b*) aprender a   (*c*) decidir

(*a*) _____   (*b*) _____   (*c*) _____

9. *¿Toma* Vd. un taxi?   (*a*) buscar   (*b*) esperar   (*c*) necesitar

(*a*) _____   (*b*) _____   (*c*) _____

10. Ana *visita* a su amiga.   (*a*) responder   (*b*) escuchar   (*c*) comprender

(*a*) _____   (*b*) _____   (*c*) _____

C. Conteste Vd. en español en frases completas.

1. ¿Canta Vd. bien? _____

2. ¿Quién explica la lección? _____

3. ¿Come Vd. mucho? _____

4. ¿Entran Vds. en la escuela a tiempo? _____

_____

5. ¿Invita Vd. a sus amigos a visitarle algunas veces? _____

_____

6. ¿Llevan falda los muchachos? _____

7. ¿Pasa Vd. mucho tiempo en la biblioteca? _____

_____

8. ¿Viaja Vd. mucho en automóvil? _____

9. ¿En qué ciudad vive Vd.? _____

10. ¿Responden Vds. en inglés o en español? _____

D. Traduzca Vd. al español las expresiones en inglés.

1. *He leaves* los libros en la mesa.   _____

2. *They suffer* mucho.   _____

3. —¿Qué hora es?—*asks* el hombre.   _____

4. Mis amigos siempre *pay*.   _____

5. *We go down* a la calle.   _____

6. *She takes away* la naranja a (from) su hermanito.   _____

7. *I fill* los bolsillos. *pockets*   _____

8. *They work* en una oficina.   _____

9. *We are traveling* a México.   _____

10. *I live* en los Estados Unidos.   _____

11. Los niños *run* en el parque.   _____

12. Cada día *he takes* una taza de té.   _____

13. *I am selling* la casa.   _____

14. ¿Qué *are you* (tú) *buying?*   _____

15. Pedro *does not help* a sus amigos.   _____

16. El profesor *teaches* bien la lección.   _____

17. La niña *drinks* mucha leche.   _____

18. Los alumnos *speak* inglés y español. -------------------------------

19. Nosotros *receive* muchas cartas. -------------------------------

20. *She is eating* una pera. -------------------------------

E. Traduzca Vd. al español.

1. They study every day. -------------------------------

2. They enter the class. -------------------------------

3. Why don't you (tú) sell the house? -------------------------------

4. She looks at the picture. -------------------------------

5. We attend this school. -------------------------------

6. They use gloves. -------------------------------

7. The pupils answer in a loud voice. -------------------------------

8. What are you* looking for? -------------------------------

9. Every year she travels. -------------------------------

10. Paul is erasing the blackboard. -------------------------------

*In these exercises, *you* as subject pronoun is to be translated by **Vd.** and *you* (*pl.*) by **Vds.,** unless otherwise indicated.

Miguel de Cervantes Saavedra (1547-1616) fue el novelista más importante de España y uno de los escritores principales del mundo. Su obra maestra, *Don Quijote de la Mancha,* ha sido traducida a casi todos los idiomas. Es una novela que nos muestra un panorama de la sociedad española del siglo XVI y de la raza humana en general.

2. PRESENT INDICATIVE OF IRREGULAR VERBS

1. The following verbs are irregular only in the first person singular of the present indicative:

caber, to fit:	*quepo,* cabes, cabe, cabemos, cabéis, caben
caer, to fall:	*caigo,* caes, cae, caemos, caéis, caen
dar, to give:	*doy,* das, da, damos, dais, dan
hacer, to do, to make:	*hago,* haces, hace, hacemos, hacéis, hacen
poner, to put:	*pongo,* pones, pone, ponemos, ponéis, ponen
saber, to know:	*sé,* sabes, sabe, sabemos, sabéis, saben
salir, to leave, to go out:	*salgo,* sales, sale, salimos, salís, salen
traer, to bring:	*traigo,* traes, trae, traemos, traéis, traen
valer, to be worth:	*valgo,* vales, vale, valemos, valéis, valen
ver, to see:	*veo,* ves, ve, vemos, veis, ven

2. Other verbs that are irregular in the present indicative are:

decir, to say, to tell:	*digo, dices, dice,* decimos, decís, *dicen*
estar, to be:	*estoy, estás, está,* estamos, estáis, *están*
ir, to go:	*voy, vas, va, vamos, vais, van*
oír, to hear:	*oigo, oyes, oye,* oímos, oís, *oyen*
ser, to be:	*soy, eres, es,* somos, sois, son
tener, to have:	*tengo, tienes, tiene,* tenemos, tenéis, *tienen*
venir, to come:	*vengo, vienes, viene,* venimos, venís, *vienen*

EJERCICIOS

A. Escriba Vd. la forma correcta de los verbos *a, b,* y *c* en lugar del verbo en letra cursiva.

EJEMPLO: Ellas *hablan* mucho.   (*a*) trabajar   (*b*) comer   (*c*) escribir

(*a*) *trabajan*   (*b*) *comen*   (*c*) *escriben*

1. Yo *escribo* la verdad.   (*a*) saber   (*b*) oír   (*c*) decir

(*a*) ------------------   (*b*) ------------------   (*c*) ------------------

2. ¿*Deseas* un regalo?   (*a*) dar   (*b*) traer   (*c*) tener

(*a*) ------------------   (*b*) ------------------   (*c*) ------------------

3. Yo *viajo* en abril.   (*a*) venir   (*b*) salir   (*c*) ir

(*a*) ------------------   (*b*) ------------------   (*c*) ------------------

4. *Valen* mucho.   (*a*) tener   (*b*) oír   (*c*) decir

(*a*) ------------------   (*b*) ------------------   (*c*) ------------------

5. Yo *aprendo* cosas interesantes.   (*a*) ver   (*b*) hacer   (*c*) comprar

(*a*) ------------------   (*b*) ------------------   (*c*) ------------------

6. Nosotros *trabajamos* en casa.   (*a*) estar   (*b*) entrar   (*c*) leer

(*a*) ------------------   (*b*) ------------------   (*c*) ------------------

7. Ella lo *prepara* en la cocina.   (*a*) hallar   (*b*) poner   (*c*) dejar

(*a*) ------------------   (*b*) ------------------   (*c*) ------------------

8. Los soldados no *sufren*.   (*a*) caer   (*b*) bajar   (*c*) ir

   (*a*) _____   (*b*) _____   (*c*) _____

9. Mi padre nunca *paga*.   (*a*) salir   (*b*) venir   (*c*) escuchar

   (*a*) _____   (*b*) _____   (*c*) _____

10. Yo *entro* en el cuarto.   (*a*) estar   (*b*) caber   (*c*) estudiar

   (*a*) _____   (*b*) _____   (*c*) _____

B. Cambie Vd. el infinitivo a las formas del presente de indicativo empleadas con los sujetos entre paréntesis.

1. *Ser* viejo.

   (tú) _____   (yo) _____   (Vd.) _____

2. *Oír* el ruido.

   (ellos) _____   (vosotros) _____   (yo) _____

3. *Ir* al parque.

   (ella) _____   (nosotros) _____   (yo) _____

4. *Decir* adiós.

   (yo) _____   (ellas) _____   (nosotros) _____

5. No *hacer* nada.

   (Juan y yo) _____   (vosotros) _____   (él) _____

6. *Venir* mañana.

   (yo) _____   (tú) _____   (nosotros) _____

7. *Estar* aquí.

   (Roberto) _____   (ellos) _____   (yo) _____

8. *Ver* el accidente.

   (nadie) _____   (yo) _____   (todos) _____

9. *Saber* bailar.

   (yo) _____   (mi profesor) _____   (ellas) _____

10. *Tener* una bicicleta.

   (nosotros) _____   (tú) _____   (ellas) _____

C. Conteste Vd. en español en frases completas.

1. ¿Es Vd. norteamericano(-a)? _____

2. ¿Trae Vd. dulces para su mamá? _____

   _____

3. ¿Cuánto vale su reloj? _____

4. ¿Sabe Vd. nadar? _____

5. ¿A qué hora sale Vd. de la escuela? _____

   _____

6. ¿Va Vd. al cine a menudo? _____

7. ¿Tiene su familia un automóvil? _____

_____

8. ¿Dice Vd. siempre la verdad? _____

_____

9. ¿Hace Vd. ejercicios todos los días? _____

_____

10. ¿Ve Vd. muchos aviones en un aeropuerto? _____

_____

11. ¿Qué dice Vd. al saludar a sus compañeros? _____

_____

12. ¿Es Vd. joven o viejo(-a)? _____

13. ¿Qué mes viene después de mayo? _____

14. ¿Pone su madre frutas en la mesa? _____

15. ¿Está Vd. cansado(-a)? _____

D. Traduzca Vd. al español las expresiones en inglés.

1. Los libros *do not fit* aquí. _____

2. Enrique y yo *are going* a España. _____

3. Yo *leave* de casa a las ocho. _____

4. *We have* un jardín bonito. _____

5. Yo *do not know* la respuesta. _____

6. Mi tío *is* rico. _____

7. Yo no *see* montañas aquí. _____

8. Él *hears* bien. _____

9. Nosotros siempre *come* temprano. _____

10. ¿Quién *is going* con Vds.? _____

E. Traduzca Vd. al español.

1. I am going to the country. _____

2. What are they saying? _____

3. The waiter is bringing coffee. _____

4. We are cousins. _____

5. How are you (tú)? _____

6. Have you many friends? _____

7. He falls down (por) the stairs. _____

8. I know how to play the piano. _____

9. He puts the newspaper on the table. _____

10. It is worth ten cents. _____

3. IDIOMATIC USE OF THE PRESENT INDICATIVE

Hace + *an expression of time* + **que** + *the present indicative* expresses an action that began in the past and continues into the present.

Hace una hora que lee.
    It   an hour that he is
   makes   reading

He has been reading for an hour.

Hace un mes que trabajo.
    It   a month that I am
  makes   working

I have been working for a month.

In asking how long someone has been doing something, *How long?* is translated by **¿Cuánto tiempo hace que . . . ?** followed by the present indicative.

¿Cuánto tiempo hace que lee?
 How   time   does that he is
 much   it   reading
               make

How long has he been reading?

¿Cuánto tiempo hace que Vd. trabaja?
 How   time   does that you are
 much   it   working
               make

How long have you been working?

EJERCICIOS

A. Escriba Vd. la forma correcta de los verbos *a*, *b*, y *c* en lugar del verbo en letra cursiva.

1. Hace una hora que *estudiamos*.   (*a*) bailar   (*b*) comer   (*c*) escribir

(*a*) ----------------------   (*b*) ----------------------   (*c*) ----------------------

2. Hace cinco días que *está* en casa.   (*a*) quedarse   (*b*) trabajar   (*c*) cenar

(*a*) ----------------------   (*b*) ----------------------   (*c*) ----------------------

3. ¿Cuánto tiempo hace que Vd. *aprende* esta lengua?   (*a*) escribir   (*b*) leer   (*c*) hablar

(*a*) ----------------------   (*b*) ----------------------   (*c*) ----------------------

4. ¿Hace mucho tiempo que no *hablas* a Tomás?   (*a*) ver   (*b*) saludar   (*c*) ayudar

(*a*) ----------------------   (*b*) ----------------------   (*c*) ----------------------

5. Hace dos años que *estudian* las matemáticas.   (*a*) enseñar   (*b*) aprender   (*c*) saber

(*a*) ----------------------   (*b*) ----------------------   (*c*) ----------------------

6. ¿Cuánto tiempo hace que *preparáis* la comida?   (*a*) comer   (*b*) cocinar   (*c*) tomar

(*a*) ----------------------   (*b*) ----------------------   (*c*) ----------------------

7. ¿Hace mucho tiempo que *descansas* aquí?   (*a*) vivir   (*b*) estar   (*c*) existir

(*a*) ----------------------   (*b*) ----------------------   (*c*) ----------------------

8. ¿Cuánto tiempo hace que el comerciante *vende* zapatos?   (*a*) comprar   (*b*) fabricar

(*c*) buscar

(*a*) ----------------------   (*b*) ----------------------   (*c*) ----------------------

9. Hace seis meses que *esperáis* en Madrid.   (*a*) vivir   (*b*) descansar   (*c*) trabajar

(*a*) ----------------------   (*b*) ----------------------   (*c*) ----------------------

10. ¿Cuánto tiempo hace que *tienen* calcetines de nilón?   (*a*) llevar   (*b*) vender   (*c*) usar

(*a*) ----------------------   (*b*) ----------------------   (*c*) ----------------------

B. Conteste Vd. en español en frases completas.

1. ¿Cuánto tiempo hace que Vd. estudia el español? _____

   _____

2. ¿Cuántas semanas hace que Vd. está en esta clase? _____

   _____

3. ¿Cuánto tiempo hace que Vd. asiste a esta escuela? _____

   _____

4. ¿Cuántos años hace que Vd. sabe nadar? _____

   _____

5. ¿Cuántos meses hace que Vd. posee un reloj? _____

   _____

6. ¿Cuánto tiempo hace que Vd. lleva anteojos? _____

   _____

7. ¿Hace mucho tiempo que Vd. toca un instrumento músico? _____

   _____

8. ¿Cuánto tiempo hace que Vd. sabe el alfabeto inglés? _____

   _____

9. ¿Cuántos años hace que nuestra nación existe? _____

   _____

10. ¿Cuánto tiempo hace que Vd. vive en este pueblo? _____

   _____

C. Complete Vd. las frases en español.

1. She has been teaching Spanish for ten years.

   Hace diez años que _____ el español.

2. How long have you been giving him money?

   ¿_____ Vd. le da dinero?

3. He has been visiting his cousin for three weeks.

   _____ a su primo.

4. How long has George been ill?

   ¿Cuánto tiempo hace que Jorge _____ enfermo?

5. Charlotte has been wanting that dress for a long time.

   Hace mucho tiempo que Carlota _____ aquel vestido.

6. They have been suffering for many years.

   _____ muchos años _____.

7. How long has he been working?

   ¿Cuánto _____?

8. You have had these books for two months.

   _____ dos meses _____ estos libros.

9. How long have you known that?

¿-- eso?

10. How long have you been going to that school?

¿-- a esa escuela?

D. Traduzca Vd. al español.

1. How long have you (tú) been reading?

----

2. How long has he been writing?

----

3. They have been traveling for six months.

----

4. I have been learning Spanish for two years.

----

5. He has been waiting for five minutes.

----

6. How long has she been talking?

----

7. We have been living here for a week.

----

8. How long has he been [a] doctor?

----

9. They have been in the room for an hour.

----

10. How long have you (pl.) been helping your friend?

----

4. PRETERITE OF REGULAR VERBS

The preterite of regular verbs is formed by:

1. dropping the infinitive ending (-ar, -er, -ir).

2. adding to the stem the following endings:

-ar verbs: *-é, -aste, -ó, -amos, -asteis, -aron*
-er verbs
-ir verbs } *-í, -iste, -ió, -imos, -isteis, -ieron*

	hablar, to speak	vender, to sell	abrir, to open
	I spoke, *did speak, etc.*	*I sold,* *did sell, etc.*	*I opened,* *did open, etc.*
yo	habl*é*	vend*í*	abr*í*
tú	habl*aste*	vend*iste*	abr*iste*
Vd., él, ella	habl*ó*	vend*ió*	abr*ió*
nosotros, -as	habl*amos*	vend*imos*	abr*imos*
vosotros, -as	habl*asteis*	vend*isteis*	abr*isteis*
Vds., ellos, -as	habl*aron*	vend*ieron*	abr*ieron*

COMMON *-AR* VERBS REGULAR IN THE PRETERITE

aceptar, to accept
acompañar, to accompany
acostarse, to go to bed
admirar, to admire
asar, to roast
cerrar, to close
cobrar, to collect
cocinar, to cook

contar, to count
conversar, to converse
copiar, to copy
desayunarse, to have breakfast
elevar, to raise, to lift
encontrar, to find, to meet
enviar, to send
espantar, to frighten, to scare
estudiar, to study

examinar, to examine
hablar, to speak
importar, to import
llorar, to cry, to weep
pensar, to think, to intend
prestar, to lend
pronunciar, to pronounce
robar, to rob

COMMON *-ER* VERBS REGULAR IN THE PRETERITE

aparecer, to appear
convencer, to convince
devolver, to return, to give back
envolver, to wrap

escoger, to choose
establecer, to establish
mover, to move
nacer, to be born
perder, to lose

reconocer, to recognize
romper, to break
vender, to sell
ver, to see

Note. The written accent is usually omitted over the following preterite forms of **ver:** *vi, vio.*

COMMON *-IR* VERBS REGULAR IN THE PRETERITE

abrir, to open

aplaudir, to applaud
interrumpir, to interrupt

recibir, to receive

11

EJERCICIOS

A. Escriba Vd. la forma correcta de los verbos *a*, *b*, y *c* en lugar del verbo en letra cursiva.

1. *Abrió* la puerta.   (*a*) cerrar   (*b*) examinar   (*c*) romper

   (*a*) _____   (*b*) _____   (*c*) _____

2. *Bebieron* té.   (*a*) vender   (*b*) enviar   (*c*) importar

   (*a*) _____   (*b*) _____   (*c*) _____

3. ¿*Vio* Vd. el monumento?   (*a*) admirar   (*b*) encontrar   (*c*) elevar

   (*a*) _____   (*b*) _____   (*c*) _____

4. No *invitasteis* a Pedro.   (*a*) acompañar   (*b*) aplaudir   (*c*) convencer

   (*a*) _____   (*b*) _____   (*c*) _____

5. *Comí* demasiado.   (*a*) cobrar   (*b*) llorar   (*c*) perder

   (*a*) _____   (*b*) _____   (*c*) _____

6. *Vimos* el cuadro.   (*a*) escoger   (*b*) copiar   (*c*) pintar

   (*a*) _____   (*b*) _____   (*c*) _____

7. Mi mamá *cocinó* el pollo.   (*a*) asar   (*b*) comer   (*c*) recibir

   (*a*) _____   (*b*) _____   (*c*) _____

8. ¿*Prestaste* el dinero?   (*a*) aceptar   (*b*) contar   (*c*) devolver

   (*a*) _____   (*b*) _____   (*c*) _____

9. No *trabajé* ayer.   (*a*) volver   (*b*) acostarse   (*c*) nacer

   (*a*) _____   (*b*) _____   (*c*) _____

10. *Entraron* en la sala.   (*a*) aparecer   (*b*) conversar   (*c*) desayunarse

    (*a*) _____   (*b*) _____   (*c*) _____

B. Cambie Vd. cada verbo del presente al pretérito.

1. ¿*Envuelve* Vd. el paquete?   _____

2. *Pensamos* ir al cine.   _____

3. *Mueven* los muebles.   _____

4. ¿*Reconoces* tu bicicleta?   _____

5. Los niños *espantan* los pájaros.   _____

6. No *interrumpo* al maestro.   _____

7. *Abrimos* la carta.   _____

8. *Establecen* una ciudad allí.   _____

9. *Roba* las joyas.   _____

10. Vosotros *habláis* demasiado.   _____

C. Conteste Vd. en español en frases completas.

1. ¿Estudió Vd. la lección para hoy?

   _____

2. ¿Tomó Vd. café esta mañana?

   _____

3. ¿Cantó la clase una canción española?

----

4. ¿Recibió Vd. buenas notas el año pasado?

----

5. ¿Pronunció Vd. bien las palabras de la lección?

----

6. ¿Bebió Vd. leche hoy?

----

7. ¿Visitó Vd. a su amigo(-a) ayer?

----

8. ¿Vio Vd. una película anoche?

----

9. ¿Compraron Vds. el libro de español?

----

10. ¿Comieron Vds. hoy en la cafetería de la escuela?

D. Traduzca Vd. al español las expresiones en inglés.

1. ¿Cuándo *did you sell* su automóvil? --------------------------------

2. *They learned* de memoria la lección. --------------------------------

3. *I entered* en el cuarto silenciosamente. --------------------------------

4. Juan y Roberto, ¿*didn't you study* la lección? --------------------------------

5. ¿A qué hora *did you leave* (vosotros) de casa? --------------------------------

6. *We wrote* a Felipe el mes pasado. --------------------------------

7. Alberto *didn't work* la semana pasada. --------------------------------

8. *I bought* dos libras de manzanas. --------------------------------

9. Vds. *did not listen* con atención. --------------------------------

10. Jorge y yo *ate* con apetito. --------------------------------

E. Traduzca Vd. al español.

1. They left the class. --------------------------------

2. Did you speak to Thomas? --------------------------------

3. I took the medicine. --------------------------------

4. We received his reply. *Recibimos la respuesta*

5. Mary helped the teacher. *a ayuda ayudó al maestro*

6. I promised to send the watch. --------------------------------

7. He saw Mr. Gómez. *Vio a el*

8. We sang Spanish songs. *Cantamos canciones españolas*

9. They did not find the house. *No encontró*

10. I opened the windows.

llevar – take
traer – bring

5. PRETERITE OF IRREGULAR VERBS

The verbs listed below are irregular in the preterite. They have the following endings with no accent marks.

$$-e,\ -iste,\ -o,\ -imos,\ -isteis,\ -ieron$$

Note

A. **-ieron** becomes **-eron** if **j** immediately precedes the ending. (See **decir, conducir, producir, traducir,** and **traer,** below.)

B. The compounds of **poner** (**componer,** etc.) and **tener** (**detener, mantener, obtener,** etc.) are conjugated like the base verbs, **poner** and **tener.**

> **andar,** to walk (preterite stem *anduv-*):
> *anduve, anduviste, anduvo, anduvimos, anduvisteis, anduvieron*

> **caber,** to fit (preterite stem *cup-*):
> *cupe, cupiste, cupo, cupimos, cupisteis, cupieron*

> **decir,** to say, to tell (preterite stem *dij-*):
> *dije, dijiste, dijo, dijimos, dijisteis, dijeron*

> **estar,** to be (preterite stem *estuv-*):
> *estuve, estuviste, estuvo, estuvimos, estuvisteis, estuvieron*

> **hacer,** to do, to make (preterite stem *hic-*):
> *hice, hiciste, hizo, hicimos, hicisteis, hicieron*

Note. The **c** changes to **z** in the 3rd person singular of **hacer.**

> **poder,** to be able, can (preterite stem *pud-*):
> *pude, pudiste, pudo, pudimos, pudisteis, pudieron*

> **poner,** to put (preterite stem *pus-*):
> *puse, pusiste, puso, pusimos, pusisteis, pusieron*

> **producir,** to produce (preterite stem *produj-*):
> *produje, produjiste, produjo, produjimos, produjisteis, produjeron*

> **querer,** to want, to wish (preterite stem *quis-*):
> *quise, quisiste, quiso, quisimos, quisisteis, quisieron*

> **saber,** to know (preterite stem *sup-*):
> *supe, supiste, supo, supimos, supisteis, supieron*

> **tener,** to have (preterite stem *tuv-*):
> *tuve, tuviste, tuvo, tuvimos, tuvisteis, tuvieron*

> **traer,** to bring (preterite stem *traj-*):
> *traje, trajiste, trajo, trajimos, trajisteis, trajeron*

> **venir,** to come (preterite stem *vin-*):
> *vine, viniste, vino, vinimos, vinisteis, vinieron*

Note. Verbs ending in **-ducir** are conjugated like **producir.**

conducir, to lead, to drive: *conduje, -iste, -o,* etc.
traducir, to translate: *traduje, -iste, -o,* etc.

The following irregular verbs have an accented **i** except in the third person (singular and plural) where **i** changes to **y.**

caer, to fall: caí, caíste, cayó, caímos, caísteis, cayeron
creer, to believe: creí, creíste, creyó, creímos, creísteis, creyeron
leer, to read: leí, leíste, leyó, leímos, leísteis, leyeron
oír, to hear: oí, oíste, oyó, oímos, oísteis, oyeron

The verbs **dar, ser,** and **ir** are also irregular in the preterite. **Dar** takes the endings of regular **-er, -ir** verbs; **ser** and **ir** have the same forms in the preterite.

dar, to give: *di, diste, dio, dimos, disteis, dieron*
ser, to be; ir, to go: *fui, fuiste, fue, fuimos, fuisteis, fueron*

EJERCICIOS

A. Escriba Vd. la forma correcta de los verbos *a*, *b*, y *c* en lugar del verbo en letra cursiva.

1. *Llegó* aquí a las tres en punto.   (*a*) estar   (*b*) venir   (*c*) presentarse

   (*a*) _____   (*b*) *Estuve vino*   (*c*) *presentó*

2. ¿Dónde *escribisteis* las cartas?   (*a*) poner   (*b*) traducir   (*c*) obtener

   (*a*) _____   (*b*) *pusisteis tradujisteis*   (*c*) *obtuvisteis*

3. Los campesinos *vendieron* legumbres.   (*a*) producir   (*b*) comprar   (*c*) traer

   (*a*) _____   (*b*) *produjeron compraron* (*c*) *trajeron*

4. No lo *hallaron.*   (*a*) creer   (*b*) hacer   (*c*) decir

   (*a*) *creyeron*   (*b*) *hicieron dijeron* (*c*) *dijeron*

5. *Prometimos* arreglar los muebles.   (*a*) poder   (*b*) querer   (*c*) lograr

   (*a*) _____   (*b*) *pudimos quisimos* (*c*) *logramos*

6. *Habló* despacio.   (*a*) andar   (*b*) leer   (*c*) ir

   (*a*) *anduvo*   (*b*) *leyó*   (*c*) _____

7. Mi padre *compró* el coche.   (*a*) conducir   (*b*) pintar   (*c*) limpiar

   (*a*) _____   (*b*) *condujo*   (*c*) *limpió*

8. ¿*Llevó* Vd. su paraguas?   (*a*) tener   (*b*) traer   (*c*) alzar

   (*a*) _____   (*b*) *tuvo trajo*   (*c*) *alzó*

9. ¿*Bajaste* por la escalera?   (*a*) caer   (*b*) subir   (*c*) ir

   (*a*) *caíste*   (*b*) *subiste*   (*c*) *fuiste*

10. *Anuncié* la noticia.   (*a*) oír   (*b*) saber   (*c*) dar

    (*a*) *oí*   (*b*) *supe di*   (*c*) _____

B. Cambie Vd. cada verbo del presente al pretérito.

1. *Van* a casa.   *fueron*

2. ¿Dónde *pongo* la maleta?   *puse*

3. *Compone* música.   *compuso*

4. *Traigo* un libro para Vd. ..... *traje* .....

5. *Da* una propina al mozo. ..... *dios* .....

6. *Es* necesario. ..... *fue* .....

7. *Detiene* el coche. ..... *detuvo detuvos* .....

8. *Leo* la revista. ..... *leyó* .....

9. *Vienen* tarde. ..... *vinieron* .....

10. No *puede* respirar. ..... *pudo* .....

11. *Tenemos* un examen. ..... *tuvimos* .....

12. *Voy* al campo. ..... *fue* .....

13. ¿Qué *hace* Vd.? ..... *hizo* .....

14. No *dicen* nada. ..... *dijeron* .....

15. *Mantiene* bien a su familia. ..... *mantuvo* .....

16. *Andamos* rápidamente. ..... *anduvimos* .....

17. Las joyas *caben* en la caja. ..... *cupimos* .....

18. *Conduce* su automóvil. ..... *condujo* .....

19. *Estamos* en el jardín. ..... *fuimos* .....

20. Los alumnos *traducen* bien. ..... *tradujeron* .....

C. Conteste Vd. en español en frases completas.

1. ¿Vino Vd. a tiempo a la escuela?

..... *Vine a tiempo* a la escuela .....

2. ¿Trajo Vd. muchos libros a la escuela hoy?

..... *Traje* .....

3. ¿Hizo Vd. el trabajo para hoy?

..... *Hice* .....

4. ¿Estuvo Vd. en casa anoche?

..... *Estuve* .....

5. ¿Fue Vd. al cine el sábado?

..... *Fui* .....

6. ¿Leyeron Vds. muchos cuentos españoles?

..... *leímos* .....

7. ¿Anduvo Vd. por el parque el domingo?

..... *anduve* .....

8. ¿Dio Vd. un regalo a su amigo para su cumpleaños?

..... *di* .....

9. ¿Tradujeron Vds. las frases al inglés?

..... *tradujimos* .....

10. ¿Puso Vd. sus libros sobre la mesa?

..... *Puse* .....

D. Traduzca Vd. al español las expresiones en inglés.

1. Nosotros *walked* por las calles de la ciudad. _____ andar anduvimos
2. Yo *read* aquella novela el año pasado. _____ leí
3. Juana y yo no *could* trabajar ayer. _____ pudimos
4. Yo no *had* bastante tiempo. _____ tuve
5. ¿Cuándo lo *did they obtain?* _____ obtuvo obtuvieron
6. Carlos y José *were* aquí el martes. _____ fueron
7. Nosotros no *brought* los discos. _____ trajimos
8. Vosotros *came* tarde. _____ vinisteis
9. Yo *wanted* comprarlo. _____ quise
10. Los alumnos *translated* las frases. _____ tradujeron
11. Juan no *went* a la escuela hoy. _____ fue
12. El niño *fell* enfermo. _____ cayó
13. Las muchachas no *said* nada. _____ dijeron
14. Tomás lo *did.* hizo _____ hizo
15. ¿*Did you hear* las noticias? _____ escuchaste
16. La dinamita *produced* la explosión. _____ produjo
17. Yo *went* a casa. _____ fue
18. El abogado lo *believed.* _____ creyó
19. Nosotros le *gave* la carta. dimos _____ dimos
20. ¿Dónde *did you (pl.) put* los libros? _____ pusieron

la noticia o news

E. Traduzca Vd. al español.

1. We went to the library. _____ Fuimos
2. She didn't hear the news. _____ oyó
3. They came on time. Vino Vinieron _____ al tiempo
4. It didn't fit in the box. _____ cupo
5. What did they bring? trajeron Qué _____ trajeron (llevar to take)
6. We couldn't see the houses. No vimos pudimos
7. Who wanted the pen? Quisimos Quien quería quisiera
8. Lincoln was a famous president. _____ fue presidente famoso
9. He made many plans. _____ hizo muchos planes
10. I gave the book to Mary. _____ Le di el libro a Mary
11. What did she say? _____ Qué dijo
12. Did you read the newspaper? _____ leyó leíste
13. He fell to the ground. _____ Se cayó al tierra
14. Where did you put the books? _____ Donde puso puso
15. They did not believe the story. _____ creyeron

6. IMPERFECT INDICATIVE

REGULAR VERBS

The imperfect indicative of regular verbs is formed by:

1. dropping the infinitive ending (**-ar, -er, -ir**).

2. adding to the stem the following endings:

> **-ar** verbs: *-aba, -abas, -aba, -ábamos, -abais, -aban*
>
> **-er** verbs ⎫
>
> **-ir** verbs ⎭ *-ía, -ías, -ía, -íamos, -íais, -ían*

	entrar, to enter	**comer,** to eat	**vivir,** to live
	I was entering, *I used to enter,* *etc.*	*I was eating,* *I used to eat,* *etc.*	*I was living,* *I used to live,* *etc.*
yo	entr*aba*	com*ía*	viv*ía*
tú	entr*abas*	com*ías*	viv*ías*
Vd., él, ella	entr*aba*	com*ía*	viv*ía*
nosotros, -as	entr*ábamos*	com*íamos*	viv*íamos*
vosotros, -as	entr*abais*	com*íais*	viv*íais*
Vds., ellos, -as	entr*aban*	com*ían*	viv*ían*

IRREGULAR VERBS

> **ir,** to go:　*iba, ibas, iba, íbamos, ibais, iban*
>
> **ser,** to be:　*era, eras, era, éramos, erais, eran*
>
> **ver,** to see:　*veía, veías, veía, veíamos, veíais, veían*

EJERCICIOS

A. Escriba Vd. la forma correcta de los verbos *a*, *b*, y *c* en lugar del verbo en letra cursiva.

1. Tomás *quería* sus juguetes.　(*a*) esconder　(*b*) reunir　(*c*) levantar

   (*a*) _quería_　　(*b*) _escondía reunía_　(*c*) _levantaba_

2. Nosotros *decíamos* la verdad.　(*a*) creer　(*b*) dudar　(*c*) saber

   (*a*) _creíamos_　　(*b*) _creíamos dudamos_　(*c*) _sabíamos_

3. Vds. *andaban* al teatro.　(*a*) ir　(*b*) correr　(*c*) acercarse

   (*a*) _ibais_　　(*b*) _corrían_　　(*c*) _acercarsean_

18

andábamos

4. Tú *tenías* las flores.   (a) oler   (b) mostrar   (c) ofrecer

(a) _olías_   (b) _mostrabas_   (c) _ofrecías_

5. Yo *veía* los animales.   (a) temer   (b) amar   (c) huir de

(a) _temía_   (b) _amaba_   (c) _huía_

6. Él *vendía* corbatas verdes.   (a) llevar   (b) preferir   (c) regalar

(a) _llevaba_   (b) _prefería_   (c) _regalaba_

7. Ella *escribía* el artículo.   (a) leer   (b) corregir   (c) entender

(a) _leía_   (b) _corregía_   (c) _entendía_

8. Yo *esperaba* el desayuno.   (a) tomar   (b) pedir   (c) comer

(a) _tomaba_   (b) _pedía_   (c) _comía_

9. ¿Qué *decíais?*   (a) tener   (b) observar   (c) padecer

(a) _teníais_   (b) _observaba_   (c) _padecía_

10. Ellos le *daban* el periódico.   (a) quitar   (b) entregar   (c) mostrar

(a) _quitaban_   (b) _entregaban_   (c) _mostraban_

B. Cambie Vd. cada verbo del presente al imperfecto.

1. *Acaban* de almorzar.   _Acaban_
2. *Obedecemos* la ley.   _obedecíamos_
3. *Se quejan* del servicio.   _Se quejaban_
4. La gente *celebra* las fiestas.   _celebraba_
5. El autor *describe* el paisaje.   _describía_
6. El muchacho *se llama* Pablo.   _se llamaba_
7. *Pasa* el día matando moscas.   _pasaba_
8. *Se bañan* todos los días.   _bañaban_
9. Siempre *evito* ese restaurante.   _evitía_
10. *Niegan* la verdad.   _negaban_

C. Cambie Vd. cada verbo del pretérito al imperfecto.

1. *Insistí* en no lavarme la cara.   _Insistía_
2. El campesino *recogió* el trigo.   _recogía_
3. ¿*Continuasteis* vuestro viaje?   _Continuíais_
4. Ayer *llovió* mucho.   _llovía_
5. Yo no *merecí* el premio.   _mercíaba_
6. No *tardé* en vestirme.   _tardía_
7. ¿*Abrazaste* a tu madre?   _abRazastía_
8. El rey no *gobernó* bien.   _gobernía_
9. *Compilaron* las listas.   _compilaban_
10. *Protegimos* a los débiles.   _Protegían_

D. Conteste Vd. en español en frases completas.

Cuando Vd. era muy joven . . .

1. ¿Tenía Vd. muchos amigos? _Tengo muchos amigos_
   Tenía mucha amigos Tuve

2. ¿Dónde pasaba Vd. las vacaciones de verano? _____
   Pasaba las v. en ingle

3. ¿Asistía Vd. a la universidad? _____
   assista a la universidado gnardo

4. ¿Decía Vd. siempre la verdad? _____
   decia

5. ¿Visitaba Vd. muchas veces a sus tíos? _____
   Visitaba

6. ¿Sabía Vd. leer y escribir? _____
   Sabia

7. ¿Siempre besaba Vd. a su mamá al salir de casa? _____
   besaba

8. ¿Salía Vd. de noche a menudo? _____
   Salia

9. ¿Iba Vd. todos los sábados al cine? _____
   No iba todos los sabados al cine

10. ¿Tenían Vds. un perro? _____
    No teniamos un perro

E. Traduzca Vd. al español.

1. We were going downtown. _Ibamos Ibamos_
2. The children were crying. _Los infantes oraan lloraan_
3. I used to visit my uncle. _Visita a mi tio_
4. We used to work there. _Trabajamos trababamos_
5. He was in the library. _era_
6. What were they doing? _¿Que hacian?_
7. We used to see Mary often. _Veiamos a Maria siempre_
8. John was my friend. _Jua era mi amigo_
9. The pupils were reading. _Los alumnos leian_
10. She was writing a letter. _Escribia una carta_

7. USES OF THE PRETERITE AND IMPERFECT

1. The *preterite* is used to indicate the *beginning* or the *end* of an action or event occurring in the past. It may also indicate the complete event (both beginning and end).

Empezó a trabajar. (beginning)	He began to work.
Cesó de llover. (end)	It stopped raining.
Visité a María ayer. (I went and returned)	I visited Mary yesterday.

2. The *imperfect* is used to indicate the *continuance* of a situation or event in the past. Neither the beginning nor the end is indicated. Thus, it is used:

   a. To express what was happening, used to happen, or happened repeatedly in the past.

¿Qué *hacían* mientras el niño *dormía?*	What were they doing while the child slept (= was sleeping)?
Vivíamos en Madrid.	We used to live in Madrid.
Yo le *veía* a menudo. often	I used to see him often.

   b. To describe persons, things, or situations in the past.

María *tenía* los ojos azules.	Mary had blue eyes.
Era una máquina útil.	It was a useful machine.

   c. To express the time of day in the past.

Eran las ocho.	It was eight o'clock.

   d. In the construction **hacía** + *an expression of time* + **que** + *the imperfect indicative*, to describe an action or event that began in the past and continued in the past. In questions, *How long?* is expressed by **¿Cuánto tiempo hacía que . . . ?** + the imperfect tense.

Hacía una hora que estudiaban. It made an hour that they were studying	They had been studying for an hour.
¿Cuánto tiempo hacía que Vd. trabajaba? How much time did it make that you were working	How long had you been working?

   e. With the preterite, to describe what was going on in the past (imperfect) when another action or event occurred, that is, began or ended (preterite).

Yo *leía* cuando mi hermano *entró.*	I was reading when my brother entered.

EJERCICIOS

A. En lugar del verbo en letra cursiva, escriba Vd. la forma correcta de los verbos *a*, *b*, y *c*, en el tiempo (tense) indicado.

1. El coronel *respetaba* al general.   (*a*) obedecer   (*b*) honrar   (*c*) creer

   (*a*) ___obedecía___   (*b*) ___honraba___   (*c*) ___creía___

2. En el verano *jugaban* mucho al aire libre.   (*a*) divertirse   (*b*) cenar   (*c*) quedarse

   (*a*) ___divertían___   (*b*) ___cenaban___   (*c*) quedaban <br> se

21

3. *Volvió* aquí a las tres de la madrugada.   (a) despertarse   (b) acostarse   (c) estar

   (a) _despertarse_   (b) _acostarse_   (c) _estaba_

4. Hacía una hora que lo *buscábamos*.   (a) aguardar   (b) seguir   (c) hacer

   (a) _aguardábamos_   (b) _seguíamos_   (c) _hacíamos_

5. El dependiente no *sabía* los precios.   (a) recordar   (b) poner   (c) establecer

   (a) _recordaba_   (b) _ponía_   (c) _establecía_

6. Elena *llevaba* una blusa blanca.   (a) tener   (b) querer   (c) preferir

   (a) _tenía_   (b) _quería_   (c) _prefería_

7. En julio *fuimos* a Europa.   (a) venir   (b) llegar   (c) visitar

   (a) _veníamos_   (b) _llegábamos_   (c) _visitábamos_

8. ¿Cuánto tiempo hacía que ellos *vivían* allí?   (a) dormir   (b) estar   (c) permanecer

   (a) _dormían_   (b) _estaban_   (c) _permanecían_

9. Desde lejos *escuchaban* la campana.   (a) oír   (b) mirar   (c) ver

   (a) _oían_   (b) _miraban_   (c) _veían_

10. Por todas partes se *veían* edificios altos.   (a) construir   (b) elevar   (c) encontrar

    (a) _construían_   (b) _elevaban_   (c) _encontraban_

11. *Odiaba* a sus enemigos.   (a) perdonar   (b) ver   (c) temer

    (a) _perdonaba_   (b) _veía_   (c) _temía_

12. ¿*Cortaste* las flores?   (a) recoger   (b) oler   (c) cultivar

    (a) _recogiste_   (b) _oliste_   (c) _cultivaste_

13. Enrique *escribía* en su cuarto.   (a) fumar   (b) comer   (c) sufrir

    (a) _fumaba_   (b) _comía_   (c) _sufría_

14. Generalmente *gastábamos* poco dinero.   (a) recibir   (b) cobrar   (c) merecer

    (a) _recibíamos_   (b) _cobrábamos_   (c) _merecíamos_

15. ¿Dónde *llenasteis* las botellas?   (a) romper   (b) sacar   (c) guardar

    (a) _rompisteis_   (b) _sacasteis_   (c) _guardasteis_

B. Complete Vd. la frase en español, subrayando (underlining) la forma correcta del verbo.

1. The examinations ended last week.
   Los exámenes (terminaron, terminaban) la semana pasada.

2. The door was open when we came.
   La puerta (estuvo, estaba) abierta cuando vinimos.

3. Every afternoon the manager signed (= used to sign) letters.
   Todas las tardes el gerente (firmó, firmaba) cartas.

4. He kissed his mother before getting on the train.
   (Besó, Besaba) a su madre antes de subir al tren.

5. We often went (= used to go) to her house.
   A menudo (fuimos, íbamos) a su casa.

6. The sky was blue.
   El cielo (fue, era) azul.

7. Without asking permission, he began to express his opinion.
   Sin pedir permiso, (comenzó, comenzaba) a expresar su opinión.

8. At three o'clock sharp it stopped raining.
A las tres en punto (cesó, cesaba) de llover.

9. He always read the newspaper at night.
Siempre (leyó, leía) el periódico de noche.

10. She was blond and had green eyes.
(Fue, Era) rubia y (tuvo, tenía) los ojos verdes.

11. He put out the light and left the room.
(Apagó, Apagaba) la luz y (salió, salía) del cuarto.

12. It was raining when we arrived.
(Llovió, Llovía) cuando (llegamos, llegábamos). *llego*

13. While the orchestra played, everybody danced (= was dancing).
Mientras la orquesta (tocó, tocaba), todo el mundo (bailó, bailaba).

14. What were you doing while I was studying?
¿Qué (hicieron, hacían) Vds. mientras yo (estudié, estudiaba)?

15. When he received the prize, he put it in his pocket.
Cuando (recibió, recibía) el premio, lo (metió, metía) en el bolsillo.

C. Conteste Vd. en español en frases completas.

1. ¿Dio Vd. un regalo a su mamá recientemente? _____
_____ *No diuse duve* _____

2. ¿Encontró Vd. a muchos amigos esta mañana mientras iba a la escuela? _____
_____

3. Cuando Vd. volvió a casa ayer, ¿colgó Vd. su abrigo en el armario? _____
_____ *volvi* _____ *colgo* _____

4. ¿Atravesó Vd. muchas calles hoy para llegar a la escuela? _____
_____ *Attravese* _____

5. ¿A qué hora se acostó Vd. anoche? _____
_____ *me acoste* _____

Cuando Vd. era niño(-a) . . .

6. ¿Soñaba Vd. con viajar? _____ *dream about* _____
_____ *Yo sonaba* _____

7. ¿Siempre obedecía Vd. a su mamá? _____
_____ *No obedicia* _____

8. ¿Poseía Vd. una bicicleta? _____
_____ *Posesa* _____

9. ¿Tiraba Vd. piedras a los otros niños? _____
_____ *No tiraba* _____

10. ¿Interrumpía Vd. a sus padres cuando ellos hablaban? _____
_____ *No* " _____

D. Traduzca Vd. al español las expresiones en inglés.

1. A menudo yo le ayudaba cuando *I was able.* _____ *pude* _____

2. ¿Cuánto tiempo hacía que Vds. *had been waiting?* _____ *esperaron esperais*

3. Hacía dos días que él *had been* enfermo cuando llegó el médico. _____ *era* _____

4. Mis primos siempre nos *used to visit* cuando vivíamos allí. _____ *visitaban* *visitan* _____

5. ¿Cuánto tiempo hacía que ellos *had been working* cuando Vd. los vio? _____ *trabajan* _____

6. Mientras yo *was going* al teatro, le encontré. _____ *iba* _____

7. Hacía siete meses que él me *had been promising* una bicicleta. _____ *prometía* _____

8. *We were talking and dancing* al mismo tiempo. _____ *hablábamos* *bailábamos* _____

9. A menudo *I saw* a Juan cuando pasaba por la calle. _____ *ve* _____

10. ¿Cuánto tiempo hacía que ellos *had been coming* a su casa? _____ *venían* _____

E. Traduzca Vd. al español.

1. I had been going to that school for five years.

_____ *Vera a ese escuela por cinco annos* _____

2. He used to visit her every day.

_____ *La visita cada dia* _____

3. They were listening to the music when I entered.

_____ *Escuchan el musica cuando entre* _____

4. My uncle often came to our house.

_____ *Mi tío siempre venía a nuestra casa* _____

5. How long had you been waiting?

_____ *Hacía Cuanto tiempo hacía espera* _____

6. We had been listening for a long time.

_____ *Escuchamos por un largo largo tiempo* _____

7. The pupils were reading and writing their lessons.

_____ *Los alumnos leían y escriban sus lecciones* _____

8. How long had he been coming here?

_____ *Cuanto tiempo hacía que venía aquí* _____

9. Mary was reading the newspaper while I listened to the radio.

_____ *Maria leía el periódico cuando escuché al radio* _____

10. He frequently wrote to us.

_____ *Frequenmente escribía a nos* _____

8. STEM-CHANGING VERBS (CLASS I)

Stem-changing verbs of the first class end in **-ar** or **-er**. These verbs change the stem vowel **e** to **ie** and **o** to **ue** in the following forms:

1. present indicative (1, 2, 3 singular and 3 plural)
2. polite commands

er ar verbs no stem change = Preterite (Past T)

	VERBS THAT CHANGE *E* TO *IE*		
	cerrar, to close	**sentarse,** to sit down	**defender,** to defend
Present Indicative	c**ie**rro c**ie**rras c**ie**rra cerramos cerráis c**ie**rran	me s**ie**nto te s**ie**ntas se s**ie**nta nos sentamos os sentáis se s**ie**ntan	def**ie**ndo def**ie**ndes def**ie**nde defendemos defendéis def**ie**nden
Polite Commands	c**ie**rre Vd. c**ie**rren Vds.	s**ié**ntese Vd. no se s**ie**nte Vd. s**ié**ntense Vds. no se s**ie**nten Vds.	def**ie**nda Vd. def**ie**ndan Vds.

No defendías Don't defend

3rd cierra tu = Closed (Command)
2nd No cierres tu — Don't"

Siente te
No te sientas

	VERBS THAT CHANGE *O* TO *UE*	
	contar, to count / tell	**volver,** to return
Present Indicative	c**ue**nto c**ue**ntas c**ue**nta contamos contáis c**ue**ntan	v**ue**lvo v**ue**lves v**ue**lve volvemos volvéis v**ue**lven
Polite Commands	c**ue**nte Vd. c**ue**nten Vds.	v**ue**lva Vd. v**ue**lvan Vds.

COMMON STEM-CHANGING VERBS (CLASS I)

E TO *IE*

atravesar, to cross	**despertarse,** to wake up	**pensar,** to think, to intend to
calentar, to heat	**empezar,** to begin	**perder,** to lose
cerrar, to close	**encender,** to light	**quebrar,** to break
comenzar, to begin	**entender,** to understand	**querer,** to want, to wish, to love
confesar, to confess	**gobernar,** to govern	**sentarse,** to sit down
defender, to defend	**nevar,** to snow	**temblar,** to tremble

O TO *UE*

acordarse (de), to remember	**envolver**, to wrap up	**poder**, to be able, can
acostarse, to go to bed	**jugar (u** to **ue)**, to play	**probar**, to prove, to try, to test
almorzar, to lunch	**llover**, to rain	**recordar**, to remember
contar, to count	**morder**, to bite	**sonar**, to sound
costar, to cost	**mostrar**, to show	**soñar**, to dream
devolver, to return, to give back	**mover**, to move	**volar**, to fly
encontrar, to find, to meet	**oler (o** to **hue)**, to smell	**volver**, to return

Important: These stem-changing verbs are identified in the vocabulary lists by the type of change (**ie** or **ue**) in parentheses next to the verb.

EJERCICIOS

A. Cambie Vd. la forma del verbo en letra cursiva, empleando los sujetos indicados.

1. El animal *muestra* los dientes.

    Nosotros _____

    Ellos _____

    Vosotros _____

2. Él *defiende* a la niña.

    Nosotros _____

    Vosotros _____

    Tú _____

3. Vds. *entienden* el español.

    Yo _____

    Tú _____

    Nosotros _entendemos_____

4. Roberto *se sienta* en el sofá.

    Vds. _____

    Tú _tú sientas_____

    Yo _me siento_____

5. Nosotros *perdemos* la batalla.

    Ellos _pierden_____

    Vd. _pierdes_____

    Yo _pierdo_____

6. Yo *cierro* la alcoba.

    Los alumnos _____

    Él _____

    Nosotros _____

7. Nosotros *encontramos* los papeles.

    Ellos _____

    Yo _____

    Tú _____

8. El estudiante *cuenta* los minutos.

    Vds. _____

    Yo _____

    Nosotros _____

9. ¿*Se acuerda* Vd. de la fecha?   *Remember*

    tú _____

    Vds. _os acordáis_____

    vosotras _____

✓ 10. Yo *me despierto* tarde.

    Su nieto _se despierta_____

    Tú _despierta_____

    Vosotros _táis_____

11. Ellas no *pueden* leer el programa.

    Vd. _____

    Vosotras _____

    Nosotros _____

12. ¿Qué *piensa* Vd.?

    Vds. _piensan_____

    él _piensa_____

    tú _piensas_____

13. Los hombres no *vuelven* a casa.

    Ella _____

    Yo _____

    Nosotros _____

14. Él *juega* al béisbol.

    Ellos _____

    Yo _____

    Nosotros _____

[handwritten notes at top: sentir Regret / u se - to feel]

[handwritten notes top right: Go "yo form" for stem when doing / ind   Hagalo = Do it]

15. Yo *me acuesto* temprano.

Ellos _____

Vosotros _____

Ella _____

B. Cambie Vd. el infinitivo a la forma indicada del imperativo.   *[handwritten: 22 new book]*

1. *Volar* Vd. como las aves.   *[handwritten: vuela]*   *[handwritten: Sit down]*
2. *Sentarse* Vds. en esas sillas.   *[handwritten: Siénten se   Siénte te]*
3. *Querer* Vd. a su patria.   *[handwritten: No defiendas]*
4. *Defender* Vd. a su hermanita.   *[handwritten: defienda (defiende)]*   *[3rd pers]*
5. *Calentar* Vds. el agua.   *[handwritten: calienten]   [Order]*
6. No *envolver* Vds. los paquetes.
7. *Oler* Vd. el perfume.   *[handwritten: Huela]*
8. No *probar* Vds. las albóndigas.   *[handwritten: No proben]*
9. *Mostrar* Vd. el mapa al explorador.   *[handwritten: Muestre Vd el mapa]*
10. *Devolver* Vd. el cuaderno a aquel alumno.   *[handwritten: Devuelva]*
11. No *mover* Vds. los muebles.   *[handwritten: No muevan]*
12. *Encender* Vd. la luz.   *[handwritten: Encienda]*
13. *Recordar* Vd. el suceso.   *[handwritten: Recuerde]*
14. No *morder* Vd. las uñas.   *[handwritten: No muerdas]*
15. *Atravesar* Vds. el río.   *[handwritten: Atraviesen]*

C. Conteste Vd. en español en frases completas.

1. ¿Dónde se sientan los alumnos?
   [handwritten: Se sientan los alumnos en sus sillas]

2. ¿A qué hora almuerza Vd.?
   [handwritten: Almuerzo a las doce]

3. ¿Juega Vd. al tenis?
   [handwritten: Juego al tenis]

4. ¿Llueve ahora?
   [handwritten: Llueve ahora]

5. ¿Cuándo empieza su primera clase?
   [handwritten: Mi clase empieza a las diez]

6. ¿Sueña Vd. con ser rico(-a)?
   [handwritten: No sueño con ser rico]

7. ¿Cuesta mucho su reloj?
   [handwritten: Su reloj cuesta mucho]

8. ¿Tiembla Vd. cuando el profesor grita?
   [handwritten: No tiemblo cuando el profesor grita]

[handwritten at bottom: Subject: Neg command - 2nd pers subjunctive / Pos   "   "   3rd   "   Singular / Everything ind]

9. ¿A qué hora se despierta Vd.?

WAKE UP

me desperto a las ocho

10. ¿En qué estación nieva?

Neva en invierno

✗ 11. ¿Cuándo se acuesta Vd.?

acosto acuesto a las once

12. ¿Confiesa Vd. siempre sus errores?

Yo Confiesa siempre mis errores

13. ¿A qué hora vuelve Vd. a casa?

Vuelvo

14. ¿Entiende Vd. esta lección?

Entiendo

15. ¿Encuentra Vd. difícil esté ejercicio?

Encuentro

D. Traduzca Vd. al español las expresiones en inglés.

1. *Do not sit down* Vds. en aquel cuarto. _No se sienten_ 21/1/

2. Clara *eats lunch* a la una. _Come_

3. *It is snowing* hoy. _Nieva_

4. La comida *smells* bien. _huela_

5. ¿Qué *do you think* de este periódico? _Que piensa_

6. *I do not understand* esa regla. _No comprenda_

7. Deseo *to go to bed.* _acostarse_

8. Los niños *wake up* temprano. _despiertan_

9. *He loses* su cartera. _Pierde_

10. Rosa *shows* un retrato de su familia a su amiga. _muestra_

E. Traduzca Vd. al español.

1. It costs four dollars.

Cuesta cuatro dolares

2. What do they think of that comedy?

Que piensen de ese Comedia

3. The soldiers are losing the battle.

Los soldados pierden la batalla

4. Are you able to sit down?

Pueden se sentarse

5. Go to bed now.

Os acostarseis acuestarsen

6. It snows in winter and rains in summer.

Nieva en invierno y llueva en verano

7. He does not understand English.

No comprende inglés

8. They defend their home.

Defienden sus casas

9. Show the dress to Mary.

Muestre el vestido a María

10. At what time does he return?

Que hora vuelve

La llama es un animal de los Andes del Perú. Es algo parecido (similar) al camello (camel), y como el camello, la llama puede andar mucho tiempo sin beber agua. Es un animal útil. Los indios lo emplean como bestia de carga (beast of burden), y usan su lana para hacer ropa.

9: STEM-CHANGING VERBS (CLASS II)

Stem-changing verbs of the second class end in **-ir** only. These verbs change the stem vowel from **e** to **ie** and from **o** to **ue** in the following forms:

1. present indicative (1, 2, 3 singular and 3 plural)
2. polite commands

They also change **e** to **i** and **o** to **u** in the following forms:

1. preterite (3 singular and 3 plural)
2. present participle (gerund)

	mentir, to lie	divertirse, to enjoy oneself	dormir, to sleep
Present Indicative	miento	me divierto	duermo
	mientes	te diviertes	duermes
	miente	se divierte	duerme
	mentimos	nos divertimos	dormimos
	mentís	os divertís	dormís
	mienten	se divierten	duermen
Polite Commands	mienta Vd.	diviértase Vd.	duerma Vd.
	mientan Vds.	no se divierta Vd.	duerman Vds.
		diviértanse Vds.	
		no se diviertan Vds.	
Preterite	mentí	me divertí	dormí
	mentiste	te divertiste	dormiste
	mintió	se divirtió	durmió
	mentimos	nos divertimos	dormimos
	mentisteis	os divertisteis	dormisteis
	mintieron	se divirtieron	durmieron
Present Participle	mintiendo	divirtiéndose	durmiendo

COMMON STEM-CHANGING VERBS (CLASS II)

E TO *IE, I*

consentir, to consent	**herir**, to wound	**preferir**, to prefer
divertirse, to enjoy oneself, to have a good time	**mentir**, to lie	**sentir**, to regret, to be sorry
		sentirse, to feel

O TO *UE, U*

dormir, to sleep	**dormirse**, to fall asleep	**morir**, to die

Important: These stem-changing verbs are identified in the vocabulary lists by the type of change (**ie, i,** or **ue, u**) in parentheses next to the verb.

30

Handwritten annotations in script, best-effort reading.

Feb. 12 Cookie

EJERCICIOS

A. Cambie Vd. la forma del verbo en letra cursiva, empleando los sujetos indicados.

1. Yo _prefiero_ descansar.

Nosotros _preferimos_

Ellos _prefieren_

Tú _prefieres_

2. Él _se divierte_ en el cine.

Vds. _os divertáis_

Ella _se divierte_

Yo _me divierto_

3. Nosotros no _mentimos_.

Los alumnos no _mienten_

Yo no _miento_

Él no _miente_

4. Ellos _duermen_ mucho.

Nosotros _dormimos_

Yo _duermo_

Tú _duermes_

5. Yo _consiento_ en acompañarle.

Su padre _consiente_

Ellos _consienten_

Vosotros _consentís_

6. Ella _se duerme_ a las ocho.

Yo _me duermo_

Tú _te duermes_

Vds. _os dormís_

7. Él y yo lo _sentimos_ mucho.   Sorry

Yo _lo siento_

Ella _lo siente_

Vds. _lo sentís_

8. El soldado _hiere_ al enemigo.   wound

Ellos _hieren_

Vd. _heris_

Nosotros _herimos_

9. Ellas _prefieren_ salir temprano.

Vosotros _preferís_

Vd. _prefiere_

Vds. _prefieren_

10. Ellos _se sienten_ bien.   sintieron sent

Nosotros _nos sentimos_

Vd. _os sentís_

Vosotros _se sienten_

B. Repita Vd. el ejercicio A, empleando el pretérito en vez del presente.

1. Yo _prefiero_ . . .

Nosotros _preferimos_

Ellos _prefiere_

Tú _prefieres_

2. Él _se divierte_ . . .

Vds. _se divirtió_

Ella _se divirtió_

Yo _me divirtió_

3. Nosotros no _mentimos_.

Los alumnos no _mintieron_

Yo no _mintió_

Él no _mintió_

4. Ellos _duermen_ . . .

Nosotros _dormimos_

Yo _duermo_

Tú _nos_

5. Yo _consiento_ . . .

Su padre _consiente_

Ellos _consiente_

Vosotros _contéis_

6. Ella _se duerme_ . . .

Yo _me duermo_

Tú _te duermes_

Vds. _se duerme_

7. Él y yo lo _sentimos_ . . .

Yo _siento_

Ella _siente_

Vds. _siente_

8. El soldado _hiere_ . . .

Ellos _hieran_

Vd. _hieres_

Nosotros _herimos_

IR verbs

9. Ellas *prefieren* . . .

Vosotros ..... *prefereis* .....

Vd. ..... *prefiere* .....

Vds. ..... *prefieران* .....

10. Ellos *se sienten* . . .

Nosotros ..... *preferemos*   Nos sentemos

Vd. ..... *prefiere* os senteén

Vosotros ..... *sentais* .....

C. Cambie Vd. el infinitivo a la forma indicada del imperativo.

1. *Dormir* Vd. bien. ..... *duerme* .....

2. *Divertirse* Vds. en la playa. ..... *Diviértase* .....

3. No *sentir* Vd. la ausencia de la maestra. ..... *No sienta,* .....

4. *Consentir* Vd. en el plan. ..... *Consienta,* .....

5. No *mentir* Vd. a su padre. ..... *No mienta.* .....

D. Conteste Vd. en español en frases completas.

1. ¿Miente Vd. algunas veces?

..... *No miento* .....

2. ¿Se divierten Vds. en el parque?

..... *No* ~~diverti~~ *divertimos* .....

3. ¿Se divirtió Vd. el domingo pasado?

Divertimos

4. ¿Qué clase prefiere Vd.?

Preferio prefiero

5. ¿En qué cuarto duerme Vd.?

duermo

6. ¿A qué hora se durmió Vd. anoche?

me ~~dorm~~ *duermio*

7. ¿Cuántas horas durmió Vd.?

duermio

8. ¿Se divierte Vd. durante las vacaciones?

divierto

9. ¿Se siente Vd. bien hoy?

me siento

10. ¿Se sintió Vd. enfermo(-a) ayer?

No me sentié

E. Escriba Vd. el infinitivo y el participio presente de cada uno de los verbos siguientes:

EJEMPLO: hablaron—*hablar, hablando*

1. prefiero ..... *preferiendo* .....

2. se divirtieron ..... *divertiendose* .....

3. se duerme ..... *de durmiendo* .....

4. murió ..... *muriendo* .....

5. sentimos ..... *sentiendo   sentiendo* .....

6. consienten ..... *consientiendo* .....

7. muere ..... *muriendo* .....

8. miente ..... *mentiendo* .....

9. se sintió ..... *sentiendose* .....

10. durmieron ..... *durmiendo* .....

6/2 ✓

F. Traduzca Vd. al español las expresiones en inglés.

1. El chico está *sleeping*. _____ *se duerme*
2. *I am sorry* decirle que no lo sé. _____ *Me siento*
3. Mi perro *died* el año pasado. _____ *murió*
4. *She preferred* aquel vestido. _____ *Prefirió*
5. *I did not sleep* bien anoche. _____ *No me dormí*
6. Mi amigo lo *regretted* mucho. _____ *sintió*
7. Los muchachos *are enjoying themselves* en el teatro. _____ *se divierten*
8. Pedro y Antonio, *do not lie* Vds. _____ *No mientan*
9. *They consent* en traerlo. _____ *consienten*
10. Carlos y yo *had a good time* ayer. _____ ~~*pasistamos*~~ *pasábamos*

G. Traduzca Vd. al español.

1. He consented to (en) sell the house.
_____ *Consintió vender la casa*
2. You regret the teacher's illness.
_____ *Siente la malada del profesor*
3. Many soldiers died in the war.
_____ *Muchos salados murieron*
4. He felt sad.
_____ *Sintió triste*
5. Do not fall asleep; enjoy yourselves.
_____ *No se duerman   se divierten*
6. They had a good time.
_____ *Pasaban una bueno tiempo*
7. Sleep in that room.
_____ *Duerma usted en ese cuarto*
8. How many hours do you sleep each night?
_____ *Cómo horas te duerme cada noche*
9. I prefer to buy this suit.
_____ *Yo prefiero comprar este traje*
10. The explosion wounded many people.
_____ *La explosión hirió muchos gente*

10. STEM-CHANGING VERBS (CLASS III)

Stem-changing verbs of the third class, like those of the second class, end in **-ir** only. These verbs change the stem vowel as follows:

e to **i** {
present indicative (1, 2, 3 singular and 3 plural)
polite commands
preterite (3 singular and 3 plural)
present participle (gerund)
}

	pedir, to ask (for)	**vestirse,** to get dressed
Present Indicative	pido pides pide pedimos pedís piden	me visto te vistes se viste nos vestimos os vestís se visten
Polite Commands	pida Vd. pidan Vds.	vístase Vd. no se vista Vd. vístanse Vds. no se vistan Vds.
Preterite	pedí pediste pidió pedimos pedisteis pidieron	me vestí te vestiste se vistió nos vestimos os vestisteis se vistieron
Present Participle	pidiendo	vistiéndose

COMMON STEM-CHANGING VERBS (CLASS III)

pedir, to ask (for)
perseguir, to pursue, to persecute
reír, to laugh

repetir, to repeat
seguir, to follow, to continue
servir, to serve

sonreír, to smile
vestir(se), to dress (oneself), to get dressed

Important: These stem-changing verbs are identified in the vocabulary lists by **(i)** next to the verb.

Note

A. The following spelling changes occur in the present indicative (1st person singular) and the polite command:

conseguir perseguir seguir } **gu** changes to **g**	corregir elegir } **g** changes to **j**

sigo, siga Vd.; corrijo, corrija Vd.

34

B. The verb **reír** (*to laugh*) is conjugated as follows:

PRESENT INDICATIVE: *río, ríes, ríe,* reímos, reís, *ríen*
COMMAND: *ría* Vd., *rían* Vds.
PRETERITE: reí, reíste, *rió,* reímos, reísteis, *rieron*
PRESENT PARTICIPLE: *riendo*

The verb **sonreír** (*to smile*) is conjugated like **reír**.

EJERCICIOS

A. Cambie Vd. la forma del verbo en letra cursiva, empleando los sujetos indicados.

1. Los alumnos *repiten* las frases.
   Vd. _repite_
   Yo _repito_
   Nosotras _repetimos_

2. La criada *sirve* el arroz con pollo.
   Tú _sirves_
   Ellos _sirven_
   Yo _sirvo_

3. Juan *sigue* buenos ejemplos.
   Yo _sigo_
   Sus hijos _siguen_
   Vosotros _seguís_

4. Nosotros *reímos* a menudo.
   Vd. _ríe_
   Ellos _ríen_
   Tú _ríes_

5. Yo *elijo* sopa de legumbres.
   Nosotros _elegimos_
   Ellos _eligen_
   Vd. _elige_

6. El mal tiempo no *impide* los coches.
   Los cocheros _impiden_
   La gente _impide_
   Nosotros _impedemos_

7. Tú *pides* permiso.
   Nosotros _pedimos_
   Yo _pido_
   Ellos _piden_

8. Él se *despide* del jefe.
   Nosotros _despedimos_
   Vds. _despiden_
   Yo _despido_

9. Nosotros *nos vestimos* con cuidado.
   Tú _te vistes_
   Ellos _se visten_
   Vd. _se viste_

10. Ella *corrige* los exámenes.
    Yo _corrijo_
    Vosotros _corregís_
    Vds. _corrigen_

B. Repita Vd. el ejercicio A, empleando el pretérito en vez del presente.

1. Los alumnos *repiten* . . .
   Vd. _repetes_ rep _repetisteis_
   Yo _repito_ _repitió_
   Nosotras _repetimos_ ✓

2. La criada *sirve* . . .
   Tú _serviste_
   Ellos _sirvieron_
   Yo _serviro_

3. Juan *sigue* . . .
   Yo _sigo_ — _seguí_
   Sus hijos _siguió_
   Vosotros _seguisteis_

4. Nosotros *reímos* . . .
   Vd. _reísteis_
   Ellos _rieron_
   Tú _reíste_

(margin notes at left:)
Repetí
Repetiste
repitió
repetimos
repetisteis
repitieron

5. Yo *elijo* . . .

Nosotros *elejimos*

Ellos *elijiera*

Vd. *elijio*

6. El mal tiempo no *impide* . . .

Los cocheros *impidieron*

La gente *impidio*

Nosotros *impedimos*

7. Tú *pides* . . . *pediste*

Nosotros *pedimos*

Yo *pide pedi*

Ellos *pidieron*

8. Él *se despide* . . .

Nosotros *nos despedemos*

Vds. *se despedisteis*

Yo *me despedi*

9. Nosotros *nos vestimos* . . .

Tú *te vestiste*

Ellos *se*

Vd. *os vestes*

10. Ella *corrige* . . .

Yo *corrigi*

Vosotros *corrigeis*

Vds. *corrigieron*

C. Cambie Vd. el infinitivo a la forma indicada del imperativo.

1. *Conseguir* Vd. un billete. — *consigas* — *consiga*

2. No *pedir* Vds. favores. — *pedisteis* — *pidan*

3. *Servir* Vd. las albóndigas ahora. — *sirva* — *sirva*

4. *Sonreír* Vd. de alegría. — *sonreisteis* — *sonria*

5. No *vestirse* Vds. rápidamente. — *vertisteis* — *vestiandose*

6. *Seguir* Vds. su camino. — *seguisteis* — *sigue*

7. No *reírse* Vd. de sus amigos. — *rio* — *reirse*

8. *Repetir* Vd. la pregunta. — *repetir* — *repite*

9. No *despedirse* Vds. ahora. — *despedisteis* — *despedirse*

10. Guardia, *perseguir* Vd. al ladrón. — *persegus* — *persenuja*

D. Conteste Vd. en español en frases completas.

1. ¿Se vistió Vd. antes de desayunarse hoy?

Me vesti

2. ¿Pide Vd. dinero a su padre?

Pedi mi

3. ¿Sonríe Vd. a menudo?

Sonri

4. ¿Quién sirvió el desayuno hoy en su casa?

Servi

5. ¿Siempre consigue Vd. lo que desea?

consigu

6. ¿Corrigió Vd. los errores en la pizarra?

corrijo

7. ¿Sigue Vd. los consejos de sus padres?

Sigo

8. ¿Ríe Vd. si está triste?

No rio si estoy triste

9. ¿Qué dice Vd. cuando se despide de sus amigos?

Cuando me despido de mis amigos digo "va"

10. ¿Repiten Vds. las frases en español?

repetimos

E. Escriba Vd. el participio presente de cada uno de los verbos siguientes:

1. repetir _____   6. conseguir _____

2. vestirse _____   7. corregir _____

3. servir _____   8. impedir _____

4. reír _____   9. sonreír _____

5. pedir _____   10. seguir _____

F. Traduzca Vd. al español las expresiones en inglés.

1. El padre *corrected* las costumbres del hijo. *corregis*

2. *Repeat* Vd. la frase. *rep*

3. El mozo está *serving* el café. *sirviendo*

4. Mi hermana *dressed herself* en seguida. *se vistio*

5. *He asked for* un paraguas. *Pidio*

6. Estábamos *getting dressed.* *nos estavistiendo*

7. ¿*Are you saying goodbye to* nosotros tan pronto? *Vds diciendo a dios a*

8. ¿Por qué *did smile* Vds.? *reisteis*

9. *Do not dress yourself* si no quiere. *No vistase usted se vista usted*

10. *They did not serve* la comida. *No sirvieron*

G. Traduzca Vd. al español.

1. I got dressed at once. *Me visti pronto* *(mismo)*

2. Serve the tea now. *Sirva el te ahora*

3. When they asked John for the money, he smiled. *Cuando pidieron Juan el dinero sonrio*

4. They elected the president. *Elegieron el president*

5. Why are you laughing? *Por que reis*

6. Ask the waiter for a cup of coffee. *Pida el mozo por una taza de te cafe*

7. He repeated the words several times. *Repitaba las palabras varias veces*

8. They continued laughing. *consiguieron rir.*

9. Correct your errors. *corrijan vos errores*

10. I promised to say goodbye to Henry. *Promi dices adios a Henry*

11. THE FUTURE TENSE

REGULAR VERBS

The future tense is formed by adding to the infinitive the following endings:

-é, -ás, -á, -emos, -éis, -án

	ayudar, to help	**aprender**, to learn	**abrir**, to open
	I shall (will) help, etc.	*I shall (will) learn, etc.*	*I shall (will) open, etc.*
yo	ayudar**é**	aprender**é**	abrir**é**
tú	ayudar**ás**	aprender**ás**	abrir**ás**
Vd., él, ella	ayudar**á**	aprender**á**	abrir**á**
nosotros, -as	ayudar**emos**	aprender**emos**	abrir**emos**
vosotros, -as	ayudar**éis**	aprender**éis**	abrir**éis**
Vds., ellos, -as	ayudar**án**	aprender**án**	abrir**án**

IRREGULAR VERBS

The following verbs drop the **e** of the infinitive ending before adding the endings of the future.

caber, to fit: *cabré, -ás, -á,* etc.
haber, to have (auxiliary verb): *habré, -ás, -á,* etc.
poder, to be able: *podré, -ás, -á,* etc.
querer, to want, to wish: *querré, -ás, -á,* etc.
saber, to know: *sabré, -ás, -á,* etc.

The following verbs replace the **e** or **i** of the infinitive ending with a **d** before adding the endings of the future.

poner, to put: *pondré, -ás, -á,* etc.
salir, to leave, to go out: *saldré, -ás, -á,* etc.
tener, to have: *tendré, -ás, -á,* etc.
valer, to be worth: *valdré, -ás, -á,* etc.
venir, to come: *vendré, -ás, -á,* etc.

The following verbs drop the **e** and **c** of the infinitive before adding the endings of the future.

decir, to say, to tell: *diré, -ás, -á,* etc.
hacer, to do, to make: *haré, -ás, -á,* etc.

USES OF THE FUTURE TENSE

The future tense is used:

1. To express future time.

¿A qué hora *llegará* el tren?   At what time will the train arrive?

2. To express wonderment or probability in the present time.

¿Qué hora *será?*   I wonder what time it is.

Será la una.   It is probably one o'clock.

EJERCICIOS

A. Escriba Vd. la forma correcta de los verbos *a*, *b*, y *c* en lugar del verbo en letra cursiva.

1. El empleado *venderá* la camisa.   (*a*) ponerse   (*b*) recibir   (*c*) quitarse

   (*a*) _pondra_   (*b*) _recibra_   (*c*) _quitarsera_

2. *Lucharán* mañana.   (*a*) llegar   (*b*) venir   (*c*) casarse

   (*a*) _llegara_   (*b*) _vendra_   (*c*) _casarsera_

3. El capitán no *mandará* atacar.   (*a*) poder   (*b*) querer   (*c*) consentir en

   (*a*) _podra_   (*b*) _querra_   (*c*) _consentira_

4. *Dormiremos* mucho tiempo.   (*a*) descansar   (*b*) tener   (*c*) continuar

   (*a*) _Nos descansaremos_   (*b*) _tendremos_   (*c*) _continuaremos_

5. ¿Qué *ganará* ella?   (*a*) decir   (*b*) permitir   (*c*) escoger

   (*a*) _dira_   (*b*) _permitira_   (*c*) _escojera_

6. Lo *principiarán* el miércoles.   (*a*) hacer   (*b*) construir   (*c*) devolver

   (*a*) _haranen_   (*b*) _construiranien_   (*c*) _devolveranien_

7. *Regresará* a las cuatro.   (*a*) partir   (*b*) pagar   (*c*) salir

   (*a*) _partira_   (*b*) _pagara_   (*c*) _saldra_

8. Lo *meteré* en la caja.   (*a*) buscar   (*b*) poner   (*c*) encontrar

   (*a*) _buscare_   (*b*) _pondre_   (*c*) _encontrare_

9. ¿Cuánto *costará*?   (*a*) valer   (*b*) durar   (*c*) llover

   (*a*) _valdra_   (*b*) _durara_   (*c*) _llovera_ Pan

10. Los soldados no *estarán* en el castillo.   (*a*) caber   (*b*) cenar   (*c*) permanecer Reman

    (*a*) _cabarran_   (*b*) ~~cabran~~ Cenaran (*c*) _Permaneceran_

B. Cambie Vd. los verbos al futuro.

1. Tomás *espera* el tren.   _____

2. ¿En qué fecha *cae* su cumpleaños?   _caera_____

3. *Tienen* muchas oportunidades.   _Tendra_____

4. ¿Me *dais* permiso para marcharme?   _dara_____

5. Pablo no *trae* el tocadiscos.   _traera_____

6. *Queremos* un consejo.   _____

7. ¿*Sufres* mucho?   _Suffrera mucho_

8. *Hay* claveles en el jardín.   _____

9. Le *vemos* todos los días.   _Lo veremos todos los dias_

10. Tú no *puedes* ir al campo conmigo.   _podras ir al campo conmigo_

C. Conteste Vd. en español en frases completas.

1. ¿A qué hora *saldrá* Vd. de la escuela hoy?

   Saldra al tres hora

2. ¿*Irá* Vd. al centro mañana?

   No ire

3. ¿Qué hará Vd. la semana que viene?

_____

4. ¿Podrá Vd. ir al cine esta noche?

_____

5. ¿A qué hora volverá Vd. a casa esta tarde?

_____

6. ¿Dónde pasará su familia las vacaciones de verano?

_____

7. ¿Cómo celebrará Vd. su cumpleaños?

_____

8. ¿Tendrá Vd. que estudiar para un examen mañana?

_____

9. ¿Cuánto tiempo durará esta clase?

_____

10. ¿Le gustará a Vd. ir a la tienda esta mañana?

_____

D. Traduzca Vd. al español las expresiones en inglés.

1. El caballero repite que *he will fulfill* con su deber. _____

2. *She is probably* unos treinta años. _____

3. No explicará por qué *he will omit* mi nombre de la lista. _____

4. El niño responde que *he will not obey* a sus padres. _____

5. ¿*I wonder if he is* alemán? _____

6. Mi madre promete que *she will divide* el pastel en tres partes. _____

7. Comprendemos que *it will be* necesario descansar. _____

8. Dicen que *they will come* mañana. _____

9. *It is probably worth* diez pesetas. _____

10. ¿*I wonder what time it is* en este momento? _____

E. Traduzca Vd. al español.

1. We will be able to go to a Mexican theater.

_____

2. We know that she will prepare the lunch.

_____

3. Tomorrow we will eat in a good restaurant.

_____

4. The maid will put the plates on the table.

_____

5. It is probably three P.M.

_____

6. She will not be able to sing this evening.

\---

7. At what time will you (*pl.*) leave tomorrow?

\---

8. The artist declares that the paintings will be worth much.

\---

9. I wonder where my books are.

\---

10. His wife thinks that he will sell the house.

\---

La Semana Santa (Holy Week) se celebra durante la semana antes del Domingo de Pascua (Easter Sunday). En Sevilla se celebra con procesiones que son famosas en todo el mundo. Centenares (hundreds) de penitentes forman la procesión, vestidos de túnicas (cloaks) como las que se ven aquí. Algunos llevan en la mano cruces o candelas, otros ayudan a llevar los pasos (floats) pintorescos.

12. THE CONDITIONAL

REGULAR VERBS

The conditional is formed by adding to the infinitive the following endings:

$$-ía, -ías, -ía, -íamos, -íais, -ían$$

	viajar, to travel	**comer,** to eat	**permitir,** to permit
	I would travel, etc.	*I would eat, etc.*	*I would permit, etc.*
yo	viajar*ía*	comer*ía*	permitir*ía*
tú	viajar*ías*	comer*ías*	permitir*ías*
Vd., él, ella	viajar*ía*	comer*ía*	permitir*ía*
nosotros, -as	viajar*íamos*	comer*íamos*	permitir*íamos*
vosotros, -as	viajar*íais*	comer*íais*	permitir*íais*
Vds., ellos, -as	viajar*ían*	comer*ían*	permitir*ían*

IRREGULAR VERBS

Like the future, the following verbs drop the **e** of the infinitive ending before adding the endings of the conditional:

caber, to fit: *cabría, -ías, -ía,* etc.

haber, to have (auxiliary verb): *habría, -ías, -ía,* etc.

poder, to be able: *podría, -ías, -ía,* etc.

querer, to want, to wish: *querría, -ías, -ía,* etc.

saber, to know: *sabría, -ías, -ía,* etc.

Like the future, the following verbs replace the **e** or **i** of the infinitive ending with a **d** before adding the endings of the conditional:

poner, to put: *pondría, -ías, -ía,* etc.

salir, to leave, to go out: *saldría, -ías, -ía,* etc.

tener, to have: *tendría, -ías, -ía,* etc.

valer, to be worth: *valdría, -ías, -ía,* etc.

venir, to come: *vendría, -ías, -ía,* etc.

Like the future, the following verbs drop the **e** and **c** of the infinitive before adding the endings of the conditional:

decir, to say, to tell: *diría, -ías, -ía,* etc.

hacer, to do, to make: *haría, -ías, -ía,* etc.

Note

When *would* is used in the sense of *used to*, it is translated by the imperfect tense, not the conditional.

Siempre nos **ayudaba.**   He always would (used to) help us.

USES OF THE CONDITIONAL

The conditional is used:

1. To express a condition (*would*).

Pagaría mucho por las joyas.   He would pay a lot for the jewels.

42

2. To express wonderment or probability in the past.

¿Qué hora **sería?**   I wonder what time it was.

Sería la una.   It was probably one o'clock.

Note

The future tense is commonly used in combination with the present or future tense; the conditional, with a past tense.

Dice que **irá.**   He says he will go.

Dijo que **iría.**   He said he would go.

EJERCICIOS

A. Escriba Vd. la forma correcta de los verbos *a*, *b*, y *c* en lugar del verbo en letra cursiva.

1. ¿Qué *aconsejaría* Vd. en tal caso?   (*a*) hacer   (*b*) contestar   (*c*) creer

    (*a*) _haría_   (*b*) _contestaría_   (*c*) _creería_

2. Ella no lo *copiaría*.   (*a*) permitir   (*b*) destruir   (*c*) escoger

    (*a*) _permitiría_   (*b*) _destruiría_   (*c*) _escogería_

3. No *irían* sin decir adiós.   (*a*) partir   (*b*) salir   (*c*) marcharse

    (*a*) _partían_   (*b*) _saldrían_   (*c*) _marcharían_

4. No *lograrían* convencerlos.   (*a*) poder   (*b*) tratar de   (*c*) insistir en

    (*a*) _podrían_   (*b*) _tratarían_   (*c*) _insistirían_

5. ¿*Respetarían* Vds. el nombre de ella?   (*a*) repetir   (*b*) acordarse   (*c*) saber

    (*a*) _repetirían_   (*b*) _acordarsían_   (*c*) _sabrían_

6. Nosotros no *viajaríamos* con ellos.   (*a*) conversar   (*b*) divertirse   (*c*) bailar

    (*a*) _conversaríamos_   (*b*) _divertiríamos_   (*c*) _bailaríamos_

7. ¿Quién *poseería* el dinero para comprarlo?   (*a*) tener   (*b*) ganar   (*c*) robar

    (*a*) _tendría_   (*b*) _ganaría_   (*c*) _robaría_

8. Yo lo *buscaría* aquí.   (*a*) poner   (*b*) esperar   (*c*) encontrar

    (*a*) _pondría_   (*b*) _esperaría_   (*c*) _encontraría_

9. *Correría* por las calles estrechas.   (*a*) andar   (*b*) caminar   (*c*) huir

    (*a*) _andaría_   (*b*) _caminaría_   (*c*) _huiría_

10. ¿*Prometerías* visitar la feria?   (*a*) querer   (*b*) preferir   (*c*) necesitar

    (*a*) _querrías_   (*b*) _preferirías_   (*c*) _necesitarías_

B. Cambie Vd. los infinitivos según los ejemplos.

EJEMPLOS: Dice (Dirá) que no *salir*.   Dice (Dirá) que no _saldrá_.

Dijo (Decía) que no *salir*.   Dijo (Decía) que no _saldría_.

1. Gritó que no *aceptar* el puesto. _aceptaría_

2. Si él no trabaja, su familia no *tener* pan. _tendrá_

3. El niño promete que no *cruzar* la calle. _cruzará_

4. Al salir, declaró que *regresar* a las nueve. _regresaría_

5. Colón creía que *descubrir* la ruta de las Indias. _descubriría_

6. Anunciarán que la biblioteca *abrirse* a las nueve. _abriría_
7. Ella preguntó si la medicina *curar* su enfermedad. _curía_
8. Prometió que todo el mundo *divertirse* allí. _divertiría_
9. No olvida que su sobrino *llegar* al día siguiente. _llegaría_
10. El comerciante declara que *emplear* a tres personas más. _empleará,_

C. Conteste Vd. en español en frases completas.

1. ¿Qué hora sería cuando Vd. se acostó anoche?
   Me acostía a las onces y notreinta

2. ¿Sabe Vd. a qué universidad asistirá?
   Se a que " asistiró

3. ¿Les aseguró el maestro que no recibirían un examen?
   El maestro no les aseguró recibirían

4. ¿Sabe Vd. a qué hora amanecerá mañana? _dawn_
   No se a qué hora amenecera

5. ¿Prometió Vd. a sus padres que estudiaría más?
   _____

6. ¿Dijo Vd. a sus amigos cuándo caería su cumpleaños?
   _____

7. ¿Adónde irá Vd. para pasar sus vacaciones?
   Iría

8. ¿Escogió Vd. un regalo que desearía dar a su mamá?
   Escogía

9. ¿Copiaría Vd. las notas de su amigo?
   No copia

10. ¿Cuánto costará un reloj como el que tiene Vd.?
    El reloj costaría   que tendrán

D. Traduzca Vd. al español las expresiones en inglés.

1. Sabe que el maestro *will notice* su ausencia. _noticaría_
2. Los niños *probably did not see* el accidente. _____
3. Estaban seguros de que el dueño *would get angry*. _se endafaarsendo_
4. ¿*I wonder if they did* el trabajo? _____
5. Dicen que *they will applaud* al actor. _____
6. *It was probably* las ocho cuando regresaron. _____
7. El mozo cree que el turista le *will give* una propina. _____
8. ¿Quién *would attack* a nuestro ejército? _____
9. La cocinera *will put* los guisantes en la sopa. _____
10. ¿*I wonder if she knows* los verbos? _____

E. Traduzca Vd. al español.

1. We would give a lot to (para) see that comedy. _____

_____

2. John said that his birthday would occur the next day. _el proxima dia_

_____

3. I know that my friends will come later. _____

_____ _vendurain_   _mas tarde_

4. They believe that the artist will create a masterpiece. _____

_____ _creara_

5. When he lived in Madrid, he would visit the museum often. _____

_____

6. The game of baseball would not interest me. _____

_____

7. Would you (tú) be able to read that book? _____

_____ _ese libro_ _____

8. I would give her two pesetas for the oranges. _buy_ _= Por = in exchange_ _(P213)_

_____

9. I wonder how much the shoes are worth. [Change to question.] _Future - "Wonder" Pres_

_____ _Condit " Past_

10. She will not serve the lunch at noon. _____

_____ _al media dia_

Past - Conditional (would)

Que eso = what this

This= Este. lapay this pencil

That=ese

eso
esto _Reserved for thgs_
that have no gender

The whole room is
= dis-array

That
this ese - It's

Francisco Pizarro (1475-1541) fue un conquistador atrevido (daring) que ganó para España el territorio del Perú. Con menos de 200 soldados venció al gran ejército de los incas, capturando y matando al rey, Atahualpa. Pizarro fue un hombre muy cruel, no sólo con los incas sino también con los españoles. Fue matado por sus propios soldados.

esa _this_
esta _that_

13. THE PRESENT PARTICIPLE (GERUND)

PRESENT PARTICIPLES OF REGULAR VERBS

hab*lar,* to speak	habl*ando,* speaking
com*er,* to eat	com*iendo,* eating
recib*ir,* to receive	recib*iendo,* receiving

PRESENT PARTICIPLES ENDING IN -*YENDO*

caer, to fall	*cayendo,* falling
construir, to construct	*construyendo,* constructing
creer, to believe	*creyendo,* believing
destruir, to destroy	*destruyendo,* destroying
huir, to flee	*huyendo,* fleeing
ir, to go	*yendo,* going
leer, to read	*leyendo,* reading
oír, to hear	*oyendo,* hearing
traer, to bring	*trayendo,* bringing

PRESENT PARTICIPLES OF STEM-CHANGING VERBS

Stem-changing verbs ending in **-ir** (classes II and III) change the stem vowel from **e** to **i,** and from **o** to **u.**

decir, to say, to tell	*diciendo,* saying, telling
despedirse, to say goodbye	*despidiéndose,* saying goodbye
divertirse, to enjoy oneself	*divirtiéndose,* enjoying oneself
dormir, to sleep	*durmiendo,* sleeping
venir, to come	*viniendo,* coming

Other verbs of this type are:

conseguir—*consiguiendo*	repetir—*repitiendo*
corregir—*corrigiendo*	seguir—*siguiendo*
mentir—*mintiendo*	sentir—*sintiendo*
morir—*muriendo*	servir—*sirviendo*
pedir—*pidiendo*	vestir—*vistiendo*

Note. The present participle of **poder** is *pudiendo.*

PROGRESSIVE TENSES

The present participle is used with **estar, seguir,** and **continuar** to denote continuous action (progressive tenses).

Siguen trabajando.	They continue working.
	(Present Progressive)
Estaba leyendo.	He was reading.
	(Past Progressive)
Continúan escribiendo.	They continue writing; they continue to write.
	(Present Progressive)

Note

The present participles of **estar, ir,** and **venir** are not used to form the progressive tenses of these verbs. Instead, the simple tenses are used.

Ella *viene* aquí.   She is coming here.
Rosa *iba* al parque.   Rose was going to the park.

EJERCICIOS

A. Escriba Vd. el participio presente de los verbos *a, b,* y *c* en lugar del verbo en letra cursiva.

1. *Andando* por el parque, le encontré.   (*a*) volver   (*b*) ir   (*c*) venir

   (*a*) _yendo_   (*b*) _volviendo_   (*c*) _viniendo_

2. Siga Vd. *trabajando.*   (*a*) divertirse   (*b*) pasearse   (*c*) estudiar

   (*a*) _sigue divirtiendo_ (*b*) _paseándose_   (*c*) _estudiando_

3. Los soldados están *saliendo* ahora.   (*a*) dormir   (*b*) despedirse   (*c*) avanzar

   (*a*) _durmiendo_   (*b*) _despidiéndose_   (*c*) _avanzando_

4. Estaban *escuchando* una historia interesante.   (*a*) leer   (*b*) escribir   (*c*) repetir

   (*a*) _leyendo_   (*b*) _escribiendo_   (*c*) _repitiendo_

5. Estamos *cantando* una canción española.   (*a*) tocar   (*b*) aprender   (*c*) traducir

   (*a*) _tocando_   (*b*) _aprendo_   (*c*) _traduciendo_

6. La criada estaba *preparando* el café en la cocina.   (*a*) beber   (*b*) servir   (*c*) calentar

   Servant   (*a*) _bebiendo_   (*b*) _sirviendo_   (*c*) _sirviendo calentando_

7. Siguen *decorando* la sala.   (*a*) buscar   (*b*) entrar en   (*c*) usar

   (*a*) _buscando_   (*b*) _entrando_   (*c*) _usando_

8. Ellos continúan *llorando.*   (*a*) comer   (*b*) esperar   (*c*) rezar

   (*a*) _comiendo_   (*b*) _esperando_   (*c*) _rezando_

9. ¿A quién estaba Vd. *hablando?*   (*a*) imitar   (*b*) molestar   (*c*) seguir

   (*a*) _imitando_   (*b*) _molestando_   (*c*) _siguiendo_

10. Los comerciantes siempre están *aumentando* los precios.   (*a*) cambiar   (*b*) arreglar
    (*c*) bajar

    (*a*) _bajando_   (*b*) _cambiando_   (*c*) _arreglando_

B. Conteste Vd. en español en frases completas.

1. ¿Está Vd. pensando en algo importante en este momento? _____

   No estoy pensando en algo importante en este momento

2. ¿Quién está enseñando la lección? _____

   Marta está enseñando la lección

3. ¿Está el maestro castigando a la clase ahora? _punish_ _____

   El no está castigando a la clase ahora

4. ¿Está acercándose la fecha de su cumpleaños? _Approach_ _____

   No está acercándose

5. ¿Oye Vd. mucho cuando está durmiendo? _____

No oyo cuando estoy

6. ¿Está lloviendo ahora? _____

No esta llorrendo

7. ¿Está Vd. escuchando atentamente las respuestas de sus compañeros? _____

Estoy escuchando   mis

8. ¿Qué están Vds. haciendo en este momento? _____

Estamos haciendo nada

9. ¿Continúa Vd. estudiando todos los días? _____

Continuo   "

10. ¿Qué están Vds. aprendiendo en esta clase? _____

Estamos aprendiendo espanial

C. Cambie Vd. cada verbo a la forma correspondiente del tiempo progresivo (presente o pasado).

EJEMPLOS: hablo—*estoy hablando*   comíamos—*estábamos comiendo*

1. leo *Estoy legendo leyendo*
2. sentían *Estan sentiendo / Estaban sintiendo*
3. decían *" diciendo*
4. se viste *Esta se vistiendo*
5. crecen *Estan creciendo*
6. traes *Estas traido*
7. caigo *Estoy caido*
8. corrigen *Estan corrigiendo*
9. creabais *Estais creabado*
10. ponían *Estaban puesto*

11. conseguimos *Estamos consiguiendo*
12. reducías *Estas reduciado*
13. creéis *Estas creeciendo*
14. destruyen *Estan destruyado*
15. nos unimos *Estamos uniado*
16. huimos *Estamos huyado*
17. moría *Estaba muriendo*
18. veo *Estaba viando*
19. construíamos *Estabamos construyendo*
20. oigo *Estaba oyendo*

D. Traduzca Vd. al español las expresiones en inglés.

1. No *being able* verlo, tuve que regresar al día siguiente. *Pudendo*
2. [By] *studying* se aprende mucho. *Estudiando*
3. *Going* a la escuela, me encontré con mis amigos. *Yendo*
4. Pasamos varias horas *playing* a la pelota. *Pasiendo*
5. *Saying* esto, se levantó y se fue. *Diciendo*
6. Pasó toda la noche *sleeping*. *durmiendo*
7. [By] *following* este camino, llegarás a Albuquerque. *consiguendo*
8. Aprendió a pronunciar [by] *repeating* las palabras del maestro. *repitiendo*
9. Vivió mucho tiempo, *dying* a la edad de noventa años. *muriendo*
10. *Entering* en la sala, se sentó. *Entrajendo*

E. Traduzca Vd. al español las expresiones en inglés, empleando el tiempo progresivo (presente o pasado).

1. Las hojas *are falling*. _estár cayendo_
2. *They keep on asking for* la misma cosa. _continua pidiendo_
3. *He continued to believe* que era una mentira. _continuó creado_
4. No es verdad; aquel hombre *is lying*. _esta mintiendo_
5. *She is buying* una novela española. _esta compriendo_
6. La criada *was covering* la mesa con un mantel. _estaba cubierto_
7. El enfermo *continues taking* la medicina. _continua pidiendo_
8. El muchacho *was playing* en la calle cuando le vi. _estaba juejado_
9. *Continue Vds. writing*. _escrito_
10. Ella *is dressing* ahora. _esta se vistiendo_

F. Traduzca Vd. al español.

1. Being a good child, he always used to obey his parents. _Estado un niño bueno el siempre obedicia sus padres_
2. She amuses herself [by] dancing. _Ella se amuse ballaiendo_
3. The boy is not lying. _El muchacho no esta mintiendo_
4. To whom is he giving the diamond? _¿A quien esta doyendo el diamante?_
5. He was opening the window. _Estaba abierto la ventana_
6. What were they saying? _¿Que estetan diciendo dicho_
7. Having enough time, I visited my friends. _Tendido bastante tiempo visíti a mis amigos_
8. It is raining. _Esta llovrando_
9. I am working in an office. _Estoy trabajando en una officina_
10. They were eating then. _Pues estaban comiado_

14. THE PAST PARTICIPLE; THE PRESENT PERFECT AND PLUPERFECT TENSES

PAST PARTICIPLES OF REGULAR VERBS

visit*ar*, to visit	visit**ado**, visited
aprend*er*, to learn	aprend**ido**, learned
viv*ir*, to live	viv**ido**, lived

PAST PARTICIPLES ENDING IN -*ÍDO*

caer, to fall	*caído,* fallen
creer, to believe	*creído,* believed
leer, to read	*leído,* read
oír, to hear	*oído,* heard
traer, to bring	*traído,* brought

IRREGULAR PAST PARTICIPLES ENDING IN -*TO*

abrir, to open	*abierto,* opened
cubrir, to cover	*cubierto,* covered
descubrir, to discover	*descubierto,* discovered
escribir, to write	*escrito,* written
morir, to die	*muerto,* died
poner, to put	*puesto,* put
romper, to break	*roto,* broken
ver, to see	*visto,* seen
volver, to return	*vuelto,* returned

IRREGULAR PAST PARTICIPLES ENDING IN -*CHO*

decir, to say, to tell	*dicho,* said, told
hacer, to do, to make	*hecho,* done, made

PRESENT PERFECT TENSE

The present perfect tense is formed by the present tense of **haber** (*to have*) plus the past participle.

I have visited (*learned, lived*)

yo	*he*	visitado (aprendido, vivido)
tú	*has*	visitado (aprendido, vivido)
Vd., él, ella	*ha*	visitado (aprendido, vivido)
nosotros, -as	*hemos*	visitado (aprendido, vivido)
vosotros, -as	*habéis*	visitado (aprendido, vivido)
Vds., ellos, -as	*han*	visitado (aprendido, vivido)

PLUPERFECT TENSE

The pluperfect tense is formed by the imperfect tense of **haber** (*to have*) plus the past participle.

I had visited (*learned, lived*)

yo	*había*	visitado (aprendido, vivido)
tú	*habías*	visitado (aprendido, vivido)
Vd., él, ella	*había*	visitado (aprendido, vivido)
nosotros, -as	*habíamos*	visitado (aprendido, vivido)
vosotros, -as	*habíais*	visitado (aprendido, vivido)
Vds., ellos, -as	*habían*	visitado (aprendido, vivido)

Note

To make a verb in the perfect tenses negative, place **no** before the verb **haber.** To make a verb interrogative, place the subject after the past participle.

No habían vivido allí.   They had not lived there.

No se han lavado todavía.   They haven't washed themselves yet.

¿ha visto Vd.?   have you seen?

EJERCICIOS

A. Escriba Vd. la forma correcta del presente perfecto de los verbos a, b, y c en lugar del verbo en letra cursiva.

1. *Hemos gastado* el dinero.   (a) pagar   (b) traer   (c) conservar

  (a) pagado   (b) traído   (c) conservado

2. Lo *han copiado* mal.   (a) hacer   (b) oír   (c) cubrir

  (a) hecho   (b) oído   (c) cubierto

3. ¿Dónde *ha comprado* Vd. el lápiz?   (a) poner   (b) arrojar   (c) esconder

  (a) puesto   (b) arrojado   (c) escondido

4. ¿No *habéis recibido* el paquete?   (a) abrir   (b) ver   (c) entregar

  (a) abierto   (b) visto   (c) entregado

5. Yo *he contestado* la carta.   (a) leer   (b) escribir   (c) romper

  (a) leído   (b) escrito   (c) roto   (escrito)

6. *Han llegado* al campo.   (a) ir   (b) viajar   (c) huir

  (a) ido   (b) viajado   (c) huido

7. Muchos soldados *han luchado*.   (a) adelantar   (b) caer   (c) morir

  (a) adelantado   (b) caído   (c) muerto

8. ¿*Has trabajado* hoy?   (a) comer   (b) salir   (c) fumar

  (a) comido   (b) salido   (c) fumado

9. No *han venido* todavía.   (a) volver   (b) acostarse   (c) almorzar

  (a) acostado   (b) vuelto   (c) almorzado

10. Mi amiga *ha dicho* la verdad.   (a) negar   (b) creer   (c) dudar

  (a) negado   (b) creído   (c) dudado

B. Escriba Vd. la forma correcta del pluscuamperfecto (pluperfect) de los verbos a, b, y c en lugar del verbo en letra cursiva.

1. Los buques *habían atacado* la isla.   (a) rodear   (b) conquistar   (c) alejarse de

  (a) rodeado   (b) conquistado   (c) alejado

2. *Habíamos jugado* en la playa.   (a) descansar   (b) divertirse   (c) desayunarse

  (a) descansado   (b) divertido   (c) desayunado

3. Ella nunca *había vivido* en Cuba.   (a) estudiar   (b) pensar   (c) estar

  (a) estudiado   (b) pensado   (c) estado

4. El policía *había encontrado* la bomba.   (a) destruir   (b) ver   (c) descubrir

  (a) destruido   (b) visto   (c) descubierto

5. Yo *había llevado* la chaqueta.   (a) admirar   (b) romper   (c) vender

(a) _admirado_   (b) _roto_   (c) _vendido_

6. *Habíamos esperado* la buena noticia.   (a) oír   (b) recibir   (c) anunciar

(a) _oído_   (b) _recibido_   (c) _anunciado_

7. *Habían asistido* el jueves.   (a) regresar   (b) terminar   (c) desaparecer _desaparecido_

(a) _regresado_   (b) _terminado_   (c) _desparido_

8. ¿*Habías buscado* una guía de teléfonos?   (a) perder   (b) compilar   (c) obtener

(a) _perdido_   (b) _compilado_   (c) _obtenido_

9. No *habíamos encontrado* leones en la selva.   (a) buscar   (b) matar   (c) hallar _find_

(a) _buscado_   (b) _matado_   (c) _hallado_

10. Los esclavos *habían deseado* la libertad.   (a) luchar por   (b) conseguir   (c) ganar

(a) _luchado_   (b) _conseguido_   (c) _ganado_

C. Cambie Vd. la forma del verbo al tiempo perfecto que corresponde (el presente al presente perfecto, el pasado al pluscuamperfecto).

Past = haber
presto estar

EJEMPLOS: *Hacemos* nuestro trabajo.   *Hemos hecho* nuestro trabajo.

Yo *hablaba* con Juan.   Yo *había hablado* con Juan.

1. Yo *visito* a mis primos en México. _he visitado visitado visitado_

2. El Sr. Valdés no *traía* su pasaporte. _traído_

3. Ellos no *leen* el periódico. _leyedo han leído_

4. Tú no *respondías* a mis preguntas. _Habías respondido_

5. Nosotros no *abrimos* (past) el baúl. _habíamos abierto_

6. Su padre *moría*. _había muerto muerto_

7. El niño *bebió* la leche. _Había bebido_

8. ¿Dónde *pones* mi pluma? _tú habías puesto_

9. Mis amigas nunca *veían* seda tan fina. _han visto_

10. Nosotros no *decimos* una mentira. _hemos dicho_ _hemos_

D. Conteste Vd. en español en frases completas.

1. ¿Ha llegado Vd. temprano a la escuela?

He llegado temprano a la escuela

2. ¿Ha muerto su abuelo?

No he muerto mi abuelo

3. ¿Había estudiado Vd. el español antes de asistir a esta escuela?

No había estudiado español antes de asistir a esta escuela

4. ¿Ha visto Vd. a sus amigos hoy?

No he visto a mis amigos hoy

5. ¿Ha escrito Vd. los ejercicios correctamente?

Siempre he escrito los ejercicios correctamente

6. ¿Ha ido Vd. al cine esta semana?

No he ido al cine esta semana

7. ¿Qué ha hecho Vd. hoy?

He estudiado y escrito español hoy

8. ¿Habían vivido sus padres en España?

No habían vivido mis padres en España

9. ¿Han preparado Vds. el trabajo?

No hemos preparado el trabajo

10. ¿He leído yo estas frases claramente?

Usted ha leído estas frases claramente

E. Traduzca Vd. al español las expresiones en inglés.

1. No sabían que *I had said* "adiós." _habían dicho_

2 Los soldados *have been* valientes. _han estado honrado_

3. *He has eaten* todas las manzanas. _He comido_

4. *¿Have you heard* la historia de su vida? _Ha oído_

5. Lo *I had covered* con un plato. _Había cubierto_

6. *They have opened* una biblioteca nueva. _Han abierto_

7. *We have not been able* ayudarle. _No hemos puesto_

8. El sastre *has made* el vestido. _He hecho_

9. *She had written* a su novio. _Había escrito_

10. Siempre *you* (tú) *have been* un amigo fiel. _habías estado_

F. Traduzca Vd. al español.

1. Who has done the work?

   ¿Quién habrá hecho el trabajo?

2. We have decided to sell the store.

   Hemos decidido a vender la tienda

3. I had opened the door.

   Había abierto la puerta   ¿La puerta está abierta? door is

4. My children have not returned.

   Mis niños no han revuelto

5. Where had they put the flowers?

   ¿Dónde habrán puesto las flores

6. That author had written interesting books.

   Ese autor había escrito los libros interesantes

7. Have you seen my nephew?

   ¿Ha usted visto mi sobrino

8. They have promised to eat the soup.

   Han prometido comer la sopa

9. What had you said to your brother?

   ¿Qué había dicho a su hermano

10. Who has read the novel?

    Quién ha leído el novel

A Rodrigo Díaz de Vivar, que vivió en el siglo XI, se le considera el héroe nacional de España. Fue una de las figuras principales en las guerras contra los moros. Éstos, que le tenían miedo, le llamaron "El Cid" (Señor). Los españoles le llamaron "El Cid Campeador" ("Champion") porque casi siempre fue victorioso en las batallas.

15. THE FUTURE PERFECT AND THE CONDITIONAL PERFECT (OPTIONAL)

FUTURE PERFECT TENSE

The future perfect tense is formed by the future of **haber** plus the past participle.

I shall (will) have visited (learned, lived)

yo	*habré*	visitado (aprendido, vivido)
tú	*habrás*	visitado (aprendido, vivido)
Vd., él, ella	*habrá*	visitado (aprendido, vivido)
nosotros, -as	*habremos*	visitado (aprendido, vivido)
vosotros, -as	*habréis*	visitado (aprendido, vivido)
Vds., ellos, -as	*habrán*	visitado (aprendido, vivido)

CONDITIONAL PERFECT

The conditional perfect is formed by the conditional of **haber** plus the past participle.

I would have visited (learned, lived)

yo	*habría*	visitado (aprendido, vivido)
tú	*habrías*	visitado (aprendido, vivido)
Vd., él, ella	*habría*	visitado (aprendido, vivido)
nosotros, -as	*habríamos*	visitado (aprendido, vivido)
vosotros, -as	*habríais*	visitado (aprendido, vivido)
Vds., ellos, -as	*habrían*	visitado (aprendido, vivido)

EJERCICIOS

A. En lugar del verbo en letra cursiva, escriba Vd. las formas correspondientes de los verbos *a, b, y c.*

1. Ellos *se habrán acercado* a la aduana con el juez. (*a*) volver (*b*) dirigirse (*c*) ir

    (*a*) ___Revuelto___ (*b*) ___dirigiendo___ (*c*) ___yendo___

2. La señorita *habrá escondido* la carta de su novio. (*a*) abrir (*b*) recibir (*c*) leer

    (*a*) ___abierto___ (*b*) ___recibrento___ (*c*) ___leyendo___

3. El enfermo *habría vivido* sin ayuda. (*a*) morir (*b*) levantarse (*c*) caer

    (*a*) ___Habrían cayendo___ (*b*) ___muerto___ (*b*) ___levantídose___

4. El pintor *habrá vendido* sus obras. (*a*) traer (*b*) mostrar (*c*) romper

    (*a*) ___trayendo___ (*b*) ___muestro___ (*c*) ___rompiendo___

5. Mi madre *habría colocado* el jugo de limón en la mesa. (*a*) señalar (*b*) poner (*c*) ver

    (*a*) ___señalando___ (*b*) ___puesto___ (*c*) ___viendo___

6. El abuelo *habría abrazado* a su nieta. (*a*) escribir (*b*) pegar (*c*) besar

    (*a*) ___escribrento___ (*b*) ___pegado___ (*c*) ___besado___

7. Los estudiantes *habrán alabado* las pinturas del gran artista. (*a*) copiar (*b*) estudiar (*c*) entender

    (*a*) ___copiado___ (*b*) ___estudiado___ (*c*) ___entendido___

8. El público no *habrá dudado* la noticia.   (a) oír   (b) escuchar   (c) creer

(a) _oyendo_   (b) _escuchado_   (c) _creyendo_

9. En Sevilla *habrían visitado* la catedral.   (a) admirar   (b) describir   (c) hallar

(a) _admirado_   (b) _describiendo_   (c) _hallarse_

10. Nosotros *habríamos contestado* lo mismo.   (a) hacer   (b) aconsejar *-se*   (c) decir

(a) _hayendo_   (b) _aconsedarse_   (c) _deyendo_

B. Subraye Vd. (Underline) la forma del verbo **haber** que traduzca correctamente la forma correspondiente en inglés.

1. they have returned   (han, habían, habrán) vuelto
2. I would have been   (había, habré, habría) sido
3. we had put   (hemos, habíamos, habríamos) puesto
4. he had covered   (habría, había, habrá) cubierto
5. we would have brought   (habíamos, hemos, habríamos) traído
6. they had discovered   (habían, habrían, han) descubierto
7. I will have seen   (he, había, habré) visto
8. you had arrived   (habrás, habrías, habías) llegado
9. they will have judged   (habrán, han, habían) juzgado
10. nothing would have happened   nada (ha, habría, había) sucedido

C. Traduzca Vd. al español las expresiones en inglés.

1. *He had paid* la cuenta. _Había pagado_
2. *They would not have read* la revista. _Habrían leído_
3. ¿Qué *would you have done* en este caso? _¿Qué habrían (habrías)_
4. Yo *had not returned* el diccionario. _Había vuelto_
5. Ana *has not returned* todavía. _No Ha vuelto todavía_
6. *We will have visited* el hospital. _Habremos visitado_
7. *They had not received* la máquina. _Habían recibido_
8. *She has not learned* mucho. _No ha aprendido_
9. La comedia *had begun* a las nueve. _Había comenzado empesado_
10. *He had gone down* al sótano. _Había (yendo) decendido_
   Había bajado

D. Traduzca Vd. al español.

1. The children had eaten the eggs.
   Los niños habían comido los huevos

2. He and I will have begun the novel.
   habremos _comenceremos la novela_

3. We would not have been able to see him.   _No habríamos puedido_
   No lo podríamos ver

4. They have gone to the movies.
   Han yendo a la / película / cine
   ido (Past perticese compro)

5. She would have died without the medicine.   *(Me di cina)*

Habría Muerta sin la medicina (femin)

6. You (Tú) had put the map on the ground.   *Puesto*

Habías el mapa al solo suelo Habrás puesto

7. They will have returned at five o'clock.   *Regresado*

Revuelvan al a las cinco

8. You (*pl.*) have not heard the truth.

Hacíais escuchado el verdad

9. They had gone out early.   *Habían salido temprano*

Había el temps temprano

10. The child would have taken the money.

El niño toma el dinero

tomaron
Robado

Hubo = (from haber)
There was a paved

La estatua de San Martín a caballo domina este monumento en Buenos Aires. José de San Martín (1778-1850) fue un general argentino que luchó por la independencia de la Argentina, Chile, y el Perú. Una de sus hazañas (exploits) más admirables fue cruzar los Andes en 1817, con un ejército de 5000 hombres, y derrotar (defeat) al ejército español en Chile.

16. *ESTAR* AND *SER*

The verbs **estar** and **ser** both mean *to be* in English.

USES OF *ESTAR*

Estar is used to express:

1. *Location or position.*

¿Dónde está Juan?	Where is John?
Madrid *está en España.*	Madrid is in Spain.

2. *Condition.*

   a. Health.

Pedro *está enfermo.*	Peter is ill.
¿Cómo está Vd.?	How are you?

   b. Change from previous state or condition.

Estoy cansado.	I am tired.
Está triste.	He is sad.

Common adjectives used with **estar** to express a change are:

abierto(-a), open	**cerrado(-a),** closed	**ocupado(-a),** busy
alegre, happy, gay	**contento(-a),** content, happy	**sentado(-a),** seated
ausente, absent	**frío(-a),** cold	**sucio(-a),** dirty
caliente, warm, hot	**limpio(-a),** clean	**triste,** sad
cansado(-a), tired	**lleno(-a),** full	**vacío(-a),** empty

3. *With the present participle to form the progressive tenses.*

Están trabajando.	They are working.

USES OF *SER*

Ser is used to express:

1. *Characteristics.*

   a. Origin, possession, and material, with **de.**

Juan *es de España.*	John is from Spain.
Esta falda *es de México.*	This skirt is from Mexico.
Es el libro *de Ana.*	It is Ann's book.
Es una corbata *de seda.*	It is a silk tie.

   b. Occupation, profession, nationality, identification.

Es médico.	He is a doctor.
Es el presidente.	He is the president.
Son españoles.	They are Spanish.
La flor *es una rosa.*	The flower is a rose.

2. *Description.*

    a. Color.

La flor *es roja.*   The flower is red.

Common adjectives of color used with **ser** are:

amarillo(-a), yellow	**blanco(-a),** white	**rojo(-a),** red
azul, blue	**negro(-a),** black	**verde,** green

    b. Other descriptive adjectives.

La casa *es grande.*   The house is large.

María *es bonita.*   Mary is pretty.

Common descriptive adjectives used with **ser** are:

alto(-a), tall	**joven,** young	**pobre,** poor
bonito(-a), pretty	**nuevo(-a),** new	**rico(-a),** rich
grande, large	**pequeño(-a),** small	**viejo(-a),** old

3. *Time and dates.*

Es la una.   It is one o'clock.

Es el dos de mayo.   It is May 2.

Note

A. The adjective **feliz** (*happy*) is used with the verb **ser.**

Es feliz.
    but   He is happy
Está contento.

B. Some adjectives may be used with either **ser** or **estar,** but differ in meaning.

Alberto *es bueno (malo).*   Albert is good (bad).   (characteristic)

Alberto *está bueno (malo).*   Albert is well (ill).   (condition)

Alberto *es listo.*   Albert is clever.   (characteristic)

Alberto *está listo.*   Albert is ready.   (condition)

C. Adjectives used with **ser** or **estar** must agree with the subject in number and gender.

María está cansada.   Mary is tired.

Son ricos.   They are rich.

EJERCICIOS

   A. Subraye Vd. la forma correcta de **ser** o **estar.**

1. Mis padres (son, están) bien.

2. Madrid (es, está) la capital de España.

3. La sopa (será, estará) caliente.

4. (Son, Están) mexicanos.

5. Mi tía (es, está) bondadosa.

6. No (soy, estoy) viejo.

7. (Soy, Estoy) muy ocupado.

8. La cesta (es, está) debajo de la mesa.

Basket

9. Mi amigo y yo (somos, estamos) felices.

10. La caja (es, está) cerrada.

11. Juan y yo (somos, estamos) tristes.

12. El profesor (es, está) delante de la clase.

13. Estos cuartos (son, están) sucios.

14. Los libros no (eran, estaban) nuevos.

15. Alberto (es, está) alto.

B. Complete Vd. cada frase, escribiendo la forma correcta de **ser** o **estar** en el presente de indicativo.

1. La comida ___este___ fría.

2. El anciano ___este___ sentado.

3. Juana ___es___ bonita.

4. Carlos ___este___ ausente.

5. Ese coche ___es___ del médico.

6. Mi tío ___es___ abogado.

7. La botella ___este___ llena de agua.

8. Este sombrero ___es___ de París.

9. La pluma ___este___ en el escritorio.

10. Las iglesias ___estan___ abiertas.

11. Ellos ___estan___ pescando.

12. ___son___ las once y media.

13. ¿ ___es___ rojo el libro?

14. El reloj ___es___ de plata.

15. Yo ___soy___ pobre.

C. Conteste Vd. en español en frases completas.

1. ¿Está Vd. contento(-a) cuando recibe buenas notas?
___Estoy contento   Recibo___

2. ¿Cuál es el primer mes del año?
___Es Janvier___

3. ¿Están cubiertos sus libros?
___Estan cubiertos___

4. ¿Cuál es su deporte favorito?
___Mi deporte favorito es tennis___

5. ¿Es Vd. gordo(-a) o delgado(-a)?
___Soy gordo___

6. ¿Cuál es el número entre diez y doce?
___Es once___

7. ¿Está su casa cerca de la escuela?
___Mi casa no esta___

8. ¿Está Vd. bueno(-a) o malo(-a) hoy?
___Estoy bueno___

9. ¿Ha estado Vd. ausente muchos días este año?
___Si He___

10. ¿De qué colores es nuestra bandera?
___el nesto Bandere es Rojo verde y blancas y amarillo___

D. Cambie Vd. las frases siguientes al plural:

1. Esta mujer es hermosa. *ESAS estan hermosa*
2. Estoy cansado. *estamos cansados*
3. La cama está limpia. *Las camas estan limpias*
4. ¿Por qué está Vd. tan alegre? *Porque estan Vd. tan alegre*
5. El chaleco es muy pequeño. *Los chalecos estan muy pequeños*
6. Tú eres muy joven. *Vosotras es*
7. El alumno es listo. *Los alumnos son listo*
8. Su traje es nuevo. *Sus trajes son nuevos*
9. Yo no soy rico. *Nosotros no somos ricos*
10. ¿Es feliz la muchacha? *Son felices las muchachas*

E. Traduzca Vd. al español las expresiones en inglés.

1. El elefante *was* muy grande. *HUBO FUE*
2. ¿Quién *is* él? *es*
3. ¿*Are* Vd. carpintero? *Este*
4. Yo no *am* francés. *Soy*
5. Mi hermana y yo *are* cantando. *estamos*
6. El vaso *is* vacío. *este*
7. El sillón *is* cerca de la puerta. *es*
8. Nosotros *were* esperando. *ESTABAMOS*
9. *It will be* el primero de mayo. *SERA*
10. ¿*Are they* aquí? *ESTAN*

F. Traduzca Vd. al español.

1. She is happy, but he is sad.
   Es felix, pero este TRISTE

2. This wine is from Spain.
   Este VINO es

3. The child is ill.   (two ways)
   EL NINO este MALO

4. They were poor, but now they are rich.
   SER POBRE pero ahora son Rico

5. That boy is not lazy; he is tired.
   Ese muchacho NO es perezoso. El es cansado

6. How is your sister? She is well, thanks.
   Como es TU Hermana ELLA este buena gracias

7. The coffee is cold.
   El cafe esto frio

8. The streets are dirty today.
   Las calles estan sucias Ahora

9. We are not young; we are old.
   No somos jovanes Nosotros somos viejos

10. Paul and Anna are very intelligent students.
    Son estudiante muy int intelligente

17. REFLEXIVE VERBS

lavarse, to wash oneself

PRESENT INDICATIVE

I wash myself, you wash yourself, etc.

yo	*me lavo*	nosotros,-as	*nos lavamos*
tú	*te lavas*	vosotros,-as	*os laváis*
Vd., él, ella	*se lava*	Vds., ellos,-as	*se lavan*

PRETERITE

I washed myself, you washed yourself, etc.

yo	*me lavé*	nosotros,-as	*nos lavamos*
tú	*te lavaste*	vosotros,-as	*os lavasteis*
Vd., él, ella	*se lavó*	Vds., ellos,-as	*se lavaron*

IMPERFECT

I was washing myself, you were washing yourself, etc.

yo	*me lavaba*	nosotros,-as	*nos lavábamos*
tú	*te lavabas*	vosotros,-as	*os lavabais*
Vd., él, ella	*se lavaba*	Vds., ellos,-as	*se lavaban*

FUTURE

I shall wash myself, you will wash yourself, etc.

yo	*me lavaré*	nosotros,-as	*nos lavaremos*
tú	*te lavarás*	vosotros,-as	*os lavaréis*
Vd., él, ella	*se lavará*	Vds., ellos,-as	*se lavarán*

CONDITIONAL

I would wash myself, you would wash yourself, etc.

yo	*me lavaría*	nosotros,-as	*nos lavaríamos*
tú	*te lavarías*	vosotros,-as	*os lavaríais*
Vd., él, ella	*se lavaría*	Vds., ellos,-as	*se lavarían*

PRESENT PERFECT

I have washed myself, you have washed yourself, etc.

yo	*me he lavado*	nosotros,-as	*nos hemos lavado*
tú	*te has lavado*	vosotros,-as	*os habéis lavado*
Vd., él, ella	*se ha lavado*	Vds., ellos,-as	*se han lavado*

PLUPERFECT

I had washed myself, you had washed yourself, etc.

yo	*me había lavado*	nosotros,-as	*nos habíamos lavado*
tú	*te habías lavado*	vosotros,-as	*os habíais lavado*
Vd., él, ella	*se había lavado*	Vds., ellos,-as	*se habían lavado*

PRESENT PARTICIPLE

lavándome, lavándote, lavándose, etc., *washing myself, washing yourself, etc.*

POLITE COMMANDS (AFFIRMATIVE)

lávese Vd., *wash yourself*   ***lávense*** Vds., *wash yourselves*

Note

A. The reflexive pronoun, like other object pronouns, normally precedes the verb. When used with (1) an affirmative command, (2) an infinitive, or (3) a present participle, the reflexive pronoun follows and is attached to the verb.

NORMAL POSITION:

Se lava.   He washes himself.

EXCEPTIONS:

1. *Affirmative Command.*

Láve**se** Vd.   Wash yourself.
(affirmative)

but

No **se** lave Vd.   Don't wash yourself.
(negative)

2. *Infinitive.*

Quiere lavar**se**. ⎫
        or   ⎬   He wants to wash himself.
Se quiere lavar. ⎭

3. *Present Participle.*

Está lavándo**se**. ⎫
        or   ⎬   He is washing himself.
Se está lavando. ⎭

B. A reflexive pronoun may either follow the infinitive or present participle, or precede the "conjugated" verb.

C. When a reflexive pronoun follows the affirmative command or the present participle, a written accent mark is required on the vowel that was stressed before the addition of the pronoun.

COMMON REFLEXIVE VERBS

asustarse, to be frightened
callarse, to be silent, to keep still
desayunarse, to eat breakfast
enfadarse ⎫
enojarse ⎬ to get angry
equivocarse, to be mistaken

irse ⎫
marcharse ⎬ to go away
levantarse, to get up
llamarse, to be called or named
pasearse, to take a walk

peinarse, to comb one's hair
ponerse, to put on, to become
quedarse, to remain
quejarse, to complain
quitarse, to take off
sentarse, to sit down

EJERCICIOS

A. Escriba Vd. la forma correcta de los verbos *a, b,* y *c* en lugar del verbo en letra cursiva.

1. El ladrón *se reía* de la policía.   (*a*) burlarse   (*b*) quejarse   (*c*) alejarse

   (*a*) _Se burla_   (*b*) _quej_   (*c*) _aleje_

2. ¿Por qué *se enojó* Vd.?   (*a*) callarse   (*b*) irse   (*c*) levantarse

   (*a*) _____   (*b*) _fue_   (*c*) _levante_

3. Alberto *se asustó.*　　(*a*) divertirse　　(*b*) sentarse　　(*c*) enfadarse

(*a*) _divertir_　　(*b*) _sentir_　　(*c*) _enfad_

4. *Nos levantaremos* temprano.　　(*a*) dormirse　　(*b*) despedirse　　(*c*) acostarse

(*a*) _____　　(*b*) _____　　(*c*) _____

5. El anciano *estaba peinándose.*　　(*a*) acercarse　　(*b*) quejarse　　(*c*) pasearse

(*a*) _Peinandose_　　(*b*) _____　　(*c*) _paseandose_

6. La enfermera no *se ha acordado* del hombre enfermo.　　(*a*) alejarse　　(*b*) olvidarse
(*c*) despedirse

(*a*) _____　　(*b*) _____　　(*c*) _____

7. ¿Cuándo *se marcharon* los actores?　　(*a*) lavarse　　(*b*) presentarse　　(*c*) desayunarse

(*a*) _____　　(*b*) _____　　(*c*) _____

8. No *se acuesten* Vds.　　(*a*) olvidarse　　(*b*) reírse　　(*c*) dormirse

(*a*) _____　　(*b*) _____　　(*c*) _____

9. Los novios *se casarán* en octubre.　　(*a*) irse　　(*b*) despedirse　　(*c*) marcharse

(*a*) _iran_　　(*b*) _despedira_　　(*c*) _____

10. Vds. *se equivocaban.*　　(*a*) vestirse　　(*b*) despertarse　　(*c*) callarse

(*a*) _se vestian_　　(*b*) _despertaban_　　(*c*) _callaban_

B.　Escriba Vd. la forma indicada del verbo en letra cursiva.

1. pres. ind.　　¿Cómo *llamarse* tú?　_____

2. imp. ind.　　Esa criada no *ocuparse* de sus deberes.　_____

3. preterite　　Los niños *ponerse* tristes.　_____

4. imperative　　¡No *equivocarse* Vds. en el uso de esas
　　　　　　　palabras!　_____

5. pres. perf.　　Ella *quejarse* del servicio.　_____

6. preterite　　Al ver el sol, la niña *alegrarse.*　_____

7. pres. ind.　　La dama *quitarse* los guantes.　_____

8. future　　Carlos y su hermana *quedarse* aquí.　_____

9. conditional　　Nosotros *hallarse* allí a las nueve.　_____

10. gerund　　Hace una hora que está *despedirse* de sus
　　　　　　compañeros.　_____

11. preterite　　No sé por qué Carlos *acostarse.*　_____

12. infinitive　　Tú debes *unirse* a los buenos.　_____

13. pres. ind.　　Todos los días mi madre *dirigirse* al mercado.　_____

14. imperative　　*Quedarse* Vds. aquí en la sala.　_Queden_

15. future　　El enemigo no *atreverse* a atacar.　_atrevera_

16. pluperfect　　Nosotros ya *desayunarse.*　_____

17. imp. ind.　　A menudo mi tía *quejarse* de su salud.　_____

18. preterite　　El torero *sorprenderse* al ver el toro.　_____

19. gerund　　Yo estaba *quitarse* los calcetines.　_____

20. infinitive　　Debemos *moverse* pronto.　_____

C. Conteste Vd. en español en frases completas.

1. ¿Se apresura Vd. a llegar a tiempo a la escuela?

----

2. ¿Desea Vd. hacerse médico?

----

3. ¿Se aprovecha Vd. de sus oportunidades?

----

4. ¿Se lavó Vd. la cara esta mañana?

----

5. ¿Se enoja Vd. a menudo?

----

6. ¿Dónde se encuentran el elefante y el león?

----

7. ¿Se mira Vd. en el espejo cuando se peina?

----

8. ¿Cómo se llama Vd.?

----

9. ¿Se sentía Vd. mal al entrar en esta clase?

----

10. ¿En qué estación se mueren las flores y las hojas?

D. Traduzca Vd. al español las expresiones en inglés.

1. *He was taking a walk* por la calle. _Se paseaba_
2. Los hombres valientes *are not frightened* fácilmente. _asustan_
3. Vds. *are mistaken* esta vez. _equivocen_
4. Roberto *used to complain* de sus vecinos. _____
5. Mi familia *has not eaten breakfast* todavía. _____
6. Todos los hombres *were silent.* _____
7. *We complained* del precio. _quejamos_
8. Mis parientes *became* tristes. _se pusieron_
9. *He put on* un gabán de lana. _puso_
10. *She has remained* en el hotel. _____
11. Roberto *did not wash* el cuello y las orejas. _No se lavó_
12. *She didn't put on* la blusa amarilla. _____
13. *¡Go away* Vd.! _Vaya se_
14. *He will get angry* si le dices eso. _enojará_
15. *They went away* satisfechos. _____

E. Traduzca Vd. al español.

1. My name is Henry; my friend's name is Robert. _____

    _____

2. They became very sick yesterday. _____

    _____

3. My sister and I got up early today. _____

    _____

4. His friends are going away. _____

5. Helen is never mistaken. _____

6. I want to sit down here. _____

7. John used to get up late. _____

8. The men became angry. _____

9. Keep still, please. _____

10. I took off my shoes. _____

La América Latina produce casi todo el café que se bebe en los Estados
Unidos. Las bayas (berries) de café crecen en un árbol, el cafeto. Antes de
exportarlas, es necesario limpiar y secarlas.

18. POLITE COMMANDS WITH *VD.* AND *VDS.*

The polite command is formed from the first person singular of the present indicative. The final -o is changed as follows:

-ar verbs:	to **-e** (Vd.) or **-en** (Vds.)
-er verbs }	to **-a** (Vd.) or **-an** (Vds.)
-ir verbs }	

	Pres. Ind., First Singular	Polite Commands
caer, to fall	caig**o**	caig**a** Vd., caig**an** Vds.
comer, to eat	com**o**	com**a** Vd., com**an** Vds.
decir, to say	dig**o**	dig**a** Vd., dig**an** Vds.
escribir, to write	escrib**o**	escrib**a** Vd., escrib**an** Vds.
hacer, to do	hag**o**	hag**a** Vd., hag**an** Vds.
huir, to flee	huy**o**	huy**a** Vd., huy**an** Vds.
oír, to hear	oig**o**	oig**a** Vd., oig**an** Vds.
poner, to put	pong**o**	pong**a** Vd., pong**an** Vds.
salir, to leave	salg**o**	salg**a** Vd., salg**an** Vds.
tener, to have	teng**o**	teng**a** Vd., teng**an** Vds.
tomar, to take	tom**o**	tom**e** Vd., tom**en** Vds.
traducir, to translate	traduzc**o**	traduzc**a** Vd., traduzc**an** Vds.
traer, to bring	traig**o**	traig**a** Vd., traig**an** Vds.
venir, to come	veng**o**	veng**a** Vd., veng**an** Vds.
ver, to see	ve**o**	ve**a** Vd., ve**an** Vds.

The following verbs form the polite commands irregularly:

dar, to give	*dé* Vd., *den* Vds.
ir, to go	*vaya* Vd., *vayan* Vds.
ser, to be	*sea* Vd., *sean* Vds.

EJERCICIOS

A. Escriba Vd. la forma correcta de los verbos *a*, *b*, y *c* en lugar del verbo en letra cursiva.

1. *Salga* Vd. de aquí.   (*a*) huir   (*b*) ir   (*c*) partir

   (*a*) _____   (*b*) _____   (*c*) _____

2. *Miren* Vds. ese árbol.   (*a*) conservar   (*b*) describir   (*c*) no cortar

   (*a*) _____   (*b*) _____   (*c*) _____

3. *Vaya* Vd. ahora mismo.   (*a*) entrar   (*b*) gritar   (*c*) obedecer

   (*a*) _____   (*b*) _____   (*c*) _____

4. *Repitan* Vds. lo que les digo.   (*a*) hacer   (*b*) no olvidar   (*c*) oír

   (*a*) _____   (*b*) _____   (*c*) _____

5. *Viva* Vd. mucho tiempo.   (*a*) estudiar   (*b*) no esperar   (*c*) descansar

   (*a*) _____   (*b*) _____   (*c*) _____

6. *Muestre* Vd. el juguete al niño.   (*a*) devolver   (*b*) dar   (*c*) quitar

(*a*) _____   (*b*) _____   (*c*) _____

7. *Defiendan* Vds. la verdad.   (*a*) decir   (*b*) creer   (*c*) descubrir

(*a*) _____   (*b*) _____   (*c*) _____

8. *Prometa* Vd. pronunciar bien.   (*a*) principiar a   (*b*) aprender a   (*c*) tratar de

(*a*) _____   (*b*) _____   (*c*) _____

9. *Traiga* Vd. los platos.   (*a*) arrojar   (*b*) romper   (*c*) contar

(*a*) _____   (*b*) _____   (*c*) _____

10. *Traduzca* Vd. la página.   (*a*) escribir   (*b*) copiar   (*c*) ver

(*a*) _____   (*b*) _____   (*c*) _____

B. Cambie Vd. cada frase empleando la forma imperativa del verbo, según los ejemplos.

EJEMPLOS: Yo no ayudo a mi mamá.   *Ayude Vd.* a su mamá.

Nosotros no ayudamos   *Ayuden Vds.* a su mamá.
a nuestra mamá.

1. Yo no leo el periódico. _____ el periódico.

2. Yo no cierro la puerta. _____ la puerta.

3. No somos diligentes. _____ diligentes.

4. No escribimos la forma correcta. _____ la forma correcta.

5. No tomo asiento. _____ asiento.

6. No cuido a mi hermano menor. _____ a su hermano menor.

7. No contestamos en voz alta. _____ en voz alta.

8. No como los bizcochos. _____ los bizcochos.

9. No cubro mi libro. _____ su libro.

10. No aprendemos las ciencias. _____ las ciencias.

C. Escriba Vd. la forma correcta (singular o plural) del imperativo.

1. (estudia) _____ Vd.   6. (da) _____ Vd.

2. (pongo) _____ Vd.   7. (veo) _____ Vd.

3. (caen) _____ Vds.   8. (vengo) _____ Vds.

4. (responde) _____ Vd.   9. (abren) _____ Vds.

5. (voy) _____ Vds.   10. (recibe) _____ Vd.

D. Traduzca Vd. al español las expresiones en inglés.

1. *Leave* Vd. de casa en seguida. _____

2. *Do not eat* Vds. tan aprisa. _____

3. *Bring* Vds. las cartas aquí. _____

4. *Buy* Vd. diez centavos de chocolate. _____

5. *Open* Vd. las ventanas, por favor. _____

6. *Give* Vd. el cuaderno al estudiante. _____

7. *Translate* Vds. bien las frases. _____

8. *Do not speak* Vd. a Dorotea.   ------------------------------

9. El profesor dijo a los alumnos:—*Read* Vds.   ------------------------------

10. *Do* Vds. el trabajo ahora.   ------------------------------

    E. Traduzca Vd. al español.

1. Listen to the teacher (Vds.).   ------------------------------

2. Do not fall (Vd.).   ------------------------------

3. Go home (Vd.).   ------------------------------

4. Write clearly (Vds.).   ------------------------------

5. Have patience (Vds.).   ------------------------------

6. Come early (Vd.).   ------------------------------

7. Tell the truth (Vd.).   ------------------------------

8. Sell the automobile (Vd.).   ------------------------------

9. Bring your books (Vds.).   ------------------------------

10. Eat slowly (Vds.).   ------------------------------

La Giralda es una famosa torre construida por los moros en Sevilla. En lo alto de la torre hay una veleta (weathervane), en forma de mujer, que "gira" (turns) con el viento. De allí (Hence) el nombre—Giralda.

19. VERBS ENDING IN *-CAR, -GAR,* AND *-ZAR*

Verbs ending in **-car, -gar, -zar** change the consonant as follows:

$$
\left.
\begin{array}{l}
\textbf{c to qu} \\
\textbf{g to gu} \\
\textbf{z to c}
\end{array}
\right\} \text{before the letter } \textbf{e}
$$

The changes therefore occur in the following forms:

1. preterite (1 singular)
2. polite commands

explicar, to explain

PRETERITE: *expliqué,* explicaste, explicó, explicamos, explicasteis, explicaron
COMMAND: *explique* Vd., *expliquen* Vds.

llegar, to arrive

PRETERITE: *llegué,* llegaste, llegó, llegamos, llegasteis, llegaron
COMMAND: *llegue* Vd., *lleguen* Vds.

rezar, to pray

PRETERITE: *recé,* rezaste, rezó, rezamos, rezasteis, rezaron
COMMAND: *rece* Vd., *recen* Vds.

Note. These changes in spelling are necessary in order to keep the original sounds of the consonants.

COMMON *-CAR* VERBS

acercarse (a), to approach
atacar, to attack
buscar, to look for
colocar, to place
dedicar, to dedicate, to devote
explicar, to explain
mascar, to chew
sacar, to take out
significar, to mean
suplicar, to beg, to implore
tocar, to touch, to play
(an instrument)

COMMON *-GAR* VERBS

cargar, to load
castigar, to punish
entregar, to deliver, to hand over
jugar (ue), to play (a game)
juzgar, to judge
llegar, to arrive
negar (ie), to deny
obligar, to obligate, to compel
pagar, to pay
rogar (ue), to beg, to request

COMMON *-ZAR* VERBS

abrazar, to embrace
alcanzar, to overtake, to reach
almorzar (ue), to lunch
alzar, to raise
avanzar, to advance
comenzar (ie), to begin
cruzar, to cross
empezar (ie), to begin
gozar, to enjoy
lanzar, to throw
realizar, to fulfill, to realize (a profit)
rezar, to pray
tropezar, to stumble

Important: Verbs with spelling changes are identified in the vocabulary lists by the type of change **(qu, gu, c)** in parentheses next to the verb.

70

EJERCICIOS

A. Conteste Vd. en español en frases completas.

1. ¿A qué hora se acercó Vd. a la escuela?

   ----

2. ¿Pagó Vd. la cuenta ayer?

   ----

3. ¿A qué hora empezó Vd. a estudiar?

   ----

4. ¿Tocó Vd. el piano anoche?

   ----

5. ¿Jugó Vd. a la pelota hoy?

   ----

6. ¿Explicó el profesor esta lección?

   ----

7. ¿Rezó Vd. anoche?

   ----

8. ¿Cuándo llegó Vd. a casa ayer?

   ----

9. ¿Buscó Vd. a su amigo(-a) la semana pasada?

   ----

10. ¿Abrazó Vd. a su madre al salir?

    ----

11. ¿Dónde colocó Vd. el sombrero?

    ----

12. ¿Cruzó Vd. la calle hoy?

    ----

13. ¿Sacó Vd. un libro de la biblioteca?

    ----

14. ¿A qué hora almorzó Vd. ayer?

    ----

15. ¿Alzó Vd. la mano hoy en la clase?

B. Cambie Vd. el infinitivo al pretérito, primera persona singular, y al imperativo (con *Vd.*).
   Ejemplo: abrazar—*abracé, abrace Vd.*

1. suplicar ------------------------------   5. gozar ------------------------------
2. obligar ------------------------------   6. juzgar ------------------------------
3. avanzar ------------------------------   7. lanzar ------------------------------
4. significar ------------------------------   8. mascar ------------------------------

9. tropezar _____

10. atacar _____

11. entregar _____

12. realizar _____

13. alcanzar _____

14. cargar _____

15. alzar _____

16. dedicar _____

17. castigar _____

18. comenzar _____

19. negar _____

20. rogar _____

C. Traduzca Vd. al español las expresiones en inglés.

1. ¿Dónde *did I place* los zapatos? _____

2. *Explain* Vd. el problema. _____

3. Ayer *I played* el piano. _____

4. *I did not play* al ajedrez. _____

5. *Advance* Vds. contra el enemigo. _____

6. ¿A qué hora *do you lunch?* _____

7. *He enjoys* de buena fama. _____

8. *I looked for* el libro pero no lo hallé. _____

9. Corrí tras él y le *overtook.* _____

10. *I took out* el dinero del banco. _____

11. *Do not approach* a aquel edificio. _____

12. *I punished* al alumno. _____

13. *¿Did they arrive* a tiempo? _____

14. *Attack* Vds. con fuerza. _____

15. *Begin* Vds. a escribir. _____

16. *Do not cross* Vd. las calles. _____

17. No puedo *reach* aquel cuadro. _____

18. Yo lo *denied.* _____

19. *He raised* los ojos. _____

20. El cartero me *delivered* el paquete. _____

D. Traduzca Vd. al español.

1. Look for the magazine. _____

2. I approached the store. _____

3. Begin the lesson. _____

4. I arrived last night. _____

5. I already lunched. _____

6. I enjoyed the music. _____

7. Do not touch that picture. _____

8. Punish the thief. _____

9. Pay the bill tomorrow. _____

10. Who plays the guitar? _____

20. VERBS ENDING IN -*GER*, -*GIR*, AND -*GUIR*

Verbs ending in **-ger, -gir, -guir** change the consonant as follows:

> **g** to **j**
> **gu** to **g** } before **o** or **a**

The changes therefore occur in the following forms:

1. present indicative (1 singular)
2. polite commands

proteger, to protect

PRES. IND.: *protejo,* proteges, protege, protegemos, protegéis, protegen
COMMAND: *proteja* Vd., *protejan* Vds.

dirigir, to direct

PRES. IND.: *dirijo,* diriges, dirige, dirigimos, dirigís, dirigen
COMMAND: *dirija* Vd., *dirijan* Vds.

seguir (i), to follow, to keep on

PRES. IND.: *sigo,* sigues, sigue, seguimos, seguís, siguen
COMMAND: *siga* Vd., *sigan* Vds.

Note. These changes in spelling are necessary in order to keep the original sounds of the consonants.

COMMON -*GER* VERBS

coger, to seize, to catch
escoger, to choose
proteger, to protect
recoger, to pick up, to gather

COMMON -*GIR* VERBS

corregir (i), to correct
dirigir, to direct
dirigirse a, to make one's way toward, to address
elegir (i), to elect

COMMON -*GUIR* VERBS

conseguir (i), to get, to obtain, to succeed in
distinguir, to distinguish
perseguir (i), to pursue
seguir (i), to follow, to keep on

Important: Verbs with these spelling changes are identified in the vocabulary lists by the type of change **(j, g)** in parentheses next to the verb.

EJERCICIOS

A. Conteste Vd. en español en frases completas.

1. ¿Escoge Vd. a sus amigos con cuidado?

----

2. ¿Distingue Vd. entre lo bueno y lo malo?

----

3. ¿Corrige Vd. sus faltas?

----

4. ¿Sigue Vd. estudiando el español?

----

5. ¿Protege Vd. a los niños?

----

6. ¿Consigue Vd. buenas notas en la clase de español?

----

7. ¿Coge Vd. muchas moscas en el verano?

----

8. ¿Recoge Vd. sus libros antes de salir de casa?

----

9. ¿A qué hora se dirige Vd. a casa?

----

10. ¿A quién eligieron presidente del país?

B. Cambie Vd. el infinitivo al presente, primera persona singular, y al imperativo (con *Vd.*).

EJEMPLO: coger—*cojo, coja Vd.*

1. dirigir	_____	6. corregir	_____
2. perseguir	_____	7. recoger	_____
3. escoger	_____	8. distinguir	_____
4. seguir	_____	9. elegir	_____
5. proteger	_____	10. conseguir	_____

C. Escriba Vd. la forma indicada del verbo en letra cursiva.

1. pres. ind.   Yo *coger* un catarro a menudo.   _____
2. command   *Corregir* Vds. las faltas.   _____
3. command   *Seguir* Vd. leyendo.   _____
4. pres. ind.   Yo *dirigirse* a su casa.   _____
5. command   *Escoger* Vd. el mejor diamante.   _____
6. preterite   Pedro *conseguir* un buen empleo.   _____
7. pres. ind.   La muchacha *recoger* el pañuelo.   _____
8. pres. ind.   Los padres siempre *proteger* a sus hijos.   _____
9. pres. ind.   Yo no *distinguir* entre los dos colores.   _____
10. pres. ind.   El policía *perseguir* al ladrón.   _____
11. pres. ind.   Yo siempre *escoger* los problemas más difíciles.   _____
12. pres. ind.   Yo no *seguir* sus consejos.   _____
13. command   *Coger* Vd. la pelota.   _____

14. pres. ind.   Antes de salir yo *recoger* mis cuadernos.   _____

15. command   *Conseguir* Vd. buenas notas.   _____

D. Traduzca Vd. al español las expresiones en inglés.

1. *Pick up* los lápices.   _____

2. *Keep on* luchando.   _____

3. El policía *seized* al ladrón.   _____

4. *He succeeded in* convencer a sus amigos.   _____

5. *He kept on* escribiendo.   _____

6. *I catch* la pelota.   _____

7. Yo siempre *follow* sus consejos.   _____

8. Ellos le *elected* presidente.   _____

9. *Correct* Vd. las frases.   _____

10. *I am addressing* a Vds.   _____

El gaucho es el "cowboy" de las pampas (plains) de la Argentina. Es una figura pintoresca y romántica. Se dice que el gaucho quiere más a su caballo que a su familia. La historia del gaucho está estrechamente (closely) unida a la de su país. En la edad moderna el gaucho va desapareciendo.

21. VERBS ENDING IN -*CER* AND -*CIR*

Most verbs ending in **-cer** and **-cir** change **c** to **zc** before **o** or **a**, if a vowel precedes the **c.** The change therefore occurs in the following forms:

      1. present indicative (1 singular)
      2. polite commands

ofrecer, to offer

PRES. IND.:   *ofrezco,* ofreces, ofrece, ofrecemos, ofrecéis, ofrecen
COMMAND: *ofrezca* Vd., *ofrezcan* Vds.

producir, to produce

PRES. IND.:   *produzco,* produces, produce, producimos, producís, producen
COMMAND: *produzca* Vd., *produzcan* Vds.

Note

A. **Decir** (*digo, diga, digan*) and **hacer** (*hago, haga, hagan*) are exceptions.

B. If a consonant precedes the **c,** the change is **c** to **z:**

vencer: *venzo, venza, venzan*

C. Verbs ending in **-ducir** are also irregular in the preterite.

produje, produjiste, produjo, produjimos, produjisteis, produjeron

COMMON -*CER* VERBS

agradecer, to thank (for)   **ofrecer,** to offer
aparecer, to appear   **padecer,** to suffer
conocer, to know (a person)   **parecer,** to seem
desaparecer, to disappear   **permanecer,** to remain
merecer, to deserve   **pertenecer,** to belong
nacer, to be born   **reconocer,** to recognize
obedecer, to obey

COMMON -*CIR* VERBS

conducir, to lead, to drive   **reducir,** to reduce
producir, to produce   **traducir,** to translate

Important: Verbs with these spelling changes are identified in the vocabulary lists by the type of change **(z, zc)** in parentheses next to the verb.

EJERCICIOS

A. Escriba Vd. las formas correctas de cada verbo en el tiempo indicado, empleando los sujetos indicados.

EJEMPLOS: ellos ofrecen: yo *ofrezco* ; Vds. *ofrecen*

           Vds. redujeron: tú *redujiste* ; él *redujo*

1. nosotros traducimos: yo _____; los alumnos _____

2. yo merezco: nosotros _____; Felipe _____

3. ellos produjeron: él _____; yo _____

4. él parece: ellos _____; yo _____

5. ¿obedece Vd.?   yo _____ ; tú _____

6. nosotros convencemos: yo _____ ; el padre _____

7. nosotros conocemos: yo _____ ; ¿quién _____ ?

8. ellos nacieron: él _____ ; yo _____

9. él condujo: ellos _____ ; nosotros _____

10. Juan padeció: nosotros _____ ; ellos _____

B. Conteste Vd. en español en frases completas.

1. ¿Cuándo nació Vd.? _____

_____

2. ¿Conoce Vd. a sus vecinos? _____

3. ¿Obedece Vd. a sus padres? _____

4. ¿Conduce Vd. un automóvil? _____

5. ¿Vence Vd. a sus rivales? _____

6. ¿Ofrece Vd. ayuda al profesor? _____

7. ¿Agradece Vd. a sus amigos los favores que ellos le hacen? _____

_____

8. ¿Traduce Vd. bien las frases de la lección? _____

_____

9. ¿Padece Vd. dolor de cabeza ahora? _____

_____

10. ¿Desaparece Vd. cuando hay algo que hacer? _____

_____

C. Cambie Vd. el infinitivo al presente, primera persona singular, y al imperativo (con *Vd.*).
EJEMPLO: obedecer—*obedezco, obedezca Vd.*

1. merecer	_____	6. pertenecer	_____
2. traducir	_____	7. reducir	_____
3. desaparecer	_____	8. vencer	_____
4. aparecer	_____	9. agradecer	_____
5. permanecer	_____	10. reconocer	_____

D. Traduzca Vd. al español las expresiones en inglés.

1. *It seems* extraño. _____

2. *I do not deserve* este premio. _____

3. Yo le *thank for* su bondad. _____

4. *Appear* Vds. ante el juez. _____

5. Yo le *led* al ascensor. _____

6. *Translate* Vds. al inglés. _____

7. *I know* a su padre. _____

8. *Obey* Vd. a la profesora. _____

9. *I was born* en agosto. _____

10. ¿*Do you recognize* a este hombre? _____

11. *They disappeared* a lo lejos. _____

12. *Offer* Vd. este dinero al pobre. _____

13. Yo le *convinced* que hoy es martes. _____

14. ¿A quién *belongs* este dinero? _____

15. *They conquered* al enemigo. _____

    E. Traduzca Vd. al español.

1. I always obey my mother. _____

2. I know her very well. _____

3. He seems intelligent. _____

4. Spain produces much wine. _____

5. I belong to this club. _____

6. I thank you [for] this gift. _____

7. He drives a new car. _____

8. It seems impossible. _____

9. Do you know that lady? _____

10. I do not recognize this man. _____

Lope de Vega (1562-1635) fue el dramaturgo principal de España y una figura prominente de la literatura universal. Escribió centenares (hundreds) de comedias, todas en verso (poetry). Su influencia fue tan grande que se dice que no sólo escribió para el teatro, sino que creó (created) el teatro nacional.

22. VERBS ENDING IN *-IAR, -UAR,* AND *-UIR*

1. Some verbs ending in **-iar** and **-uar** have a written accent mark on the **i** (**í**) or the **u** (**ú**) in the following forms:

    1. present indicative (1, 2, 3 singular and 3 plural)
    2. polite commands

PRESENT INDICATIVE

enviar, to send		**continuar,** to continue	
envío	enviamos	contin**ú**o	continuamos
envías	enviáis	contin**ú**as	continuáis
envía	envían	contin**ú**a	contin**ú**an

POLITE COMMAND

envíe Vd.	envíen Vds.
contin**ú**e Vd.	contin**ú**en Vds.

Like **enviar**: guiar; like **continuar**: situar, graduarse.

Note. The verbs **anunciar, averiguar, cambiar, copiar, estudiar, iniciar, limpiar, odiar, principiar,** and **pronunciar** are exceptions and have no accents on the **u** or the **i**.

2. Verbs ending in **-uir** (but not **-guir**) change as follows: Drop the infinitive ending (**-ir**) and insert **y** in the:

    a. present indicative (1, 2, 3 singular and 3 plural)
    b. polite commands
    c. preterite (3 singular and 3 plural)
    d. present participle

huir, to flee

PRESENT INDICATIVE

hu**y**o	huimos
hu**y**es	huís
hu**y**e	hu**y**en

POLITE COMMAND

hu**y**a Vd.	hu**y**an Vds.

PRETERITE

huí	huimos
huiste	huisteis
hu**y**ó	hu**y**eron

PRESENT PARTICIPLE

hu**y**endo

Like **huir**: concluir, construir, contribuir, destruir, distribuir, influir, sustituir.

EJERCICIOS

A. Cambie Vd. la forma del verbo en letra cursiva, empleando los sujetos indicados.

1. Yo *envío* el regalo.

   Nosotros _____

   Ella _____

   Vosotros _____

2. Ella *distribuye* los premios.

   Ellos _____

   Yo _____

   Nosotras _____

3. Nosotros *contribuimos* (present) a menudo.

   Él _____

   María y yo _____

   Yo _____

4. Ellas *odian* el trabajo.

   Tú y yo _____

   Mi hermano _____

   Vd. _____

5. Nosotras *continuamos* (present) andando.

   Tú _____

   Vosotros _____

   Ellos _____

6. Tú *averiguas* la distancia.

   Vosotros _____

   Yo _____

   Ellos _____

7. Vds. *construyeron* un ferrocarril.

   Vd. _____

   Tú _____

   Nosotros _____

8. Tú *guías* el coche.

   Nosotros _____

   Vd. _____

   Ellos _____

9. Él *anuncia* la llegada del tren.

   Los empleados _____

   Vd. _____

   Vosotros _____

10. Ella y yo *limpiamos* (preterite) la habitación.

    Luisa _____

    Ellas _____

    Tú _____

B. Escriba Vd. la forma correcta de los verbos *a*, *b*, y *c* en lugar del verbo en letra cursiva.

1. *Anda* por el bosque.   (*a*) huir   (*b*) correr   (*c*) avanzar

   (*a*) _____   (*b*) _____   (*c*) _____

2. Un soldado *limpia* las armas.   (*a*) destruir   (*b*) distribuir   (*c*) enviar

   (*a*) _____   (*b*) _____   (*c*) _____

3. *Colocaron* el hospital en la avenida principal.   (*a*) situar   (*b*) construir   (*c*) alzar

   (*a*) _____   (*b*) _____   (*c*) _____

4. Están *mirando* un gran edificio.   (*a*) construir   (*b*) destruir   (*c*) limpiar

   (*a*) _____   (*b*) _____   (*c*) _____

5. Sale *gritando*.   (*a*) correr   (*b*) cantar   (*c*) huir

   (*a*) _____   (*b*) _____   (*c*) _____

6. *Rompió* las cortinas.   (*a*) limpiar   (*b*) cambiar   (*c*) destruir

   (*a*) _____   (*b*) _____   (*c*) _____

7. El general está *regresando* del combate.   (*a*) retirarse   (*b*) huir   (*c*) alejarse

   (*a*) _____   (*b*) _____   (*c*) _____

8. *Pronúncielo* con cuidado.   (*a*) copiar   (*b*) situar   (*c*) estudiar

   (*a*) _____   (*b*) _____   (*c*) _____

9. *Arreglaron* el asunto.   (*a*) terminar   (*b*) estudiar   (*c*) concluir

(*a*) ----------------------   (*b*) ----------------------   (*c*) ----------------------

10. *Terminan* el negocio.   (*a*) cambiar   (*b*) continuar   (*c*) concluir

(*a*) ----------------------   (*b*) ----------------------   (*c*) ----------------------

C. Conteste Vd. en español en frases completas.

1. ¿Mueve Vd. los labios cuando pronuncia las palabras? ----------------------------------

----

2. ¿Continúa Vd. escuchando los programas de radio todo el día? ----------------------

----

3. ¿Cuándo se gradúa Vd.? --

4. ¿Construyen muchos rascacielos en esta ciudad? ----------------------------

----

5. ¿Guía Vd. el automóvil de su familia? --

----

6. ¿Huye Vd. de la escuela los días de exámenes? ----------------------------

----

7. ¿Inicia Vd. el día dando un paseo rápido? ----------------------------------

----

8. ¿Cambian a menudo las modas? --

----

9. ¿Contribuye Vd. mucho dinero para los pobres? ----------------------------

----

10. ¿Destruye Vd. los nidos de los pájaros? ----------------------------------

----

11. ¿Influye Vd. en las decisiones de sus padres? ----------------------------

----

12. ¿Estudia Vd. el latín también? --

----

13. ¿Se limpia Vd. los dientes todos los días? --------------------------------

----

14. ¿Envía Vd. tarjetas de cumpleaños a sus amigos? --------------------------

----

15. ¿Odia Vd. los huevos? --

D. Traduzca Vd. al español las expresiones en inglés.

1. Mi prima *did not graduate* el año pasado.   ----------------------------------

2. Los indios de México *constructed* muchas pirámides.   ----------------------------

3. Ellos *contributed* mucho para defender a su patria.   ------------------------------------

4. Estaban *destroying* la ciudad.   ------------------------------------

5. *Send it* Vd. lo más pronto posible.   ------------------------------------

6. El ingeniero *copied* los planes.   ------------------------------------

7. *He guided* a los turistas al museo.   ------------------------------------

8. Al ver al policía, el ladrón *began* a gritar.   ------------------------------------

9. *Substitute* Vd. esta palabra por otra.   ------------------------------------

10. El director *concluded* su discurso.   ------------------------------------

E. Traduzca Vd. al español.

1. Do not hate (Vds.) your neighbors.

----

2. She continues speaking.

----

3. Pronounce (Vd.) the word clearly.

----

4. I sent him the gift.

----

5. A pupil distributed the papers.

----

6. She found out the price of the article.

----

7. The maid cleans the room every day.

----

8. The soldiers don't flee from the battle.

----

9. An employee announces the hour.

----

10. Charles didn't study the lesson last night.

----

23. THE PASSIVE EXPRESSED BY A REFLEXIVE CONSTRUCTION; INDEFINITE *SE*

1. The passive voice is often expressed by the reflexive construction when the agent (doer) is not mentioned and the subject is a thing.

Aquí **se habla** español. (singular) (singular)	Spanish is spoken here.
Se abren las tiendas a las nueve. (plural) (plural)	The stores are opened at nine o'clock.
Se terminó el trabajo. (singular) (singular)	The work was finished.
Se construyeron muchas casas. (plural) (plural)	Many houses were built.

Note

A. The third person singular form of the verb is used when the subject is singular; the third person plural is used when the subject is plural.

B. The subject often follows the verb.

2. The pronoun **se** is used also with indefinite meaning (*one, people, they, you,* etc.). As an indefinite pronoun it is always used with a verb in the third person singular.

Se cree que él es rico.	(It is believed, People believe, One believes, They believe) that he is rich.
Se paga al entrar.	(One pays, People pay, You pay) upon entering.

EJERCICIOS

A. Escriba Vd. la forma reflexiva de los verbos *a*, *b*, y *c* en lugar del verbo en letra cursiva.

1. Aquí *se vende* tabaco.   (*a*) fumar   (*b*) comprar   (*c*) cultivar

   (*a*) _____   (*b*) _____   (*c*) _____

2. Los billetes *se compran* allí.   (*a*) echar   (*b*) distribuir   (*c*) cobrar

   (*a*) _____   (*b*) _____   (*c*) _____

3. Esas flores *se encuentran* en el campo.   (*a*) ver   (*b*) buscar   (*c*) hallar

   (*a*) _____   (*b*) _____   (*c*) _____

4. La fiesta *se celebrará* la semana que viene.   (*a*) omitir   (*b*) observar   (*c*) acabar

   (*a*) _____   (*b*) _____   (*c*) _____

5. *Se cree* que la bomba atómica puede destruir una ciudad entera.   (*a*) saber
   (*b*) comprender   (*c*) anunciar

   (*a*) _____   (*b*) _____   (*c*) _____

6. *Se ven* muchas cosas pintorescas en México.   (*a*) notar   (*b*) fabricar   (*c*) conservar

   (*a*) _____   (*b*) _____   (*c*) _____

7. No *se escribe* así.   (*a*) pronunciar   (*b*) jugar   (*c*) pintar

   (*a*) _____   (*b*) _____   (*c*) _____

8. No *se puede* hablar de esta manera.   (*a*) deber   (*b*) soler   (*c*) permitir

(*a*) ----------------------   (*b*) ----------------------   (*c*) ----------------------

9. La cuenta *se ha pagado* ya.   (*a*) arreglar   (*b*) cobrar   (*c*) entregar

(*a*) ----------------------   (*b*) ----------------------   (*c*) ----------------------

10. *Se necesitan* armas allí.   (*a*) enviar   (*b*) obtener   (*c*) usar

(*a*) ----------------------   (*b*) ----------------------   (*c*) ----------------------

B. Conteste Vd. en español en frases completas.

1. ¿Qué lengua se habla en España?

----

2. ¿Cuándo se celebra la Navidad?

----

3. ¿A qué hora se abre la escuela?

----

4. ¿Qué se vende en una panadería?

----

5. ¿Qué se compra en una carnicería?

----

6. ¿A qué hora se cierran las tiendas?

----

7. ¿A qué hora se sirve el almuerzo?

----

8. ¿Cómo se dice "road" en español?

----

9. ¿Dónde se hallan edificios altos?

----

10. ¿Se permite fumar en el cine?

C. Traduzca Vd. al español las expresiones en inglés.

1. Desde lejos *are heard* las campanas. ----------------------
2. *It is believed* que es un hombre valiente. ----------------------
3. El primer capítulo *was read* en voz alta. ----------------------
4. En Cuba *are produced* el azúcar y el café. ----------------------
5. En aquella fábrica *they work* hasta las cinco. ----------------------
6. En España *are eaten* muchos cereales. ----------------------
7. En aquel autobús *you pay* al entrar. ----------------------
8. Nada *is known* de su vida. ----------------------
9. Aquí *one enters* por la puerta. ----------------------

10. Poco a poco *one learns* mucho. --------------------------------------

11. En aquella tienda *are sold.* pañuelos. ----------------------------------

12. *People know* que el mundo es redondo. --------------------------------

13. Hoy día *one travels* mucho. ---

14. *They say* que él es muy rico. ---------------------------------------

15. En mi casa *we eat* a las seis. ---------------------------------------

16. Aquí *are spoken* español y francés. ----------------------------------

17. Muchos edificios *have been built.* ------------------------------------

18. En este país *people smoke* mucho. ------------------------------------

19. ¿A qué hora *is opened* esta tienda? ----------------------------------

20. Muchos monumentos *are seen* en aquel país. ----------------------------

D. Traduzca Vd. al español.

1. The national holiday of Mexico is celebrated September 16. ---------------
----

2. Many newspapers are read every day. ----------------------------------
----

3. Spanish is taught in many schools. ------------------------------------
----

4. Books are sold here. --
----

5. Much money is needed. ---
----

6. The doors are closed at noon. ---------------------------------------
----

7. It is believed that he is innocent. ------------------------------------
----

8. Many flags were seen on the streets. ----------------------------------
----

9. They say that he used to have much money. -----------------------------
----

10. How does one enter that building? -------------------------------------
----

24. THE PASSIVE VOICE (OPTIONAL)

When the agent (doer) is mentioned, the passive voice is formed by the verb **ser** followed by the past participle.

El hombre fue atacado por el perro.
The   man   was   attacked   by   the dog.

La puerta fue abierta por el alumno.
The   door   was   opened   by   the pupil.

Las ventanas fueron cerradas por el profesor.
The   windows   were   closed   by   the   teacher.

María es amada de todos.
Mary   is   loved   by   all.

Pedro amado Note

A. The past participle is used here as an adjective and agrees with the subject in gender and number.

B. *By* is translated by **por** if a physical action is expressed **(atacar, abrir, cerrar)** and by **de** if a state of mind, a feeling, or an opinion is expressed **(amar).**

C. The passive voice in Spanish is a word-for-word translation of the English passive voice.

EJERCICIOS

A. Cambie Vd. cada frase, empleando los sujetos indicados y haciendo los otros cambios necesarios.

1. *Las líneas* fueron fijadas por un comité.

   La fecha _fue fijada_

   El día _fue fijado_

   Los límites _fueron fijados_

2. *La comida* será preparada por la criada.

   Los pollos _fueron preparados_

   El rosbif _fue preparado_

   Las patatas _fueron preparadas_

3. *El alcalde* es amado de todos.

   Los extranjeros _son amados de_

   Nosotras _somos amadas de_

   Mi tía _es amada de_

4. *El acueducto* fue guardado por los soldados.

   Las calles _fueron guardadas por_

   Los puentes _fueron guardados por_

   La aduana _fue guardada por_

5. *Este cuadro* fue pintado por un gran artista.

   La obra _fue pintada_

   Los retratos _fueron pintados_

   Las escenas _" pintadas_

6. *Los gritos* fueron oídos por los habitantes.

El ruido _fue oído_

La música _fue oída_

Las canciones _fueron oídas_

7. *El presidente* es respetado de la gente.

Los jueces _son respetados_

Las leyes _son respetadas_

Su memoria _es respetada_

8. *Los soldados americanos* son admirados de todo el mundo.

El vino español _es admirado_

Las bailarinas _son admiradas_

Isabel _es admirada_

9. *Una nueva compañía* será fundada por ellos.

Dos colonias _serán fundadas_

Un teatro y un museo _serán fundados_

Un gobierno _será fundado_

10. *Las banderas* fueron tomadas por el enemigo.

La fábrica _fue tomada_

El país _fue tomado_

Los tesoros _fueron tomados_

B. Cambie Vd. las frases siguientes a la voz pasiva:

EJEMPLO: { Juan abrió las ventanas.
{ Las ventanas *fueron abiertas por* Juan.

1. La gente admira al general.

El general _es admirado de_ la gente.

2. Su hermano cerró la puerta.

La puerta _fue cerrado por_ su hermano.

3. María no invitó a Juan.

Juan no _fue invitado por_ María.

4. Cervantes escribió *Don Quijote*.

Don Quijote _fue escribado por_ Cervantes.

5. Los niños respetan a los profesores.

Los profesores _son respetados de_ los niños.

6. Pedro firmó la carta.

La carta _fue firmada_ Pedro.

7. José ayudará a mis hermanas.

Mis hermanas _serán ayudaras por_ José.

8. Antonio ama a Isabel.

Isabel __es amada de_____ Antonio.

9. La maestra castigó al niño.

El niño ___fue castigado_____ la maestra.

10. Un autor español escribió estas novelas.

Estas novelas _____ un autor español.

C. Traduzca Vd. al español las expresiones en inglés.

1. La ciudad *will be taken by* los soldados. _____

2. Teresa *was not invited by* sus amigas. _____

3. Estos estudiantes *are admired by* sus profesores. _____

4. América *was discovered by* Colón. _____

5. El soldado *was wounded by* el enemigo. _____

6. El héroe *was praised by* el presidente. _____

7. La cuenta *will be paid by* el señor Pardo. _____

8. Los hijos *are loved by* sus padres. _____

9. Los documentos *were received by* el abogado. _____

10. *She is feared by* los estudiantes. _____

D. Traduzca Vd. al español.

1. The child was saved by the dog.

_____

2. The exercises were explained by the teacher.

_____

3. They are respected by their friends.

_____

4. The town was captured by the soldiers.

_____

5. The lesson was learned by the pupils.

_____

6. The father was loved by his children.

_____

7. He is employed by the government.

_____

8. The captain was hated by his soldiers.

_____

9. The president is admired by the people.

_____

10. The books were bought by my father.

_____

25. FORMATION OF THE PRESENT SUBJUNCTIVE

The present subjunctive is formed from the stem of the present indicative, first person singular. The final **-o** is changed as follows:

> **-ar** verbs: *-e, -es, -e, -emos, -éis, -en*
> **-er** verbs⎫
> **-ir** verbs⎭ *-a, -as, -a, -amos, -áis, -an*

REGULAR VERBS

hablar, to speak		**comer**, to eat		**abrir**, to open	
habl*e*	habl*emos*	com*a*	com*amos*	abr*a*	abr*amos*
habl*es*	habl*éis*	com*as*	com*áis*	abr*as*	abr*áis*
habl*e*	habl*en*	com*a*	com*an*	abr*a*	abr*an*

	Pres. Ind., *First Singular*	*Present Subjunctive*
caber, to fit	quep**o**	*quepa, quepas, quepa, quepamos, quepáis, quepan*
caer, to fall	caig**o**	*caiga, caigas, caiga, caigamos, caigáis, caigan*
conocer, to know	conozc**o**	*conozca, conozcas, conozca, conozcamos, conozcáis, conozcan*
decir, to say	dig**o**	*diga, digas, diga, digamos, digáis, digan*
hacer, to do	hag**o**	*haga, hagas, haga, hagamos, hagáis, hagan*
huir, to flee	huy**o**	*huya, huyas, huya, huyamos, huyáis, huyan*
oír, to hear	oig**o**	*oiga, oigas, oiga, oigamos, oigáis, oigan*
poner, to put	pong**o**	*ponga, pongas, ponga, pongamos, pongáis, pongan*
salir, to leave	salg**o**	*salga, salgas, salga, salgamos, salgáis, salgan*
tener, to have	teng**o**	*tenga, tengas, tenga, tengamos, tangáis, tengan*
traducir, to translate	traduzc**o**	*traduzca, traduzcas, traduzca, traduzcamos, traduzcáis, traduzcan*
traer, to bring	traig**o**	*traiga, traigas, traiga, traigamos, traigáis, traigan*
valer, to be worth	valg**o**	*valga, valgas, valga, valgamos, valgáis, valgan*
vencer, to conquer	venz**o**	*venza, venzas, venza, venzamos, venzáis, venzan*
venir, to come	veng**o**	*venga, vengas, venga, vengamos, vengáis, vengan*
ver, to see	ve**o**	*vea, veas, vea, veamos, veáis, vean*

STEM-CHANGING VERBS

cerrar, to close	cierr**o**	*cierre, cierres, cierre,* cerremos, cerréis, *cierren*
contar, to count	cuent**o**	*cuente, cuentes, cuente,* contemos, contéis, *cuenten*
perder, to lose	pierd**o**	*pierda, pierdas, pierda,* perdamos, perdáis, *pierdan*
poder, to be able	pued**o**	*pueda, puedas, pueda,* podamos, podáis, *puedan*
querer, to want	quier**o**	*quiera, quieras, quiera,* queramos, queráis, *quieran*
volver, to return	vuelv**o**	*vuelva, vuelvas, vuelva,* volvamos, volváis, *vuelvan*
sentir, to regret	sient**o**	*sienta, sientas, sienta, sintamos, sintáis, sientan*
dormir, to sleep	duerm**o**	*duerma, duermas, duerma, durmamos, durmáis, duerman*
pedir, to ask for	pid**o**	*pida, pidas, pida, pidamos, pidáis, pidan*
enviar, to send	enví**o**	*envíe, envíes, envíe,* enviemos, enviéis, *envíen*
continuar, to continue	continú**o**	*continúe, continúes, continúe,* continuemos, continuéis, *continúen*

Note

A. In **-ar** and **-er** verbs, the stem changes in the present subjunctive are the same as those in the present indicative.

B. Stem-changing **-ir** verbs (**sentir, dormir, pedir**) also change in the first and second persons plural (**e** to **i**, **o** to **u**).

C. Some verbs ending in **-iar** or **-uar** stress the **i** or the **u** (**í, ú**) in all forms except those for **nosotros** and **vosotros**.

CONSONANT-CHANGING VERBS

avanzar, to advance	*avance, avances, avance, avancemos, avancéis, avancen*
buscar, to look for	*busque, busques, busque, busquemos, busquéis, busquen*
coger, to seize	*coja, cojas, coja, cojamos, cojáis, cojan*
dirigir, to direct	*dirija, dirijas, dirija, dirijamos, dirijáis, dirijan*
distinguir, to distinguish	*distinga, distingas, distinga, distingamos, distingáis, distingan*
empezar, to begin	*empiece, empieces, empiece, empecemos, empecéis, empiecen*
juzgar, to judge	*juzgue, juzgues, juzgue, juzguemos, juzguéis, juzguen*
llegar, to arrive	*llegue, llegues, llegue, lleguemos, lleguéis, lleguen*
pagar, to pay	*pague, pagues, pague, paguemos, paguéis, paguen*
sacar, to take out	*saque, saques, saque, saquemos, saquéis, saquen*
seguir, to follow	*siga, sigas, siga, sigamos, sigáis, sigan*
tocar, to touch	*toque, toques, toque, toquemos, toquéis, toquen*

Note. Some verbs are both stem changing and consonant changing (**empezar, seguir**).

IRREGULAR VERBS

dar, to give	*dé,* des, *dé,* demos, deis, den
estar, to be	*esté, estés, esté,* estemos, estéis, *estén*
haber, to have	*haya, hayas, haya, hayamos, hayáis, hayan*
ir, to go	*vaya, vayas, vaya, vayamos, vayáis, vayan*
saber, to know	*sepa, sepas, sepa, sepamos, sepáis, sepan*
ser, to be	*sea, seas, sea, seamos, seáis, sean*

EJERCICIOS

A. Cambie Vd. cada infinitivo a las formas siguientes: (1) presente de indicativo, 1 sing.; (2) presente de subjuntivo, 3 sing.; y (3) presente de subjuntivo, 1 plural.

EJEMPLO: valer   (1) *valgo*   (2) *valga*   (3) *valgamos*

1. destruir   (1) destruyo   (2) destruya   (3) destruyamos
2. prometer   (1) prometo   (2) prometa   (3) prometamos
3. vivir   (1) vivo   (2) viva   (3) vivamos
4. conducir   (1) conduzco   (2) conduzca   (3) conduzcamos
5. oír   (1) oigo   (2) oiga   (3) oigamos
6. venir   (1) vengo   (2) venga   (3) vengamos
7. comprar   (1) compro   (2) compre   (3) compremos
8. parecer   (1) parezco   (2) parezca   (3) parezcamos
9. ver   (1) veo   (2) vea   (3) veamos
10. decir   (1) digo   (2) diga   (3) digamos

11. tener	(1) _tenga_	(2) _tenga_	(3) _tengamos_
12. convencer	(1) _convenza_	(2) _convenza_	(3) _convenzamos_
13. recibir	(1) _reciba_	(2) _reciba_	(3) _recibamos_
14. correr	(1) _corra_	(2) _corra_	(3) _corramos_
15. visitar	(1) _visite_	(2) _visite_	(3) _visitemos_
16. hablar	(1) _hable_	(2) _hable_	(3) _hablemos_
17. caer	(1) _caiga_	(2) _caiga_	(3) _caigamos_
18. traer	(1) _traiga_	(2) _traiga_	(3) _traigamos_
19. salir	(1) _salga_	(2) _salga_	(3) _salgamos_
20. hacer	(1) _haga_	(2) _haga_	(3) _hagamos_
21. escribir	(1) _escriba_	(2) _escriba_	(3) _escribamos_
22. vender	(1) _venda_	(2) _venda_	(3) _vendamos_
23. entrar	(1) _entre_	(2) _entre_	(3) _entremos_
24. poner	(1) _ponga_	(2) _ponga_	(3) _pongamos_
25. proteger	(1) _proteja_	(2) _proteja_	(3) _protejamos_

B. Escriba Vd. las formas del presente de subjuntivo, empleando los sujetos entre paréntesis.

1. servir

(él) _sirva_   (nosotros) _sirvamos_

(yo) _sirva_   (tú) _sirvas_

2. extender

(Vd.) _extienda_   (ellas) _extiendan_

(nosotros) _extendamos_   (tú) _extiendas_

3. morir

(ella) _muera_   (nosotros) _muramos_

(ellos) _mueran_   (vosotros) _muráis_

4. soñar

(nosotros) _soñemos_   (Vd.) _sueñe_

(vosotras) _soñéis_   (yo) _sueñe_

5. encontrar _encuentres_

(tú) _encuentres_   (nosotros) _encontremos_

(él) _encuentre_   (vosotros) _encontréis_

6. dormir

(nosotros) _durmamos_   (él) _duerma_

(Vds.) _duerman_   (yo) _duerma_

7. pedir

(ellos) _pidan_   (vosotros) _pidáis_

(Vd.) _pida_   (yo) _pida_

8. contar

(vosotros) _contéis_   (ellos) _cuenten_

(tú) _cuentes_   (yo) _cuente_

9. despertarse

(él) _se despierte_   (yo) _me despierte_

(nosotros) _despertemos_   (ellos) _se despierten_

10. sentir

(yo) _sintie_   (nosotros) _sintamos_

(ellos) _sintien_   (tú) _sinties_

11. perder

(él) _pierda_   (yo) _pierda_

(nosotros) _perdamos_   (Vds.) _pierdan_

12. reír

(yo) _ría_   (él) _ría_

(nosotros) _riamos_   (tú) _rías_

13. cerrar

(yo) _cierre_   (nosotros) _cerremos_

(ellos) _cierren_   (tú) _cierres_

14. volver

(Vds.) _volváis_   (nosotros) _volvamos_

(yo) _vuelve_   (vosotros) _volváis_

15. divertirse

(yo) _divertiría_   (ella) _divierta_

(nosotros) _divertamos_   (ellos) _diviertan_

C. Cambie Vd. cada infinitivo a las formas siguientes: (1) pretérito, 1 sing.; (2) presente de subjuntivo, 3 plural; y (3) presente de subjuntivo, 1 plural.

EJEMPLO: atacar   (1) *ataqué*   (2) *ataquen*   (3) *ataquemos*

1. comenzar   (1) _____   (2) _____   (3) _____

2. continuar   (1) _____   (2) _____   (3) _____

3. abrazar   (1) _____   (2) _____   (3) _____

4. acercarse   (1) _____   (2) _____   (3) _____

5. juzgar   (1) _____   (2) _____   (3) _____

6. almorzar   (1) _____   (2) _____   (3) _____

7. sacar   (1) _____   (2) _____   (3) _____

8. llegar   (1) _____   (2) _____   (3) _____

9. alcanzar   (1) _____   (2) _____   (3) _____

10. buscar   (1) _____   (2) _____   (3) _____

11. seguir   (1) _____   (2) _____   (3) _____

12. pagar (1) _____ (2) _____ (3) _____

13. tocar (1) _____ (2) _____ (3) _____

14. distinguir (1) _____ (2) _____ (3) _____

15. dirigirse (1) _____ (2) _____ (3) _____

16. jugar (1) _____ (2) _____ (3) _____

17. explicar (1) _____ (2) _____ (3) _____

18. corregir (1) _____ (2) _____ (3) _____

19. avanzar (1) _____ (2) _____ (3) _____

20. coger (1) _____ (2) _____ (3) _____

D. Cambie Vd. cada infinitivo a las formas siguientes: (1) presente de indicativo, 1 sing.; (2) presente de subjuntivo, 1 plural; y (3) presente de subjuntivo, 3 plural.

EJEMPLO: agradecer (1) *agradezco* (2) *agradezcamos* (3) *agradezcan*

1. caber (1) _____ (2) _____ (3) _____

2. empezar (1) _____ (2) _____ (3) _____

3. vestirse (1) _____ (2) _____ (3) _____

4. estar (1) _____ (2) _____ (3) _____

5. valer (1) _____ (2) _____ (3) _____

6. mentir (1) _____ (2) _____ (3) _____

7. saber (1) _____ (2) _____ (3) _____

8. vencer (1) _____ (2) _____ (3) _____

9. coger (1) _____ (2) _____ (3) _____

10. dar (1) _____ (2) _____ (3) _____

11. repetir (1) _____ (2) _____ (3) _____

12. haber (1) _____ (2) _____ (3) _____

13. acostarse (1) _____ (2) _____ (3) _____

14. ser (1) _____ (2) _____ (3) _____

15. sufrir (1) _____ (2) _____ (3) _____

16. traducir (1) _____ (2) _____ (3) _____

17. ir (1) _____ (2) _____ (3) _____

18. caer (1) _____ (2) _____ (3) _____

19. pensar (1) _____ (2) _____ (3) _____

20. sonar (1) _____ (2) _____ (3) _____

21. huir (1) _____ (2) _____ (3) _____

22. castigar (1) _____ (2) _____ (3) _____

23. conocer (1) _____ (2) _____ (3) _____

24. pedir (1) _____ (2) _____ (3) _____

25. enviar (1) _____ (2) _____ (3) _____

26. FORMATION OF THE IMPERFECT SUBJUNCTIVE (OPTIONAL)

The imperfect subjunctive of all verbs is formed by dropping the **-ron** from the third person plural of the preterite and adding either the **-se** endings (-se, -ses, -se, '-semos, -seis, -sen) or the **-ra** endings (-ra, -ras, -ra, '-ramos, -rais, -ran).

Not emphasized

Infinitive	**tomar**	**vender**	**vivir**
Preterite, 3rd Plur.	toma**ron**	vendie**ron**	vivie**ron**
Stem	toma-	vendie-	vivie-
Imperfect Subjunctive, -se form	toma**se**	vendie**se**	vivie**se**
	toma**ses**	vendie**ses**	vivie**ses**
	toma**se**	vendie**se**	vivie**se**
	tomá**semos**	vendié**semos**	vivié**semos**
	toma**seis**	vendie**seis**	vivie**seis**
	toma**sen**	vendie**sen**	vivie**sen**
-ra form	toma**ra**	vendie**ra**	vivie**ra**
	toma**ras**	vendie**ras**	vivie**ras**
	toma**ra**	vendie**ra**	vivie**ra**
	tomá**ramos**	vendié**ramos**	vivié**ramos**
	toma**rais**	vendie**rais**	vivie**rais**
	toma**ran**	vendie**ran**	vivie**ran**

add Ra Res ra ramos rais ran
to 3rd. pl. preterite

STEM-CHANGING *-IR* VERBS

sentir, to regret

sintieron: sintiese, sintieses, etc.
sintiera, sintieras, etc.

dormir, to sleep

durmieron: durmiese, durmieses, etc.
durmiera, durmieras, etc.

pedir, to ask for

pidieron: pidiese, pidieses, etc.
pidiera, pidieras, etc.

94

IMPERFECT SUBJUNCTIVE OF VERBS IRREGULAR IN THE PRETERITE

	-SE Form	-RA Form
andar, to walk:	anduviese, etc.	anduviera, etc.
caber, to fit:	cupiese, etc.	cupiera, etc.
caer, to fall:	cayese, etc.	cayera, etc.
creer, to believe:	creyese, etc.	creyera, etc.
dar, to give:	diese, etc.	diera, etc.
decir, to say:	dijese, etc.	dijera, etc.
estar, to be:	estuviese, etc.	estuviera, etc.
haber, to have:	hubiese, etc.	hubiera, etc.
hacer, to do:	hiciese, etc.	hiciera, etc.
huir, to flee:	huyese, etc.	huyera, etc.
ir, to go; ser, to be:	fuese, etc.	fuera, etc.
leer, to read:	leyese, etc.	leyera, etc.
oír, to hear:	oyese, etc.	oyera, etc.
poder, to be able:	pudiese, etc.	pudiera, etc.
poner, to put:	pusiese, etc.	pusiera, etc.
producir, to produce:	produjese, etc.	produjera, etc.
querer, to want:	quisiese, etc.	quisiera, etc.
saber, to know:	supiese, etc.	supiera, etc.
tener, to have:	tuviese, etc.	tuviera, etc.
traer, to bring:	trajese, etc.	trajera, etc.
venir, to come:	viniese, etc.	viniera, etc.

EJERCICIOS

A. Cambie Vd. cada infinitivo a las formas siguientes: (1) pretérito, 3 plural; (2) imperfecto de subjuntivo, forma **-se**, 3 sing.; y (3) imperfecto de subjuntivo, forma **-se**, 1 plural.

EJEMPLO: hablar   (1) *hablaron*   (2) *hablase*   (3) *hablásemos*

1. estudiar   (1) _estudieron_   (2) _estudiase_   (3) _estudiésemos_
2. responder   (1) _respondieron_   (2) _respondiese_   (3) _respondiésemos_
3. abrir   (1) _abrieron_   (2) _abriese_   (3) _abriésemos_
4. mezclar   (1) _mezclaron_   (2) _mezclase_   (3) _mezclásemos_
5. ser   (1) _fueron_   (2) _fuera_   (3) _fuéramos_ X
6. desear   (1) _desearon_   (2) _desease_   (3) _deseasen_
7. saber   (1) _supieron_   (2) _supiera_   (3) _supieran_
8. dar   (1) _dieron_   (2) _diera_   (3) _dieran_
9. sentir   (1) _sintieron_   (2) _sintiese_   (3) _sintiésemos_
10. leer   (1) _leyeron_   (2) _leyesen_   (3) _leyesen_

En 11–20, escriba Vd. la forma **-ra** del imperfecto de subjuntivo.

EJEMPLO: hablar   (1) *hablaron*   (2) *hablara*   (3) *habláramos*

11. volver   (1) _volvieron_   (2) _volviera_   (3) _volviéramos_
12. poner   (1) _pusieron_   (2) _pusiera_   (3) _pusiéramos_
13. perder   (1) _perdieron_   (2) _perdiera_   (3) _perdiéramos_
14. morir   (1) _murieron_   (2) _muriera_   (3) _murieran_

X irregulas

fuéramos X

15. poder (1) _pudiera_ (2) _pudiera_ (3) _pudieran_

16. tener (1) _tuviera_ (2) _tuviera_ (3) _tuvieran_

17. encantar (1) _encantara_ (2) _encantara_ (3) _encantaran_

18. subir (1) _subiera_ (2) _subiera_ (3) _subieran_

19. beber (1) _bebiera_ (2) _bebiera_ (3) _bebieran_

20. caer (1) _cayera_ (2) _cayera_ (3) _cayeran_

B. Escriba Vd. los infinitivos de los verbos siguientes:

1. diéramos _dar_

2. quisiesen _querer_

3. condujera _conducir_

4. hiciéramos _hacer_

5. dijeras _decir_

6. pidiesen _pedir_

7. riera _reír_

8. supiéramos _saber_

9. tuviésemos _tener_

10. perdiera _perder_

11. pudiéramos _poder_

12. trajesen _traer_

13. sonriese _ser_ _sonreír_

14. hubiésemos _haber_

15. pusiesen _poner_

La Piedra del Sol es un ejemplo admirable del arte antigua de los aztecas de México. Es de forma circular y pesa 57.000 libras. En el centro se ve la figura del Dios del Sol. Se ven también otras figuras que representan los días de la semana, los elementos, etc. Los aztecas la emplearon como calendario.

27. POLITE AND INDIRECT COMMANDS

The present subjunctive is used to express:

1. Polite commands with **Vd.** and **Vds.,** affirmative and negative.

Salga Vd. en seguida.	Leave immediately.
Vayan Vds. a casa.	Go home.
No lean Vds. aquel libro.	Don't read that book.

2. Indirect commands introduced in English by *let* or *may*.

Que *entre* él.	Let him enter.
Que *vengan* mañana.	Let them come tomorrow.
Que Dios le *proteja.*	May God protect you.
Vendamos la casa.	Let us sell the house.
but	
Vamos.	Let us go.

Note

A. In indirect commands, **que** generally precedes the subjunctive but is omitted when expressing *let us.*

B. *Let us go* is expressed by **vamos** instead of **vayamos.**

C. *Let us* may also be expressed by **vamos a** + the infinitive.

Vamos a entrar (or *Entremos*).	Let us enter.
Vamos a correr (or *Corramos*).	Let us run.

EJERCICIOS

A. Escriba Vd. la forma correcta de los verbos *a*, *b*, y *c* en lugar del verbo en letra cursiva.

1. *Aprendan* Vds. la dirección.   (*a*) copiar   (*b*) leer   (*c*) no olvidar

   (*a*) _____   (*b*) _____   (*c*) _____

2. *Subamos* la colina.   (*a*) ver   (*b*) bajar   (*c*) buscar

   (*a*) _____   (*b*) _____   (*c*) _____

3. Que Dios le *ayude.*   (*a*) guardar   (*b*) proteger   (*c*) castigar

   (*a*) _____   (*b*) _____   (*c*) _____

4. *Siga* Vd. adelante.   (*a*) pasar   (*b*) correr   (*c*) ir

   (*a*) _____   (*b*) _____   (*c*) _____

5. *Cierre* Vd. la puerta.   (*a*) abrir   (*b*) destruir   (*c*) pintar

   (*a*) _____   (*b*) _____   (*c*) _____

6. *Miren* Vds. los aviones.   (*a*) contar   (*b*) observar   (*c*) ver

   (*a*) _____   (*b*) _____   (*c*) _____

7. *Escuchemos* la canción.   (*a*) empezar   (*b*) aprender   (*c*) enseñar

   (*a*) _____   (*b*) _____   (*c*) _____

8. *Salga* Vd. con el gato.   (*a*) quedarse   (*b*) jugar   (*c*) volver

(*a*) _____   (*b*) _____   (*c*) _____

9. *Traiga* Vd. la cuenta.   (*a*) entregar   (*b*) devolver   (*c*) cobrar

(*a*) _____   (*b*) _____   (*c*) _____

10. Que *descansen* en paz.   (*a*) dormir   (*b*) rezar   (*c*) soñar

(*a*) _____   (*b*) _____   (*c*) _____

B. Cambie Vd. cada infinitivo a la forma del imperativo empleada con (1) *Vd.*, (2) *Vds.*, y (3) *nosotros*.

EJEMPLO: comer   (1) *coma*   (2) *coman*   (3) *comamos*

1. poner   (1) _____   (2) _____   (3) _____

2. encender   (1) _____   (2) _____   (3) _____

3. abrazar   (1) _____   (2) _____   (3) _____

4. conseguir   (1) _____   (2) _____   (3) _____

5. impedir   (1) _____   (2) _____   (3) _____

6. atravesar   (1) _____   (2) _____   (3) _____

7. enviar   (1) _____   (2) _____   (3) _____

8. atacar   (1) _____   (2) _____   (3) _____

9. continuar   (1) _____   (2) _____   (3) _____

10. concluir   (1) _____   (2) _____   (3) _____

11. mostrar   (1) _____   (2) _____   (3) _____

12. elegir   (1) _____   (2) _____   (3) _____

13. describir   (1) _____   (2) _____   (3) _____

14. morir   (1) _____   (2) _____   (3) _____

15. detener   (1) _____   (2) _____   (3) _____

16. morder   (1) _____   (2) _____   (3) _____

17. coger   (1) _____   (2) _____   (3) _____

18. mezclar   (1) _____   (2) _____   (3) _____

19. agradecer   (1) _____   (2) _____   (3) _____

20. apagar   (1) _____   (2) _____   (3) _____

C. Complete Vd. las frases siguientes, empleando en vez del infinitivo la forma indicada del imperativo:

1. (Hablar) Vd. despacio.   _____

2. (Ir) nosotros al centro.   _____

3. Que (vivir) ellos mil años.   _____

4. (Examinar) Vd. el lápiz.   _____

5. (Seguir) Vds. luchando.   _____

6. Que no (sufrir) él.   _____

7. Que (reír) ellos.   _____

8. No (engañar) nosotros a los inocentes. _____

9. (Cumplir) Vd. con su deber. _____

10. (Limitar) Vds. sus gastos. _____

D. Traduzca Vd. al español.

1. Tell (Vds.) the truth. _____

2. Give (Vd.) the money to the man. _____

3. Do not leave (Vds.) the house. _____

4. Let us go to the movies. _____

5. Do (Vd.) the work now. _____

6. Let them enter the museum. _____

7. Let us be good neighbors. _____

8. Do not put (Vd.) your feet on the sofa. _____

9. Let her see the book. _____

10. Mr. González, wrap the packages. _____

El Escorial, cerca de Madrid, fue construido por el rey Felipe II. Es un edificio inmenso que contiene un palacio, un monasterio, una biblioteca, un museo, y un Panteón (burial place) de Reyes. Felipe II estableció aquí su corte, y desde aquí gobernó el país.

[handwritten at top:] Imposy will = Calls for subjunctive. *(Same duty anf I want to work)*

28. THE SUBJUNCTIVE AFTER CERTAIN VERBS

The subjunctive is used in a dependent clause when the verb in the main clause expresses:

1. A *wish:* **desear** (to wish), **querer** (to want), **preferir** (to prefer)

   Quiero que Vd. *trabaje* mañana.   I want you to work (that you work) tomorrow.
   (main)   (dependent)

2. A *command* or *advice:* **mandar** (to order), **prohibir** (to forbid), **aconsejar** (to advise), **decir** (to tell, in the sense of *to order*)

   Manda que ellos lo *hagan.*   He orders them to do it (that they do it).
   (main)   (dependent)

3. A *request:* **pedir** (to ask, to request), **rogar** (to request, to beg), **suplicar** (to implore, to beg)

   Me **pide** que le *pague.*   He asks me to pay him (that I pay him).
   (main)   (dependent)

4. *Emotion:* **esperar** (to hope), **sentir** (to be sorry, to regret), **alegrarse (de)** (to be glad), **temer** (to fear)

   Espero que *compren* la casa.   I hope they buy the house.
   (main)   (dependent)

5. *Doubt* or *denial:* **dudar** (to doubt), **negar** (to deny)

   Dudo que *vengan* temprano.   I doubt that they will come early.
   (main)   (dependent)

   Niega que *sea* la verdad.   She denies that it is the truth.
   (main)   (dependent)

6. A *belief* (when negative or interrogative): **pensar** (to think), **creer** (to believe)

   [handwritten:] Subj.   ¿**Piensa** Vd. que él *sea* sincero?   Do you think he is sincere?
   (main)   (dependent)

   No creo que él *tenga* el dinero.   I don't believe he has the money.
   (main)   (dependent)

   but

   Creo que él **tiene** el dinero.   I believe that he has the money.
   (main)   (dependent)

Note

In each of the above sentences, the subject of the main verb is different from the subject of the dependent verb. If the subjects are the same, **que** is omitted and the infinitive form of the dependent verb is used.

Quiero trabajar mañana.   I want to work tomorrow.

Espera comprar la casa.   He hopes to buy the house.

EJERCICIOS

A. Subraye Vd. la forma correcta del verbo entre paréntesis. Después, traduzca Vd. la frase al inglés.

1. Mandan que yo (voy, vaya).   *[handwritten:]* me mandan R

- -

2. Espero que Vd. (tiene, tenga) mucha suerte.

- -

[handwritten at bottom:] Never used present subjunctive after IF.

[handwritten notes in top margin: mandar, silles subj, prohibir or, dejar permitir inf., No te permitto usar mi coche, objes krono, No te permitto que usas]

3. Teme que Tomás no (llegará, *llegue*) a tiempo.

----

4. Dudo que él (traerá, *traiga*) el dinero.   *I doubt.*

----

5. ¿Creen Vds. que él (apagará, apague) la luz?
    apague   *Don you think he will turn out the light apaga Do you believe he turned out the light.*

6. Deseo que Vds. (vienen, *vengan*) mañana.

----

7. No creo que María (es, *sea*) tan cruel.

----

8. ¿Desea Vd. (*comprar*, compre) una corbata?   (*No change of subjects*

----

9. Prefieren que yo lo (hago, *haga*).
    subjunctive

----

10. Dudo que él lo (recordará, *recuerde*).
  Se   *I doubt that he will remember*
  If it is positive — "I'm sure he will remember it"

B. Escriba Vd. la forma correcta de los verbos entre paréntesis.

1. El padre prohibe que su hija (fumar, bailar, casarse, salir).
  fume baille fumar, saleja,

2. Deseo que Vds. (ir, quedarse, rezar, cenar) conmigo. *recen = pray*
  vayan vengan, vayan, cenen, queda

3. Siento que ella (estar, caer, parecer, sentirse) enferma.
  este, parece paresca,

4. Me alegro de (oír, saber, poseer, averiguar) eso.
  sabes   No chng of subjes

5. Dígale que lo (poner, parar, dejar, esconder) aquí.
  pone pones para,

6. Esperan que su hijo (ir, visitar, consultar, llamar) a un buen médico.
  vaya, consulte,   andar-watch using plan

7. No creo que este reloj (costar, valer, durar, adelantar) mucho.
  costas cueste valga, dure - adalente

8. Manda que Vds. lo (traer, arreglar, beber, cobrar).   *cobre*
  trajes bebes, arreglen traige beban

9. Te suplico que (tú) lo (creer, construir, explicar, guardar).   *Subjunctive*
  creyes creas, construas explis guarda

10. Yo prefiero (ir, desayunarse, principiar, acostarse) a las siete.
  desayunarme acostarme,
  To form the endig "parga" (Vos)

C. Conteste Vd. en español en frases completas.

1. ¿Aconseja Vd. a sus compañeros que dediquen más tiempo al estudio? _____

_____

2. ¿Se alegra Vd. de que haga buen (mal) tiempo hoy? _____

_____

3. ¿Cree Vd. que haya un examen mañana? _____

4. ¿Espera Vd. graduarse este año? _____

_____

5. ¿Desea Vd. que sus amigos le respeten? _____

_____

6. ¿Le prohiben sus padres que Vd. fume? _____

_____

7. ¿Siente Vd. que hoy no sea día de vacaciones? _____

_____

8. ¿Teme Vd. que sus padres no le permitan salir de noche? _____

_____

9. ¿Prefiere Vd. que el profesor (la profesora) no dé exámenes? _____

_____

10. ¿Quiere Vd. que el maestro (la maestra) explique el subjuntivo otra vez? _____

_____

D. Traduzca Vd. al español las expresiones en inglés.

1. ¿Cree Vd. que yo *will arrive* allí a tiempo? _____

2. ¿Piensan Vds. que yo *believe* eso? _____

3. Queremos que Vds. *come* aquí. _____

4. Espero que Dolores *will be able* venir. _____

5. Creemos que ellos *will come* mañana. _____

6. Pida Vd. al mozo *to serve* la comida. _____

7. Temo que ella *will die.* _____

8. Prefiero que los niños *leave* en seguida. _____

9. Le ruego que *he explain* todo. _____

10. Niega que nosotros *are telling* la verdad. _____

E. Traduzca Vd. al español.

1. I doubt that it will rain tomorrow.

_____

2. I do not believe that he is a lawyer.

_____

3. Do you believe that he is poor?

----

4. I want you to come to my room.

----

5. He thinks that she is intelligent.

----

6. Ask him to bring his guitar.

----

7. I hope to see that movie.

----

8. I am glad that she is well.

----

9. We hope that you will believe us.

----

10. We fear that he is ill.

Jai-alai es el deporte tradicional de las Provincias Vascongadas, en el norte de España. Se juega en una cancha (court) de tres paredes llamada "frontón." Es algo semejante a nuestro "handball," pero en jai-alai se usa una cesta atada a la mano para coger y lanzar la pelota. Con esta cesta lanzan la pelota contra las paredes con mucha fuerza. Jai-alai es muy popular en España, México, y Cuba, y también en la Florida.

[handwritten: Roya Ratalondo]

29. SEQUENCE OF TENSES (OPTIONAL)

1. The present subjunctive is generally used if the verb in the main clause is in the present indicative, the future, or the command.

Manda (Mandará, Mande Vd.) que lo *hagan.*   He orders (He will order, Order) them to do
(present)   (future)   (command)   (present subjunctive)   it (that they do it).

2. The imperfect subjunctive is generally used if the verb in the main clause is in one of the past tenses or in the conditional.

[handwritten above hiciesen: hicieran]

Mandó (Mandaba, Mandaría) que lo *hiciesen.*   He ordered (He was ordering, He would
(preterite)   (imperfect)   (conditional)   (imperfect subjunctive)   order) them to do it (that they do it).

3. The perfect subjunctive is formed by the present subjunctive of **haber** and the past participle (**haya hablado,** has spoken). The perfect subjunctive is used if the verb in the main clause is in the present tense, and the dependent verb represents an event that *has* taken place.

No creo que *hayan salido.*   I do not believe that they (have) left.
(present)   (perfect subjunctive)

4. The pluperfect subjunctive is formed by the imperfect subjunctive of **haber** and the past participle (**hubiese** or **hubiera hablado,** had spoken). The pluperfect subjunctive is used if the verb in the main clause is in a past tense and the dependent verb represents an event that *had* taken place previously.

No creía que *hubiesen salido.*   I did not believe that they had left.
(past)   (pluperfect subjunctive)

EJERCICIOS

A. Subraye Vd. la forma correcta del verbo entre paréntesis. Después, traduzca Vd. la frase al inglés.

1. Sentía que Vds. no (puedan, pudiesen, pueden) venir.

------------- *[handwritten: Pudieran]* ---

2. Quiere que nosotros lo (paguemos, pagaremos, pagáramos).

----

3. Le dije que (salga, saliera, sale).

----

4. Pidió al músico que (toque, tocara, toca) una canción española.

----

5. Se alegró de que Vds. se (diviertan, divirtieron, hubieran divertido).

----

6. No creíamos que él (mienta, mintiese, miente).

----

7. Negó que su hermano (hubiese vuelto, vuelva, volvería).

----

8. Piden al mozo que (sirva, sirviera, servía) la comida.

104

Past o Imp Subj

9. Me rogó que (almuerce, almorzara, almuerzo) con él.

----

10. Temo que él me (castigue, castigase, castigará).

B. Escriba Vd. la forma correcta de los verbos entre paréntesis.

Past 1. Me aconsejó que (ver, aplaudir, hablar, alabar) a aquel actor. *Praise*
_____ , *viere* , *aplaudier* , *hablar* ,

2. Dudan que él (decir, saber, confesar, descubrir) la verdad.
I ver. _____ , *sepa* , *conf* , *descubre* ,

3. No creía que mi hermano lo (hacer, comprender, escoger, olvidar). *Past Subj*
ver _____ , *hiciere* , *comprender* , *escoger* , *olvidara*

4. Temían que el niño (caer, despedirse, llorar, huir).
cayera , *despedir* , *llore* , *huer*

5. No quiero (molestar, saludar, obedecer, ayudar) al profesor.

----------- , ----------- , -----------° , -----------

6. Él quería que nosotros (ir, estar, quedarse, aguardar) allí anoche.

----------- , ----------- , ----------- , -----------

7. ¿Cree Vd. que yo (poder, saber, desear, necesitar) hacerlo?

----------- , ----------- , ----------- , -----------

8. Negó que su amigo (haber robado, haber escondido, haber examinado, haber visto) las joyas.

----------- , ----------- , ----------- , -----------

9. El maestro siente mucho que nosotros no (callarse, aprender, escribir, leer) en la clase.

----------- , ----------- , ----------- , -----------

10. Dudo que ellos (haber leído, haber cubierto, haber usado, haber olvidado) sus libros.

----------- , ----------- , ----------- , -----------

21 words **C.** Traduzca Vd. al español las expresiones en inglés.

1. El policía mandó que *they wait*. _____ *entiendieren* ,
2. El médico dudaba que el paciente *would live*. _____ *vivera*
3. Se alegró de que nosotros *came* a verle. _____ *elegier*
4. No creíamos que *they would sell* la casa. _____ *vendrían ellos*
5. Nos dijo *to see* aquella película. _____ *ver*
6. ¿Cree Vd. que él nos *will give* la revista? _____ *da*
7. Quiero *to buy* una novela. _____ *comprar*
8. Dudo que este alumno *does* su trabajo. _____ *hiciese*
9. Mi madre prohibe que yo *eat* manzanas verdes. _____ *comes*
10. Quería *them to learn* el español. _____ *ellos aprenden*
11. Sienten que nosotros no *have seen* aquel monumento. _____ *no vieron*
12. Desean que yo *go* a la playa con ellos. _____ *iba*

13. Me pidió *to bring* la cesta. _____ traer _____

14. Teme que ellos lo *know*. _____ conozca _____

15. Manda *us to return* a casa. _____ nos volver amos _____

D. Traduzca Vd. al español.

1. The general ordered his army to attack.

_____

2. We are glad that you have arrived.

_____

3. They doubted that we had waited.

_____

4. She begged him to go to school.

_____

5. Do you think that they will come on time?

_____

6. Does Henry think that she is stupid?

_____

7. She wants to see the house.

_____

8. I am sorry that the doctor cannot see you today.

_____

9. They feared that he would leave.

_____

10. He wanted us to know the truth.

_____

30. THE SUBJUNCTIVE AFTER IMPERSONAL EXPRESSIONS

The subjunctive is used after certain impersonal expressions if the dependent verb has an expressed subject.

es dudoso, it is doubtful	**es imposible,** it is impossible
es importante, it is important	**es necesario** ⎱ it is necessary
es lástima, it is a pity	**es preciso** ⎰
es posible, it is possible	**es probable,** it is probable

Es dudoso que lo *compre.*	It is doubtful that he will buy it.
Es importante que lo *hagamos.*	It is important for us to do it (that we do it).
Es necesario que Vd. *coma.*	It is necessary for you to eat (that you eat).
but	
Es necesario comer.	It is necessary to eat.

Note

The subjunctive is *not* used after impersonal expressions that express certainty.

es cierto, it is certain
es evidente, it is evident
es verdad, it is true
es claro, it is clear

Es cierto que **estudia** mucho.	It is certain that he studies much.
Es verdad que mañana **es** su cumpleaños.	It is true that tomorrow is his birthday.
but	
No es cierto que *estudie* mucho.	It is not certain that he studies much.

EJERCICIOS

A. Subraye Vd. la forma correcta del verbo entre paréntesis. Después, traduzca Vd. la frase al inglés.

1. Es posible que ella no (quiere, querrá, quiera) ir.

- -

2. Es importante que Vds. (oyen, oigan, oirán) el cuento.

- -

3. Es preciso que nosotros (recibiremos, recibamos, recibimos) la carta.

- -

4. Es dudoso que yo lo (hallo, halla, halle). Discover it.

- -

5. Es probable que Carmen (está, esté, estará) enferma.

- -

6. Es verdad que él (comprar, compre, comprará) la casa.

  _____

7. No es necesario que ellos (salen, salgan, saldrán).

  _____

8. Es importante que Vd. lo (hace, hará, haga).

  _____

9. Es necesario que Pedro y su amigo lo (ven, vean, vayan).

  _____

10. Es imposible (decida, decide, decidir) ahora.

  _____

  B. Escriba Vd. la forma correcta de los verbos entre paréntesis.

1. Es preciso que ellos (admirar, construir, establecer, terminar) la casa.

  _____, _____, _____, _____

2. Es verdad que su papá le (dar, prestar, comprar, devolver) el automóvil la semana que viene.

  _____, _____, _____, _____

3. Es necesario (estudiar, trabajar, leer, escribir) para aprender.

  _____, _____, _____, _____

4. Es preciso que nosotros lo (llevar, conducir, enviar, acompañar) a la librería.

  _____, _____, _____, _____

5. Es claro que el propietario (ganar, deber, gastar, comprender) mucho.

  _____, _____, _____, _____

6. ¿Será posible que él me lo (dar, mostrar, entregar, mandar) mañana?

  _____, _____, _____, _____

7. Será imposible que ellas (andar, aparecer, caminar, ir) por allí.

  _____, _____, _____, _____

8. No es importante que nosotros le (imitar, aconsejar, obedecer, invitar).

  _____, _____, _____, _____

9. Es lástima que ella no (poder, pensar, querer, consentir en) asistir al baile.

  _____, _____, _____, _____

10. Es probable que él (tener, poseer, comprar, obtener) una buena colección de cuadros.

  _____, _____, _____, _____

  C. Conteste Vd. en español en frases completas.

1. ¿Es cierto que la luna es de queso verde?

  _____

2. ¿Es posible que una persona ciega vea claramente?

  _____

3. ¿Es preciso llevar sobretodo en el verano?

  _____

4. ¿Es verdad que Vd. tiene un resfriado hoy?

----

5. ¿Es importante que una persona haga sus tareas?

----

6. ¿Es necesario comer para vivir?

----

7. ¿Es verdad que Vd. tiene un hermano menor?

----

8. ¿Es dudoso que haga buen tiempo mañana?

----

9. ¿Es posible que Vd. no venga a la escuela mañana?

----

10. ¿Es probable que Vd. reciba una buena nota en esta clase?

D. Traduzca Vd. al español las expresiones en inglés.

1. Es imposible que yo *visit* a mi abuelo.   -------------------------

2. Es probable que Felipe lo *will want*.   -------------------------

3. Es preciso que el médico *come* inmediatamente.   -------------------------

4. Es evidente que *they do not want* venir.   -------------------------

5. Es cierto que Vds. *do not understand* el problema.   -------------------------

6. Es posible que *we will learn* a nadar.   -------------------------

7. Es necesario que los niños *drink* más leche.   -------------------------

8. Es lástima que su hermano *is suffering* tanto.   -------------------------

9. Es dudoso que él *will remember* la dirección.   -------------------------

10. Es lástima que ella *has* dolor de cabeza.   -------------------------

E. Traduzca Vd. al español.

1. It is true that we are brothers.

----

2. It is important for you to leave now.

----

3. It is possible that he will live.

----

4. It is impossible for him to stay there.

----

5. It is important for you to be here.

----

6. It is necessary for the soldiers to obey.

----

7. It is impossible for him to study with another student.

----

8. It is important to tell the truth.

----

9. It is possible that they cannot come.

----

10. It is probable that she will invite us.

Cerca de Madrid se encuentra el Valle de los Caídos (Valley of the Fallen), un monumento enorme construido en memoria de los soldados que murieron en la Guerra Civil española de 1936–39. La iglesia tiene la forma de una cruz, y detrás de ella hay una cruz de 500 pies de alto.

31. THE SUBJUNCTIVE AFTER
CERTAIN CONJUNCTIONS (OPTIONAL)

1. The subjunctive is used after the following conjunctions:

> **antes (de) que,** before
> **a menos que,** unless
> **para que,** in order that, so that
> **con tal que,** provided that
> **en caso de que,** in case
> **sin que,** without

Voy a hacerlo **antes de que** *lleguen.*	I am going to do it before they arrive.
Trajo los cuadros **para que** todos *pudiesen* verlos.	He brought the pictures in order that all could see them.
Salió **sin que** yo le *viera.*	He left without my seeing him.

Note. If the subjects of the main verb and the dependent verb are the same, **que** is omitted and the infinitive is used.

Lo haré **antes de salir.**	I shall do it before leaving.
Trajo los cuadros **para venderlos.**	He brought the pictures in order to sell them.
Salió **sin decir** adiós.	He left without saying goodbye.

2. The subjunctive is used after the following conjunctions only if uncertainty, doubt, anticipation, or indefiniteness is implied. Otherwise, the indicative is used.

> **así que**
> **luego que** ⎫ as soon as
> **en cuanto** ⎭
> **cuando,** when
> **hasta que,** until

Le hablaré **cuando** *vuelva.*	I shall speak to him when he returns. (whenever that may be)
Comprarán el automóvil **luego que** *reciban* el dinero.	They will buy the automobile as soon as they receive the money. (It is not known when or if they will receive the money.)

but

Le hablé **cuando volvió.**	I spoke to him when he returned. (He did return.)
Compró la bicicleta **luego que** la **vio.**	He bought the bicycle as soon as he saw it. (He did see it.)

EJERCICIOS

A. Subraye Vd. la forma correcta del verbo entre paréntesis. Después, traduzca Vd. la frase al inglés.

1. Espere Vd. hasta que yo le (llamo, llama, llame).

   ----

2. Saldremos en cuanto (podemos, podremos, podamos).

   ----

3. No iría a menos que ellos (fueran, fueron, vayan) también.

   ----

4. En caso de que Pedro (viene, vendrá, venga), llámeme.

   ----

5. Lo haremos antes de que (salgan, salen, salieran).

   ----

6. Vino a vernos luego que (llegue, llegó, llegase).

   ----

7. Se quitó el sombrero antes de (entrar, entre, entró).

   ----

8. No puedo salir de casa hasta que (vuelvan, vuelven, volverán) mis padres.

   ----

9. No irá a menos que (tendrá, tenga, tuviese) un vestido nuevo.

   ----

10. Se lo explicó a ellos para que (comprendieran, comprendieron, comprendan).

    ----

11. Cuando (entré, entre, entrase) en el cuarto, ella estudiaba.

    ----

12. Escríbame a menudo para que (sé, sepa, sea) dónde comunicarme con Vd.

    ----

13. Cuando (vuelvo, vuelva, vuelve) del campo, la veré.

    ----

14. Tomó el libro sin que nosotros lo (sabemos, sepamos, supiéramos).

    ----

15. Le daré el libro con tal que Vd. (prometa, promete, prometerá) devolvérmelo.

B. Traduzca Vd. al español las expresiones en inglés.

1. A menos que ellos *have* mucho dinero, no serán felices. _____

2. Irá a su casa con tal que Vds. le *invite*. _____

3. La criada preparó la comida antes que nosotros *went* a la feria. _____

4. En caso de que *I am* ocupado mañana, venga a verme el sábado. _____

5. Lo haré *without his helping me*. _____

6. Cuando *I am* presidente, ayudaré a los pobres. _____

7. Luego que él me *saw*, comenzó a llorar. _____

8. No vaya Vd. hasta que yo *return*. _____

9. El profesor enseña para que los estudiantes *will learn*. _____

10. Lo recibirán el lunes con tal que nosotros lo *send* hoy. _____

C. Traduzca Vd. al español.

1. I shall wait until noon in case you come late. _____

_____

2. They did not want to leave unless we accompanied them. _____

_____

3. Give this letter to your father as soon as he arrives. _____

_____

4. We must eat in order to live. _____

_____

5. He will not buy the automobile until I see it. _____

_____

6. My father gave me five dollars so that I might buy the shirt. _____

_____

7. He will attend school unless he is ill. _____

_____

8. My friends did not visit me in order that I might study for the examinations. _____

_____

9. The children ate before we left. _____

_____

10. When you visit Spain, you will find many interesting customs. _____

_____

32. THE SUBJUNCTIVE AFTER AN INDEFINITE
OR NEGATIVE ANTECEDENT (OPTIONAL)

1. The subjunctive is used after an indefinite antecedent.

Busco **una criada que** *sepa* cocinar bien. I am looking for a maid that knows how to cook well.
<small>(I may never find such a person.)</small>

but

Conozco a **una criada que sabe** cocinar bien. I know a maid who knows how to cook well.
<small>(There is such a person; I know her.)</small>

Note. Since the object **(criada)** is indefinite in the first example, the personal **a** is not used.

2. The subjunctive is used after compounds of **-quiera** and similar indefinite expressions.

---

quienquiera, whoever
(a) dondequiera, wherever
cualquiera, cualquier, whatever
por + *adjective or adverb* + **que** + *subjunctive,* however, no matter how

---

Quienquiera que *diga* eso, tiene razón. Whoever says that, is right.

Cualquier vestido **que** Vd. *compre* en esa tienda es importado de Francia. Whatever dress you buy in that store is imported from France.

Por valiente que *sea,* no lo hará. However brave he may be, he will not do it.

3. The subjunctive is used after a negative antecedent.

No hay nadie que lo *crea.* There is no one who will believe it.

No hay nada que Vd. *pueda* hacer. There is nothing that you can do.

EJERCICIOS

A. Escriba Vd. la forma correcta del verbo en vez del infinitivo.

1. Busco una casa que *tener* un jardín grande. _____

2. Halló un hotel que *tener* cuartos grandes y claros. _____

3. Quiero comprar una novela que *ser* interesante. _____

4. Compró un libro que *ser* interesante. _____

5. Dondequiera que Vds. *ir,* no verán tal cosa. _____

6. No hay persona que *creer* eso. _____

7. Quienquiera que *poder* hacerlo, recibirá un premio. _____

8. Por viejo que *ser,* es muy fuerte. _____

9. No hay nadie que lo *hacer.* _____

10. Cualquier ciudad que nosotros *visitar,* hallaremos monumentos interesantes. _____

B. Traduzca Vd. al español las expresiones en inglés.

1. Tengo una gramática que *has* muchos ejercicios. _____

2. Quienquiera que *he may be*, no se lo daré. _____

3. Cualquier hombre que *does* eso, será castigado. _____

4. Por mucho que nosotros *suffer*, no nos ayudará. _____

5. ¿Hay alguien que no *admires* su belleza? _____

6. ¿Hay un museo en Nueva York que *has* cuadros de Velázquez? _____

7. ¿Existe una persona que no lo *has* visto? _____

8. Buscaba un hombre que *could* guiarle a la hacienda. _____

9. Dondequiera que *they may be*, los encontraré. _____

10. No había nadie que *knew* la respuesta. _____

C. Traduzca Vd. al español.

1. We are looking for a man who wants to work. _____

_____

2. He will help me no matter how difficult it is. _____

_____

3. There is no one who speaks to him. _____

_____

4. I shall follow you wherever you go. _____

_____

5. I know a guide who speaks English. _____

_____

6. Whatever book you read, you will learn much. _____

_____

7. Whoever says that, is telling a lie. _____

_____

8. Wherever you find Henry, you will find his cousin. _____

_____

_____

9. However rich they may be, they will never be happy. _____

_____

_____

10. He wants to buy a magazine that has many interesting stories. _____

_____

33. "IF" CLAUSES (OPTIONAL)

The imperfect subjunctive and the pluperfect subjunctive are used in "if" clauses that are contrary to fact. The imperfect subjunctive indicates present time; the pluperfect subjunctive indicates past time. Such clauses may be identified by the word *would* in the result clause.

Si *tuviese* (or *tuviera*) el dinero **iría** a México.	If I had the money, I would go to Mexico. (But I don't have the money. *present*)
Si *hubiesen* (or *hubieran*) venido, los **habría-** **mos** visto.	If they had come, we would have seen them. (But they had not come. *past*)

but

Si tengo el dinero, **iré** a México.	If I have the money, I shall go to Mexico.
Si vienen, los **veremos.**	If they come, we will see them.

Note

A. The **-ra** form of the imperfect subjunctive may be used instead of the conditional in the result clause.

Si tuviese el tiempo, le *visitara.*	If I had the time, I would visit him.

B. The present subjunctive is never used in "if" clauses. *always Subj.*

C. The "if" clause is not necessarily the first clause of the sentence.

Yo iría a México **si tuviera** (or **tuviese**) **el** **dinero.**	I would go to Mexico if I had the money.

EJERCICIOS

A. Escriba Vd. la forma correcta del verbo en vez del infinitivo.

1. Si él me *dar* un regalo, no lo aceptaría. ------------------------------
2. Si nosotros *estudiar*, saldremos bien en los exámenes. ------------------------------
3. Nosotros le ayudaríamos, si él *ser* pobre. ------------------------------
4. Si *tener* un automóvil, iría al campo. ------------------------------
5. Yo *venir*, si ellos me invitasen. ------------------------------
6. Si Vds. *buscar* el reloj, lo hallarían. ------------------------------
7. Ella habría muerto, si el médico no *llegar* a tiempo. ------------------------------
8. Si *hacer* calor, no saliera. ------------------------------
9. Si nosotros *ganar* bastante dinero, habríamos ido a México. ------------------------------
10. Si ellos *querer* el libro, nosotros se lo daríamos. ------------------------------

B. Traduzca Vd. al español las expresiones en inglés.

1. Si nosotros *went* al campo, nos divertiríamos. ------------------------------
2. Yo leyera aquella novela si *it were* en la biblioteca. ------------------------------
3. Yo *would be able* hacerlo si tuviese la ocasión. ------------------------------
4. Si *we had gone* al cine, habríamos visto una película interesante. ------------------------------

5. Si yo *knew* la respuesta, yo se la diría.   ----------------------------

6. Si Vd. desea ir a su casa, *I shall go* también.   ----------------------------

7. Si Teresa no *is* cansada, vendrá a la fiesta.   ----------------------------

8. Lo haría si *I had* el tiempo.   ----------------------------

9. Si nosotros *had prepared* la lección, la hubiéramos sabido.   ----------------------------

10. Si fuera importante, lo *he would send*.   ----------------------------

11. Si Vds. *study* el español, sabrán hablarlo.   ----------------------------

12. Si *I received* una carta de él, la contestaría.   ----------------------------

13. Si Vd. lo *want*, se lo daré.   ----------------------------

14. Si *they had left* a las ocho, hubieran llegado a las nueve.   ----------------------------

15. Si Felipe *had found* el libro, él se lo habría devuelto.   ----------------------------

16. Le *we would have helped* si hubiésemos sabido eso.   ----------------------------

17. Si Vd. *came*, me alegraría mucho.   ----------------------------

18. Si *I were* con él, yo no le permitiría hacerlo.   ----------------------------

19. Si hubiese llovido, *she would not have gone out*.   ----------------------------

20. Yo comprara la casa si *it were not* tan cara.   ----------------------------

C. Traduzca Vd. al español.

1. If I sell the house, they will buy it.

----

2. If I sold the house, they would buy it.

----

3. If I had sold the house, they would have bought it.

----

4. If you were rich, what would you do?

----

5. We would believe it, if we saw it.

----

6. If he studied, he would learn much.

----

7. We would have done it, if we had had the time.

----

8. If you study Spanish, you will understand it.

----

9. If I were you, I would see him.

----

10. We'll go if we have the money.

----

34. FAMILIAR COMMANDS

REGULAR VERBS

	AFFIRMATIVE		NEGATIVE	
	Singular	*Plural*	*Singular*	*Plural*
tomar, to take	take		don't take	
	toma (tú)	tomad (vosotros)	no tomes (tú)	no toméis (vosotros)
comer, to eat	eat		don't eat	
	come (tú)	comed (vosotros)	no comas (tú)	no comáis (vosotros)
escribir, to write	write		don't write	
	escribe (tú)	escribid (vosotros)	no escribas (tú)	no escribáis (vosotros)

Note

A. The singular form of the familiar affirmative command is the same as the third person singular of the present indicative.

B. The plural form of the familiar affirmative command is formed by changing the final **-r** of the infinitive to **-d.**

C. All the negative forms of the familiar command are expressed by the present subjunctive.

IRREGULAR VERBS

decir, to say:	*di* (tú)	**poner,** to put:	*pon* (tú)	**tener,** to have:	*ten* (tú)
hacer, to do:	*haz* (tú)	**salir,** to leave:	*sal* (tú)	**valer,** to be worth:	*val* (tú)
ir, to go:	*ve* (tú)	**ser,** to be:	*sé* (tú)	**venir,** to come:	*ven* (tú)

Note

Irregular verbs in the familiar commands are irregular in the **tú** form only. The other forms are regular.

decir: *di* (tú), **decid** (vosotros), **no digas** (tú), **no digáis** (vosotros)
hacer: *haz* (tú), **haced** (vosotros), **no hagas** (tú), **no hagáis** (vosotros)

EJERCICIOS

A. Escriba Vd. las formas afirmativa y negativa del imperativo íntimo (familiar) de cada verbo, según el ejemplo.

	AFFIRMATIVE		NEGATIVE	
	tú	*vosotros*	*tú*	*vosotros*
hablar	habla	hablad	no hables	no habléis
1. cantar	Canta	Cantad	4 Cantes	Canteis
2. vender	vende	vended	vendes	vendes
3. recibir	recibe	recibid	recibes	recibes

118

4. salir _Sal_ —— —— ——
5. tener _ten_ —— —— ——
6. dar _dé_ _decid_ —— ——
7. ser _sé_ —— —— ——
8. ir _ve_ —— —— ——
9. dormir _duerme_ _duermad_ —— ——
10. venir _ven_ —— —— ——

B. Cambie Vd. la forma del verbo a la forma correspondiente del imperativo íntimo.

1. entre Vd. _Entra_ tú   6. ponga Vd. _Pon_ tú
2. miren Vds. _mirad_ vosotros   7. salgan Vds. _Salgáis_ vosotros
3. escriba Vd. _escriba_ tú   8. no vaya Vd. no _vayas_ tú
4. aprendan Vds. _aprendáis_ vosotros   9. no tomen Vds. no _toméis_ vosotros
5. haga Vd. _Hagan_ tú   10. no diga Vd. no _tomas_ tú

C. Cambie Vd. la forma del verbo a la forma correspondiente del imperativo formal.

1. sal (tú) _salgáis_ Vd.   6. dad (vosotros) —— Vds.
2. id (vosotros) —— Vds.   7. no traigáis (vosotros) no —— Vds.
3. no hables (tú) no _hablais_ Vd.   8. haz (tú) _hagáis_ Vd.
4. promete (tú) _prometéis_ Vd.   9. ve (tú) _vejáis_ Vd.
5. di (tú) _decid_ Vd.   10. tened (vosotros) _tenéis_ Vds.

D. Traduzca Vd. al español las expresiones en inglés.

1. *Leave* (tú) de casa en seguida. _Sal_
2. *Eat* (tú) la ensalada. _Come_
3. *Do not speak* (vosotros) a Dolores. _No hableis_
4. *Read* (vosotros) las revistas. _Leis_
5. *Do not enter* (tú) en la sala. _No entre_
6. *Go* (tú) allá ahora. _Ve_
7. *Do not be* (tú) tonto. _No se_
8. *Put* (tú) el libro aquí. _Pon_
9. *Tell* la verdad a tu madre. _Di_
10. *Be* bueno, hijo mío. _Se_

(No comas Don't) Come lo = Eat it

No compres Don't Compra lo   Buy it

35. MASTERY EXERCISES

A. Traduzca Vd. al español las expresiones en inglés.

1. José *was going* a casa. — *Estaba yendo*
2. *Put* tú el dinero en el cajón. — *Pone*
3. El pañuelo *fell* al suelo. — *cayó*
4. *Tell* la verdad siempre, mi hijita. — *Dice*
5. They *were living* en Inglaterra. — *Estaban corriendo*
6. Lo *he put* en el bolsillo. — *Lo pone*
7. They *had bought* una alfombra. — *Han comprado*
8. Lo *they have received.* — *Lo han recibiendo*
9. ¿*Do you see* aquel calendario? — *¿ Ve*
10. She *is going* a la oficina. — *Esta yendo*
11. *I saw* a Enrique ayer. — *Ve*
12. *I will visit* a mis parientes. — *Visitaré*
13. No lo *we have done.* — *No lo hemos puesto*
14. They *were* enemigos. — *Estaban*
15. *I waited* hasta las nueve. — *Espere*
16. *Go* Vd. al mercado. — *Iba*
17. El carnicero nos *gave* la carne. — *da*
18. Siempre *we will tell* la verdad. — *Diremos*
19. *Give me* Vd. la cuchara, por favor. — *Da*
20. *He brought* una botella de leche. — *Compro*
21. *I know* al compositor. — *Conozco*
22. *Let's be* buenos vecinos. — *Vamos a ser*
23. *Don't tell* tú tantas mentiras. — *No dias = No digas*
24. She *won't be able* salir. — *No podra Podra*
25. *Leave* tú de aquí. — *Sal Sal*
26. They *sat down* en el sofá. — *se sentaron*
27. No le *I gave* nada. — *Di*
28. ¿Dónde lo *have you put?* — *Donde ha Puesto*
29. They *were walking* despacio. — *Estaban andando (tu.)*
30. *Close* Vd. el laboratorio. — *Cierre (No cierres (tu.))*
31. *I came* tarde. — *Vine*
32. *It is probably* las tres. — *Serán las tres*
33. *He entered* en un monasterio. — *Entró*
34. *We are going to* nadar en el océano. — *Ibamos*

120

Present   future
Pred —

35. *They probably went* hacia el oeste.   _Irían_
36. *Be careful,* hermanito.   _Tenga   Ten cuidado_
37. *They will come* mañana.   _Vendrá_
38. Dijo que lo *he would buy.*   _compra_
39. Lo *he did* con cuidado.   _Haz_
40. *We sold* el pescado.   _Vendimos_
41. *Come* mañana, hijo mío.   _Venga   Ven_
42. *Don't be* tontos, niños.   _No estén seas_
43. Hace una hora que *he is sleeping.*
44. *Come* vosotros mañana a las tres.
45. *They smell* las flores.
46. *Keep on* Vds. avanzando.   _Sigan_
47. *They became* pálidos.   _Pusieron Palador_
48. *He takes off* la ropa.   _Toma / de gente_
49. Le *he led* a la cárcel.   _Le conduj_
50. *He was born* en Europa.   _Nació_

B. Escriba Vd. los verbos siguientes en el presente, el imperfecto, y el pretérito, en las formas indicadas:

	Present	Imperfect	Preterite
yo (hablar)	hablo	hablaba	hablé
1. él (entrar)			
2. nosotros (comer)			
3. yo (vivir)			
4. ella (querer)			
5. yo (tener)			
6. ellos (salir)			
7. yo (decir)			
8. Pedro (hacer)			
9. él (pensar)			
10. ellos (volver)			
11. yo (ir)			
12. el niño (dormir)			
13. Vds. (ver)			
14. él (ser)			
15. yo (estar)			
16. nosotros (saber)			
17. yo (poder)			
18. los niños (venir)			
19. Vds. (traer)			

20. Ana (dar) ---------------------------- ---------------------------- ----------------------------

21. yo (conocer) ---------------------------- ---------------------------- ----------------------------

22. él (levantarse) ---------------------------- ---------------------------- ----------------------------

23. nosotros (pedir) ---------------------------- ---------------------------- ----------------------------

24. él (oír) ---------------------------- ---------------------------- ----------------------------

25. yo (llegar) ---------------------------- ---------------------------- ----------------------------

C. Escriba Vd. los verbos siguientes en el futuro y el presente perfecto, en las formas indicadas:

	Future	*Present Perfect*
yo (visitar)	visitaré	he visitado
1. él (invitar)		
2. yo (vender)		
3. nosotros (recibir)		
4. ellos (volver)		
5. yo (abrir)		
6. Pedro (salir)		
7. nosotros (ver)		
8. yo (decir)		
9. Vds. (venir)		
10. ¿quién (hacer)?		
11. yo (escribir)		
12. nosotros (tener)		
13. él (caer)		
14. yo (poner)		
15. nosotros (querer)		
16. yo (saber)		
17. él (morir)		
18. nosotros (ir)		
19. yo (traer)		
20. Vd. (dar)		

D. Escriba Vd. los infinitivos de los verbos siguientes:

1. trajo ----------------------------

2. vimos ----------------------------

3. busqué ----------------------------

4. huyó ----------------------------

5. conozco ----------------------------

6. pierde ----------------------------

7. digo ----------------------------

8. cayendo ----------------------------

9. roto ----------------------------

10. pongo ----------------------------

11. oyen ----------------------------

12. se acuesta ----------------------------

13. empiezo ----------------------------

14. produjo ----------------------------

15. murieron ----------------------------

16. doy ----------------------------

17. siguen _____   19. venga _____

18. era _____   20. pide _____

E. Escriba Vd. la tercera persona singular (*él*) y la primera persona plural (*nosotros*) del presente de subjuntivo de los verbos siguientes:

| | *Present Subjunctive* | |
escribir	*3 Singular* escriba	*1 Plural* escribamos
1. tomar		
2. venir		
3. ser		
4. cerrar		
5. decir		
6. parecer		
7. haber		
8. dar		
9. poner		
10. comer		
11. seguir		
12. saber		
13. ir		
14. volver		
15. llegar		
16. tener		
17. estar		
18. jugar		
19. perder		
20. traer		
21. contar		
22. salir		
23. querer		
24. ver		
25. sentir		

F. Escriba Vd. la forma correcta del verbo en letra cursiva.

1. Habían *volver* a casa. _____

2. Yo *acercarse* a la estatua y la miré. _____

3. Dudo que ellos lo *tener*. _____

4. Hace tres horas que *nevar*. _____

5. Mientras ella *cantar*, el público hablaba. _____

6. Continúe Vd. *leer*. _____

7. Anoche mi hermano y yo *ir* al teatro. _____

8. Hacía mucho tiempo que yo no los *ver*. _____

9. Mientras yo leía, él *escuchar*. _____

10. Siguen *venir* de todas partes. _____

11. Yo no *poder* ir a su oficina la semana que viene. _____

12. ¿Dónde lo han *poner?* _____

13. ¿Cuánto tiempo hace que *llover?* _____

14. ¿Cree Vd. que ellos lo *saber?* _____

15. Nos ruega que *ir* a su casa. _____

16. ¿Cuánto tiempo hacía que Vds. le *conocer?* _____

17. Estoy *vestirse*. _____

18. Los niños están *dormir*. _____

19. Ana y Juan *ser* amigos cuando yo los conocía. _____

20. Ella desea *ir* al cine. _____

21. Me pide que *volver* mañana. _____

22. Ellos *divertirse* ayer en la playa. _____

23. Creen que él *ser* sabio. _____

24. Él me estaba *pedir* dinero. _____

25. Prohiben que nosotros *salir* de casa. _____

G. Traduzca Vd. al español.

1. He went to the store. _____

2. They left the room. _____

3. Sit down, please. _____

4. We can't sleep. _____

5. I would do it gladly. _____

6. It rains much in April. _____

7. I shall come tonight. _____

8. What did you say? _____

9. Do not get up. _____

10. Let us work together. _____

11. What have you done? _____

12. Do not bring it. _____

13. I do not want to stay here. _____

14. I am looking for a good hotel. _____

15. We used to live here. _____

16. They have gone to the country. _____

17. He didn't study the lesson. _____

18. We came early. _____

19. Did you hear a noise? _____

20. At what time do you go to bed? _____

21. I am going to the station. _____

22. I wonder if it is true. _____

23. Dinner is served at six o'clock. _____

24. Where are they? _____

25. What would you do? _____

26. He is probably tired. _____

27. I know his parents. _____

28. It is believed that he is dead. _____

29. What do you think of her? _____

30. He has lost the jewels. _____

El Castillo del Morro es una fortaleza (fortress) construida por los españoles en el puerto de La Habana para proteger la ciudad contra los ataques (attacks) de los piratas. Hay fortalezas semejantes, también llamadas "Castillo del Morro," en los puertos de Santiago de Cuba y San Juan de Puerto Rico.

Part II—*Grammatical Structures*

1. FORMS AND CONTRACTIONS OF THE ARTICLES; POSSESSION

FORMS OF THE DEFINITE AND INDEFINITE ARTICLES

	SINGULAR		PLURAL	
	Masculine	*Feminine*	*Masculine*	*Feminine*
the	el	la	los	las
a, an; *pl.*, some, a few	un	una	unos	unas

AGREEMENT OF ARTICLES

Articles agree in number and gender with the nouns they modify.

MASCULINE	FEMININE
el muchacho, the boy	**la muchacha,** the girl
los muchachos, the boys	**las muchachas,** the girls
un muchacho, a boy	**una muchacha,** a girl
unos muchachos, some boys	**unas muchachas,** some girls

Note

El is used instead of **la** before a feminine singular noun that begins with a *stressed* **a** or **ha.**

| **el agua** | the water |
| **el hacha** | the ax |

but

la alumna	the pupil
las aguas	the waters
las hachas	the axes

REPETITION OF ARTICLES

The article is generally repeated before each noun.

| Tiene **una** pluma y **un** lápiz. | He has a pen and (a) pencil. |
| **El** hombre y **la** mujer son amigos. | The man and (the) woman are friends. |

CONTRACTIONS OF THE ARTICLE *EL*

The article **el** contracts as follows:

| **a + el = al** | to the |
| **de + el = del** | of (from) the |

| Va **al** cine. | He goes to the movies. |
| Habla **del** niño. | He speaks of the child. |

The articles do not contract in any other case.

Habla **a las** mujeres.   He speaks to the women.

Recibe cartas **de los** alumnos.   He receives letters from the pupils.

POSSESSION

Possession is expressed in Spanish by **de** or **de** + the article before the possessor. There is no apostrophe *s* in Spanish.

el perro **de** Juan   John's dog (the dog of John)

el perro **del** muchacho   the boy's dog (the dog of the boy)

el perro **de la** muchacha   the girl's dog (the dog of the girl)

EJERCICIOS

A. Cambie Vd. el artículo al plural.

1. el año _____ años
2. un lápiz _____ lápices
3. la flor _____ flores
4. el alma _____ almas
5. un balcón _____ balcones
6. una corrección _____ correcciones
7. el águila _____ águilas
8. un libro _____ libros
9. una pluma _____ plumas
10. la boca _____ bocas

B. Cambie Vd. el artículo al singular.

1. unas familias _____ familia
2. los sombreros _____ sombrero
3. unos meses _____ mes
4. las aldeas _____ aldea
5. unos cursos _____ curso
6. las niñas _____ niña
7. las aguas _____ agua
8. las hachas _____ hacha
9. los diablos _____ diablo
10. las almohadas _____ almohada

C. Complete Vd. la frase con la forma correcta: **de, del, de la, de los, o de las.**

1. La esposa _____ médico es maestra.
2. Una _____ muchachas es inglesa.
3. Hablan _____ hombres.
4. Es el sombrero _____ Ana.
5. Son los hijos _____ vecina.
6. Es una carta _____ mi amigo.
7. Fue el mejor dramaturgo _____ época.
8. Estaba en el centro _____ grupo.
9. Lima es la capital _____ peruanos.
10. La sal cayó _____ mesa.

D. Complete Vd. la frase con la forma correcta: **a, al, a la, a los, o a las.**

1. Da el libro _____ alumno.
2. Hablo _____ profesor.
3. ¿Quién enseña la regla _____ estudiantes?

4. El profesor explica la gramática _____ clase.

5. Escribo _____ Tomás.

6. Trae juguetes _____ niñas.

7. El tren llegó _____ día siguiente.

8. Tuve que ir _____ sastrería.

9. El jefe habló _____ trabajadores.

10. Aplaudimos _____ bailarina.

E. Traduzca Vd. al español las expresiones en inglés.

1. Tomo *a pencil and a ruler*. _____

2. *The boy's father* va a la peluquería. _____

3. *Some* hombres son cobardes. _____

4. *The* viaje fue agradable. _____

5. *The children's maid* es francesa. _____

6. Es *a* ciudad moderna. _____

7. *The* árboles son grandes. _____

8. Abro *the* ventanas. _____

9. *Some* flores son caras. _____

10. *The* mujer es bella. _____

11. Hablo *to the* alumno. _____

12. *The* agua está caliente. _____

13. Hoy es el primer día *of the* semana. _____

14. Hace *a* mes que no le veo. _____

15. *Some* ciudades son pequeñas. _____

16. *The men and women* bajan. _____

17. *Some* familias son numerosas. _____

18. El tintero está en *the teacher's desk*. _____

19. Enviamos cartas *to the* escuelas de México. _____

20. Las puertas *of the* aulas están abiertas. _____

21. *John's sister* es mi amiga. _____

22. Este cepillo es *Mary's*. _____

23. Enero es el primer mes *of the* año. _____

24. Recibió un regalo *from the* estudiantes. _____

25. El director habla *to the* clase. _____

2. USES OF THE DEFINITE ARTICLE

The definite article is generally used before:

1. *Names of languages and other subjects of study* (except after **hablar, en,** or **de**).

El **español** es una lengua importante.	Spanish is an important language.
Estudia *el* **francés.**	He studies French.
Me gusta *la* **historia.**	I like history.

  but

Habla español.	He speaks Spanish.
Escribe **en inglés.**	He writes in English.
Es un profesor **de alemán.**	He is a German teacher.

2. *Parts of the body and articles of clothing.*

Se lava *la* **cara.**	He washes his face.
Se pone *la* **camisa.**	He puts on his shirt.

3. *Titles* (except in direct address).

El **señor** Pardo es alto.	Mr. Pardo is tall.
El **doctor** Pérez está aquí.	Doctor Pérez is here.

  but

Buenos días, **señor** Pardo.	Good morning, Mr. Pardo.

4. *Seasons.*

Hace frío en *el* **invierno.**	It is cold in winter.

5. *Days of the week, to express "on."*

Voy al centro *el* **lunes.**	I am going downtown on Monday.
No vamos a la escuela *los* **sábados.**	We do not go to school on Saturdays.

6. *Nouns in a general or abstract sense.*

Los **libros** son útiles.	Books are useful.
La **altura** me espanta.	Height frightens me.

7. *Nouns of weight or measure.*

Cuesta diez centavos *la* **libra.**	It costs ten cents a pound.

8. *Certain time expressions.*

el **mes próximo**	next month
la **semana pasada**	last week

9. *The words* **escuela, clase,** *and* **iglesia** *when they follow a preposition.*

Voy a *la* **escuela.**	I go to school.
Está en *la* **iglesia.**	She is in church.

10. *Certain geographical names.*

la Argentina	el Japón
el Brasil	el Perú
el Canadá	la América del Norte (or Norte América)
los Estados Unidos	la América del Sur (or Sud América)
la Habana	la América Central (or Centro América)

but

España, Spain	México, Mexico	Europa, Europe
Francia, France	Alemania, Germany	Asia, Asia
Inglaterra, England	Italia, Italy	África, Africa

EJERCICIOS

A. Complete Vd. la frase con la forma correcta del artículo definido, si hace falta (if it is needed).

1. Se pone _____ guantes.

2. _____ Canadá y _____ México están situados en _____ América del Norte.

3. Vino a mi casa _____ año pasado.

4. Estudio _____ historia.

5. _____ señorita Owens es mi profesora de _____ español.

6. Contesta en _____ inglés.

7. Se lava _____ manos.

8. ¿Cómo está Vd., _____ señor Jackson?

9. Habla _____ francés.

10. Vamos a _____ iglesia _____ domingos.

11. _____ señora Harding es hermosa.

12. _____ pan es necesario.

13. _____ primavera y _____ otoño son estaciones populares.

14. Vendremos _____ mes próximo.

15. _____ general Pershing fue americano.

16. Va a la escuela _____ martes.

17. Se quitó _____ zapatos.

18. Iré al circo _____ sábado.

19. Cuesta seis dólares _____ docena.

20. _____ Argentina y _____ Brasil son países de _____ América del Sur.

B. Conteste Vd. en español en frases completas.

1. ¿Sabe Vd. hablar en español e inglés?

_____

2. ¿Va Vd. a la escuela los sábados?

_____

3. ¿Prefiere Vd. visitar la América del Sur o México?

_____

4. ¿Se limpia Vd. los dientes todos los días?

_____

5. ¿Es más barato el oro o la plata?

_____

6. ¿A qué hora abre Vd. los ojos generalmente?

_____

7. ¿Le gusta a Vd. la leche?

_____

8. ¿Lleva Vd. sobretodo en el invierno o en el verano?

_____

9. ¿Cuáles de los países europeos desea Vd. ver?

_____

10. ¿Vio Vd. una película la semana pasada?

_____

C. Traduzca Vd. al español las expresiones en inglés.

1. Me quito _my_ zapatos. _____

2. _Mr._ Hall está enfermo. _____

3. _Dogs_ son animales útiles. _____

4. Buenos días, _Mrs._ González. _____

5. _Doctor_ Jones es célebre. _____

6. Se lava _his face._ _____

7. Visitaré a mi amigo _on Wednesday_ o _on Friday._ _____

8. _Havana_ es la capital de Cuba. _____

9. _England, Italy, Spain, France,_ y _Germany_ son países de _Europe._ _____

_____

10. _Next week_ celebro mi cumpleaños. _____

11. Voy _to church on Sundays._ _____

12. Valen cinco pesos _a dozen._ _____

13. _Last month_ estaba en el campo. _____

14. Le veo _on Thursdays._ _____

15. _Summer_ y _winter_ son mis estaciones favoritas. _____

16. Vamos a la playa _on Tuesday._ _____

17. Me gustan _pies,_ pero no me gusta _bread._ _____

18. _Captain_ Smith fue un soldado valiente. _____

19. Paga cinco centavos _a libra._ _____

20. Escriben los ejercicios en _Spanish._ _____

D. Traduzca Vd. al español.

1. President López went to Argentina last year. _____

_____

2. They will arrive from Japan next Thursday. _____

_____

3. Guatemala is in Central America. _____

_____

4. She takes off her hat. _____

5. Children are good. _____

6. Spring is the season of the flowers. _____

_____

7. He speaks English. _____

8. Do you have my Spanish book? _____

_____

9. I washed my face. _____

10. Miss Shaw is studying Spanish. _____

_____

3. OMISSION OF THE ARTICLES

OMISSION OF THE DEFINITE ARTICLE

The definite article is omitted:

1. *Before a noun in apposition.*

Lima, **capital** del Perú, es una ciudad interesante.	Lima, the capital of Peru, is an interesting city.

2. *With names of rulers.*

Carlos Quinto fue un rey español.	Charles the Fifth was a Spanish king.

OMISSION OF THE INDEFINITE ARTICLE

The indefinite article is omitted:

1. *Before an unmodified predicate noun expressing nationality, religion, rank, or occupation.*

Soy norteamericano.	I am an American.
¿Es Vd. protestante?	Are you a Protestant?
Es princesa.	She is a princess.
Es dentista.	He is a dentist.

but

Es *un* abogado *famoso*.	He is a famous lawyer.

2. *With certain words.*

cien dólares	a hundred dollars
cierta persona	a certain person
mil habitantes	a thousand inhabitants
otro alumno	another pupil
¡Qué lástima!	What a pity!
tal hijo	such a son

EJERCICIOS

A. Traduzca Vd. cada frase al inglés, y explique Vd. por qué se omite el artículo, subrayando la letra correcta, (*a*), (*b*), (*c*), o (*d*).

> (*a*) = a noun in apposition
> (*b*) = a name of a ruler
> (*c*) = an unmodified predicate noun
> (*d*) = a word that generally omits the indefinite article

1. Es abogado. (*a*) (*b*) (*c*) (*d*) _____

2. Tal hombre no existe. (*a*) (*b*) (*c*) (*d*) _____

3. Buscan otro camino. (*a*) (*b*) (*c*) (*d*) _____

4. Alfonso Trece fue el último rey de España. (*a*) (*b*) (*c*) (*d*) _____

_____

5. Hablo de cierto caballero. (*a*) (*b*) (*c*) (*d*) _____

_____

6. Es cristiano. (*a*) (*b*) (*c*) (*d*) ------------------------------------

7. Tengo cien pesos. (*a*) (*b*) (*c*) (*d*) ------------------------------

8. Es norteamericano. (*a*) (*b*) (*c*) (*d*) ----------------------------

9. María, hermana de mi amigo, es bonita. (*a*) (*b*) (*c*) (*d*) ----------

----

10. No soy médico. (*a*) (*b*) (*c*) (*d*) -----------------------------------

11. ¡Qué árbol alto! (*a*) (*b*) (*c*) (*d*) ----------------------------------

12. El vino, producto importante de España, se vende en todas partes. (*a*) (*b*) (*c*) (*d*) --------------

----

13. Hay mil estudiantes. (*a*) (*b*) (*c*) (*d*) ------------------------------

14. Felipe Segundo fue rey de España. (*a*) (*b*) (*c*) (*d*) ----------------

----

15. Madrid, capital de España, es una ciudad importante. (*a*) (*b*) (*c*) (*d*) -----------------

----

B. Traduzca Vd. al español las expresiones en inglés.

1. Es *a lawyer* rico. ---

2. Soy *a soldier*. --

3. ¡*What a* muchacha bonita! ------------------------------------

4. Este pueblo tiene *a thousand* habitantes. --------------------

5. Tengo *a hundred* libros en mi biblioteca. --------------------

6. Es *a doctor*. ---

7. ¿Es Vd. *a tailor?* --

8. *George the Sixth* fue rey de Inglaterra. --------------------

9. Es *a Catholic*. ---

10. Es *a teacher* inteligente. --------------------------------

11. La señorita Moreno era *a teacher*. ------------------------

12. Valparaíso, *the principal port* de Chile, es una ciudad encantadora. --------------------

13. No creerá *such a* cuento. ---------------------------------

14. Busca *a certain* libro. ------------------------------------

15. Es *a Spaniard*. --

C. Traduzca Vd. al español.

1. What a pretty tree! ---------------------------------------

2. I am a lawyer; he is a judge. ----------------------------

3. He is a famous doctor. -----------------------------------

4. Have you another pencil? ---------------------------------

5. They want to buy a certain book. _____

6. Mr. White is a baker; Mr. Brown is a butcher. _____

_____

7. I don't want to have such a friend. _____

8. A hundred men and a thousand women attended. _____

_____

9. I am an American; he is a Frenchman. _____

_____

10. I want to be a soldier. _____

El 12 de octubre de 1492 Colón desembarcó (landed) en la isla de San Salvador. Dio gracias a Dios por su ayuda y plantó en la playa la bandera de España, tomando posesión de la isla en nombre de los Reyes Católicos, Fernando e Isabel. Ese día, que en los países hispánicos se llama el Día de la Raza, fue glorioso para España porque fue el día en que comenzó la difusión (spread) en el Nuevo Mundo de la cultura y civilización españolas.

4. THE NEUTER ARTICLE *LO*

The neuter article **lo** is used (1) before the masculine singular form of an adjective used as a noun, and (2) before a past participle.

lo bueno y **lo malo**	the good and the bad
lo dicho	what has been said

Lo + an adjective (or adverb) + **que** = *how*.

Vd. no sabe *lo difícil que* es.	You don't know how difficult it is.
Me sorprende *lo bien que* juega.	It surprises me how well he plays.

EJERCICIOS

A. Traduzca Vd. al inglés.

1. Lo contrario de "rico" es "pobre."

   ----

2. "Lo bueno" y "lo malo" son antónimos.

   ----

3. Hice lo mismo que Vd.

   ----

4. ¿No ven Vds. lo necesario que es?

   ----

5. Vd. sabe lo aplicado que es.

   ----

6. ¿Notó Vd. lo mal que habla?

   ----

7. Quiero lo mejor.

   ----

8. Hay una gran diferencia entre lo dicho y lo hecho.

   ----

9. ¿Ha notado Vd. lo bien que toca el piano?

   ----

10. Lea Vd. lo escrito.

B. Conteste Vd. en español en frases completas.

1. ¿Distingue Vd. entre lo bueno y lo malo?

   ----

2. ¿Cree Vd. que lo caro es siempre preferible a lo barato?

   ----

3. ¿Sabe Vd. lo importante que es el estudio del español?

----

4. ¿Son iguales "lo dicho" y "lo hecho"?

----

5. ¿Prefiere Vd. comprar lo americano o lo extranjero?

----

6. ¿Cuál dura más, lo escrito o lo hablado?

----

7. ¿Ha notado Vd. lo fácil que es esta lección?

----

8. Como turista, ¿le gustaría más ver lo hermoso o lo feo?

----

9. ¿Corrige Vd. lo escrito en la pizarra?

----

10. ¿Qué es lo contrario de "silencio"?

C. Traduzca Vd. al español las expresiones en inglés.

1. No puedo hacer *the impossible*. ------------------------

2. Haré *the best* que puedo. ------------------------

3. ¿Sabe Vd. *how* pobre que es? ------------------------

4. No debemos imitar *the bad*. ------------------------

5. ¿Ve Vd. *how pleasant* será? ------------------------

6. Copien Vds. *what has been written*. ------------------------

7. Pensaba en *how kind* era. ------------------------

8. Prefiero *the useful* a *the beautiful*. ------------------------

9. Sé *how strong he is*. ------------------------

10. Vd. no puede imaginarse *how tired I am*. ------------------------

D. Traduzca Vd. al español.

1. He admires the good and the noble.

----

2. They know how intelligent he is.

----

3. I saw how cruel he was.

----

4. She prefers the easy to the difficult.

----

5. We do not know how rich he is.

----

6. What is said is not always what is done.

----

7. They would do the same.

----

8. We understand how important it is.

----

9. I can only do the possible.

----

10. Did you notice how sad he was?

El Cristo de los Andes es una estatua enorme situada en la frontera entre Chile y la Argentina. Fue construida en 1904 como símbolo de paz y amistad, para celebrar el arreglo (settlement) pacífico de una disputa acerca de la frontera entre los dos países. El monumento contiene la inscripción: "Se desplomarán primero estas montañas antes que argentinos y chilenos rompan la paz jurada a los pies del Cristo Redentor." ("Sooner shall these mountains crumble into dust than Argentines and Chileans break the peace sworn at the feet of Christ the Redeemer.")

5. NOUNS

GENDER OF NOUNS

Nouns ending in **-o** or referring to male beings are generally masculine.

el sombrero, the hat   **el hombre,** the man

Nouns ending in **-a, -d, -ción, -z** or referring to female beings are generally feminine.

la casa, the house   **la voz,** the voice

la verdad, the truth   **la madre,** the mother

la nación, the nation

Exceptions in Gender

1. Feminine nouns ending in **-o.**

   la mano, the hand   **la radio,** the radio

2. Masculine nouns ending in **-a.**

   el tranvía, the streetcar   **el problema,** the problem

   el clima, the climate   **el programa,** the program

   el drama, the drama   **el mapa,** the map

   el idioma, the language   **el poeta,** the poet

PLURAL OF NOUNS

Nouns ending in a vowel add **-s.**

el libro, the book   **los libros,** the books

Nouns ending in a consonant add **-es.**

la flor, the flower   **las flores,** the flowers

Nouns ending in **-z** change **z** to **c** and add **-es.**

el lápiz, the pencil   **los lápices,** the pencils

Nouns ending in **-n** or **-s** with an accent mark in the last syllable generally drop the accent mark in the plural.

la lección, the lesson   **las lecciones,** the lessons

el inglés, the Englishman   **los ingleses,** the Englishmen

　　but

el país, the country   **los países,** the countries

(The accent mark is required in **países** to preserve the stress.)

Nouns of more than one syllable ending in **-n** with no accent mark in the last syllable generally add an accent mark in the plural.

el crimen, the crime   **los crímenes,** the crimes

la orden, the order   **las órdenes,** the orders

　　but

el plan, the plan   **los planes,** the plans

Nouns ending in -s where the final syllable is unstressed remain the same in the plural.

el paraguas, the umbrella	**los paraguas,** the umbrellas

but

el mes, the month	**los meses,** the months

The masculine plural form of a noun may refer to both the male and the female members of a group.

los padres	the father and mother, the parents
los hijos	the son and daughter, the children
los niños	the little boy and girl, the children
los reyes	the king and queen, the rulers
los señores Luna	Mr. and Mrs. Luna

NOUNS DESCRIBING MATERIALS OR CONTENTS

Nouns describing the materials or ingredients of which something is made are preceded by **de.**

un anillo *de oro*	a gold ring (a ring of gold)
una corbata *de seda*	a silk tie (a tie of silk)
un pastel *de manzana*	an apple pie (a pie of apple)
un sandwich *de pollo*	a chicken sandwich (a sandwich of chicken)

EJERCICIOS

A. Traduzca Vd. al inglés de dos maneras.

1. los niños _____
2. los padres _____
3. los muchachos _____
4. los hijos _____
5. los abuelos _____
6. los reyes _____
7. los tíos _____
8. los hermanos _____
9. los nietos _____
10. los chicos _____

B. Escriba Vd. la forma correcta del artículo definido.

1. _____ libertad   5. _____ región   8. _____ ley
2. _____ mano   6. _____ hacha   9. _____ crimen
3. _____ agua   7. _____ idioma   10. _____ clima
4. _____ problema

C. Cambie Vd. al plural los siguientes sustantivos:

1. el amigo _____   4. el jardín _____
2. el lunes _____   5. la voz _____
3. el lápiz _____   6. la lección _____

7. el examen ----------------------------   12. la luz ----------------------------

8. el viaje ----------------------------   13. el inglés ----------------------------

9. el mes ----------------------------   14. el ángel ----------------------------

10. el francés ----------------------------   15. la ciudad ----------------------------

11. el país ----------------------------

D. Cambie Vd. al singular los siguientes sustantivos:

1. las cruces ----------------------------   6. los problemas ----------------------------

2. las flores ----------------------------   7. los alemanes ----------------------------

3. las naciones ----------------------------   8. los jueves ----------------------------

4. los profesores ----------------------------   9. las leyes ----------------------------

5. las órdenes ----------------------------   10. unos días ----------------------------

E. Traduzca Vd. al español.

1. the drama ----------------------------   19. vanilla ice cream ----------------------------

2. the furniture ----------------------------   20. the vacation ----------------------------

3. a silk dress ----------------------------   21. the candy ----------------------------

4. the water ----------------------------   22. the program ----------------------------

5. the poet ----------------------------   23. apple pie ----------------------------

6. an iron box ----------------------------   24. the priest ----------------------------

7. a gold watch ----------------------------   25. the streetcar ----------------------------

8. the information ----------------------------   26. chicken salad ----------------------------

9. the voices ----------------------------   27. the examinations ----------------------------

10. the map ----------------------------   28. the angel ----------------------------

11. a diamond ring ----------------------------   29. the umbrella ----------------------------

12. a woolen suit ----------------------------   30. tomato soup ----------------------------

13. the lights ----------------------------   31. the parents ----------------------------

14. the radio ----------------------------   32. the children ----------------------------

15. the business ----------------------------   33. Mr. and Mrs. Pereda ----------------------------

16. a cotton blouse ----------------------------   34. the brother and sister ----------------------------

17. the news ----------------------------   35. the king and queen ----------------------------

18. the gardens ----------------------------

6. THE PERSONAL *A*

The preposition **a** is required before the direct object of a verb if the direct object is:

1. *A definite person or persons.*

       Invita **a su amigo.**   He invites his friend.

2. *A domestic animal* (*pet,* etc.).

       Admira **al perro.**   He admires the dog.

3. *A geographic name* (unless preceded by the definite article).

       Quiere visitar **a México.**   He wants to visit Mexico.

          but

       Quiere visitar **la Argentina.**   He wants to visit Argentina.

4. *A pronoun referring to a person* (**nadie, alguien,** etc.).

       No veo **a nadie.**   I don't see anyone.

Note

A. The personal **a** is not translated into English.

B. The personal **a** is not used with the verb **tener.**

      Tengo un amigo.   I have a friend.

      Tiene un caballo.   He has a horse.

EJERCICIOS

A. En cada frase, escriba Vd. la preposición **a** si es necesario:

1. Ayuda _____ Ana.
2. El médico curó _____ enfermo.
3. Visitaré _____ México el año que viene.
4. No comprendo _____ la lección.
5. Tiene _____ muchos primos.
6. No encontraron _____ sus amigos.
7. Aguardaban _____ tren.
8. No agradeció _____ su hermana.
9. Juanito cubrió _____ la cabeza.
10. Tengo _____ dos perritos.
11. Me escribió _____ una carta.
12. No vi _____ mi amigo ayer.
13. Busca _____ su gato.
14. ¿Visitó Vd. _____ la Argentina el año pasado?
15. ¿Conoce Vd. _____ aquel hombre?

B. Conteste Vd. en español en frases completas.

1. ¿Piensa Vd. ver a Madrid algún día? _____

_____

2. ¿Acompaña Vd. a sus amigos a menudo? _____

_____

3. ¿Quién fundó a Lima? [Pizarro] _____

_____

4. ¿Besa Vd. a su mamá al salir de casa? _____

_____

5. ¿Ama Vd. a su perrito? _____

_____

6. ¿Le permitirán sus padres visitar a España este verano? _____

_____

7. Andando a la escuela, ¿ve Vd. a alguien que conoce? _____

_____

8. ¿Espera Vd. visitar a sus parientes durante la Navidad? _____

_____

9. ¿Saluda Vd. a sus amigos todos los días? _____

_____

10. ¿Contribuye Vd. para ayudar a los pobres? _____

_____

C. Traduzca Vd. al español las expresiones en inglés.

1. Admiro *Henry*. _____

2. Quiere ver *the teacher*. _____

3. No veo *anyone*. _____

4. Llama *the horse*. _____

5. ¿Ha visitado Vd. *Buenos Aires?* _____

6. Tengo *a sister*. _____

7. El maestro enseña *the pupils*. _____

8. Leo *a magazine*. _____

9. Contesta *the man*. _____

10. Visitó *Peru*. _____

11. El público aplaudió *the actor*. _____

12. Ayer celebré *my birthday*. _____

13. Ella despertó *her son*. _____

14. Honraron *the heroes*. _____

15. El niño imita *his father*. _____

D. Traduzca Vd. al español.

1. He understands the exercises because he understands the teacher. _____

_____

2. I visited Spain last year. _____

_____

3. Henry is helping his mother. _____

_____

4. The teacher asked Arthur if the lesson was easy. _____

_____

5. I do not see my friends in the garden. _____

_____

6. Are you looking for someone? _____

_____

7. I do not know anyone in the class. _____

_____

8. Have you a brother? _____

_____

9. We visited England last month. _____

_____

10. The children love their parents. _____

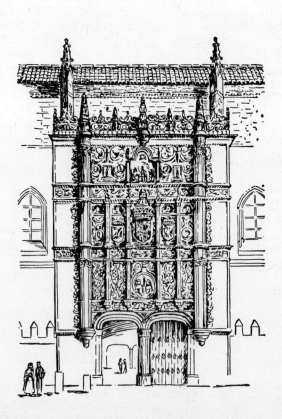

La Universidad de Salamanca es la universidad más vieja de España. Fue establecida en el siglo XIII. En los siglos XV y XVI fue una de las universidades más famosas de toda Europa. Muchos estudiantes vinieron a Salamanca de todas partes para continuar sus estudios.

7. POSITION AND AGREEMENT OF ADJECTIVES

FORMS OF ADJECTIVES

Adjectives whose masculine singular ends in **-o** and adjectives of nationality have four forms. Other adjectives have two forms.

| | SINGULAR | | PLURAL | |
	Masculine	*Feminine*	*Masculine*	*Feminine*
rich:	**rico**	**rica**	**ricos**	**ricas**
Spanish:	**español**	**española**	**españoles**	**españolas**
but				
large:	**grande**	**grande**	**grandes**	**grandes**
easy:	**fácil**	**fácil**	**fáciles**	**fáciles**

Adjectives ending in **-z** change **z** to **c** in the plural.

    feliz, felices   happy

A few adjectives drop their accent in the plural, while a few others add an accent in the plural.

    cortés, corteses   courteous, polite

    joven, jóvenes   young

Adjectives of nationality that have an accent mark on the last syllable, drop the accent mark in the feminine singular and in both plural forms.

    francés, francesa, franceses, francesas   French

    inglés, inglesa, ingleses, inglesas   English

    alemán, alemana, alemanes, alemanas   German

POSITION OF ADJECTIVES

Descriptive adjectives generally follow the nouns they modify.

    un hombre *alto*   a tall man

    una casa *grande*   a large house

Adjectives of number or quantity generally precede the nouns they modify.

    pocos hombres   few men

    todos los niños   every child

Common adjectives of quantity are:

mucho (-a), much	**cada,** each, every	**todos los (todas las),** every
poco (-a), little	**muchos (-as),** many	**varios (-as),** several
todo (-a), all	**pocos (-as),** few	**algunos (-as),** some

AGREEMENT OF ADJECTIVES

Adjectives agree in number and gender with the nouns they modify.

    Tiene **libros** *interesantes.*   He has interesting books.

    Ana es *perezosa.*   Ann is lazy.

Note

A. An adjective modifying two or more masculine nouns is in the masculine plural.

    Alberto y Juan son **perezosos.**   Albert and John are lazy.

B. An adjective modifying two or more feminine nouns is in the feminine plural.

    María y Ana son **bonitas.**   Mary and Anne are pretty.

C. An adjective modifying two or more nouns of different gender is in the masculine plural.

    Alberto y Ana son **ricos.**   Albert and Anne are wealthy.

EJERCICIOS

A. Escriba Vd. la forma correcta de los adjetivos *a, b, y c* en vez del adjetivo en letra cursiva.

1. Son lecciones *difíciles.*   (*a*) interesante   (*b*) breve   (*c*) corto

    (*a*) _____ (*b*) _____ (*c*) _____

2. Sevilla es una ciudad *pintoresca.*   (*a*) español   (*b*) alegre   (*c*) bello

    (*a*) _____ (*b*) _____ (*c*) _____

3. Tengo cuatro trajes *oscuros.*   (*a*) pardo   (*b*) claro   (*c*) azul

    (*a*) _____ (*b*) _____ (*c*) _____

4. Vive en una casa *blanca.*   (*a*) humilde   (*b*) modesto   (*c*) grande

    (*a*) _____ (*b*) _____ (*c*) _____

5. Son estudiantes *aplicados.*   (*a*) cortés   (*b*) necio   (*c*) perezoso

    (*a*) _____ (*b*) _____ (*c*) _____

6. Veo a las mujeres *altas.*   (*a*) alemán   (*b*) simpático   (*c*) amable

    (*a*) _____ (*b*) _____ (*c*) _____

7. Mi hermana es una muchacha *sincera.*   (*a*) hermoso   (*b*) débil   (*c*) modesto

    (*a*) _____ (*b*) _____ (*c*) _____

8. Compró dos sombreros *bonitos.*   (*a*) gris   (*b*) barato   (*c*) amarillo

    (*a*) _____ (*b*) _____ (*c*) _____

9. Es una caja *ancha.*   (*a*) grande   (*b*) cuadrado   (*c*) verde

    (*a*) _____ (*b*) _____ (*c*) _____

10. Tienen *cinco* plumas.   (*a*) alguno   (*b*) poco   (*c*) mucho

    (*a*) _____ (*b*) _____ (*c*) _____

B. Cambie Vd. cada expresión a la forma femenina.

1. algunos profesores ingleses   _____ profesoras _____

2. un hombre leal   _____ mujer _____

3. un padre bueno   _____ madre _____

4. el marido cortés   _____ esposa _____

5. los alumnos jóvenes   _____ alumnas _____

6. el abuelo cariñoso   _____ abuela _____

7. los bailarines andaluces   _____ bailarinas _____

8. el cocinero agradable   _____ cocinera _____

9. el esclavo infeliz   _____ esclava _____

10. el rey portugués   _____ reina _____

C. Cambie Vd. cada expresión a la forma masculina.

1. cada muchacha inglesa   _____ muchacho _____

2. todas las hijas   _____ _____ hijos

3. algunas mujeres españolas   _____ hombres _____

4. varias niñas hermosas   _____ niños _____

5. la vaca gorda   _____ toro _____

6. una poetisa famosa   _____ poeta _____

7. las princesas inglesas   _____ príncipes _____

8. la cordera flaca   _____ cordero _____

9. una gallina asada   _____ gallo _____

10. la burra trabajadora   _____ burro _____

D. Traduzca Vd. al español las expresiones en inglés.

1. Elena es *a polite girl*.   _____

2. Isabel es *Spanish*.   _____

3. Dé Vd. un libro a *each* alumno.   _____

4. Estos hombres son *English*.   _____

5. Son *weak children*.   _____

6. Carlos y Alberto son *French*.   _____

7. Tiene *little* inteligencia.   _____

8. Son *courteous boys*.   _____

9. Berlín es *a German city*.   _____

10. Viven en *a yellow house*.   _____

11. Luisa y Ana son *tall*.   _____

12. Hay *seven days* en una semana.   _____

13. Hay *many difficult exercises* en este libro.   _____

14. Sabe *the easy words*.   _____

15. Mañana será *another day*.   _____

16. Voy al cine *every Saturday*.   _____

17. Carlos y yo somos *young*.   _____

18. Hay *a small door* en *each room*.   _____

19. Nos visitan *every week*.   _____

20. Carlota y su hermano son muy *lazy*.   _____

E. Traduzca Vd. al español.

1. every city   --

2. the English language   --

3. green eyes   --

4. every port   --

5. few persons   --

6. an intelligent boy   --

7. each day   --

8. the easy lessons   --

9. five large windows   --

10. several weeks   --

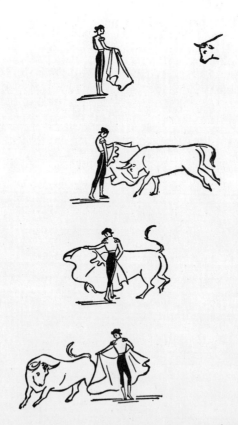

La corrida de toros es un espectáculo tradicional en España y en muchas partes del mundo hispánico. Tiene su origen en el siglo XII. A los españoles les gusta asistir a la plaza de toros para admirar la destreza (skill), el arte, y la osadía (boldness) del torero, que lucha contra un toro feroz que trata de matar al torero con sus cuernos (horns).

8. ADVERBS

1. Adverbs are regularly formed from adjectives by adding **-mente** to the feminine singular form of the adjective.

ADJECTIVE	ADVERB
cariñoso, -a, affectionate	**cariñosamente,** affectionately
inteligente, intelligent	**inteligentemente,** intelligently
rápido, -a, rapid	**rápidamente,** rapidly
cortés, polite, courteous	**cortésmente,** politely, courteously
fácil, easy	**fácilmente,** easily

Note. Adjectives that bear a written accent mark keep the accent mark when changed to adverbs.

2. When two or more adverbs ending in **-mente** occur in a series, **-mente** is used only with the last of the series.

Juan escribe **rápida** y *correctamente.*   John writes rapidly and correctly.

3. Some adverbs have special forms.

aprisa, quickly	**despacio,** slowly
bien, well	**mal,** badly

4. Many adverbs are formed by **con** + a noun.

con alegría, happily = **alegremente**

con atención, attentively = **atentamente**

con cariño, affectionately = **cariñosamente**

con cortesía, courteously = **cortésmente**

con cuidado, carefully = **cuidadosamente**

con frecuencia, frequently = **frecuentemente**

con (mucho) gusto, gladly = **gustosamente**

con inteligencia, intelligently = **inteligentemente**

con paciencia, patiently = **pacientemente**

con tristeza, sadly = **tristemente**

EJERCICIOS

A. Forme Vd. adverbios de los siguientes adjetivos, añadiendo **-mente:**

1. bondadoso _____   6. lento _____

2. científico _____   7. perfecto _____

3. cierto _____   8. probable _____

4. frecuente _____   9. terrible _____

5. hábil _____   10. típico _____

B. Forme Vd. expresiones sinónimas de los adverbios siguientes:

EJEMPLO: cuidadosamente—*con cuidado*

1. cariñosamente _____
2. frecuentemente _____
3. tristemente _____
4. fácilmente _____
5. cortésmente _____

6. bondadosamente _____
7. inteligentemente _____
8. pacientemente _____
9. alegremente _____
10. inocentemente _____

C. Traduzca Vd. al español las expresiones en inglés.

1. El piloto se acercaba *slowly* al aeropuerto. _____
2. La secretaria copiará la lista *carefully*. _____
3. Soltó *quickly* el vaso de agua caliente. _____
4. Adondequiera que él vaya le tratarán *badly*. _____
5. Mi madre sabe cocinar *well*. _____
6. Habló a su cuñado *politely and patiently*. _____
7. *Frequently* tomaban la merienda en algún café. _____
8. El maestro explicó la gramática *clearly and correctly*. _____
9. El peluquero dijo que me cortaría el pelo *gladly*. _____
10. *Generally* compraba carne en un supermercado. _____

9. POSSESSIVE ADJECTIVES

	SINGULAR	PLURAL
my	*mi* libro	*mis* libros
your (*fam.*)	*tu* hermano	*tus* hermanos
your, his, her, its, their	*su* casa	*sus* casas
our	*nuestro* profesor	*nuestros* profesores
	nuestra profesora	*nuestras* profesoras
your (*fam. pl.*)	*vuestro* hijo	*vuestros* hijos
	vuestra hija	*vuestras* hijas

Note

Possessive adjectives agree in gender and number with the person or thing possessed, *not* with the possessor.

nuestra abuela	our grandmother
mis libros	my books
sus lecciones	his (her, their, your) lessons

1. The definite article often replaces the possessive adjective when referring to parts of the body and articles of clothing, especially when used with a reflexive verb.

Me lavo *la* cara.	I wash my face.
Se quita *el* sombrero.	He takes off his hat.

2. Since **su** and **sus** have several meanings, the intended meaning may be clarified by replacing **su** or **sus** with the definite article and by adding **de él, de ella, de Vd. (Vds.),** or **de ellos (ellas)** after the noun.

el libro *de él*	his book
la casa *de ellos*	their house

EJERCICIOS

A. Complete Vd. cada frase con la forma correcta del adjetivo entre paréntesis.

1. _____ padres son buenos. (Su, Sus)

2. Carlota no ve a _____ perro. (nuestro, -a, -os, -as)

3. ¿Dónde está _____ lápiz? (su, sus)

4. _____ profesores son simpáticos. (Nuestro, -a, -os, -as)

5. No tengo _____ llaves. (mi, mis)

6. Estoy en _____ cuarto. (mi, mis)

7. _____ hijas son muy bonitas. (Vuestro, -a, -os, -as)

8. ¿Has comprado _____ libros? (tu, tus)

9. _____ ventanas están sucias. (Su, Sus)

10. _____ escuela es grande. (Nuestro, -a, -os, -as)

B. Cambie Vd. cada frase al plural.

1. Nuestro amigo es mexicano. _____

2. Tu hermana es bonita. _____

3. Mi lección es fácil. _____

4. Su casa es muy pequeña. _____

5. Vuestro tío es bueno. _____

6. Mi brazo es fuerte. _____

7. Nuestra alfombra costó mucho. _____

8. Su hijo es aplicado. _____

9. Mi bolsillo está vacío. _____

10. Nuestro compañero averiguó la verdad. _____

_____

C. Cambie Vd. cada frase al singular.

1. Sus hermanas son simpáticas. _____

2. ¿Tienen Vds. sus libros? _____

3. Tus compañeros son muy inteligentes. _____

4. ¿Son españoles vuestros vecinos? _____

5. Mis profesores son buenos. _____

6. No aceptaron mis consejos. _____

7. Sus decisiones son sabias. _____

8. Tus corbatas no son nuevas. _____

9. Nuestros diamantes son preciosos. _____

10. Nuestros discos están rotos. _____

D. Conteste Vd. en español en frases completas.

1. ¿Es grande su escuela? _____

2. ¿Tiene Vd. mis llaves? _____

3. ¿Vive Vd. cerca de sus amigos? _____

4. ¿Desea Vd. comprar mi automóvil? _____

5. ¿Se lava Vd. las manos todos los días? _____

_____

6. En la clase ¿levanta Vd. la mano antes de hablar? _____

_____

7. ¿Besa Vd. a su mamá al volver a casa? _____

_____

8. ¿Me ha devuelto Vd. mis libros? _____

_____

9. ¿Debe Vd. respetar a sus padres? _____

10. ¿Sabe su mamá cocinar bien? _____

E. Traduzca Vd. al español las expresiones en inglés.

1. *Our* ciudad es grande. _____

2. *Your* sillas no son cómodas. _____

3. No se lava *his ears*. _____

4. *My* hermanos están en el ejército. _____

5. *Our* cuartos son grandes. _____

6. *Your* puerta está abierta. _____

7. *Their* padre es abogado. _____

8. *Our* jardín es pequeño. _____

9. *Her* amigas son bonitas. _____

10. Se pone *his* sombrero. _____

11. ¿Tienes *your* libros? _____

12. *Her sister* y *his sister* son maestras. _____

13. *His* padres son bondadosos. _____

14. *Our* primos vienen mañana. _____

15. Cada país tiene *its* costumbres. _____

Hernán Cortés (1485-1547) fue tal vez el más grande de los conquistadores españoles. En 1519 llegó a la costa de México con menos de 500 soldados, y avanzó hacia la capital de los aztecas, Tenochtitlán (hoy la Ciudad de México). Hizo prisionero al emperador azteca, Moctezuma. Después de luchas sangrientas (bloody) que duraron dos años, Cortés logró vencer a los aztecas. En 1521 tomó posesión de la nueva colonia en nombre del rey Carlos V, y le dio el nombre de Nueva España.

10. POSSESSIVE PRONOUNS

	SINGULAR	PLURAL
mine	el mío la mía	los míos las mías
yours (*fam.*)	el tuyo la tuya	los tuyos las tuyas
his, hers, yours, theirs	el suyo la suya	los suyos las suyas
ours	el nuestro la nuestra	los nuestros las nuestras
yours (*fam. pl.*)	el vuestro la vuestra	los vuestros las vuestras

Note

Possessive pronouns agree in gender and number with the nouns they replace, *not* with the possessor.

mis amigos y *los suyos*   my friends and his (yours, hers, theirs)

su casa y *la nuestra*   his house and ours

1. The article of the possessive pronoun is generally omitted after the verb **ser** and in such expressions as *a friend of mine, a cousin of ours*, etc.

Esta pluma es **mía**.   This pen is mine.

Juan es **un amigo suyo**.   John is a friend of his (yours, hers, theirs).

Note. In **un amigo suyo**, the word **suyo** is really an adjective, since it is used with the noun **amigo**.

2. Since **el suyo, la suya**, etc., have several meanings, the intended meaning may be clarified by using instead the definite article followed by **de él, de ella, de Vd. (Vds.)**, or **de ellos (ellas)**.

mi casa y *la de él*   my house and his

nuestro cuarto y *el de ellos*   our room and theirs

EJERCICIOS

A. Subraye Vd. la forma correcta del pronombre posesivo.

1. Su armario es más grande que (el mío, la mía, las mías).

2. Mi bicicleta es vieja. (El suyo, La suya, Las suyas) es nueva.

3. Su escuela es más pequeña que (el nuestro, la nuestra, los nuestros).

4. Nuestros cuartos son más claros que (la suya, los suyos, las suyas).

5. Estos libros son (mío, míos, mías).

6. Nuestra casa es tan bonita como (el de Vd., la de Vd., los de Vd.).

7. Mi familia es más pobre que (el suyo, la suya, los suyos).

8. Juan es un vecino (nuestro, nuestra, nuestras).

9. Mi reloj es más caro que (el tuyo, la tuya, las tuyas).

10. Compre Vd. sus billetes y yo compraré (la mía, los míos, las mías).

B. Cambie Vd. cada frase, empleando pronombres posesivos en lugar de las expresiones en letra cursiva.

EJEMPLO: Tiene *mi pluma, su lápiz, nuestras revistas, tu dinero.*

Tiene *la mía, el suyo, las nuestras, el tuyo.*

1. Hay muchas rosas en *mi jardín, su cuarto, nuestro patio, tu cesta.*

----

2. ¿Dónde están *sus libros, tus discos, mis anteojos, sus joyas?*

----

3. Pagó a *nuestra criada, su cocinera, nuestros compañeros, sus dependientes.*

----

4. *Tu perro, Mi maleta, Su mesa, Nuestra nación* es grande.

----

5. No tengo *tu corbata, sus papeles, mi paquete, su retrato.*

----

6. *Nuestra profesora, Mi sobrino, Tu caballo, Nuestro alcalde* es joven.

----

7. ¿Tiene Vd. *mi revista, mi baúl, su billete, mis camisas?*

----

8. Hemos vendido *nuestra casa, nuestros diamantes, nuestro coche, nuestras cosas.*

----

9. Vive cerca de *su casa, sus suegros, nuestra iglesia, su fábrica.*

----

10. *Mi abuela, Tu nieto, Su papá, Nuestro presidente* no vive en California.

C. Traduzca Vd. al español las expresiones en inglés.

1. Busque Vd. sus libros y yo buscaré *mine.*   ------------------------------

2. Habla de mi profesor y *of yours.*   ------------------------------

3. Nuestra familia es más grande que *his.*   ------------------------------

4. Sus hermanas y *mine* son amigas.   ------------------------------

5. Mis guantes son más caros que *hers.*   ------------------------------

6. Mi tía y *hers* son maestras.   ------------------------------

7. Halló su pluma, pero yo no hallé *mine.*   ------------------------------

8. Son amigos *of his;* no son amigos *of mine.*   ------------------------------

9. Mi hermano es médico; *hers* es abogado; *his* es ingeniero. -------------------------------------

10. Invitaré a mi prima y a *his*. -------------------------------------

11. Quiero tinta negra; *yours* es verde y *his* es roja. -------------------------------------

12. Nuestro ejército es más poderoso que *theirs*. -------------------------------------

13. Tomás es *a cousin of mine*. -------------------------------------

14. Sus trenes son más cómodos que *ours*. -------------------------------------

15. Perdió su pelota y *mine*. -------------------------------------

16. Compramos nuestros zapatos donde ella compró *hers*. -------------------------------------

17. Su escuela es más grande que *theirs*. -------------------------------------

18. Estos libros son *his*. -------------------------------------

19. Nuestras tropas son más valientes que *theirs*. -------------------------------------

20. Yo estudio mis lecciones. ¿Estudia Vd. *yours?* -------------------------------------

D. Traduzca Vd. al español.

1. our neighbor and his ---

2. your children and ours ---

3. an aunt of theirs ---

4. his watch and mine ---

5. your dog and theirs ---

6. their sisters and mine ---

7. my ideas and his ---

8. a brother of hers ---

9. her picture and ours ---

10. my uncle and yours ---

11. their story and yours ---

12. our school and theirs ---

13. her pen and mine ---

14. my rooms and yours ---

15. his house and ours ---

16. my family and yours ---

17. our cousins and theirs ---

18. your books and mine ---

19. my wife and his ---

20. his sisters and yours

11. DEMONSTRATIVE ADJECTIVES

	Masculine	*Feminine*
this these	**este** cuarto **estos** cuartos	**esta** tienda **estas** tiendas
that (near you) those (near you)	**ese** cuarto **esos** cuartos	**esa** tienda **esas** tiendas
that (at a distance) those (at a distance)	**aquel** cuarto **aquellos** cuartos	**aquella** tienda **aquellas** tiendas

EJERCICIOS

A. Subraye Vd. la forma correcta del adjetivo entre paréntesis.

1. *This* caballo es hermoso.   (Este, Ese)

2. *Those* lápices escriben bien.   (Estos, Esos)

3. *Those* casas son pequeñas.   (Aquellas, Estas)

4. *That* libro es una gramática española.   (Este, Ese)

5. *This* tienda es de mi tío.   (Este, Esta)

6. *Those* (over there) estudiantes son perezosos.   (Aquellos, Esos)

7. *This* lección es fácil.   (Este, Esta)

8. *These* calles son estrechas.   (Estos, Estas)

9. *Those* soldados son valientes.   (Estos, Esos)

10. *That* (yonder) cuadro es bonito.   (Ese, Aquel)

B. Cambie Vd. las frases del singular al plural o viceversa.

1. Este sombrero es bonito. ------------------------------------ son bonitos.

2. Aquellos libros son interesantes. ------------------------------ es interesante.

3. Esos trajes son baratos. ------------------------------------ es barato.

4. Aquel hombre es cortés. ------------------------------------ son corteses.

5. Esas mujeres son inglesas. ----------------------------------- es inglesa.

6. Estos lápices son míos. ------------------------------------- es mío.

7. Ese niño es español. -------------------------------------- son españoles.

8. Aquellas flores son raras. ----------------------------------- es rara.

9. Este árbol es grande. -------------------------------------- son grandes.

10. Esta casa es hermosa. ------------------------------------- son hermosas.

C. Traduzca Vd. al español las palabras en inglés.

1. Compré *that* cuaderno. _____

2. Prefiero *this* silla. _____

3. ¿Ve Vd. *that* buque a lo lejos? _____

4. Quiero *that* lámpara cerca de Vd. _____

5. *These* sombreros son más caros. _____

6. *That* hombre que está sentado allí es famoso. _____

7. No vive en *that* calle. _____

8. *Those* exámenes son difíciles. _____

9. ¿Cuándo se abren *those* tiendas? _____

10. *This* lápiz no escribe bien. _____

11. *This* monumento es antiguo. _____

12. *Those* frutas son amargas. _____

13. *This* bebida es excelente. _____

14. *That* cantidad no es bastante. _____

15. No puedo encender *these* fósforos. _____

D. Traduzca Vd. al español.

1. those gloves (near you) _____

2. that watch _____

3. those girls (near you) _____

4. this water _____

5. that man (near you) _____

6. these books _____

7. this map _____

8. that week _____

9. these soldiers _____

10. those mountains (at a distance) _____

11. this trip _____

12. that country (far away) _____

13. this year _____

14. these rivers _____

15. those rooms _____

12. DEMONSTRATIVE PRONOUNS

	Masculine	Feminine	Neuter
this [one] these	éste éstos	ésta éstas	esto
that [one] (near you) those (near you)	ése ésos	ésa ésas	eso
that [one] (at a distance) those (at a distance)	aquél aquéllos	aquélla aquéllas	aquello

Note. Demonstrative pronouns, with the exception of the neuter forms, are distinguished from the demonstrative adjectives by a written accent mark on the first **e**.

1. Demonstrative pronouns must agree in number and gender with the nouns they replace.

este hombre y **aquél**	this man and that one
esos alumnos y **éstos**	those pupils and these

2. The neuter forms are used when referring to a statement, an idea, or something vague, indefinite, or not mentioned. They are used only in the singular and do not bear an accent mark.

No me gusta **esto.**	I don't like this.
Eso es importante.	That is important.

EJERCICIOS

A. Subraye Vd. la forma correcta del pronombre entre paréntesis.

1. No comprendo *this.*   (esto, éste, eso)
2. Aquellos ejercicios son más fáciles que *these.*   (ésos, éstos, estos)
3. Esta mujer es joven; *that one* es vieja.   (aquélla, esa, ésta)
4. ¿Escribió Vd. *that?*   (aquél, ése, aquello)
5. Esa clase es más grande que *this one.*   (está, ésta, esa)
6. Estos zapatos son más caros que *those.*   (aquéllos, éstos, aquello)
7. ¿Qué silla prefiere Vd., ésta o *that one?*   (aquél, esa, ésa)
8. Este alumno es aplicado; *that one* (*over there*) es perezoso.   (aquello, aquél, ése)
9. *That* es difícil.   (Ése, Aquél, Eso)
10. ¿Quién necesita *this?*   (esto, eso, aquello)

B. Cambie Vd. cada frase, empleando un pronombre demostrativo en vez de la expresión en letra cursiva.

EJEMPLO: Va a *este mercado.*

Va a ___éste.___

1. Prefiero *esa corbata.*   Prefiero _____.
2. Quiero ver *aquellos zapatos.*   Quiero ver _____.
3. *Esos muebles* son viejos.   _____ son viejos.

4. *Aquella ciudad* es famosa.   _____ es famosa.

5. No leo *aquel periódico*.   No leo _____.

6. *Esta tinta* es verde.   _____ es verde.

7. No hallamos *aquel libro*.   No hallamos _____.

8. *Este reloj* es de oro.   _____ es de oro.

9. *Estos pantalones* son cortos.   _____ son cortos.

10. *Estas mujeres* son habladoras.   _____ son habladoras.

11. *Ese aduanero* examinó mis maletas.   _____ examinó mis maletas.

12. *Aquellas águilas* vuelan muy alto.   _____ vuelan muy alto.

13. ¿Son dulces *estas cerezas?*   ¿Son dulces _____?

14. *Esas sillas* parecen cómodas.   _____ parecen cómodas.

15. *Aquella bandera* es de mi patria.   _____ es de mi patria.

C. Traduzca Vd. al español las expresiones en inglés.

1. No creo *this*.   _____

2. Esa iglesia fue construida antes que *this one*.   _____

3. Se habla español en estos países y en *those*.   _____

4. Estas ventanas son más grandes que *those*.   _____

5. *That* es imposible.   _____

6. Este hombre y *that one* que está sentado allí son primos.   _____

7. Ese perro es más feroz que *this one*.   _____

8. Estos árboles son manzanos; *those* a lo lejos son perales.   _____

9. Esos cuadros y *these* fueron pintados por ese artista.   _____

10. Esta pluma escribe mejor que *that one*.   _____

D. Traduzca Vd. al español.

1. these roses and those   _____

2. that library and this one   _____

3. those cities and these   _____

4. this store and that one   _____

5. I do not understand this.   _____

6. these universities and those   _____

7. those towns and these   _____

8. When did you hear that?   _____

9. that garden and this one   _____

10. this automobile and that one   _____

13. COMPARISON OF ADJECTIVES

tall:	alto(-a, -os, -as)
taller:	más alto(-a, -os, -as)
(the) tallest:	el . . . más alto, la . . . más alta
	los . . . más altos, las . . . más altas
popular:	popular (populares)
more popular:	más popular (populares)
(the) most popular:	el . . . más popular, la . . . más popular
	los . . . más populares, las . . . más populares
interesting:	interesante (interesantes)
less interesting:	menos interesante (interesantes)
(the) least interesting:	el . . . menos interesante, la . . . menos interesante
	los . . . menos interesantes, las . . . menos interesantes

Note

A noun modified by the superlative form of the adjective follows the definite article and precedes **más** or **menos.**

el *hombre* **más popular**	the most popular man
la *revista* **menos interesante**	the least interesting magazine

1. A possessive adjective may replace the article in the superlative.

su amigo **más alto**	his tallest friend

2. After a superlative, *in* is translated by **de.**

Es el alumno más inteligente *de* la clase.	He is the most intelligent pupil in the class.

TRANSLATION OF *THAN*

Than is generally translated by **que.**

Juan es más alto *que* Enrique.	John is taller than Henry.

Than is translated by **de** before a number, except when the sentence is negative.

Gastó más *de* diez dólares.	He spent more than ten dollars.
Cuesta menos *de* treinta centavos.	It costs less than thirty cents.

but

No gastó más **que** diez dólares.	He did not spend more than ten dollars. (He spent only ten dollars.)

ADJECTIVES COMPARED IRREGULARLY

good:	bueno (-a, -os, -as)	large (great):	grande (-s)
better:	mejor (mejores)	greater, older:	mayor (mayores)
best:	el mejor, la mejor	greatest, oldest:	el mayor, la mayor
	los mejores, las mejores		los mayores, las mayores
bad:	malo (-a, -os, -as)	small:	pequeño (-a, -os, -as)
worse:	peor (peores)	lesser, younger:	menor (menores)
worst:	el peor, la peor	least, youngest:	el menor, la menor
	los peores, las peores		los menores, las menores

Note

A. **Mejor** and **peor** generally precede the nouns they modify.

el *mejor* libro   the best book

la *peor* clase   the worst class

B. **Mayor** and **menor** generally follow the nouns they modify.

el hijo *mayor*   the oldest son

mi hermana *menor*   my youngest sister

EJERCICIOS

A. Complete Vd. cada frase, empleando el adjetivo entre paréntesis en la forma comparativa.

EJEMPLO: (hermoso)   Ana es *más hermosa que* Conchita.

1. (barato)   Aquellas corbatas son _____ éstas.

2. (bonito)   Estos árboles son _____ ésos.

3. (alto)   La hija del señor Molina es _____ Vd.

4. (grande)   Su escuela es _____ la nuestra.

5. (azul)   Sus ojos son _____ el cielo.

6. (caliente)   El café está _____ la leche.

7. (guapo)   Lola no es _____ Carlota.

8. (largo)   Mi discurso es _____ el del señor González.

9. (natural)   Su voz parece hoy _____ ayer.

10. (estrecho) Esta calle es _____ aquélla.

B. Complete Vd. cada frase según los ejemplos, empleando el adjetivo entre paréntesis en la forma superlativa.

EJEMPLOS: (muchacha) (bonito)   Elena es *la muchacha más bonita* de la clase.

(popular)   Mi maestro es *el más popular* de la escuela.

1. (alumno) (inteligente)   Arturo y Carlos son _____ de la escuela.

2. (muchacha) (hermoso)   Rosa es _____ de la clase.

3. (difícil)   Este problema es _____ del libro.

4. (hija) (mayor)   Ella es _____ de la familia.

5. (aplicado)   Ana y Juana son _____ de las hermanas.

6. (estudiante) (mejor)   Jorge es _____ de todos mis amigos.

7. (peor)   Este libro es _____ de todos.

8. (grande)   Este árbol es _____ del jardín.

9. (menor)   Soy _____ de la familia.

10. (libro) (interesante)   Éstos son _____ de la biblioteca.

C. Complete Vd. cada frase, empleando la forma correcta de *than*.

1. Este niño es más débil _____ ése.

2. Hace más calor en el verano _____ en el invierno.

3. Tengo menos _____ veinte dólares.

4. José es más popular _____ Enrique.

5. Gasté más _____ cuatro pesos.

6. Había más _____ cien personas.

7. Esta puerta es más fuerte _____ ésa.

8. Menos _____ treinta alumnos asistieron a la clase.

9. No compré más _____ dos camisas.

10. Comió más _____ seis manzanas.

D. Conteste Vd. en español en frases completas.

1. ¿Es Vd. más alto(-a) que sus compañeros?

_____

2. ¿Quién es el (la) más inteligente de la clase de español?

_____

3. ¿Es Vd. mayor que su hermano(-a)?

_____

4. ¿Quién es el menor de su familia?

_____

5. ¿Cómo se llama su mejor amigo(-a)?

_____

6. ¿Tiene Vd. más de cincuenta dólares en el banco?

_____

7. ¿Cuál es el estado más grande de los Estados Unidos?

_____

8. ¿Es Vd. más aplicado(-a) que los otros alumnos?

_____

9. ¿Cuál es la peor estación del año?

_____

10. ¿Quién es el muchacho (la muchacha) más popular de la escuela?

_____

E. Traduzca Vd. al español las expresiones en inglés.

1. Eso no tiene *the least* importancia. _____

2. Buenos Aires es *the largest city in* la Argentina. _____

3. Paquita es *older than* su prima. _____

4. Son *the highest mountains in the* continente. _____

5. Su traje es *cheaper than* el mío. _____

6. Estas niñas son *lazier than* aquéllas. _____

7. Mis amigos son *more faithful than* los suyos. _____

8. Esta revista es *less interesting than* aquélla. ------------------------------

9. Esta novela es *more famous than* ésa. ------------------------------

10. Nuestros soldados son *the bravest in the* mundo. ------------------------------

11. Escribió *more than* mil artículos. ------------------------------

12. Esta camisa es *better than* aquélla. ------------------------------

13. Es *the richest in* la clase. ------------------------------

14. Washington, D.C., es la *greatest* capital del mundo. ------------------------------

15. Llegó en *less than* cuatro horas. ------------------------------

16. Estas canciones son *worse than* aquéllas. ------------------------------

17. Esos cuartos son *less expensive than* éstos. ------------------------------

18. Son *the most studious in* la escuela. ------------------------------

19. Ésa fue *the best* representación. ------------------------------

20. Paco es *the youngest in the* club. ------------------------------

F. Traduzca Vd. al español.

1. Winter is the worst season in the year.

----

2. Our house is better than his.

----

3. Uruguay is not the smallest country in South America.

----

4. Arthur is the youngest son.

----

5. He is more popular than his friend.

----

6. His brother is older than you.

----

7. Her cousin is younger than Rose.

----

8. Those lessons are less difficult.

----

9. Joseph is my best friend.

----

10. February is the shortest month in the year.

----

14. EXPRESSIONS OF EQUALITY

Tan + adjective (or adverb) + **como** = as . . . as.

Es *tan fuerte como* Vd.   He is as strong as you.

Baila *tan bien como* su hermano.   He dances as well as his brother.

Tanto, -a (tantos, -as) + noun + **como** = as much (as many) . . . as.

Tengo *tanto dinero como* Vd.   I have as much money as you.

Lee *tantos libros como* su amigo.   He reads as many books as his friend.

Tanto, -a (tantos, -as) + **como** = as much (as many) as.

¿Cuántas manzanas comió? Comió *tantas*   How many apples did he eat? He ate as many
como Juan.   as John.

No hace *tanto como* yo.   He doesn't do as much as I.

EJERCICIOS

A. Complete Vd. cada frase, empleando **tan . . . como** con la forma correcta del adjetivo entre paréntesis.

1. (nuevo)   Mis trajes son _____ los suyos.

2. (pobre)   Soy _____ Vd.

3. (pequeño)   Esta niña es _____ ésa.

4. (fácil)   Estas lecciones son _____ aquéllas.

5. (perezoso)   Es _____ su hermano.

6. (ancho)   Estas cajas son _____ ésas.

7. (joven)   Sus padres son _____ los míos.

8. (cansado)   Estamos _____ ellos.

9. (alto)   Esas alumnas son _____ éstas.

10. (diligente) Pedro no es _____ su amigo.

B. Complete Vd. cada frase, empleando **tanto(-a, -os, -as) . . . como.**

1. No usé _____ tinta _____ Vd.

2. Compró _____ pescado _____ carne.

3. Abril tiene _____ días _____ junio.

4. Tiene _____ cuartos _____ nosotros.

5. Necesita _____ madera _____ hierro.

6. Trajo _____ flores _____ ellos.

7. Perdí _____ dinero _____ mi padre.

8. Hay _____ alumnas _____ alumnos.

9. Tengo _____ amigos _____ Vds.

10. Había _____ mujeres _____ hombres.

C. Conteste Vd. en español en frases completas.

1. ¿Es tan profundo el río como el océano? _____

_____

2. ¿Va Vd. al teatro tan frecuentemente como sus padres? _____

_____

3. ¿Tiene nuestra bandera tantas estrellas como el cielo? _____

_____

4. ¿Es Vd. tan fuerte como su papá? _____

_____

5. ¿Gasta Vd. tanto como sus amigos? _____

_____

6. ¿Es Vd. tan inteligente como sus compañeros? _____

_____

7. ¿Son tan blandas las piedras como las almohadas? _____

_____

8. ¿Tiene Chicago tantos habitantes como Nueva York? _____

_____

9. ¿Hace tanto frío en septiembre como en enero? _____

_____

10. ¿Sabe Vd. tantas palabras como el maestro? _____

_____

D. Traduzca Vd. al español las expresiones en inglés.

1. Vicente sabe *as much as* Ramón.   _____
2. Leyó *as many books as* yo.   _____
3. Su casa es *as large as* la mía.   _____
4. Compro *as much milk as* Vd.   _____
5. Ese camino es *as short as* éste.   _____
6. Trajimos *as many flowers as* ellas.   _____
7. Estas calles son *as long as* ésas.   _____
8. Gana *as much money as* el presidente.   _____
9. Ana recibió tres cartas y yo recibí *as many as* ella. _____
10. María es *as tall as* su amiga.   _____

E. Traduzca Vd. al español.

1. This novel is as interesting as that one. _____

_____

2. He has as many sisters as brothers. _____

_____

3. His parents are as rich as mine. --
----

4. They did not buy as much meat as we. ------------------------------------
----

5. Those exercises are as difficult as these. ---------------------------------
----

6. I ate as much as you. ---

7. He spends as much time in the country as in the city. -----------------------
----

8. We ate as soon as he came. --
----

9. January has as many days as March. --------------------------------------
----

10. He knows as much as I. ---

**La Dama de Elche es una estatua antigua descubierta en 1897 cerca de
la ciudad de Elche en España. Se cree que es una estatua de una diosa
(goddess) o princesa de los iberos, un pueblo antiguo de España.**

15. THE ABSOLUTE SUPERLATIVE (OPTIONAL)

1. The absolute superlative (no comparison involved) is formed by using **muy** before an adjective or adverb, or by attaching **-ísimo (-a, -os, -as)** to it. If a word ends in a consonant, **-ísimo** is attached directly to it. If a word ends in a vowel, the vowel is dropped before adding **-ísimo**. The ending **-ísimo** is translated by *very* or *extremely*.

un libro **muy popular**
or } a very popular book
un libro **popularísimo**

una casa **muy grande**
or } an extremely large house
una casa **grandísima**

2. *Very much* is expressed in Spanish by **muchísimo** and never by "muy mucho."

Juan quiere *muchísimo* a su novia.   John loves his sweetheart very much.

3. Adjectives ending in **-co, -go,** or **-z** change **c** to **qu, g** to **gu,** and **z** to **c** before adding **-ísimo**.

muy rico or **riquísimo**   very rich

muy largo or **larguísimo**   very long

muy feliz or **felicísimo**   very happy

EJERCICIOS

A. Complete Vd. cada frase, escribiendo el adjetivo entre paréntesis en la forma **-ísimo(-a, -os, -as)**.

EJEMPLO: (triste)   María está *tristísima*.

1. (grande)   Son edificios _____.
2. (inteligente)   Es una alumna _____.
3. (breve)   Es un ejercicio _____.
4. (pobre)   Luisa es una muchacha _____.
5. (cruel)   Es un hombre _____.
6. (hermoso)   Es una mujer _____.
7. (poco)   El niño comió _____.
8. (largo)   Estas avenidas son _____.
9. (mucho)   Estudia _____.
10. (rico)   Mi tío es un hombre _____.

B. En cada frase, escriba Vd. de otra manera la expresión en letra cursiva.

1. Este hombre es *muy alto*.   _____
2. Esas mujeres son *muy ricas*.   _____
3. Es una novela *muy importante*.   _____
4. Los perros son *muy feroces*.   _____
5. La tiza es *muy blanca*.   _____

6. Felipe está *muy triste*.   ------------------------------------

7. Estas calles son *muy anchas*.   ------------------------------------

8. La lección es *muy interesante*.   ------------------------------------

9. Estos alumnos son *muy inteligentes*.   ------------------------------------

10. Es una familia *muy feliz*.   ------------------------------------

C. Traduzca Vd. al español las expresiones en inglés, empleando la forma **-ísimo(-a, -os, -as)**.

1. Su casa es *very small*.   ------------------------------------

2. Este hombre está *very sick*.   ------------------------------------

3. Los edificios de Nueva York son *extremely tall*.   ------------------------------------

4. Lee *very much*.   ------------------------------------

5. Tiene *very many* amigos.   ------------------------------------

6. Juan está *extremely tired*.   ------------------------------------

7. Mi abuelo es *very old*.   ------------------------------------

8. Estas máquinas son *very expensive*.   ------------------------------------

9. Elena es una muchacha *very pretty*.   ------------------------------------

10. Las manzanas son *very sweet*.   ------------------------------------

Diego Velázquez (1599-1660) fue el pintor más importante de España. Fue el pintor de cámara (court painter) del rey Felipe IV, e hizo muchos retratos de la familia real. Lo más característico de sus obras es el realismo: "verdad y no pintura" ("truth, not painting"), como él mismo lo expresó. *Las meninas* y *La rendición de Bredá* son dos de sus obras más importantes.

16. SHORTENING OF ADJECTIVES

The following adjectives drop the final **-o** *before* a masculine singular noun:

Adjective	Shortened Form Before a Masculine Singular Noun
uno, a, an, one	**un** centavo, a (one) cent
bueno, good	un **buen** hotel, a good hotel
malo, bad	un **mal** niño, a bad child
primero, first	el **primer** mes, the first month
tercero, third	el **tercer** día, the third day
alguno, some	**algún** muchacho, some boy
ninguno, no	**ningún** hombre, no man

but

un hotel **bueno**

un niño **malo**

el mes **primero**

Santo becomes **San** before a masculine name of a saint, unless the name begins with **To-** or **Do-**.

San Juan	Saint John
San Pedro	Saint Peter

but

Santo Tomás	Saint Thomas
Santo Domingo	Saint Dominic
Santa Bárbara	Saint Barbara

Grande becomes **gran** before a singular noun of either gender and means *great*. When **grande** follows the noun, it means *large* or *big*.

un *gran* **héroe**	a great hero
una *gran* **heroína**	a great heroine

but

un **edificio grande**	a large building

Ciento becomes **cien** before a plural noun of either gender and before the numbers **mil** (*thousand*) and **millones** (*millions*). In combination with any other number, it remains **ciento.**

cien libros	one (a) hundred books
cien sillas	one (a) hundred chairs
cien mil soldados	one hundred thousand soldiers

but

ciento veinte sillas	one hundred twenty chairs

EJERCICIOS

A. Complete Vd. cada frase, escribiendo la forma correcta del adjetivo entre paréntesis.

1. (tercero) Vino el _____ día

2. (primero) Es la _____ vez que lo veo.

3. (ciento) Había _____ alumnos y _____ treinta alumnas.

4. (ninguno)   No vimos a _____ soldado.

5. (malo)   No es una _____ película.

6. (alguno)   Lo haré _____ día.

7. (grande)   Vive en una casa _____.

8. (bueno)   Es un _____ muchacho.

9. (Santo)   _____ José es la capital de Costa Rica.

10. (grande)   Wáshington fue un _____ hombre.

B. Complete Vd. cada frase, escribiendo la forma correcta de uno de los adjetivos siguientes: **uno, bueno, malo, primero, tercero, ninguno, Santo, grande, ciento.**

1. Enero es el _____ mes del año.

2. Martes es el _____ día de la semana.

3. Un niño que no obedece a sus padres es un _____ niño.

4. Noventa dólares y diez dólares son _____ dólares.

5. _____ Domingo es un país.

6. Lo contrario de un mal muchacho es un _____ muchacho.

7. Siete y _____ son ocho.

8. _____ Francisco es una ciudad en los Estados Unidos.

9. No tengo _____ dinero.

10. El Cid fue un _____ héroe español.

C. Conteste Vd. en español en frases completas.

1. ¿Cuál es el primer mes del año? ¿El tercero? _____

_____

2. ¿Qué lengua se habla en Santo Domingo? _____

_____

3. ¿Cuántos son sesenta dólares y cuarenta dólares? _____

_____

4. ¿Cuál de éstos fue un gran héroe de la América del Sur: Bolívar o el Cid? _____

_____

5. ¿Es Vd. un(-a) buen(-a) muchacho(-a)? _____

_____

6. ¿Tiene Vd. algún dinero? (Conteste Vd. en sentido negativo.) _____

_____

7. ¿Cuál es la ciudad más grande de los Estados Unidos? _____

_____

8. ¿Asiste Vd. a una escuela grande? _____

_____

9. ¿Cuántos son ochenta y sesenta? _____

_____

10. ¿En qué estado está San Francisco? _____

_____

D. Traduzca Vd. al español las expresiones en inglés.

1. Alfonso es un *bad* muchacho.   _____

2. María es una *good* niña.   _____

3. Nueva York es una *great* ciudad.   _____

4. Río de Janeiro es una ciudad *large*.   _____

5. Marzo es el *third* mes del año.   _____

6. Se habla español en *Saint* José y *Saint* Domingo.   _____

7. *Some* alumnos son perezosos.   _____

8. La ciudad tiene una población de *100,000*.   _____

9. Gastó más de *one hundred fifty* dólares.   _____

10. *A hundred* mujeres fueron a la feria.   _____

E. Traduzca Vd. al español.

1. It is a good hotel. _____

2. I bought one pair of shoes. _____

3. Take the third seat. _____

4. No man is perfect. _____

5. It is the first road to the right. _____

6. I shall return some day. _____

7. He earned one hundred thousand dollars. _____

8. Saint Mary and Saint Thomas are famous saints. _____

_____

9. Many American cities bear the name of some saint. _____

_____

10. Napoleon was a great man; he was not a big man. _____

_____

17. PERSONAL PRONOUNS AFTER PREPOSITIONS

sin *mí*	without *me*
de *ti*	from *you* (*fam.*)
para *Vd.*	for *you*
con *él*	with *him, it* (*m.*)
delante de *ella*	in front of *her, it* (*f.*)
para *sí*	for *himself* (*herself, yourself, themselves*)
detrás de *nosotros* (*-as*)	behind *us*
después de *vosotros* (*-as*)	after *you* (*fam. pl.*)
antes de *Vds.*	before *you*
cerca de *ellos*	near *them* (*m.*)
lejos de *ellas*	far from *them* (*f.*)

Note. With the exception of **mí, ti,** and **sí,** these pronouns are identical with the subject pronouns.

The preposition **con** combines with **mí, ti,** and **sí** to form **conmigo, contigo,** and **consigo.** These three forms do not change in gender or number.

conmigo	with me
contigo	with you (*fam.*)
consigo	with him(self), her(self), you(rself), them(selves)

EJERCICIOS

A. Subraye Vd. la expresión entre paréntesis que traduzca correctamente la expresión en inglés.

1. Está cerca de *me*.   (yo, mi, mí)

2. Traje un regalo para *them*.   (su, ellos, sus)

3. Fue sin *us*.   (nuestros, nuestro, nosotros)

4. No hablo de *him*.   (él, ello, su)

5. Estaba delante de *you*.   (Vd., su, tu)

6. Vive *with me*.   (con mi, con mí, conmigo)

7. Iré *with you*.   (con tú, contigo, con ti)

8. Está sentado entre *him and her*.   (el suyo y la suya, su y su, él y ella)

9. Viene con *you*.   (vosotros, vuestros, tuyo)

10. Lleva dos maletas *with her*.   (con la suya, consigo, con suya)

B. Cambie Vd. a pronombres las expresiones en letra cursiva.

EJEMPLO: Sale con *María*.   Sale con *ella*.

1. Es para *los niños*.   ------------------------------------

2. Llegó después de *Elena*.   ------------------------------------

3. Quiero ir con *Juan*.   ------------------------------------

4. Entraron en *el cuarto*.   ------------------------------------

5. Vive con *su madre*.   ------------------------------------

6. El director camina con *el profesor*.   ------------------------------

7. Sale de *la casa*.   ------------------------------------

8. Regresó antes de *Alberto y Pedro*. _____

9. Habla *del presidente*. _____

10. ¿Quiere Vd. jugar con *Luisa y su hermana?* _____

C. Conteste Vd. en español en frases completas, empleando pronombres en vez de las expresiones en letra cursiva.

EJEMPLO: ¿Compra Vd. regalos para *su mamá?*

Sí, compro regalos para *ella*.

1. ¿Tiene Vd. un calendario cerca de *su escritorio?*

_____

2. ¿Habla Vd. mucho con *sus amigos?*

_____

3. ¿Hay un campo detrás de *la escuela?*

_____

4. ¿Distingue Vd. entre *lo bueno y lo malo?*

_____

5. ¿Vuelve Vd. a casa antes de *la puesta del sol?*

_____

6. ¿Le gusta a Vd. nadar en *el lago?*

_____

7. ¿Vive Vd. lejos de *la estación del ómnibus?*

_____

8. ¿Se aleja Vd. de *los malos amigos?*

_____

9. ¿Tiene Vd. mucho dinero en *el banco?*

_____

10. ¿Corta Vd. la carne con *el cuchillo?*

_____

D. Traduzca Vd. al español las expresiones en inglés.

1. Es para *me*. _____

2. Había una disputa entre *him* y *her*. _____

3. No vayan Vds. sin *them*. _____

4. Está delante de *us*. _____

5. Trae un paquete *with her* (with herself). _____

6. Viven lejos de *you*. _____

7. Quiero hablar *with you* (fam. sing.). _____

8. Viene hacia *us*. _____

9. Recibí una carta de *him*. _____

10. ¿Viene Vd. *with me* o *with him?* _____

E. Traduzca Vd. al español.

1. They live near you (fam. sing.). _____

2. She is running towards us. _____

3. What do you know about them? _____

4. They are not far from me. _____

5. He will not go without her. _____

6. They are seated behind them. _____

_____

7. What were you doing with him? _____

8. I brought a box of candy with me. _____

_____

9. The gift is for him. _____

10. They are going with you. _____

En España cada región tiene sus propios bailes y costumbres tradicionales.
Aquí hay un grupo de bailarines de Zamora, en el noroeste del país.

18. SINGLE OBJECT PRONOUNS

DIRECT OBJECT PRONOUNS

Ana no *me* visita.	Ann does not visit *me*.
Ana no *te* visita.	Ann does not visit *you (fam.)*.
Ana no *le* visita.	Ann does not visit *him, you (m.)*.
Ana no *lo* visita.	Ann does not visit *him, it (m.)*.
Ana no *la* visita.	Ann does not visit *her, it, you (f.)*.
Ana no *nos* visita.	Ann does not visit *us*.
Ana no *os* visita.	Ann does not visit *you (fam. pl.)*.
Ana no *los* visita.	Ann does not visit *them, you (m. pl.)*.
Ana no *las* visita.	Ann does not visit *them, you (f. pl.)*.

Note

Either **le** or **lo** may be used to translate *him*. The plural of **le** or **lo** is **los**.

No *le* visito.	I do not visit him (you).
No *los* visito.	I do not visit them (you).

INDIRECT OBJECT PRONOUNS

Ana no *me* habla.	Ann does not speak *to me*.
Ana no *te* habla.	Ann does not speak *to you (fam.)*.
Ana no *le* habla.	Ann does not speak *to him, to her, to you*.
Ana no *nos* habla.	Ann does not speak *to us*.
Ana no *os* habla.	Ann does not speak *to you (fam. pl.)*.
Ana no *les* habla.	Ann does not speak *to them, to you (pl.)*.

Since **le** and **les** have several meanings, the intended meaning may be clarified by adding **a él, a ella, a Vd., a ellos (-as),** or **a Vds.** after the verb.

Ana le habla *a él.*	Ann speaks to him.

Note

The preposition **a** before a noun object does not always indicate an indirect object. The noun may be a direct object with the personal **a**. (See Grammar Lesson 6.)

Veo *a María.*	(direct object)	*La* veo.
Hablo *a María.*	(indirect object)	*Le* hablo (a ella).

POSITION OF OBJECT PRONOUNS

Object pronouns generally precede the verb.

Pedro no *la* ve.	Peter doesn't see her.
Carmen *les* escribe.	Carmen writes to them.

Exceptions

1. Affirmative command.

Tóme*lo* Vd.	Take it.
(affirmative)	

but

No lo tome Vd.	Don't take it.
(negative)	

2. Infinitive.

Voy a **tomar*lo*.**
   or
Lo voy a tomar.
                                  I am going to take it.

3. Present participle.

Dolores está **tomándo*lo*.**
   or
Dolores ***lo*** está tomando.
                                  Dolores is taking it.

Note

A. Object pronouns follow and are attached to the affirmative command (but precede the negative command).

B. Object pronouns may either follow the infinitive and present participle or precede the "conjugated" verb.

C. When an object pronoun is attached to the affirmative command or the present participle, a written accent mark is generally required on the vowel that is stressed.

EJERCICIOS

A. Complete Vd. la traducción al inglés.

1. Lo tengo.   I have _____.
2. No le comprendo.   I do not understand _____.
3. Carmen los invita.   Carmen invites _____.
4. No puedo verlo.   I can't see _____.
5. No nos responde.   He does not answer _____.
6. Le visita.   He visits _____.
7. No le conozco a Vd.   I do not know _____.
8. Ayúdele Vd.   Help _____.
9. Le escribe a ella.   He writes _____.
10. No les dé Vd. el dinero. Do not give _____ the money.

B. Cambie Vd. cada frase a la forma negativa.

1. Escríbanles Vds. _____
2. Escúchenle Vds. _____
3. Ayúdenos Vd. _____
4. Los he comprado. _____
5. Tómelo Vd. _____
6. Léalo Vd. _____
7. Invítenle Vds. _____
8. Búsquelas Vd. _____
9. Visítenla Vds. _____
10. Cómprelo Vd. _____

C. Cambie Vd. cada frase a la forma afirmativa.

1. No me diga Vd. _____

2. No lo coma Vd. _____

3. No le pregunte Vd. _____

4. No los tomen Vds. _____

5. No lo haga Vd. _____

6. No le escriban Vds. _____

7. No la enseñe Vd. _____

8. No les hable Vd. _____

9. No lo den Vds. _____

10. No lo abran Vds. _____

D. Cambie Vd. cada frase, empleando pronombres en lugar de las expresiones en letra cursiva.

EJEMPLO: Grita *a su hermano, a nosotros, a Juan y Pedro.*

Le grita, *Nos* grita, *Les* grita.

1. Deseo vender *la hacienda, los instrumentos, las joyas.*

_____

2. Hablo *a María, a los viajeros, al zapatero.*

_____

3. No abran Vds. *los cuadernos, el despacho, las maletas.*

_____

4. ¿Conoce Vd. *a la niña, al panadero, a nuestro presidente?*

_____

5. No visitaré *a mis amigos, a Pablo, a la señora.*

_____

6. Él no habló *al profesor, a los vendedores, a nosotros.*

_____

7. Espere Vd. *a Ana y Dolores, a Ramón y Roberto, al amo.*

_____

8. Está escuchando *al escritor, el tocadiscos, las voces.*

_____

9. Explicará el caso *a sus padres, a Vd., a la bailarina.*

_____

10. Deben respetar *a las mujeres, al capitán, a la dama.*

_____

E. Conteste Vd. en español, empleando pronombres en lugar de los sustantivos.

1. ¿Desea Vd. vender su reloj? _____

2. ¿Ve Vd. a sus amigos todos los días? _____

3. ¿Tiene Vd. las maletas? _____

4. ¿Ayuda Vd. a su madre? _____

5. ¿Escribe Vd. a sus primos? _____

6. ¿Habla Vd. a su enemigo? _____

7. ¿Comprende Vd. la lección? _____

8. ¿Conoce Vd. a la señora Gómez? _____

9. ¿Invitó Vd. a Pablo y a Rosa? _____

10. ¿Aprende Vd. el español? _____

F. Escriba Vd. las frases siguientes, colocando en la posición correcta la traducción de las expresiones entre paréntesis:

1. El profesor explica (*it*). _____

2. Pedro siempre ayuda (*me*). _____

3. Vds. se levantaron; por eso, yo pude ver (*you*). _____

_____

4. Traiga Vd. (*them*). _____

5. Vendió el caballo (*to us*). _____

6. Ana admira (*her*). _____

7. El maestro está leyendo un cuento (*to them*). _____

_____

8. Si vas al teatro, veré (*you*). _____

9. Tomen Vds. (*it*). _____

10. Si no sale esta noche, vendré a visitar (*him*). _____

_____

11. No ha escrito (*to me*). _____

12. ¿Oye Vd. (*us*)? _____

13. No preste Vd. el dinero (*to her*). _____

14. Estoy hablando (*to you*); ¿por qué no me contesta Vd.? _____

_____

15. No habla (*to him*). _____

G. Traduzca Vd. al español.

1. Write to me, señorita. _____

2. I do not understand her. _____

3. Will you (*tú*) invite me? _____

4. We sent the money to them. _____

5. I will not lend her the newspaper. _____

6. Speak to them, sir; do not speak to her. _____

_____

7. Do you want to sell them (*f.*)? ---

----

8. Tell her the truth, gentlemen. ---

----

9. Why are you (*pl.*) looking at it (*f.*)? ---

----

10. You were waiting for us. ---

El Alcázar de Segovia es un castillo antiguo construido en el siglo XI.
Contiene muchos tesoros artísticos de la Edad Media (Middle Ages).

19. DOUBLE OBJECT PRONOUNS

When a verb has two object pronouns, the indirect object (usually the object pronoun referring to the person) precedes the direct object pronoun (usually the object pronoun referring to a thing).

Juan *me lo* (*la*) da.	John gives *it to me.*
Juan *me los* (*las*) da.	John gives *them to me.*
Juan *te lo* (*la*) da.	John gives *it to you* (*fam.*).
Juan *te los* (*las*) da.	John gives *them to you* (*fam.*).
Juan *se lo* (*la*) da.	John gives *it to him* (*her, you, them*).
Juan *se los* (*las*) da.	John gives *them to him* (*her, you, them*).
Juan *nos lo* (*la*) da.	John gives *it to us.*
Juan *nos los* (*las*) da.	John gives *them to us.*
Juan *os lo* (*la*) da.	John gives *it to you* (*fam. pl.*).
Juan *os los* (*las*) da.	John gives *them to you* (*fam. pl.*).

Since **se** has several meanings, the intended meaning may be clarified by adding **a él, a ella, a Vd., a ellos (-as),** or **a Vds.** after the verb.

Juan se lo da *a ella.*	John gives it to her.

Note

A. **Se** replaces **le** or **les** before **lo, la, los, las.**

Juan **le** da el libro.	John gives the book to him.
Juan **se** lo da.	John gives it to him.

B. When two object pronouns are used, the direct object pronoun is usually **lo, la, los, las.**

POSITION OF DOUBLE OBJECT PRONOUNS

Double object pronouns, like single object pronouns, generally precede the verb.

Juan no *se lo* vende.	John does not sell it to him.

Exceptions

1. Affirmative command.

Vénda*selo* Vd. (affirmative)	Sell it to him.

but

No se lo venda Vd. (negative)	Don't sell it to him.

2. Infinitive.

Voy a **vendér*selo.*** *or* *Se lo* voy a vender.	I am going to sell it to him.

3. Present participle.

Alberto está **vendiéndo*selo.*** *or* Alberto *se lo* está vendiendo.	Albert is selling it to him.

Note

A. Double object pronouns follow and are attached to the affirmative command (but precede the negative command).

B. Object pronouns may either follow the infinitive and present participle or precede the "conjugated" verb.

C. When two object pronouns are attached to the verb, a written accent mark is required on the vowel that is stressed.

EJERCICIOS

A. Complete Vd. la traducción al inglés.

1. El niño me los trae.   The child brings _____
2. No quiere vendérselos.   He does not wish to sell _____
3. Escríbaselo Vd.   Write _____
4. Nos lo explica.   He explains _____
5. Tráigamela Vd.   Bring _____
6. Estoy explicándoselo a Vd.   I am explaining _____
7. No se lo diga Vd.   Do not tell _____
8. Voy a enviárselos.   I am going to send _____
9. Démelo Vd.   Give _____
10. ¿Desea Vd. mostrárnosla?   Do you wish to show _____?
11. Alberto se las presenta.   Albert presents _____
12. Se lo estoy leyendo.   I am reading _____
13. No te la he escrito.   I have not written _____
14. Os los dio.   He gave _____
15. Se la entregaremos.   We will deliver _____

B. Subraye Vd. la frase que traduzca correctamente lo inglés.

1. He sells it to them.
   ✓ a. Se lo vende.
   b. Se los vende.
   c. Véndaselo.

2. Bring them to me.
   a. Me los trae.
   b. Tráigamelos Vd.
   ✓ c. Tráigamelo Vd.

3. I want to show it to you.
   ✓ a. Quiero mostrárselo.
   b. Quiere mostrárselo.
   c. Quiero mostrárselos.

4. Do not lend it to her.
   a. No la preste Vd.
   b. No se lo preste Vd.
   ✓ c. No se la presta.

5. The teacher is reading it to us.
   ✓ a. El profesor está leyéndonoslo.
   b. El profesor está leyéndonoslos.
   c. El profesor está leyéndomelo.

C. Cambie Vd. las frases siguientes a la forma afirmativa o negativa:

1. Ofrézcansela Vds. _____
2. No nos lo diga Vd. _____
3. No se la den Vds. _____
4. Regáleselo Vd. _____
5. Mándenmela Vds. _____
6. No me los envíe Vd. _____
7. No se las preste Vd. _____
8. Confiésemela Vd. _____
9. Descríbaselas Vd. _____
10. No se los lea Vd. _____

D. Conteste Vd. en español en frases completas, empleando pronombres en lugar de las expresiones en letra cursiva.

1. ¿Expresa Vd. claramente *sus pensamientos a sus amigos?* _____
_____
2. ¿Debe Vd. *dinero al profesor?* _____
3. ¿Muestra Vd. *cortesía a los ancianos?* _____
4. ¿Da Vd. *un beso a su mamá* al salir de casa? _____
_____
5. ¿Paga Vd. *impuestos al gobierno?* _____
6. ¿Presta Vd. *ayuda a sus amigos?* _____
7. ¿Da Vd. *limosna a los pordioseros?* _____
8. ¿Es verdad que el maestro les da a Vds. *muchas pruebas?* _____
_____
9. ¿Da Vd. *huesos a su perrito?* _____
10. ¿Sabe Vd. explicar *esta lección a la clase?* _____

E. Escriba Vd. las frases siguientes, empleando pronombres en lugar de las expresiones en letra cursiva:

EJEMPLO: Vendió *la casa a Juan.* *Se la* vendió.

1. Ha enviado *los paquetes a Ana.* _____
2. Nos enseña *el cuaderno.* _____
3. El profesor está explicando *el ejercicio al alumno.* _____
4. Al dar *el periódico a Manuel,* se sentó. _____
5. Me vendió *el automóvil.* _____
6. Prometí *el libro a mi prima.* _____
7. Les explica *las lecciones.* _____
8. Venda Vd. *la casa a su tío.* _____
9. Debe escribir *las cartas a sus amigos.* _____
10. Le prestó *el lápiz.* _____

F. Escriba Vd. las frases siguientes, colocando en la posición correcta la traducción de las expresiones entre paréntesis:

1. Felipe lee (*it to me*). _____

2. No escriban Vds. (*it to him*). _____

3. Dé Vd. (*them to me*). _____

4. Ha enseñado (*them to her*). _____

5. No venda Vd. (*them to us*). _____

6. Estoy trayendo (*them to you* [*fam. sing.*]). _____

7. Escribe (*it to him*). _____

8. Traeremos (*them to them*). _____

9. Estamos enviando (*it to her*). _____

10. Léalos Vd. (*to her*). _____

11. ¿Mandaron Vds. (*it to them*)? _____

12. Voy a mostrar (*it to you* [*pl.*]*). _____

13. Explicaremos (*them to you**). _____

14. Presten Vds. (*them to him*). _____

15. Prometieron dar (*it to us*). _____

G. Traduzca Vd. al español.

1. I want to explain it (*f.*) to you. _____

2. Do not bring them (*f.*) to him. _____

3. Sell them (*m.*) to me. _____

4. We can't tell it (*m.*) to her. _____

5. They have given them (*f.*) to us. _____

6. He promised it (*m.*) to me. _____

7. We shall not send them (*m.*) to you. _____

8. I am bringing it (*m.*) to you (*fam. sing.*). _____

9. They must explain them (*m.*) to you. _____

10. Give it (*m.*) to them. _____

*In these exercises, *you* as object pronoun is to be translated by a polite form of the direct or indirect object pronoun (**le, la, los, les,** or **se**), unless otherwise indicated.

20. INTERROGATIVE WORDS

¿qué?, what?	**¿cuándo?**, when?
¿quién, -es?, who?	**¿cuánto, -a?**, how much?
¿a quién, -es?, whom? to whom?	**¿cuántos, -as?**, how many?
¿de quién, -es?, whose? of whom?	**¿cómo?**, how?
¿con quién, -es?, with whom?	**¿por qué?**, why?
¿cuál, -es?, which? which one(s)?	**¿dónde?**, where?

Note

A. All interrogative words have a written accent mark.

B. **Qué** is used instead of **cuál** to translate *which* before a noun.

¿Qué vestido prefiere Vd.?	Which dress do you prefer?

C. **Cuál** is used instead of **qué** to translate *what* before the verb **ser** (*to be*), except when asking for a definition of a word.

¿Cuál es la capital de México?	What is the capital of Mexico?
¿Cuáles son los productos importantes de Cuba?	What are the important products of Cuba?

but

¿Qué es la astronomía?	What is astronomy?

D. **¿De quién, -es?** (*whose?*) is used as follows:

¿De quién es el sombrero? Of whom is the hat	Whose hat is it?
¿De quiénes son estos libros? Of whom are these books	Whose books are these?

E. **A dónde** is used instead of **dónde** to indicate motion to a place (*to where*).

¿A dónde va Vd.?	Where are you going?

EJERCICIOS

A. Complete Vd. la traducción al español, subrayando la expresión interrogativa correcta.

1. Whom are you visiting?   ¿(Quién, A quién) visita Vd.?

2. What did you buy?   ¿(Qué, Cuál) compró Vd.?

3. Where are you running?   ¿(Dónde, A dónde) corre Vd.?

4. Who are these men?   ¿(Quién, Quiénes) son estos hombres?

5. Whose pen is this?   ¿(De quién, A quién) es esta pluma?

6. Which hat do you prefer?   ¿(Cuál, Qué) sombrero prefiere Vd.?

7. What is the capital of Peru?   ¿(Cuál, Qué) es la capital del Perú?

8. What is geometry?   ¿(Cuál, Qué) es la geometría?

9. Which one of the books do you want?   ¿(Cuál, Qué) de los libros desea Vd.?

10. With whom do you play?   ¿Con (quién, a quién) juega Vd.?

B. Traduzca Vd. al español las expresiones en inglés.

1. ¿*Who* es Vd.? _____

2. ¿*Which* son los más cómodos? _____

3. ¿*What* lee Vd.? _____

4. ¿*Whom* ve Vd.? _____

5. ¿*With whom* jugaban Vds.? _____

6. ¿*What* es la capital del Brasil? _____

7. ¿*Whose* es este sombrero? _____

8. ¿*How* está su padre? _____

9. ¿*Which* traje prefiere Vd.? _____

10. ¿*Why* lloran Vds.? _____

11. ¿*Which one* es el mejor? _____

12. ¿*Who* son esos muchachos? _____

13. ¿*Where* vive su familia? _____

14. ¿*How many* mujeres asistieron? _____

15. ¿*Which ones* son sus hermanas? _____

16. ¿*How many* libros tiene Vd.? _____

17. ¿*Where* va Vd.? _____

18. ¿*Which* de los caballos es árabe? _____

19. ¿*How much* cuesta? _____

20. ¿*When* llega el tren? _____

C. Forme Vd. preguntas, empleando expresiones interrogativas en lugar de las palabras en letra cursiva.

Ejemplo: Leen *el libro*.

¿*Qué* leen?

1. Estudia *la lección*.   ¿_____ estudia?

2. *Jorge* está ausente.   ¿_____ está ausente?

3. Es el libro *del profesor*.   ¿_____ es el libro?

4. Hablan *de la señorita Brown*.   ¿_____ hablan?

5. Prefiere *los zapatos negros*.   ¿_____ prefiere?

6. *Los soldados* vienen.   ¿_____ vienen?

7. Irán *mañana*.   ¿_____ irán?

8. Va *a la playa*.   ¿_____ va?

9. Recibió *una carta*.   ¿_____ recibió?

10. Tiene *dos* hijos.   ¿_____ hijos tiene?

11. No vino *porque estaba enfermo*. ¿_____ no vino?

12. Perdió *un peso*.   ¿_____ perdió?

13. Trabaja con *su padre*.   ¿Con _____ trabaja?

14. Está *en casa*.   ¿---------------------- está?

15. *Madrid* es la capital de España.   ¿---------------------- es la capital de España?

   D. Traduzca Vd. al español.

1. Whose is this ball? _____

2. Who is going to the movies? _____

3. What did you say? _____

4. Whom are you calling? _____

5. Which one of these books is yours?_____

6. With whom is he speaking? _____

7. Where is it? _____

8. How many pupils are there in the class? _____

9. How do you do that? _____

10. When are they leaving? _____

11. How much is it worth? _____

12. Why are they shouting? _____

13. To whom were you speaking? _____

14. What is a charro? _____

15. Which hotel do you prefer? _____

21. RELATIVE PRONOUNS AND ADJECTIVES

que, who, whom, which, that

El hombre *que* entró es mi vecino.	The man who entered is my neighbor.
El muchacho *que* Vd. vio es mi primo.	The boy whom you saw is my cousin.
La casa en *que* vivo es pequeña.	The house in which I live is small.

Note. The relative pronoun may sometimes be omitted in English, but it is never omitted in Spanish.

Las novelas *que* escribe son interesantes.	The novels (that, which) he writes are interesting.
La persona *que* admiro es mi tío Felipe.	The person (that, whom) I admire is my uncle Philip.

quien, -es, whom (after a preposition)

La mujer *con quien* trabajo es española.	The woman with whom I work is Spanish.
Las mujeres *de quienes* hablo son españolas.	The women of whom I am speaking are Spanish.

lo que, what (that which)

No comprendo *lo que* dice.	I do not understand what he says.

cuyo, -a, -os, -as, whose (never used as an interrogative)

El alumno *cuya* pluma se perdió ayer está ausente.	The pupil whose pen was lost yesterday is absent.

Note. **Cuyo** agrees in gender and number with the thing possessed, *not* with the possessor.

EJERCICIOS

A. Subraye Vd. la palabra correcta entre paréntesis.

1. Ésta es la casa en (que, cual) vivo.

2. No me dijo (que, lo que) hizo.

3. Las personas (cuyas, que) hablan demasiado no son inteligentes.

4. Los soldados de (cuales, quienes) hablamos son americanos.

5. Esta casa es bonita, pero las casas (que, a quienes) vimos ayer eran más bonitas.

6. El hombre (que, quien) está sentado allí es el presidente.

7. Allí está la mujer (de quien, cuyo) hijo murió el año pasado.

8. La novela (que, de quien) leo es muy interesante.

9. La mujer de (que, quien) hablo estaba aquí.

10. El espejo (que, cual) cayó es suyo.

B. Emplee Vd. una de las expresiones siguientes para traducir lo inglés: **qué, que, quién, quien, a quién, de quién, lo que, cuyo, cuál.**

1. ¿*What* hace Vd. esta noche?   ------------------------------

2. No sé *what* haré.   ------------------------------

3. El hombre *who* habló es un abogado famoso.   ------------------------------

4. Pedro es el niño *whose* tío es profesor.

5. ¿*Who* habla?

6. ¿*Whose* es esta pelota?

7. La mujer con *whom* trabajo es muy bonita.

8. ¿*Whom* vio Vd. anoche?

9. El reloj *which* compré es de oro.

10. ¿*Which* prefiere Vd., éste o ése?

C. Traduzca Vd. al español las expresiones en inglés.

1. No leí el libro *that* recibí de mi tío.

2. La casa en *which* vivo es pequeña.

3. El hombre *whom* vimos ayer está aquí ahora.

4. Éste es el muchacho *whose* hermanas son tan bellas.

5. ¿Ha comprado Vd. *what* le dije?

6. Los hombres *who* son ricos no son siempre felices.

7. Es una pequeña aldea *whose* nombre he olvidado.

8. Mi pluma escribe bien, pero la pluma *that* Vd. me regaló escribe mejor.

9. El alumno *who* no lo sabe es tonto.

10. Tomás y Enrique son los muchachos con *whom* juego.

11. ¿Conoce Vd. al hombre *whose* casa compré?

12. Me dijo *what* quería.

13. Muéstreles los vestidos *that* Vd. compró.

14. La mujer con *whom* hablé es profesora.

15. El soldado *who* está entre los dos generales es el capitán Moreno.

D. Traduzca Vd. al español.

1. The child who is laughing is my cousin.

2. He did not understand what he read.

3. Mr. Hernández is the man whose daughter I met last month.

4. These are the soldiers whom we admire so much.

5. The Spanish novel I was reading was very interesting.

6. I know the men of whom you were speaking.

7. The picture of which I spoke to you is here.

----

8. We do not believe what he says.

----

9. Do you know the lawyers to whom I was speaking?

----

10. What you need is a large room.

El charro es el "cowboy" mexicano. Su bonita compañera de baile
lleva un vestido pintoresco al estilo llamado "la china poblana." El baile
típico del charro es el jarabe tapatío.

22. NEGATIVE WORDS

> **nadie,** no one, nobody, not . . . anyone, not . . . anybody
> **nada,** nothing, not . . . anything
> **nunca,** never, not . . . ever
> **jamás,** never, not . . . ever, ever
> **ninguno, -a, -os, -as,** no, none, not . . . any
> **tampoco,** neither, not . . . either
> **ni . . . ni,** neither . . . nor, not . . . either . . . or

Note

A. All negative sentences have a negative word preceding the verb. Unlike English, a sentence in Spanish may have two negative words. In such cases, **no** must precede the verb, and the other negative word must follow it.

Nadie vino.
  or
No vino *nadie.*

No one (Nobody) came.

Nada sospecha.
  or
No sospecha *nada.*

He suspects nothing.
(*Or* He doesn't suspect anything.)

B. When **nadie** is the object of the verb, it is preceded by the personal **a.**

A nadie vimos.
  or
No vimos *a nadie.*

We saw no one.
(*Or* We didn't see anyone.)

C. **Jamás** in an affirmative question means *ever*.

¿Ha estado Vd. *jamás* en San Francisco?   Have you ever been in San Francisco?

D. **Ningún** drops its -o when coming immediately before a masculine singular noun.

Ningún hombre es perfecto.   No man is perfect.
  but
Ninguna mujer es perfecta.   No woman is perfect.

E. Negatives are used after such expressions as **más que** (*more than*), **mejor que** (*better than*), **peor que** (*worse than*), **sin** (*without*), to express an affirmative idea.

más que nunca   more than ever
mejor que nadie   better than anyone
sin hacer nada   without doing anything

IDIOMATIC NEGATIVE EXPRESSIONS

ni yo tampoco   nor I either
Ya no vive aquí.   He no longer lives here.
No me cobró **más que** un dólar.   He charged me only a dollar.
de ninguna manera
de ningún modo   by no means
ni siquiera   not even

EJERCICIOS

A. Complete Vd. las frases en español.

1. I can't go either.   No puedo ir _____.

2. No one left.   _____ salió.

3. He doesn't know anything.   No sabe _____.

4. He would never sell it.   _____ lo vendería.

5. They never speak to us.   _____ nos hablan.

6. He doesn't ever visit his brother.   _____ visita a su hermano.

7. Have you ever traveled to Europe?   ¿Ha viajado Vd. _____ a Europa?

8. None of them returned.   _____ de ellos volvió.

9. I don't need either shirts or ties.   No necesito _____ camisas _____ corbatas.

10. Nor I either.   _____ tampoco.

11. By no means.   De _____ manera.

12. He left without saying anything.   Salió sin decir _____.

13. They no longer work here.   _____ trabajan aquí.

14. His pronunciation is worse than ever.   Su pronunciación es peor que _____.

15. It is worth only fifty cents.   No vale _____ cincuenta centavos.

B. Cambie Vd. cada frase según los ejemplos, empleando la otra forma negativa.

EJEMPLOS: No tengo nada.   Nunca trabaja.

Nada tengo.   *No trabaja nunca.*

1. No le hablaré nunca. _____

2. Jamás lo habría creído. _____

3. A nadie conocimos. _____

4. Nada quiero. _____

5. Ninguno de sus amigos vino. _____

6. No nos ayudó tampoco. _____

7. No tiene ningunos enemigos. _____

8. Nadie le escuchó. _____

9. No compré ni pan ni leche. _____

10. No dije nada. _____

C. Conteste Vd. en español en sentido negativo, empleando una de las expresiones siguientes: **nadie, nada, nunca, ninguno, ni . . . ni, tampoco.**

1. ¿Cuándo estuvo Vd. en España?

_____

2. ¿Qué hacen Vds. hoy?

_____

3. ¿Aprende Vd. el latín o el francés?

_____

4. ¿Ha viajado Vd. jamás a Guatemala?

----

5. ¿Va Vd. al museo o a la biblioteca?

----

6. ¿Tiene su amigo algunos libros interesantes?

----

7. ¿Qué tiene Vd. en la mano?

----

8. ¿Cuándo van sus amigos a Sudamérica? ¿Va Vd. también?

----

9. ¿Tiene Vd. algún problema?

----

10. ¿A quién visitó Vd. ayer?

D. Escriba Vd. las frases siguientes en sentido negativo:

1. Tiene algunos amigos.

----

2. Vienen a mi casa o a su casa.

----

3. Alguien duerme.

----

4. Siempre trabajan.

----

5. Tome Vd. algo.

----

6. Se atreve a hacer todo.

----

7. Posee una bicicleta.

----

8. Se esconderán en algún sitio.

----

9. Ella vendía agujas y alfileres.

----

10. El cartero nos dio algunas cartas.

E. Traduzca Vd. al español las expresiones en inglés.

1. *Nobody* está aquí.   _____

2. No vemos *anything*.   _____

3. No jugó con nosotros *either*.   _____

4. *No* persona inteligente diría eso.   _____

5. *Nothing* le gusta.   _____

6. *Neither* Juana *nor* su prima lo sabe.   _____

7. No veo *anyone*.   _____

8. ¿Ha visto V.d. *ever* tal pájaro?   _____

9. *None* de los paquetes llegó.   _____

10. *He never* escribe a sus parientes.   _____

11. ¿Lo haría Vd.? *By no means*.   _____

12. No le creen *either*.   _____

13. Ahora está ausente *more than ever*.   _____

14. Salió *without saying anything*.   _____

15. Cantó *better than anyone*.   _____

16. *I saw only* dos aviones.
    (Do not use **sólo** or **solamente**.)   _____

17. *Nothing* me dijo.   _____

18. Él no lo hizo; *nor I either*.   _____

19. Enrique *no longer* viene a vernos.   _____

20. No tiene *either* lápiz *or* pluma.   _____

23. CARDINAL NUMBERS

0–10

0	cero	6	seis
1	uno (-a)	7	siete
2	dos	8	ocho
3	tres	9	nueve
4	cuatro	10	diez
5	cinco		

11–19

11	once	16	diez y seis
12	doce	17	diez y siete
13	trece	18	diez y ocho
14	catorce	19	diez y nueve
15	quince		

20–99

20	veinte	60	sesenta
21	veinte y uno	70	setenta
22	veinte y dos	80	ochenta
30	treinta	90	noventa
40	cuarenta	99	noventa y nueve
50	cincuenta		

100–900

100	ciento (cien)	600	seiscientos, -as
200	doscientos, -as	700	*setecientos,* -as
300	trescientos, -as	800	ochocientos, -as
400	cuatrocientos, -as	900	*novecientos,* -as
500	*quinientos,* -as		

1,000–100,000,000

1,000	mil	1,000,000	un millón (de)
2,000	dos mil	2,000,000	dos millones (de)
100,000	cien mil	100,000,000	cien millones (de)

Note

A. **Y** is used only in compound numbers from 16 to 99.

> 35   treinta *y* cinco
> 142   ciento **cuarenta** *y* dos

but

> 115   ciento **quince**

B. Cardinal numbers are invariable, except **uno** and combinations of **ciento** (the hundreds).

cuatro docenas	four dozen
setenta profesores	seventy teachers

but

un muchacho	one boy
una muchacha	one girl
treinta y un muchachos	thirty-one boys
treinta y una muchachas	thirty-one girls
trescientos coches	three hundred cars
quinientas páginas	five hundred pages

C. **Ciento** is shortened to **cien** before a noun of either gender, and before **mil** and **millones.**

cien soldados	one hundred soldiers
cien mil	one hundred thousand
cien millones	one hundred million

but

ciento cinco   one hundred five

D. **Un** is not used with **ciento** and **mil,** but **un** must be used with **millón,** which requires **de** when a noun follows.

ciento veinte	a hundred twenty
mil asientos	a thousand seats

but

un millón *de* habitantes   a million inhabitants

ARITHMETIC EXPRESSIONS

y, plus (+)	**por,** (multiplied) by, "times" (×)
menos, minus (−)	**son,** equal(s) (=)

EJERCICIOS

A. Escriba Vd. en inglés los números siguientes:

1. seis _____
2. catorce _____
3. veinte y dos _____
4. ciento doce _____
5. quinientos noventa _____
6. cuarenta y ocho _____
7. doscientos veinte _____
8. ochenta y uno _____
9. trescientos setenta _____
10. sesenta y nueve _____
11. setecientos treinta y ocho _____
12. noventa y seis _____
13. cien mil _____
14. veinte y siete _____
15. treinta y cinco _____
16. diez mil _____
17. setenta y cuatro _____
18. cuatrocientos trece _____
19. cincuenta y siete _____
20. diez y nueve _____

B. Escriba Vd. en español los números siguientes:

5	86	
7	97	
12	110	
15	209	
18	321	
27	436	
33	547	
44	658	
52	765	
61	882	
78	973	

5,746 _____   1,000,000 _____

100,000 _____   3,000,000 _____

C. Conteste Vd. en español en frases completas.

1. ¿Cuántos zapatos hay en un par de zapatos?

_____

2. ¿Cuántas personas hay en un equipo de béisbol?

_____

3. ¿Cuántas letras hay en el alfabeto inglés?

_____

4. ¿Cuántos centavos hay en un dólar?

_____

5. ¿Cuántos estados hay en los Estados Unidos?

_____

6. ¿Cuántos días hay en un año?

_____

7. ¿Cuántos días hay en el mes de marzo?

_____

8. ¿Cuántos días hay en el mes de febrero?

_____

9. ¿Cuántas preguntas hay en este ejercicio?

_____

10. ¿En qué lección está este ejercicio?

_____

11. ¿Cuántos años hay en un siglo?

_____

12. ¿Cuántos dedos tiene Vd. en cada mano?

_____

13. ¿Cuántas naranjas hay en una docena?

_____

14. ¿Cuántas horas hay en un día?

_____

15. ¿Cuántas estaciones hay en un año?

_____

D. Complete Vd. las frases siguientes:

1. Cuatro y nueve son _____.

2. Veinte menos catorce son _____.

3. Cuatro por ocho son _____.

4. Treinta menos cinco son _____.

5. Cincuenta menos _____ son dos.

6. Nueve por siete son _____.

7. Cuarenta y treinta son _____.

8. Setenta y cinco menos _____ son diez.

9. Cuarenta por dos son _____.

10. Setenta menos sesenta son _____.

11. _____ menos treinta son cincuenta.

12. Ciento menos uno son _____.

13. Noventa y trece son _____.

14. Doce por doce son _____.

15. Cuatrocientos y trescientos son _____.

16. Novecientos menos _____ son cuatrocientos.

17. _____ cajas y doscientas cajas son ochocientas cajas.

18. Quinientos por dos son _____.

19. Dos mil y tres mil son _____.

20. Cincuenta mil por dos son _____.

21. Setecientos y _____ son mil seiscientos.

22. Ochocientos mil y doscientos mil son _____.

23. _____ mil menos seis mil son catorce mil.

24. Treinta docenas y _____ docenas son ciento treinta docenas.

25. Setenta pesos y cincuenta pesos son _____ pesos.

26. Un millón de habitantes y un millón de habitantes son _____ habitantes.

27. Ochenta libras y once libras son _____ libras.

28. Nueve por seis son _____.

29. Siete hombres y catorce hombres son _____ hombres.

30. Mil dólares por mil dólares son _____ dólares.

E. Traduzca Vd. al español.

1. one thousand dollars   _____

2. five hundred tickets   _____

3. a hundred students   _____

4. page seventy-nine   _____

5. eighty-one women   _____

6. five million inhabitants   _____

7. ninety-two days   _____

8. one million soldiers   _____

9. one week   _____

10. one hundred thirty pounds   _____

11. seven hundred pages   _____

12. one dollar   _____

13. one hundred nine men   _____

14. one hundred pesos   _____

15. forty-one horses   _____

Machu Picchu, situado muy alto en los Andes, fue una ciudad antigua, tal vez la capital de los incas antes de la llegada de los españoles. Durante siglos no se sabía que tal ciudad existía. En 1911, un explorador norteamericano, Hiram Bingham, descubrió las ruinas pintorescas de la ciudad. Hoy día muchos turistas visitan el lugar.

24. ORDINAL NUMBERS

1st **primero, -a (primer)**	6th **sexto, -a**
2nd **segundo, -a**	7th **séptimo, -a**
3rd **tercero, -a (tercer)**	8th **octavo, -a**
4th **cuarto, -a**	9th **noveno, -a**
5th **quinto, -a**	10th **décimo, -a**

Note

A. **Primero** and **tercero** drop their **-o** before a masculine singular noun.

el *primer* hombre	the first man
el *tercer* mes	the third month
but	
la **primera** semana	the first week
el libro **tercero**	the third book

B. Ordinal numbers are used through *tenth;* cardinal numbers are used above *tenth* and generally follow the noun.

la *sexta* lección	the sixth lesson
Felipe *Segundo*	Philip the Second
but	
la lección **catorce**	the fourteenth lesson
Alfonso **Doce**	Alphonse the Twelfth

EJERCICIOS

A. Subraye Vd. la traducción correcta de la expresión en inglés.

1. Preparó la comida por *first* vez.

   (*a*) primera   (*b*) primer   (*c*) una

2. He leído el *first* capítulo.

   (*a*) primero   (*b*) primer   (*c*) uno

3. Luis *the Fifteenth* fue un rey francés.

   (*a*) Quince   (*b*) el Quinto   (*c*) Cinco

4. Está sentado en *the fourth* asiento.

   (*a*) cuatro   (*b*) cuarto   (*c*) el cuarto

5. Celebraron su *ninth* aniversario.

   (*a*) novena   (*b*) nueve   (*c*) noveno

6. El capítulo *twelfth* es muy importante.

   (*a*) doce   (*b*) docena   (*c*) dos

7. ¿A dónde fue Vd. el *third* día?

   (*a*) tres   (*b*) tercer   (*c*) tercero

8. Felipe *the Second* fue un famoso rey español.

    (*a*) Según   (*b*) Segundo   (*c*) Dos

9. Tengo boletos (tickets) para la *tenth* fila.

    (*a*) diez   (*b*) décima   (*c*) décimo

10. Aquel autor vivió en *the nineteenth century*.

    (*a*) el siglo diez y nueve   (*b*) el diez y nueve siglo   (*c*) el siglo décimo y nueve

B. Conteste Vd. en español en frases completas.

1. ¿Cuál es el primer día de la semana?

----

2. ¿Cuál es el tercer mes del año?

----

3. ¿Cuál es el nombre de un famoso rey español?

----

4. ¿Qué lección estudia Vd. en el libro de español?

----

5. ¿Qué fila precede a la octava fila?

----

6. ¿Qué año de español estudia Vd.?

----

7. ¿En qué fecha comienza el año?

----

8. ¿Cuál es el décimo mes del año?

----

9. ¿Cuál es el quinto día de la semana?

----

10. ¿Qué avenida sigue a la Sexta?

C. Traduzca Vd. al español las expresiones en inglés.

1. *Philip the Third* siguió a Felipe Segundo. -----------------------------

2. Abril es el *fourth* mes del año. -----------------------------

3. Vive en la *Fifth* Avenida. -----------------------------

4. Estudien Vds. la *eighth* lección. -----------------------------

5. Enero es el *first* mes del año. -----------------------------

6. Murió en *the seventeenth century*. -----------------------------

7. Están sentados en la *second* fila. -----------------------------

8. *Henry the Eighth* fue un rey inglés. -----------------------------

9. El último rey de España fue *Alphonso XIII*. -----------------------------

10. Vivimos en *the twentieth century*. -----------------------------

D. Traduzca Vd. al español.

1. Forty-second Street ....

2. Napoleon the First ....

3. Philip the Second ....

4. Charles V ....

5. the eighth paragraph ....

6. Seventh Avenue ....

7. the tenth chapter ....

8. Louis XIV ....

9. the fourth lesson ....

10. the third seat ....

11. the first man ....

12. the sixth word ....

13. the ninth volume ....

14. the first time ....

15. the third row ....

**Mate es un té hecho de la "yerba mate." Se usa mucho en la Argentina
y el Paraguay. Se bebe en una calabaza (gourd) por medio de una
bombilla (tube).**

25. DATES

¿Cuál es la fecha de hoy?	What is today's date?
Es el primero de enero.	It is January 1.
Es el dos (tres, cuatro, etc.) de enero.	It is January 2 (3, 4, etc.).
El veinte y cinco de marzo de mil novecientos cincuenta y tres.	March 25, 1953.

Note

A. In dates, cardinal numbers are used instead of ordinal numbers except for *first* (**primero**).

B. The year is expressed in Spanish by thousands and hundreds and not by hundreds, as in English.

mil novecientos cuarenta y dos	1942

C. Another common way of expressing dates is as follows:

¿A cuántos estamos hoy?	What is today's date?
Estamos a cinco de mayo.	It is May 5.

D. With dates, the English word *on* is not expressed in Spanish.

Se casaron el quince de octubre.	They were married on October 15.

MONTHS OF THE YEAR

enero, January	**mayo,** May	**septiembre,** September
febrero, February	**junio,** June	**octubre,** October
marzo, March	**julio,** July	**noviembre,** November
abril, April	**agosto,** August	**diciembre,** December

Note. The months of the year in Spanish are not capitalized.

EJERCICIOS

A. Traduzca Vd. al inglés.

1. ¿A cuántos estamos hoy? Estamos a primero de octubre.

2. Ayer fue el doce de enero.

3. Mañana será el treinta de abril.

4. el catorce de agosto de mil novecientos cuarenta y siete

5. el trece de julio de mil setecientos setenta y siete

6. el doce de octubre de mil cuatrocientos noventa y dos

7. Es el veinte y uno de septiembre.

8. Nació el quince de enero de mil ochocientos noventa y cuatro.

9. La guerra duró desde el año mil novecientos cuarenta y uno hasta el año mil novecientos cuarenta y seis.

10. Nací en mil novecientos cincuenta y dos.

B. Conteste Vd. en español en frases completas.

1. ¿Cuál es la fecha de hoy?

2. ¿Cuál fue la fecha de ayer?

3. ¿Cuál será la fecha de mañana?

4. ¿Cuándo se celebra el día de la independencia de los Estados Unidos?

5. ¿Cuál es la fecha del descubrimiento de América?

6. ¿Cuándo cae la fiesta de Navidad?

7. ¿Cuándo cae el día de Año Nuevo?

8. ¿Cuándo se celebra el cumpleaños de Jorge Wáshington?

9. ¿Cuándo se celebra el cumpleaños de Abrahán Lincoln?

10. ¿Cuándo nació Vd.?

C. Traduzca Vd. al español las fechas siguientes:

1. October 4, 1936
2. July 14, 1789
3. January 22, 1941
4. August 3, 1914
5. February 13, 1370
6. November 25, 1912
7. September 14, 1953

8. December 31, 1848 _____

9. April 1, 1931 _____

10. October 8, 1212 _____

11. May 2, 1808 _____

12. March 30, 1660 _____

13. April 19, 1898 _____

14. June 18, 1967 _____

15. November 4, 1955 _____

    D. Traduzca Vd. al español.

1. What is today's date? _____

_____

2. It is the third of June, 1956. _____

_____

3. Cervantes was born in 1547 and died in 1616. _____

_____

4. Tomorrow will be the first of March. _____

_____

5. Yesterday was the second of January. _____

_____

6. He received my letter on February 6, 1955. _____

_____

7. I paid the bill on December 11, 1954. _____

_____

8. We lived there from August 5, 1941 until October 1, 1951. _____

_____

9. The war between Spain and France began in 1808 and ended in 1814. _____

_____

10. Spain was a very powerful nation from 1516 to 1598. _____

_____

26. TIME EXPRESSIONS

1. In time expressions, *it is* is expressed by **es** for *one o'clock* and by **son** for *two o'clock* on.

¿Qué hora *es?*	What time is it?
***Es* la una.**	It is one o'clock.
***Son* las dos (tres, cuatro, etc.).**	It is two (three, four, etc.) o'clock.

2. In Spanish, the hour is given first and then the minutes.

Es *la una* y *cinco.*	It is five after (past) one.
Son *las dos* menos *diez.*	It is ten to (of) two.
Son *las tres* y *cuarto.*	It is a quarter after three.
Son *las cuatro* y *media.*	It is half past four.

Note

A. *After* or *past* is expressed by **y**; *to* or *of* by **menos**; *a quarter* by **cuarto**; and *half past* by **y media.**

B. After *half past*, minutes are expressed with the following hour minus **(menos)** the minutes.

a las ocho *menos* diez	at 7:50

OTHER TIME EXPRESSIONS

¿a qué hora?	at what time?
a la una	at one o'clock
a las dos (**tres,** etc.)	at two (three, etc.) o'clock
de la mañana	A.M., in the morning
de la tarde	P.M., in the afternoon
de la noche	P.M., in the evening
en punto	exactly, sharp
a tiempo	on time
a eso de las siete	at about seven o'clock
Es mediodía.	It is noon.
Es medianoche.	It is midnight.

EJERCICIOS

A. Traduzca Vd. al inglés.

1. Son las nueve y cinco. --

2. Es la una menos cuarto. --

3. Son las diez y media. --

4. Son las cuatro en punto. --

5. Son las once de la noche. --

6. Nunca llega a tiempo. --

7. Vino a eso de las seis. --

8. Es mediodía. --

9. Va a la escuela desde las ocho hasta las tres. ------------------------

10. Es medianoche. --

11. Salió a las dos. --

12. Son las siete de la mañana. --

13. Era la una cuando ocurrió. --

14. ¿A qué hora va Vd. al cine? --

15. Pronto serán las diez. --

B. Complete Vd. las frases en español.

1. What time is it?   ¿Qué _____ es?

2. It is one o'clock.   Es _____.

3. It is ten minutes after three.   _____ las tres _____.

4. It is a quarter past eight.   Son las ocho _____.

5. It is five minutes to four.   Son las cuatro _____.

6. It is twenty minutes of six.   Son las seis _____.

7. It is half past twelve.   Son las doce _____.

8. It is 8:40 A.M.   Son las _____.

9. It is half past one.   Es la una _____.

10. It is 11:00 P.M.   Son las once _____.

11. It is noon.   Es _____.

12. He left at about three o'clock.   Salió _____.

13. It is exactly 5 o'clock.   Son las cinco _____.

14. It is midnight.   Es _____.

15. It was four o'clock when he arrived.   _____ cuando llegó.

C. Conteste Vd. en español en frases complétas.

1. ¿A qué hora se levanta Vd.?

_____

2. ¿A qué hora se desayuna Vd.?

_____

3. ¿Cuándo llega Vd. a la escuela?

_____

4. ¿A qué hora comienzan las clases?

_____

5. ¿A qué hora almuerza Vd.?

_____

6. ¿Cuándo sale Vd. de la escuela?

_____

7. ¿A qué hora cena Vd.?

_____

8. ¿Cuándo estudia Vd. sus lecciones?

_____

9. ¿Cuándo terminan las clases?

_____

10. ¿A qué hora se acuesta Vd.?

_____

D. Escriba Vd. en español.

EJEMPLOS: 1:20 P.M.   la una y veinte de la tarde
8:40 A.M.   las nueve menos veinte de la mañana

1. 1:15 --

2. 2:50 P.M. --

3. 8:45 P.M. --

4. 9:20 A.M. --

5. 7:30 --

6. 6:40 --

7. 10:55 A.M. --

8. 11:18 P.M. --

9. 12:05 --

10. 8:35 A.M. --

11. 3.30 P.M. --

12. 2:10 --

13. 1:25 --

14. 8:15 A.M. --

15. 6:20 P.M. --

E. Traduzca Vd. al español.

1. It begins at four o'clock in the afternoon. ------------------------------

----

2. He gets up at eleven in the morning. -----------------------------------

----

3. At what time do you wake up in the morning? ----------------------------

----

4. It was one o'clock when he came. ---------------------------------------

----

5. He came on time. ---

----

6. It is 8 P.M. ---

----

7. It will soon be nine o'clock. --

----

8. I attend school from half past eight until three. ----------------------

----

9. I do not study after 10:45 o'clock. ------------------------------------

----

10. He remained until 2:15 o'clock. --

----

27. THE USE OF PREPOSITIONS BEFORE INFINITIVES

The *only* form of the verb that may follow a preposition is the infinitive.

VERBS REQUIRING THE PREPOSITION *A* BEFORE AN INFINITIVE

Verbs of *beginning, motion, teaching,* and *learning,* and a few other verbs, require the preposition **a** before a following infinitive.

comenzar (ie) a ⎫ empezar (ie) a ⎬ to begin to principiar a ⎭ ir a, to go to venir a, to come to salir a, to go out to apresurarse a, to hurry to, to hasten to enseñar a, to teach to	aprender a, to learn to ayudar a, to help to invitar a, to invite to atreverse a, to dare to negarse (ie) a, to refuse to volver (ue) a, to (*verb*) again

El niño *empieza a* llorar.	The child begins to cry.
Voy a estudiar.	I am going to study.
No *se atreve a* atacar.	He does not dare to attack.
Se niega a obedecer.	He refuses to obey.
Vuelven a correr.	They run again.

VERBS REQUIRING THE PREPOSITION *DE* BEFORE AN INFINITIVE

acabar de, to have just acordarse (ue) de, to remember to alegrarse de, to be glad to cesar de, to stop, to cease	dejar de, to stop, to fail to olvidarse de, to forget to tratar de, to try to

Acaba (Acababa) de hablar.	He has just (had just) spoken.
Deja de trabajar.	He stops working (fails to work).
Se olvidaron de traerlo.	They forgot to bring it.
Trata de trabajar.	He tries to work.

VERBS REQUIRING THE PREPOSITION *EN* BEFORE AN INFINITIVE

consentir (ie) en, to consent to consistir en, to consist of	insistir en, to insist on tardar en, to be long in, to delay in

Consiente en venir.	He consents to come.
Tarda en llegar.	He is long in arriving.

OTHER COMMON PREPOSITIONS

al (= a el) + inf., on, upon	en vez de, instead of
antes de, before	sin, without
después de, after	

al entrar   upon entering

antes de llegar   before arriving

VERBS REQUIRING NO PREPOSITION BEFORE AN INFINITIVE

deber, ought to, must	oír, to hear
dejar, to let, to allow	pensar (ie), to intend
desear, to desire	poder (ue), to be able, can
esperar, to hope, to expect	querer (ie), to want
hacer, to make, to have (something done)	saber, to know (how)
lograr, to succeed in	soler (ue), to be in the habit of
	ver, to see

Debe hacer el trabajo.	He ought to do the work.
No me *dejó* entrar.	He did not let me enter.
Me *hace* reír.	He makes me laugh.
Hizo construir una casa.	He had a house built.
Logró convencerle.	He succeeded in convincing him.
No le *oímos* salir.	We did not hear him leave.
Quiero comprar un traje.	I want to buy a suit.
¿*Sabe* Vd. tocar el piano?	Do you know how to play the piano?
Suele venir temprano.	He is in the habit of coming early.
Le *vi* jugar.	I saw him playing.

EJERCICIOS

A. Complete Vd. cada frase, empleando una preposición *si es necesario*.

1. Me enseñó _____ nadar.
2. Le ayudan _____ caminar.
3. Cesó _____ llover.
4. Vino _____ visitarnos.
5. ¿No puede Vd. _____ verlo?
6. ¿Quién le invitó _____ entrar?
7. No tardaron _____ llegar.
8. Consintieron _____ ayudarnos.
9. Los vi _____ salir.
10. Hizo _____ decorar el cuarto.
11. Vuelven _____ hacerlo.
12. Se negaron _____ contestarle.
13. Empieza _____ bailar.
14. Logra _____ hacerlo.
15. No se atrevió _____ moverse.
16. Acaba _____ llegar.
17. Suelen _____ pasar por aquí cada día.
18. Se apresuró _____ verlo.
19. Va _____ cantar.
20. La felicidad no consiste _____ tener mucho dinero.

B. Conteste Vd. en español en frases completas.

1. ¿Va Vd. a escribir una carta a su amigo(-a) hoy?

----

2. ¿Qué desea Vd. hacer esta tarde?

----

3. ¿Piensa Vd. hacer un viaje el año que viene?

----

4. ¿Se olvidó Vd. de traer su libro hoy?

----

5. ¿Qué lengua aprende Vd. a hablar?

----

6. ¿Sabe Vd. conducir un coche?

----

7. ¿Piensa Vd. antes de hablar?

----

8. ¿Trata Vd. de conversar en español con sus amigos?

----

9. ¿Se alegra Vd. de vivir en los Estados Unidos?

----

10. ¿Le gusta a Vd. divertirse en vez de trabajar?

C. Traduzca Vd. al español las expresiones en inglés.

1. *We shall try to* venir. ------------------------------------

2. *On opening* la puerta, vio al criado. --------------------

3. *They had just* hacer el trabajo. ----------------------------

4. *He refused to* vendérselo. --------------------------------

5. *He has just* llegar de Cuba. ------------------------------

6. *It stopped* nevar. --

7. *She remembered to* traerlo. ------------------------------

8. *They expect* viajar por España. --------------------------

9. Si Vd. viene, *don't fail to* traerlo. ----------------------

10. Le oímos *singing*. --

11. *We didn't dare to* contestarle. ----------------------------

12. *It is beginning to* llover. --------------------------------

13. *I ought to* estudiar. --------------------------------------

14. *They insist on* pagar la cuenta. --------------------------

15. Salió *without saying* nada. ------------------------------

16. *He succeeded in* vencer al enemigo. ----------------------

17. *After reading* el periódico, se acostó. ---

18. *They did not let me* pasar. ---

19. El niño *cries again*. ---

20. Escuche Vd. *instead of speaking*. ---

D. Traduzca Vd. al español.

1. Upon entering his house, he did not see anyone. -------------------------------

----

2. He is learning to play the piano. ---

3. Miss Davis is teaching me to dance. ---

----

4. I forgot to bring the toys. ---

5. The child began to play. ---

6. They were not long in coming to the party. -------------------------------

----

7. He left the room without doing anything. -------------------------------

----

8. When are you going to send the letter? -------------------------------

----

9. She helped me serve the dinner. ---

10. Do you know how to swim? ---

28. *PARA* AND *POR*

USES OF *PARA*

Para is used to indicate: (1) purpose, (2) use, (3) destination, (4) for a time in the future, (5) considering the fact that (in spite of the fact that). **Para** is usually translated *to, in order to, for,* or *by*.

1. Comemos *para* vivir.
   (purpose)

   We eat to (in order to) live.

2. Es una caja *para* dulces.
   (use)

   It is a box for candy (a candy box).

3. Salen *para* México.
   (destination)

   They are leaving for Mexico.

4. Lo necesito *para* mañana a las tres.
   (future time)

   I need it for (by) tomorrow at three o'clock.

5. *Para* un viejo, es muy fuerte.
   (in spite of being)

   For an old man, he is very strong.

USES OF *POR*

Por is used when *for* means: (1) in exchange for, (2) for a period of time, (3) for the sake of.

1. Pagué cinco dólares *por* la pluma.
   (exchange)

   I paid five dollars for the pen.

2. Estudió *por* una hora.
   (period of time)

   He studied for an hour.

3. Lo hago *por* Vd.
   (for the sake of)

   I am doing it for you.

Por is used after the verbs **ir** (*to go*), **enviar** (*to send*), **luchar** (*to fight*).

Voy por leche.

I am going for milk.

Envía por el médico.

He sends for the doctor.

Luchan por su patria.

They fight for their country.

Por also means *by* or *through*.

Fue enviado *por* el presidente.

He was sent by the president.

Viajaron *por* avión.

They traveled by plane.

Entró *por* la ventana.

He entered by (through) the window.

ESTAR PARA AND *ESTAR POR*

Estar para + infinitive means *to be about to*.

Están para salir.

They are about to leave.

Estar por + infinitive means *to be in favor of*.

Están por salir.

They are in favor of leaving.

Note

The word *for* is not translated with the following verbs: **buscar** (*to look for*), **esperar** (*to wait for*), **pedir** (*to ask for*).

Buscan un hotel.

They are looking for a hotel.

Esperé el tren.

I waited for the train.

Pidió un vaso de leche.

She asked for a glass of milk.

213

EJERCICIOS

A. Complete Vd. cada frase, empleando correctamente la preposición **para** o **por** en el espacio.

1. Sale _____ Inglaterra mañana.

2. Pagué dos pesos _____ un paraguas.

3. Caminaron _____ el bosque.

4. Mi madre preparó la cena _____ el día siguiente.

5. Irá al campo _____ pasar dos semanas allí.

6. Lo cambié _____ un reloj de oro.

7. Es una caja _____ juguetes.

8. _____ un niño, lee muy bien.

9. Va a la escuela _____ tranvía.

10. Aquella novela fue escrita _____ un escritor famoso.

B. Conteste Vd. en español en frases completas.

1. ¿Prefiere Vd. viajar por tren o por avión?

_____

2. ¿A quién visita Vd. para curar un dolor de muelas?

_____

3. ¿Está Vd. por comenzar sus vacaciones ahora mismo?

_____

4. ¿Ha estudiado Vd. la lección para hoy?

_____

5. ¿Tiene Vd. que correr a la escuela para llegar a tiempo?

_____

6. ¿Ha viajado Vd. alguna vez por el Canadá?

_____

7. ¿Para qué es el jabón?

_____

8. ¿Hay un estante para libros en su cuarto?

_____

9. ¿Lucharía Vd. por la justicia?

_____

10. ¿Envía Vd. por el médico cuando tiene fiebre?

_____

C. Traduzca Vd. al español las expresiones en inglés.

1. El soldado fue atacado *by* el enemigo.   _____

2. Respiramos *in order to* vivir.   _____

3. Viajaron *through* Europa.   _____

4. Muchos *are in favor of* ayudar a Tomás.   _____

5. *We are waiting for* un autobús. _____

6. Salieron *for* La Habana. _____

7. América fue descubierta *by* Colón. _____

8. Ella *is looking for* su pluma. _____

9. Los pasajeros *are about to* subir al tren. _____

10. Enviaron *for* el médico. _____

D. Traduzca Vd. al español.

1. It is necessary to study in order to learn. _____

2. The train is about to leave. _____

3. We traveled for six months. _____

4. They will study for the examination. _____

5. He spoke for an hour. _____

6. I am looking for my brother. _____

7. After eating, the man asked for the check. _____
_____

8. Mary sent for the package. _____

9. They found an empty candy box. _____
_____

10. He paid fifty dollars for the suit. _____
_____

Felipe II (1527-1598) reinó en España desde 1556 hasta su muerte. Fue muy religioso y creyó que su deber era proteger la religión católica contra sus enemigos. Así, empleó la mayor parte del oro que recibió de las colonias en guerras constantes contra otros países de Europa. En 1588 envió la Gran Armada Invencible para invadir a Inglaterra. La Armada sufrió una derrota (defeat) completa. Con aquella derrota comenzó la decadencia (decline) de España como poder europeo importante.

29. MASTERY EXERCISES

A. Traduzca Vd. al español las expresiones en inglés. (See Grammar Lessons 1 to 5.)

1. *Peru and Argentina* son dos naciones de *South America.* ---------------------------------
2. *The king's army* protegió el palacio. ---
3. Escribió un resumen del ensayo en *a hundred* palabras. ------------------------------
4. Ella se lavó *her face* con agua y jabón. ---
5. En el gabinete había *a wooden desk.* --
6. *Philip the Second* tenía muchas posesiones en el Nuevo Mundo. ------------------------
7. *In autumn* las hojas se vuelven pardas. ---
8. *The boys and girls* asistieron a la reunión. --
9. *Mary's brother* no es muy inteligente. --
10. Para el almuerzo, generalmente comía *a chicken salad.* -----------------------------
11. *The art of* Velázquez vive todavía. --
12. *Mr.* Muñoz es *a Galician.* --
13. Las fresas cuestan cincuenta centavos *a box.* --------------------------------------
14. Los niños saben distinguir entre *the good* y *the bad.* -----------------------------
15. No podían imaginarse *how high* era la torre. ---------------------------------------
16. Santiago, *the capital* de Chile, tiene un clima agradable. --------------------------
17. *Automobiles* son muy comunes hoy día. ---
18. Sabe hablar *Spanish* porque estudia el vocabulario y la gramática. -----------------
19. *On Tuesdays* los trabajadores se reúnen con el dueño. ------------------------------
20. Es *a doctor,* pero no sabe curar *a stomach ache.* ---------------------------------

B. Traduzca Vd. al español las expresiones en inglés. (See Grammar Lesson 6.)

1. El director no expulsó *anyone* de la escuela. ---------------------------------
2. Todo el mundo alababa *the hero.* ---------------------------------
3. Un grupo de cincuenta estados forman *the United States.* ---------------------------------
4. Nombraron *George* presidente del club. ---------------------------------
5. Dondequiera que vivas, tendrás *neighbors.* ---------------------------------
6. Deseo acompañar *someone* al baile. ---------------------------------
7. La niña aceptó *the rose* de su primo. ---------------------------------
8. El año pasado visitaron *Germany.* ---------------------------------
9. Un pescador salvó *the girl.* ---------------------------------
10. Una luz eléctrica alumbraba *the street.* ---------------------------------

C. Complete Vd. cada frase, subrayando la expresión correcta entre paréntesis. (See Grammar Lessons **9** to **12**.)

1. *That* niño es cubano.   (Eso, Ese)

2. Ningún maestro es tan bueno como *theirs*.   (el suyo, los suyos)

3. Las aventuras del Cid y *Pizarro's* no eran semejantes.   (los Pizarros, las de Pizarro)

4. Las monedas que él halló son *mine*.   (mío, mías)

5. *Her* boda tuvo lugar el domingo pasado.   (Su, Suya)

6. Mi respuesta no fue tan falsa como *his*.   (el suyo, la suya)

7. Los huevos que yo compré son buenos; *those* no están frescos.   (ésos, éstos)

8. ¿Qué sabe Vd. acerca de *this?*   (esto, éste)

9. No puedo aceptar *those* condiciones.   (estas, esas)

10. Esta mujer es simpática; *that one* tiene un carácter desagradable.   (aquélla, eso)

11. Pasó una hora peinándose *her* cabello.   (su, el)

12. *This* cerezo no da buenas frutas.   (Este, Esta)

13. *Their* acento es extranjero.   (Su, Sus)

14. Las industrias de España no son tan importantes como *ours*.   (nuestras, las nuestras)

15. Una hermana *of mine* tiene miedo de los ratones.   (la mía, mía)

D. Traduzca Vd. al español las expresiones en inglés. (See Grammar Lessons **7, 8, 13, 14, 15, 16**.)

1. La pimienta es *stronger than* la sal.

2. Hoy día los negocios tienen un *bad* aspecto.

3. La cocinera dividió el pastel *carefully*.

4. El asno es tal vez *the most hard-working animal in the* mundo.

5. El alumno quedó mudo *more than* dos minutos.

6. Por dos días el enfermo no tomó *no* alimento.

7. Para celebrar el día de *Saint* Tomás, asistió a un concierto.

8. El contador no ganaba *as much money as* merecía.

9. El perro sigue a su amo *faithfully*.

10. Su impermeable es *less expensive than* el mío.

11. Cortés fue un *great* conquistador.

12. Francia ya no tiene *as many colonies as* antes.

13. El doctor es un hombre *very rich* [one word].

14. El algodón no es *as strong as* el rayón.

15. Las uvas de este año son *better than* las del año pasado.

E. Escriba Vd. las frases siguientes, empleando pronombres en lugar de las expresiones en letra cursiva: (See Grammar Lessons **17, 18, 19**.)

1. Indique Vd. *a los viajeros el camino correcto.*

2. La bomba atómica es un gran peligro para *el mundo.*

3. Entró en el comedor y se sentó al lado de *las señoras.*

4. Dentro de *la maleta* vio una espada de acero fino. _____

5. El ladrón confesó *sus crímenes al juez.* _____

6. La actriz demostró *al público su talento.* _____

7. Se puso la gorra, y salió entre *los dos policías.* _____

8. No pudo expresar *su gran amor a la señorita.* _____

9. El peluquero estaba cortando *el pelo a la niña.* _____

10. No preste Vd. *la pintura a Pablo.* _____

F. Subraye Vd. la expresión entre paréntesis que traduzca correctamente la expresión en inglés.

1. Soy *as* alta *as* Vd.   (tan . . . como, tanto . . . como, tanta . . . como)

2. No *you* conozco.   (ti, Vd., le)

3. Mi hermano es más religioso que *yours.*   (su, el suyo, Vds.)

4. *It is* las cinco.   (Es, Son, Está)

5. No comen *as many* legumbres como nosotros.   (muchas, tan, tantas)

6. Lolita es la niña más hermosa *in* la familia.   (en, de, por)

7. Ganó más *than* mil pesos.   (que, de, como)

8. Sancho fue un *good* escudero.   (bien, buen, bueno)

9. Había *one hundred* pupitres en la sala.   (cien, ciento, cientos)

10. Tiene *twenty-one* años.   (veinte y uno, veinte y un, veinte y una)

11. El profesor *to her* enseña la historia.   (le, la, se)

12. Está sentado detrás de *her.*   (la, ella, su)

13. Este sarape es más barato que *hers.*   (el suyo, la suya, sus)

14. Jaime *them to him* envía.   (se los, los se, le los)

15. Se puso *his* suéter.   (su, el suyo, el)

16. Le visitó *every* meses.   (todos los, todas las, cada)

17. Es el *first* de noviembre.   (uno, primero, primer)

18. Voy a *give it to them.*   (dárselo, dárselos, se los dar)

19. No *them* veo.   (los, se, ellos)

20. Mi voluntad es más fuerte que *theirs.*   (el suyo, la suya, las suyas)

21. *There are* dos mapas en la clase.   (Son, Están, Hay)

22. *Saint* Tomás fue un gran escritor.   (San, Santo, Santa)

23. Si Vd. ve una corbata bonita, *buy it.*   (cómprelo, cómprela, la compra)

24. No quiere *to work.*   (trabajar, trabaje, a trabajar)

25. Estudia *for* un examen.   (por, para que, para)

26. Antes de *eating,* me lavo las manos y la cara.   (comer, comido, comiendo)

27. Antonio *has just* entrar.   (acaba de, acababa de, ha acabado de)

28. Venga Vd. con *us.*   (nos, nosotros, él y yo)

29. *Those* hombres insisten en eso.   (Aquéllos, Esos, Los)

30. *These* mesas están sucias.   (Estas, Esas, Aquellas)

31. ¿Recibió Vd. la carta *that* envié?   (ese, aquél, que)

32. No creo *that*.   (esto, ése, eso)

33. Es *a doctor*.   (un médico, un doctor, médico)

34. ¿*Whose* es esta huerta?   (A quién, De quién, Cuya)

35. *Upon* entrar en el cuarto, vi a la criada.   (En, Sobre, Al)

36. Van a la iglesia *on* domingos.   (en, el, los)

37. *Our* placeres son sencillos.   (Nosotros, Nuestros, Nos)

38. No me gusta *either*.   (ni, también, tampoco)

39. ¿*Which* de los niños es americano?   (Qué, Cuál, Cuáles)

40. Robaron *what* pudieron hallar.   (qué, cuál, lo que)

41. La mujer *who* entró es puertorriqueña.   (que, a quien, quién)

42. Es el *third* de diciembre.   (tres, tercero, tercer)

43. *Bring them* Vd. mañana.   (Los traiga, Tráigalos, Los traen)

44. Estudia *with me*.   (conmigo, con me, con mí)

45. Es un amigo *of mine*.   (mío, de mío, mí)

46. ¿Tiene Vd. *my* gafas?   (mi, mí, mis)

47. *No one* quería al dictador.   (Ningún, Nadie, Nada)

48. Los hombres con *whom* hablaba son periodistas.   (que, quien, quienes)

49. *None* de los huéspedes pudo dormir.   (Ninguno, No, Nada)

50. Mi casa está cerca de *his*.   (el de ella, la de él, el de él)

    G. Traduzca Vd. al español las expresiones en inglés.

1. *Mr.* Gómez tiene dolor de cabeza.   ---

2. Los claveles son *pretty*.   ---

3. *This* ejercicio es inútil.   ---

4. No aguardé *anyone*.   ---

5. *Charles the Fifth* fue un emperador español.   ---

6. Van *to school*.   ---

7. María *him* visita todos los días.   ---

8. El hierro es más pesado *than* la madera.   ---

9. ¿Ha visto Vd. *ever* tal espectáculo?   ---

10. Sus brazos son más largos que *mine*.   ---

11. Tomás fue el *first* hermano que se casó.   ---

12. Aquella camisa está más limpia que *this one*.   ---

13. Fabricaron *green blouses* allí.   ---

14. Los perros entienden *very much*.   ---

15. La guerra terminó en *1945*.   ---

16. Necesito *one hundred twenty* dólares.   ---

17. Le presentaron *a gold watch*.   ----------------------------

18. Cuesta cuarenta centavos *a dozen*.   ----------------------------

19. No dijo *anything*.   ----------------------------

20. Se graduó *on Wednesday*.   ----------------------------

21. *Frequently* visitaban el Gran Cañón.   ----------------------------

22. Salió sin *saying* nada.   ----------------------------

23. Imita *his neighbors*.   ----------------------------

24. *Dogs* son animales útiles.   ----------------------------

25. ¿Quién tiene *the teacher's book?*   ----------------------------

26. Pagó dos pesos *for* una libra de dulces.   ----------------------------

27. *I know how to* mejorarlo.   ----------------------------

28. Vino a *see us* ayer.   ----------------------------

29. Pidió *chocolate ice cream*.   ----------------------------

30. *It to them* dimos.   ----------------------------

31. Casi siempre anda *slowly*.   ----------------------------

32. Juan es *older than* yo.   ----------------------------

33. Granada y Valencia son ciudades *Spanish*.   ----------------------------

34. No puedo hacer *the impossible*.   ----------------------------

35. Voy a Alemania *next week*.   ----------------------------

36. Comió el emparedado *rapidly*.   ----------------------------

37. *Don't buy it* Vd.   ----------------------------

38. *After reading* el próximo capítulo, se acostó.   ----------------------------

39. Este vestido es más bonito que *that one*.   ----------------------------

40. Juana es la muchacha *whose* retrato Vd. vio.   ----------------------------

41. Está *showing them to him*.   ----------------------------

42. María no va a la fiesta; *nor I either*.   ----------------------------

43. Los castellanos vencieron a los moros en *1492*.   ----------------------------

44. ¿*What* es la capital de Cuba?   ----------------------------

45. *No* hombre es perfecto.   ----------------------------

46. Este templo costó *a million dollars*.   ----------------------------

47. *He is going to see* a sus amigos.   ----------------------------

48. Los soldados fueron heridos *by* las fuerzas enemigas.   ----------------------------

49. Ella *no longer* vive aquí.   ----------------------------

50. ¿*Where* va Vd. el viernes?   ----------------------------

Part III—*Idioms*

1. IDIOMS WITH *DAR*

dar a, to face

    Mi ventana *da a* la avenida.   My window faces the avenue.

dar con alguien (or **algo**), to meet, to come upon, to find someone (or something)

    Di con mi amigo en la calle.   I met my friend on the street.

dar cuerda (al reloj), to wind (the watch)

    Todos los días *doy cuerda a mi reloj.*   Every day I wind my watch.

dar de comer a, to feed

    Dan de comer a los caballos.   They feed the horses.

dar la hora (las siete), to strike the hour (seven)

    El reloj *dio las siete.*   The clock struck seven.

dar la mano a alguien, to shake hands with someone

    Le *dio la mano.*   He shook hands with him.

darse la mano, to shake hands (with each other)

    Los amigos *se dan la mano.*   The friends shake hands.

dar las gracias a, to thank

    Dio las gracias al hombre por su bondad.   He thanked the man for his kindness.

dar los buenos días (las buenas noches) a alguien, to say good morning (good night) to someone

    Da los buenos días a su amigo.   He says good morning to his friend.

dar un paseo, to take a walk or a ride

    Da un paseo por el parque.   He takes a walk (a ride) through the park.

dar un paseo en automóvil (a caballo), to take an automobile ride (to go horseback riding)

    Dan un paseo en automóvil.   They take an automobile ride.

EJERCICIOS

A. Complete Vd. cada frase correctamente con una de las expresiones siguientes:

a	en coche
buenos días	la hora
con	la mano
cuerda	las gracias
de comer	un paseo

1. A las nueve en punto, el reloj dio _____ _____.

2. Mi madre me dará _____ una tortilla y un panecillo.

3. Al entrar, el cura dio los _____ a la gente.

4. La ventana de mi dormitorio da _____ la calle.

5. El senador va a dar un paseo _____ por el parque.

221

6. Al verse, se dieron ---------------------------------------.

7. Se olvidó de dar ------------------------------------- a su reloj.

8. El chófer aceptó la propina, y dio ------------------------------- al pasajero.

9. En la tienda dio ------------------------------- el caballero que buscaba.

10. Por las tardes dan ------------------------- de media hora.

B. Conteste Vd. en español en frases completas.

1. ¿Da Vd. un paseo por la mañana? --------------------------------
   ----

2. ¿Le gusta a Vd. un cuarto que da a la calle? ------------------
   ----

3. ¿Da Vd. de comer a los pájaros? ---------------------------------
   ----

4. Si Vd. da con su amigo(-a) en la calle, ¿se dan Vds. la mano? ------
   ----

5. ¿Da Vd. las gracias a las personas que le ayudan? --------------
   ----

6. ¿Da Vd. cuerda a su reloj todos los días? ----------------------
   ----

7. ¿Da Vd. las buenas noches a su familia antes de acostarse? --------
   ----

8. ¿Prefiere Vd. dar un paseo en automóvil o a caballo? -----------
   ----

9. Al despedirse de un amigo, ¿le da Vd. la mano? -----------------
   ----

10. ¿Qué hora da el reloj cuando Vd. se despierta? -----------------
    ----

C. Traduzca Vd. al español las palabras en inglés, empleando una expresión con el verbo **dar.**

1. La catedral *faces* un palacio magnífico. ----------------------

2. El cocinero *feeds* al gato. -----------------------------------

3. Por fin *we found* la entrada. --------------------------------

4. Por la noche ella *goes horseback riding.* ---------------------

5. *They shook hands* y salieron. --------------------------------

6. *I took an automobile ride* ayer. -----------------------------

7. El reloj *struck* las once. -----------------------------------

8. Antes de salir, *he said good night.* -------------------------

9. *He didn't wind* a su reloj, y el reloj se paró. ---------------

10. Jaime no quiere *to shake hands with* Luis. ------------------

D. Traduzca Vd. al español.

1. Do you want to take a walk? ---------------------------------

2. He shook hands with me. ---------------------------------

3. The clock struck one. ---------------------------------

4. My room faces the park. ---------------------------------

5. She is feeding her child. ---------------------------------

6. Upon meeting, they shook hands. ---------------------------------

7. Every day he says "good morning" to me. ---------------------------------

----

8. In the street I found a gold ring. ---------------------------------

9. Don't forget to wind your watch. ---------------------------------

10. I often take an automobile ride in the afternoon. ---------------------------------

----

El Guadalquivir es el río más navegable e importante de España. Pasa por las ciudades andaluzas de Córdoba y Sevilla antes de desembocar (empty) en el Atlántico. Durante la época colonial todo el comercio español con las colonias solía partir de la ciudad de Sevilla y volver a ella, pasando por el Guadalquivir.

2. THE VERB *GUSTAR*

Me gusta el libro.
to me   is
        pleasing

I like the book.

Me gustan los libros.
to me   are
        pleasing

I like books.

Le gusta la flor.
to you   is
to him pleasing
to her

{ You like the flower.
{ He (She) likes the flower.

Le gustan las flores.
to you   are
to him pleasing
to her

{ You like (the) flowers.
{ He (She) likes (the) flowers.

Nos gusta la novela.
to us   is
        pleasing

We like the novel.

Nos gustan las novelas.
to us   are
        pleasing

We like novels.

Les gusta cantar.
to you   is
to them pleasing

You (*pl.*) (They) like to sing.

A María no le gusta el cuarto.
to   Mary   (to her) is not
                pleasing

Mary doesn't like the room.

A los niños les gusta la escuela.
to the children (to them) is
            pleasing

The children like the school.

Note

A. The verb **gustar** (*to be pleasing*) is used to express the English verb *to like*. "I like the book" must be rendered in Spanish by "The book is pleasing to me"; "He likes books" by "The books are pleasing to him."

B. The verb **gustar** usually occurs only in the third person singular or the third person plural.

C. The thing *liked* is the object in English, but becomes the subject in Spanish. Since the verb must agree with the subject, **gustar** must be singular if the Spanish subject is singular; if the subject is plural, **gustar** must be plural.

D. The subject usually follows the verb **gustar**.

E. The indirect object pronouns (**me, te, le, nos, os, les**) must always be used with the verb **gustar**, even if the object nouns are expressed.

EJERCICIOS

A. Subraye Vd. la frase en español que traduzca correctamente lo inglés.

1. I like the watch.

   a. Me gusta el reloj.

   b. Yo gustan el reloj.

2. We like coffee.

   a. Nos gustan el café.

   b. Nos gusta el café.

3. I like comedies.

   a. Me gusta las comedias.

   b. Me gustan las comedias.

4. Do you like the room?

   a. ¿Le gusta el cuarto?

   b. ¿Gusta Vd. el cuarto?

224

5. Tom liked the shirt.

    a. A Tomás le gustó la camisa.

    b. Tomás gustó la camisa.

6. Would you like to see it?

    a. ¿Le gustaría verlo?

    b. ¿Gustaría Vd. verlo?

7. She does not like tea.

    a. No le gusta el té.

    b. No la gusta el té.

8. They liked the picture.

    a Les gustó el cuadro.

    b. Les gustaron el cuadro.

9. He likes to dance.

    a. Él gusta a bailar.

    b. Le gusta bailar.

10. Boys like sports.

    a. Los muchachos gustan los deportes.

    b. A los muchachos les gustan los deportes.

B. Conteste Vd. en español en frases completas.

1. ¿Le gustan a Vd. las naranjas?

----

2. ¿Le gusta a Vd. jugar al fútbol?

----

3. ¿Les gustan a los alumnos las vacaciones?

----

4. ¿Le gustaría a Vd. viajar a México?

----

5. ¿Le gusta a Vd. obtener buenas notas?

----

6. ¿Le gustaría a Vd. vivir en un país extranjero?

----

7. ¿Le gustan a Vd. las corridas de toros?

----

8. ¿Cómo le gusta a Vd. pasar las vacaciones?

----

9. ¿Le gustaría a Vd. vivir bajo una dictadura?

----

10. ¿Qué le gusta a Vd. comer más?

C. Traduzca Vd. al español las palabras en inglés.

1. *We like* la música.

2. *They like* el invierno.

3. *I like it* muchísimo.

4. *He likes* jugar a la pelota.

5. ¿*Do you like* nadar en el lago?

6. *Philip likes* las vacaciones.

7. *I would like* verlo.

8. *Julia doesn't like* este libro. ---

9. *¿Do you like* los perros? --

10. *The men liked* el hotel. ---

11. *She likes* los vestidos bonitos. --

12. *We liked* mucho la película. ---

13. *¿Did you like* la comedia? ---

14. *She liked* las rosas. ---

15. *Children like* los cuentos. --

16. *We like* los caballos. --

17. *He likes* los melocotones. ---

18. *Helen likes* los dulces. --

19. *I like* la leche. --

20. *They do not like* los pájaros. ---

D. Traduzca Vd. al español.

1. I do not like vegetables. ---

2. Do you like coffee? ---

3. She likes tea. --

4. They like to read Spanish stories. ---

5. You will like it very much. --

6. Women like pretty things. --

7. The boy liked the trip. --

8. They do not like the hotel. ---

9. I like books. ---

10. Do you like potatoes? --

3. IDIOMS WITH *HABER*

hay, there is, there are

había ⎫
hubo ⎭ there was, there were

habrá, there will be

habría, there would be

ha habido, there has (have) been

Había muchos clientes en la tienda.	There were many customers in the store.

haber lodo (luna, sol, neblina, polvo), to be muddy (moonlight, sunny, foggy, dusty)

Hay (mucho) lodo hoy.	It is (very) muddy today.
Había neblina anoche.	It was foggy last night.

haber de + infinitive, to be to, to be supposed to

Han de venir mañana.	They are to come tomorrow. (They're supposed to come tomorrow.)

hay que + infinitive, one must

Hay que tener paciencia.	One must have patience.

hay + noun + **que** + infinitive, there is (there are) + noun + verb

Hay trabajo que hacer.	There is work to do.

No hay de qué. Don't mention it. (You're welcome.)

Note

A. **Hay** is a special form used in the present tense.

B. The third person singular form is used to translate the singular forms "there *is*," "there *was*," etc., and the plural forms "there *are*," "there *were*," etc.

EJERCICIOS

A. Complete Vd. cada frase con una de las expresiones siguientes:

había	hay luna
ha de	hay neblina
han de	había polvo
no hay de qué	hay que
hay lodo	hay . . . que

1. Jaime _____ venir al anochecer.

2. Cuando alguien me dice "muchas gracias," yo siempre contesto "_____."

3. _____ callarse para oír.

4. No me gusta dar un paseo después de la lluvia, cuando _____ en las calles.

5. _____ una caja de dulces en la mesa.

6. En una noche clara _____.

7. _____ en el aire ayer.

8. Hoy _____; no se ve el sol.

9. En el campo _____ muchas cosas interesantes _____ ver.

10. Ellos _____ estar allí a las once.

B. Conteste Vd. en español en frases completas.

1. ¿Cuántos alumnos hay en esta escuela? _____

_____

2. ¿Hace buen tiempo cuando hay neblina? _____

_____

3. ¿Hay que llamar a un carpintero para cortar la hierba? _____

_____

4. ¿Cuándo dice Vd. "no hay de qué"? _____

_____

5. ¿A qué hora ha Vd. de estar en la escuela? _____

_____

6. ¿Hay sol hoy? _____

_____

7. Cuando llueve, ¿hay lodo o hay polvo en las calles? _____

_____

8. ¿Hay mucho que ver en un museo? _____

_____

9. ¿Cuántas semanas hay en un año? _____

_____

10. ¿Hay luna a mediodía? _____

_____

C. Traduzca Vd. al español las palabras en inglés.

1. *There will be* mucha gente en la tienda. _____

2. *There are* millones de soldados en el ejército. _____

3. *There were* tres sillas en la sala. _____

4. *There have been* muchos cambios. _____

5. *You're welcome*, Isabel. _____

6. Me gusta la noche cuando *there is moonlight*. _____

7. *One must* observar bien para aprender. _____

8. *I am to* llegar a las doce. _____

9. *¿Is there* baile esta noche? _____

10. *It was very dusty* ayer. _____

D. Traduzca Vd. al español.

1. He is to be there this afternoon. _____

2. In the battle there were many soldiers. _____

_____

3. The capital is beautiful; one must admire it. _____

_____

4. In the museum there are many things to see. ----------------------------------

----

5. After the rain it is muddy. ----------------------------------

6. There is much to do now. ----------------------------------

7. It is dusty today. ----------------------------------

8. The man answered, "Don't mention it." ----------------------------------

9. There was an employee in the store. ----------------------------------

10. It is sunny today. ----------------------------------

El acueducto de Segovia es una de las obras más admirables de la arquitectura romana. Fue construido hace 2000 años y siguió llevando agua a los habitantes hasta 1958. Tiene media milla de largo y está sostenido (supported) en 170 arcos (arches). Los romanos construyeron tan bien que en España se usa la expresión "obra de romanos" para describir un trabajo muy difícil.

4. IDIOMS WITH *HACER*

Weather Expressions:

¿Qué tiempo hace?	How is the weather?
Hace buen (mal) tiempo.	{ It is good (bad) weather. { The weather is fine (bad).
Hace (mucho) calor.	It is (very) warm.
Hacía frío.	It was cold.
Hará viento (fresco, sol).	It will be windy (cool, sunny).

hacer el favor de + infinitive, please

Haga Vd. *el favor de pasar* la sal.	Please pass the salt.

hacer de + noun of occupation, to act as

Hace de presidente.	He acts as president.

hacer el baúl (la maleta), to pack one's trunk (suitcase)

Hizo la maleta en seguida.	He packed his suitcase at once.

hacerle falta, to need, to be lacking to someone

Le hace falta un cuaderno. <small>to you is lacking to him to her</small>	{ You need a notebook. { He (She) needs a notebook.
Le hacen falta dos cuadernos. <small>to you are lacking to him to her</small>	{ You need two notebooks. { He (She) needs two notebooks.
A Juan y María les hace falta un cuaderno. <small>to John and Mary (to them) is lacking</small>	John and Mary need a notebook.

Note

A. The expression **hacerle falta** (*to be lacking to someone*) is used to express the English verb *to need*. "I need a notebook" is rendered by "A notebook is lacking to me"; "He needs two pencils" by "Two pencils are lacking to him."

B. Like **gustar,** the expression **hacerle falta** usually occurs only in the third person singular or third person plural.

C. Since the object *needed* in English becomes the subject in Spanish, the form of **hacer** must agree with it. Thus, if the thing needed is singular, use the third person singular of **hacer;** if it is plural, use the plural form.

D. The subject (the thing needed) usually follows **hacerle falta.**

E. The indirect object pronouns (**me, te, le, nos, os, les**) must be used with **hacerle falta,** even if the object nouns are expressed.

hace + time expression + preterite, ago

Le hablé *hace una semana.*	I spoke to him a week ago.

hacer una pregunta, to ask a question

El alumno *hizo una pregunta* al profesor.	The pupil asked the teacher a question.

hacer un viaje, to take a trip

 Hace un viaje a México.   He takes a trip to Mexico.

hacer una visita, to pay a visit

 Hice una visita a mi tío.   I paid a visit to my uncle.

hacerse, to become (through one's own efforts)

 Se hizo famoso.   He became famous.

hacerse tarde, to be getting late

 Se hace tarde.   It is getting late.

EJERCICIOS

A. Complete Vd. cada frase con una de las palabras o expresiones siguientes: (Cada expresión debe usarse solamente una vez.)

de	tiempo
el favor	un viaje
falta	una pregunta
mucho frío	una semana
tarde	una visita

1. En el invierno hace _____.

2. Haga Vd. _____ de callarse.

3. Él me hizo _____, y yo la contesté.

4. En la primavera harán _____ a Alemania.

5. Luis hacía _____ abogado.

6. ¿Qué _____ hace hoy?

7. Me hace _____ un tenedor.

8. Debo volver a casa porque se hace _____.

9. Le vi hace _____.

10. Sus conocidos le hicieron _____ el domingo.

B. Conteste Vd. en español en frases completas.

1. ¿Qué tiempo hace hoy?

   _____

2. ¿Le hace falta a Vd. dinero de vez en cuando?

   _____

3. ¿Hace mucho frío en el verano?

   _____

4. ¿Desea Vd. hacerse rico(-a) algún día?

   _____

5. ¿Qué tiempo hace en el otoño?

   _____

6. ¿Ha hecho Vd. un viaje a México?

   _____

7. ¿En qué estación hace mucho sol?

_____

8. ¿Hace Vd. muchas preguntas al maestro?

_____

9. ¿Hace Vd. su maleta antes o después de un viaje?

_____

10. ¿Qué tiempo hace en el invierno?

_____

C. En cada frase, emplee Vd. un sinónimo de la expresión en letra cursiva.

1. *Viajaron* por Europa.   _____

2. *Visita* a sus padres.   _____

3. *Abra Vd.* la puerta, *por favor*.   _____

4. *Necesito* un paraguas.   _____

5. *Hay sol* hoy.   _____

D. Traduzca Vd. al español las expresiones en inglés.

1. *It was fine weather* la semana pasada.   _____

2. *It is very warm* hoy.   _____

3. *It was windy* en las montañas.   _____

4. *The weather is bad* en el norte.   _____

5. *Please answer* a mi carta.   _____

6. Le vi *a month ago*.   _____

7. *He became* autor.   _____

8. *We need* el dinero.   _____

9. *He paid a visit* a su amigo.   _____

10. *It will be sunny* en el oeste.   _____

E. Traduzca Vd. al español.

1. It is cool here. _____

2. She needs thirty cents. _____

3. It is very cold today. _____

4. How was the weather yesterday? _____

5. The student acted as teacher. _____

6. Pack your trunk at once. _____

7. She needs a pen. _____

8. The teacher asks many questions. _____

9. In summer it is warm. _____

10. He wishes to take a trip to Europe. _____

5. IDIOMS WITH *TENER*

IDIOMS IN WHICH *TENER* = TO BE

tener . . . años, to be . . . years old

Tiene veinte años.	He is twenty years old.
¿Cuántos años tiene Vd.? *¿Qué edad tiene Vd.?*	How old are you?

tener (mucho) calor, to be (very) warm

Tiene (mucho) calor.	He is (very) warm.

tener (mucho) frío, to be (very) cold

Tengo (mucho) frío.	I am (very) cold.

Note

To be warm and to be cold are translated by **hacer calor** and **hacer frío** when referring to the weather, and by **estar caliente** and **estar frío(-a)** when referring to things.

Hace calor (frío).	It is (The weather is) warm (cold).
La sopa está caliente (fría).	The soup is warm (cold).

tener (mucha) hambre, to be (very) hungry

¿Tiene Vd. *(mucha) hambre?*	Are you (very) hungry?

tener (mucha) sed, to be (very) thirsty

Tengo (mucha) sed.	I am (very) thirsty.

tener éxito, to be successful

Siempre *tiene éxito.*	He is always successful.

tener razón, to be right; **no tener razón,** to be wrong

Alfredo *tiene razón.*	Alfred is right.
Pablo *no tiene razón.*	Paul is wrong.

tener sueño, to be sleepy

¿Tiene Vd. *sueño?*	Are you sleepy?

tener cuidado, to be careful

Tenga Vd. *cuidado.*	Be careful.

tener prisa, to be in a hurry

El hombre *tiene prisa.*	The man is in a hurry.

tener (mucho) gusto en, to be (very) glad to

Tengo (mucho) gusto en conocerle.	I am (very) glad to know you.

tener miedo de + infinitive, to be afraid to

tener miedo a + noun, to be afraid of

Tiene miedo de tocarlo.	She is afraid to touch it.
Tiene miedo al perro.	She is afraid of the dog.

OTHER IDIOMS WITH *TENER*

tener dolor de cabeza, to have a headache

 Tengo dolor de cabeza.   I have a headache.

tener que + infinitive, to have to, must

 Tengo que estudiar.   I have to (must) study.

tener mucho (poco, algo, etc.**) que hacer,** to have much (little, something, etc.) to do

 Tengo mucho que hacer.   I have much to do.

tener la bondad de + infinitive, please

 Tenga Vd. la bondad de esperar un momento. Please wait a moment.

tener las manos frías (los ojos cansados), to have cold hands (tired eyes)

 Tiene las manos frías (calientes). His hands are cold (warm).

 Tengo los ojos cansados.   My eyes are tired.

¿Qué tiene Vd.? What is the matter with you?

EJERCICIOS

A. A la izquierda de cada frase de la lista *A*, escriba Vd. la letra de su traducción que aparece en la lista *B*.

A	B
_____ **1.** ¿Cuántos años tiene Vd.?	*a.* I am very warm.
_____ **2.** Tiene trece años.	*b.* You were wrong.
_____ **3.** Tengo mucho calor.	*c.* I have nothing to do.
_____ **4.** Tienen razón.	*d.* Are you thirsty?
_____ **5.** Tenían sueño.	*e.* His eyes are tired.
_____ **6.** Tiene los ojos cansados.	*f.* The woman was cold.
_____ **7.** Tienen miedo al hombre.	*g.* How old are you?
_____ **8.** ¿Tienen Vds. sed?	*h.* I am very glad to know you.
_____ **9.** Tenga Vd. la bondad de salir.	*i.* They are right.
_____ **10.** Tengo mucho gusto en conocerle.	*j.* He is afraid to enter.
_____ **11.** Tengan Vds. cuidado.	*k.* Why are you in a hurry?
_____ **12.** Tengo las manos frías.	*l.* We are very hungry.
_____ **13.** ¿Por qué tiene Vd. prisa?	*m.* My hands are cold.
_____ **14.** Tiene miedo de entrar.	*n.* She is thirteen years old.
_____ **15.** Tenemos mucha hambre.	*o.* They are afraid of the man.
_____ **16.** ¿Tiene Vd. dolor de cabeza?	*p.* Please leave.
_____ **17.** La mujer tenía frío.	*q.* They were sleepy.
_____ **18.** ¿Qué tiene Vd.?	*r.* What's the matter with you?
_____ **19.** Vds. no tenían razón.	*s.* Have you a headache?
_____ **20.** No tengo nada que hacer.	*t.* Be careful.

B. En cada frase, emplee Vd. un sinónimo de la expresión en letra cursiva.

1. *Haga Vd. el favor de* alejarse. _____

2. *¿Qué edad* tiene aquel actor? _____

3. *Debo* doblar el papel. _____

4. *Temo* llegar tarde. _____

5. Vd. *se equivoca.* _____

C. Complete Vd. cada frase con la forma correcta de una de las expresiones siguientes:

tener calor	tener miedo
tener frío	tener prisa
tener mucho gusto	tener que
tener hambre	tener sed
tener la bondad	tener sueño

1. En el otoño ellos _____ volver a la escuela.

2. _____ ; sin embargo, no se acuesta.

3. Bebemos agua cuando _____ .

4. Llevaba ropa pesada, y _____ .

5. Ella come cuando _____ .

6. Estudian porque _____ de salir mal.

7. Se acercaron al fuego porque _____ .

8. Andaban lentamente porque no _____ .

9. _____ en conocerle, señor.

10. Camarero, _____ de darme una servilleta.

D. Conteste Vd. en español en frases completas.

1. ¿Cuántos años tiene Vd.? _____

_____

2. ¿Toma Vd. té cuando tiene dolor de cabeza? _____

_____

3. ¿Tiene Vd. frío hoy? _____

_____

4. ¿Tiene Vd. que estudiar esta noche para un examen? _____

_____

5. ¿Tiene Vd. razón siempre? _____

_____

6. ¿Tiene Vd. hambre por la tarde? _____

_____

7. ¿Qué bebe Vd. cuando tiene sed? _____

_____

8. ¿Qué hace Vd. cuando tiene sueño? _____

_____

9. ¿Tiene Vd. cuidado al cruzar la calle? _____

_____

10. ¿Tiene Vd. algo que hacer esta tarde? _____

_____

E. Traduzca Vd. al español las expresiones en inglés.

1. *I must learn it* de memoria. _____

2. Su marido *is thirty years old.* _____

3. *She was afraid of* los animales. _____

4. *He has much to do* hoy. _____

5. *We shall be very glad to* decorar la sala. _____

6. Nunca *they are in a hurry.* _____

7. Isabel y Elena *are very hungry.* _____

8. ¿*What is the matter with* su primo? _____

9. Los trabajadores *were sleepy.* _____

10. *He had to* marcharse a las once. _____

F. Traduzca Vd. al español.

1. My father has a headache. _____

2. You (*pl.*) are wrong. _____

3. Do you drink when you are thirsty? _____

4. I have something to do today. _____

5. Please read it to the class. _____

6. The children were sleepy. _____

7. The boy is right. _____

8. Be careful, George. _____

9. He is afraid to enter the house. _____

10. I am very warm today. _____

6. MISCELLANEOUS VERBAL IDIOMS—I

acabar de, to have just

    Acaba (acababa) de entrar.   He has just (had just) entered.

aprovecharse de, to take advantage of (an opportunity)

    Se aprovecha de cada oportunidad.   He takes advantage of each opportunity.

asistir a, to attend

    Asistimos a la escuela.   We attend school.

bajar de, to get off (the train, bus, etc.)

    Baja del tren.   He gets off the train.

burlarse de, to make fun of

    Se burla de la muchacha.   He makes fun of the girl.

cambiar de, to change (seat, train, mind)

    Cambia de asiento con su amigo.   He changes seats with his friend.

    Cambió de opinión.   He changed his mind.

casarse con, to marry

    Se casó con Isabel.   He married Elizabeth.

contar con, to rely on, to count on

    Cuento con mis amigos.   I rely on my friends.

creer que sí (no), to think so (not)

    Creo que sí.   I think so.

cumplir . . . años, to be . . . years old

    Hoy *cumple* quince *años.*   Today he is fifteen years old.

cumplir con (su promesa, su palabra), to fulfill, to keep (one's promise, one's word)

    Es un hombre que siempre *cumple con su*   He is a man who always keeps his word.
       palabra.

dedicarse a, to devote oneself to

    Se dedica al trabajo.   He devotes himself to the work.

dejar caer, to drop

    Dejó caer los platos.   He dropped the plates.

dejar de + infinitive, to stop, to fail to

    Dejó de comer.   He stopped eating.

    No *deje* Vd. *de hacer*lo.   Don't fail to do it.

despedirse de, to take leave of, to say goodbye to

    En la estación *se despidió de* sus amigos.   In the station he said goodbye to his friends.

echarse a + infinitive, to begin to, to start to

    Se echa a llorar.   He begins to cry.

echar de menos, to miss

    Echa de menos a sus amigos.   He misses his friends.

echar una carta al correo, to mail a letter

    Eché la carta al correo ayer.   I mailed the letter yesterday.

EJERCICIOS

A. Complete Vd. cada frase con una de las expresiones siguientes:

asisto	de tren
bajaron	echo
cuento	que no
cumplió	se casó
dejó	se dedica

1. _____ del tranvía.

2. Ayer _____ cincuenta años.

3. _____ de menos a los amigos de la niñez.

4. _____ a la carrera de enfermera.

5. La taquígrafa _____ caer el sacapuntas.

6. Para aprender, _____ con la ayuda del maestro.

7. Los pasajeros cambiaron _____.

8. ¿Hace frío? Creo _____.

9. No _____ a la escuela los sábados.

10. Luis _____ con Elena.

B. A la izquierda de cada frase de la lista *A*, escriba Vd. la letra de su traducción que aparece en la lista *B*.

A	*B*
_____ 1. Creo que sí.	*a.* He has just stolen them.
_____ 2. Se echó a correr.	*b.* Taking advantage of a free hour, he studied the lesson.
_____ 3. Siempre cumple con su deber.	
_____ 4. Aprovechándose de una hora libre, estudió la lección.	*c.* I think so.
	d. The truckmen dropped the trunk.
_____ 5. No deje Vd. de apagar la luz.	*e.* Don't fail to put out the light.
_____ 6. Echó la carta al correo.	*f.* He always does (ful lls) his duty.
_____ 7. Acaba de robarlas.	*g.* He makes fun of his aunt.
_____ 8. Los carreteros dejaron caer el baúl.	*h.* She began to run.
_____ 9. Se despidió de todos.	*i.* He mailed the letter.
_____ 10. Se burla de su tía.	*j.* He took leave of everyone.

C. Conteste Vd. en español en frases completas.

1. ¿Baja Vd. de un autobús con cuidado?

_____

2. ¿Se dedica Vd. al estudio?

_____

3. ¿Se burla Vd. de los locos?

_____

4. ¿Asiste Vd. a la escuela los lunes?

_____

5. ¿Se aprovecha Vd. de cada ocasión?

----

6. ¿Deja Vd. de hacer sus tareas a menudo?

----

7. ¿Siempre cumple Vd. con su promesa?

----

8. ¿Puede Vd. contar con el cariño de su familia?

----

9. ¿Echa Vd. una carta al correo antes o después de escribirla?

----

10. Al oír una broma, ¿se echa Vd. a llorar?

D. Traduzca Vd. al español las expresiones en inglés.

1. *I shall not fail to* decorar el árbol.   -------------------------

2. *She mails the letters* por la tarde.   -------------------------

3. No desean *to attend* la universidad.   -------------------------

4. *She changes* opinión a menudo.   -------------------------

5. ¿Pueden Vds. *rely on* aquel dependiente?   -------------------------

6. *She misses* a sus parientes.   -------------------------

7. ¿Es sabio el filósofo? *I think so.*   -------------------------

8. *They have just* volver de Italia.   -------------------------

9. *He will marry* la hija del gobernador.   -------------------------

10. Mañana *she will be* quince años.   -------------------------

E. Traduzca Vd. al español.

1. Is she leaving tonight? I think so.

----

2. Do not drop the book.

----

3. In the street he began to run.

----

4. She attends church on Sundays.

----

5. He says goodbye to his mother.

----

6. He never keeps his promise.

----

7. They take advantage of their opportunities.

----

8. She devotes herself to helping the poor.

---

9. He makes fun of his enemies.

---

10. A beautiful girl got off the train.

En San Juan de Puerto Rico se ve lo antiguo al lado de lo moderno. Desde la antigua Fortaleza (Fort) de San Gerónimo, se ve la playa lujosa (luxurious) de El Condado, con sus hoteles grandes y modernos, a donde vienen miles de turistas cada año.

7. MISCELLANEOUS VERBAL IDIOMS—II

enamorarse de, to fall in love with

    Se enamoró de Dolores.   He fell in love with Dolores.

entrar en, to enter

    Entró en el cuarto.   He entered the room.

estar a punto de
estar para } to be about to

    Estaban a punto de salir.   They were about to leave.

estar de pie, to be standing

    Todos *estaban de pie.*   All were standing.

estar por, to be in favor of

    Yo estoy por ir al cine.   I am in favor of going to the movies.

faltarle, to need, to be lacking

    Me falta el tiempo para estudiar.   I need the time to study.
    _{to me   is}
          _{lacking}

    Le faltan los libros necesarios.   You lack (He, She lacks) the necessary books.
    _{to you   are}
    _{to him lacking}
    _{to her}

    Note. Like **gustar,** the verb **faltar** is used here only in the third person singular and the third person plural.

gozar de, to enjoy

    Goza de buena salud.   He enjoys good health.

jugar a, to play (a game)

    Juegan al tenis.   They play tennis.

llegar a ser + noun, to become

    Llegó a ser presidente.   He became president.

llevar a cabo, to carry out

    El capitán *llevó a cabo* las órdenes del general.   The captain carried out the general's orders.

negarse a + infinitive, to refuse to

    Se niega a firmar el cheque.   He refuses to sign the check.

ocuparse de, to busy oneself with, to be concerned with, to attend to

    La criada *se ocupa de* los niños.   The maid attends to the children.

pensar de, to think of (have an opinion about)

    ¿Qué *piensa* Vd. *de* mi nueva bicicleta?   What do you think of my new bicycle?

pensar en, to think of, to think about (direct one's thoughts to)

    Nunca *piensa en* sus amigos.   He never thinks of his friends.

poner la mesa, to set the table

    María *pone la mesa.*   Mary sets the table.

241

ponerse + article of clothing, to put on

   Se pone el abrigo.   He puts on his coat.

ponerse + adjective, to become (involuntarily)

   Se puso pálido.   He became pale.

ponerse a + infinitive, to begin to

   Se pusieron a correr.   They began to run.

ponerse el sol, to set (referring to the sun)

   ¿A qué hora *se pone el sol?*   At what time does the sun set?

ponerse en camino (en marcha), to start out, to set out

   Se pusieron en camino (en marcha) tarde.   They started out late.

EJERCICIOS

A. Complete Vd. cada frase con una de las expresiones siguientes:

de pie	se negó a
enamora	se ocupa
entró	se pone
goza	se pusieron
llegó	se puso

1. El sol _____ temprano en el invierno.

2. Ellos _____ en camino a mediodía.

3. _____ a ser famoso.

4. _____ de buena fama.

5. La princesa se _____ del soldado.

6. La madre _____ de la casa.

7. El banco _____ prestarme dinero.

8. Ella _____ la blusa azul y salió.

9. _____ en una botica y pidió la medicina.

10. Estoy _____ porque no hay asientos.

B. A la izquierda de cada frase de la lista *A*, escriba Vd. la letra de su traducción que aparece en la lista *B*.

A	*B*
_____ 1. Pensaba en los días de su juventud.	*a.* The milkman was in favor of leaving.
_____ 2. El lechero estaba a punto de marcharse.	*b.* A button is missing on his jacket.
_____ 3. Al anochecer, ella puso la mesa.	*c.* He thought of the days of his youth.
_____ 4. Se puso pálida.	*d.* She became pale.
_____ 5. Se puso a curar la herida.	*e.* I don't know what to think of the situation.
_____ 6. Logró llevar a cabo sus planes.	*f.* He began to treat the wound.
_____ 7. No sé qué pensar de la situación.	*g.* He succeeded in carrying out his plans.
_____ 8. Le falta a la chaqueta un botón.	*h.* At nightfall, she set the table.
_____ 9. El lechero estaba por marcharse.	*i.* The milkman was about to leave.
_____ 10. Estaba de pie en la acera, esperando.	*j.* He was standing on the sidewalk, waiting.

C. Conteste Vd. en español en frases completas.

1. ¿Piensa Vd. mucho en los placeres de las vacaciones? _____

_____

2. ¿Quién pone la mesa en su casa? _____

_____

3. ¿Juega Vd. al jai-alai? _____

_____

4. ¿Le falta el dinero para comprar un helado? _____

_____

5. ¿Goza Vd. de buena salud? _____

_____

6. ¿Se niega Vd. a hacer actos peligrosos? _____

_____

7. ¿En dónde entra Vd. para ver objetos de arte? _____

_____

8. ¿A qué hora se puso el sol ayer? _____

_____

9. ¿Se ocupa Vd. de los problemas de sus amigos? _____

_____

10. ¿Se pone Vd. enfermo(-a) cuando come frutas verdes? _____

_____

D. Traduzca Vd. al español las expresiones en inglés.

1. *They refused to* subir la escalera.   _____

2. La madre *is concerned with* la casa.   _____

3. El ejército *was about to* avanzar.   _____

4. El caballero *fell in love with* la dama.   _____

5. El mozo *didn't set* la mesa.   _____

6. La niña *became* muy contenta.   _____

7. Después de un descanso, los turistas *set out.*   _____

8. No me dice lo que *he thinks of* la nueva ley.   _____

9. Algún día *he will become* gobernador.   _____

10. En seguida, *he began to* comer el pavo asado.   _____

E. Traduzca Vd. al español.

1. I fell in love with the beautiful girl. _____

_____

2. They play baseball every Saturday. _____

_____

3. The teacher was standing behind his desk. _____

4. She entered the school at nine o'clock. _____

5. He needs patience. _____

_____

6. The sun will set early today. _____

_____

7. He put on his coat and hat. _____

_____

8. After many years, he became a lawyer. _____

_____

9. They are about to leave. _____

_____

10. She is thinking of her children. _____

8. MISCELLANEOUS VERBAL IDIOMS—III

prestar atención, to pay attention

No *presta atención* en la clase. · · · · He does not pay attention in class.

quedarle algo a alguien, to have something left, to remain to someone

Le queda un dólar. · · · · You have (He, She has) a dollar left.

to you remains
to him
to her

Me quedan dos dólares. · · · · I have two dollars left.

to me remain

Note. Like **gustar,** the verb **quedar** is used here only in the third person singular and the third person plural.

querer a, to love

Quiero a mis padres. · · · · I love my parents.

querer decir, to mean

¿Qué *quiere* Vd. *decir?* · · · · What do you mean?

quitarse + article of clothing, to take off

Se quita el sombrero. · · · · He takes off his hat.

reírse de, to laugh at

Se ríe de la muchacha. · · · · He laughs at the girl.

salir bien (mal), to come out well (poorly), to pass (fail)

Salió bien en el examen. · · · · He came out well on (passed) the examination.

salir de, to leave, to go out of

Salgo de la escuela a las tres. · · · · I leave school at three.

salir el sol, to rise (referring to the sun)

El sol sale temprano. · · · · The sun rises early.

servirse de, to use, to make use of

Se sirve de la madera para hacer una mesa. · · · · He uses the wood to make a table.

soñar con, to dream of

Sueña con su amigo. · · · · He dreams of his friend.

subir a, to get on (the train, bus, etc.)

Sube al autobús. · · · · He gets on the bus.

subir (bajar) la escalera, to go upstairs (downstairs)

Sube la escalera. · · · · He goes upstairs.

Baja la escalera. · · · · He goes downstairs.

tardar en + infinitive, to delay in

El tren *tardó en llegar.* · · · · The train delayed in arriving.

tocarle a uno, to be one's turn

Les toca hacerlo. · · · · It is their turn to do it.

Note. The verb **tocar,** when used in the above expression, appears only in the third person singular.

245

tratar de + infinitive, to try to

    Trata de trabajar.   He tries to work.

volver a + infinitive, to (*verb*) again

    Vuelve a cantar.   He sings again.

EJERCICIOS

A. Complete Vd. cada frase con una de las palabras siguientes:

decir	sirven
presten	soñó
quedan	toca
quiere	trató
salieron	volvió

1. Su novio _____ a decorar el comedor.

2. Bolívar _____ con la libertad.

3. El dependiente _____ de envolver los guantes.

4. Los alumnos se _____ del laboratorio.

5. Sólo me _____ dos libras de azúcar.

6. _____ mucho a su novia.

7. ¡_____ Vds. atención!

8. ¿Qué quiere _____ este párrafo?

9. _____ bien en los negocios.

10. Le _____ a Vd. leer.

B. Escoja Vd. de la lista siguiente un antónimo de cada una de las expresiones en letra cursiva, y escríbalo en la forma correcta:

            quitarse
            salir bien
            salir de
            salir el sol
            subir a

1. *Entraron en* la zapatería. _____

2. Los pasajeros *bajaron del* autobús. _____

3. *Salió mal* en el examen. _____

4. *El sol se pone* a las seis. _____

5. Ella *se puso* la blusa amarilla. _____

C. Escoja Vd. de la lista siguiente un sinónimo de cada una de las expresiones en letra cursiva, y escríbalo en la forma correcta:

            prestar atención
            querer a
            querer decir
            reírse de
            servirse del

1. Los alumnos suelen *escuchar con atención.* _____

2. *Se burla de* Pablo. _____

3. *Ama a* Rosa. _____

4. El alumno *usa el* sacapuntas. _____

5. ¿Qué *significan* estas líneas? _____

D. A la izquierda de cada frase de la lista *A*, escriba Vd. la letra de su traducción que aparece en la lista *B*.

<table>
<tr><td align="center">A</td><td align="center">B</td></tr>
</table>

_____ 1. Se rió del fracaso de su enemigo.

_____ 2. Para llegar al vestíbulo, bajaron la escalera.

_____ 3. Le quedan unas lágrimas en la mejilla.

_____ 4. Volvió a colgar la chaqueta en el armario.

_____ 5. El bailarín trató de esconderse en las sombras.

_____ 6. Estando fatigados, subieron a un taxi.

_____ 7. El marinero se quitó el impermeable.

_____ 8. Subiendo la escalera llegaron arriba.

_____ 9. El cochero tardó en llegar a la fonda.

_____ 10. Le toca a Vd. comprar los sellos.

a. The dancer tried to hide in the shadows.

b. The sailor took off his raincoat.

c. To get to the vestibule, they went downstairs.

d. The driver delayed in reaching the inn.

e. She still has some tears on her cheek.

f. Being tired, they got into a taxi.

g. They got upstairs by climbing the stairs.

h. It is your turn to buy the stamps.

i. She again hung the jacket in the closet.

j. He laughed at his enemy's failure.

E. Conteste Vd. en español en frases completas.

1. ¿Qué quiere decir "amistad"? _____

_____

2. Para llegar al quinto piso, ¿hay que subir o bajar la escalera? _____

_____

3. ¿Tarda Vd. en atender a sus deberes? _____

_____

4. ¿Sueña Vd. con hacerse célebre? _____

_____

5. ¿A qué hora salió el sol ayer? _____

_____

6. ¿Trata Vd. de cocinar algunas veces? _____

_____

7. ¿Se quita Vd. el abrigo al entrar en casa? _____

_____

8. ¿Sale Vd. de casa después de la cena? _____

_____

9. ¿De qué se sirve Vd. para cortar la carne? _____

_____

10. ¿Quiere Vd. a sus parientes? _____

F. Traduzca Vd. al español las expresiones en inglés.

1. El hombre tuvo que *again* trabajar, porque *he had left* menos de un dólar. ------------------

2. Se apresuró a *get on the* tren, pero el tren *delayed in* salir. ------------------

3. Dorotea *didn't pay attention*, y *failed* en los exámenes. ------------------

4. Para *leave* la casa, es necesario *to descend the stairs*. ------------------

5. *He tries to* trabajar bien, y *dreams of* el futuro. ------------------

6. Para saber lo que *means* una palabra, *I use the* diccionario. ------------------

7. Luisa *loves* sus amigas, y nunca *laughs at* sus faltas. ------------------

8. Al entrar, *he took off* los zapatos y *went upstairs*. ------------------

9. *It is her turn* preparar el desayuno cuando *the sun rises*. ------------------

10. *He passes* en los exámenes porque *he pays attention* en la clase. ------------------

G. Traduzca Vd. al español.

1. He studies because he doesn't want to fail (in) the examination. ------------------

2. The enemy attacked again at noon. ------------------

3. At (En) the station he got on the train. ------------------

4. All the pupils passed the test last week. ------------------

5. It is my turn to pay the bill. ------------------

6. He delayed fifteen minutes in leaving the office. ------------------

7. We never laugh at the teacher's jokes. ------------------

8. The sun rose at 6 A.M. today. ------------------

9. Why don't you (tú) pay attention, Johnny? ------------------

10. Yesterday she had only four dollars left. ------------------

9. IDIOMS WITH *A*

a caballo, on horseback

    Los vaqueros montan *a caballo.*   The cowboys ride on horseback.

a casa, home

    Va *a casa.*   He goes home.

a causa de, on account of, because of

    Llegó tarde *a causa de* la tempestad.   He arrived late because of the storm.

a eso de, at about (+ time expression)

    Vino *a eso de* las tres.   He came at about three.

a la derecha, to (on, at) the right

    Vaya Vd. *a la derecha.*   Go to the right.

a la izquierda, to (on, at) the left

    Su cuarto está *a la izquierda.*   His room is on the left.

a menudo, often

    Nos visita *a menudo.*   He often visits us.

a pesar de, in spite of

    Lo hace *a pesar de* ella.   He does it in spite of her.

a pie, on foot

    Van a la ciudad *a pie.*   They go to the city on foot.

a tiempo, on time

    Llegan *a tiempo.*   They arrive on time.

al aire libre, in the open air, outdoors

    Jugaban *al aire libre.*   They were playing in the open air.

al día siguiente, on the following day

    Vino *al día siguiente.*   He came on the following day.

al fin, finally, at last

    Al fin lo vieron.   Finally they saw it.

al lado de, beside, next to

    Está sentado *al lado de* su esposa.   He is seated beside his wife.

al + infinitive, on, upon

    Al ver a su hermano, Alicia empezó a llorar.   On seeing her brother, Alice began to cry.

EJERCICIOS

A. Complete Vd. cada frase con una de las expresiones siguientes:

a casa	a pesar de
a causa de	al aire libre
a eso de	al día siguiente
a la derecha	al llegar
a menudo	al fin

1. No sabiendo qué dirección tomar, fue _____

2. _____ abajo, se echó a correr.

3. _____ la lluvia, se puso el impermeable.

4. Los pájaros y las abejas viven _____.

5. _____, a las seis, cesó de nevar.

6. El baile termina _____ las once.

7. No volvió _____ antes de medianoche.

8. Se lava _____, varias veces al día.

9. _____ su enfermedad, pudo subir la escalera.

10. Esperamos dos horas; _____ llegó el autobús.

B. Escriba Vd. un sinónimo de cada expresión en letra cursiva, escogiéndolo de la lista siguiente:

a menudo
al aire libre
al día siguiente
al fin
al lado de

1. Sintió la necesidad de dar un paseo *fuera de la casa.* _____

2. La sastrería está *junto a* la carnicería. _____

3. *Muchas veces* repiten respuestas incorrectas. _____

4. *Al día próximo* el suelo estaba cubierto de nieve. _____

5. *Por fin* llegó el médico con un remedio. _____

C. Escriba Vd. un antónimo de cada expresión en letra cursiva, escogiéndolo de la lista siguiente:

a caballo
a la izquierda
a menudo
a pesar de
a tiempo

1. Tiene miedo de ir *a pie.* _____

2. El piloto *nunca* trata de viajar cuando hay neblina. _____

3. Mi casa se encuentra *a la derecha* del hospital. _____

4. *A causa de* su salud, no podía jugar al tenis. _____

5. Ambos llegaron *tarde* al mercado. _____

D. Conteste Vd. en español en frases completas.

1. ¿Se siente Vd. triste al ponerse el sol? _____

_____

2. ¿Habla Vd. con sus amigos a menudo? _____

_____

3. ¿A qué hora vuelve Vd. a casa? _____

_____

4. ¿Le gusta a Vd. dar largos paseos a pie? _____

_____

5. ¿Cómo se llama el alumno a la izquierda de Vd.? _____

6. ¿Qué edificio hay al lado de su casa? _____

7. ¿Toma Vd. alimento a causa de o a pesar de tener hambre? _____

8. ¿Siempre llega Vd. a tiempo a la clase? _____

9. ¿Prefiere Vd. dar paseos en auto o a caballo? _____

10. ¿Le gusta a Vd. pasar los días al aire libre? _____

E. Traduzca Vd. al español las expresiones en inglés.

1. El actor miró *to the right*. _____
2. Muchos sufren *because of* la guerra. _____
3. Puso el baúl *beside* la cama. _____
4. Está sentado *next to* la mujer bella. _____
5. Está débil *on account of* su enfermedad. _____
6. *Upon returning home*, dio un beso a su mamá. _____
7. Subió el monte *in spite of* la dificultad. _____
8. Viaja a Europa *often*. _____
9. *At last* pudo establecer un negocio en el pueblo. _____
10. El juez le examinó *on the following day*. _____
11. El comedor está *at the left*. _____
12. Tenemos que ir *on foot*. _____
13. El barco nunca sale *on time*. _____
14. Llegamos *at about* las once. _____
15. Va montado *on horseback*. _____

F. Traduzca Vd. al español.

1. The actor often arrives at the theater on time. _____

2. On the following day he left at about three o'clock. _____

3. We returned home on horseback. _____

4. Because of his illness, he spent much time outdoors. _____

5. At last he decided to go there on foot. _____

_____

6. In spite of the snow, the army advanced on the following day. _____

_____

7. Upon approaching the corner, we went to the right. _____

_____

8. During the battle the captain often fought beside the soldiers. _____

_____

9. At last he reached the building, which was to the left of the park. _____

_____

10. In spite of the rain, he returned home on foot. _____

_____

El padre Miguel Hidalgo (1753-1811), cura del pueblo mexicano de Dolores, en 1810 inició la revolución contra España. Salió victorioso en varias batallas contra los españoles, pero al fin fue capturado y condenado a muerte. Otros patriotas continuaron la lucha y lograron la independencia. Hasta hoy se venera (is venerated) el nombre de Hidalgo, a quien los mexicanos consideran padre de la independencia mexicana. En México se celebra el 15 de septiembre, aniversario de la revolución, con fiestas en que se repite el "Grito (War Cry) de Dolores": "¡Viva Nuestra Señora de Guadalupe y mueran los gachupines!" ("Long live Our Lady of Guadalupe and death to the Spaniards!")

10. IDIOMS WITH *DE*

de buena gana, willingly

    Lo hace *de buena gana.*   He does it willingly.

de mala gana, unwillingly

    Lo hizo *de mala gana.*   He did it unwillingly.

de cuando en cuando, from time to time

    Se escribían *de cuando en cuando.*   They wrote to each other from time to time.

de día, by day, in the daytime

    Trabaja *de día.*   He works by day (in the daytime).

de noche, at night, in the nighttime

    Trabaja *de noche.*   He works at night (in the nighttime).

de esta (esa) manera, in this (that) way

    Hágalo Vd. *de esta (esa) manera.*   Do it in this (that) way.

de este (ese) modo, in this (that) way

    No lo haga Vd. *de este (ese) modo.*   Don't do it in this (that) way.

de la mañana (tarde, noche), in the morning (afternoon, evening); a.m. (p.m.)

    Salió a las tres *de la tarde.*   He left at 3 p.m.

de memoria, by heart

    Aprendió la regla *de memoria.*   He learned the rule by heart.

de moda, in style, in fashion

    Este vestido ya no está *de moda.*   This dress is no longer in style.

de nada, you're welcome, don't mention it

    Respondió:—*De nada.*   He answered, "You're welcome."

de nuevo, again

    Lo hace *de nuevo.*   He does it again.

de pronto, suddenly, all of a sudden

    De pronto apareció.   Suddenly he appeared.

de repente, suddenly, all of a sudden

    Murió *de repente.*   He died suddenly.

EJERCICIOS

A. Escriba Vd. un sinónimo de cada expresión en letra cursiva, escogiéndolo de la lista siguiente:

                de esa manera
                de este modo
                de nada
                de nuevo
                de repente

1. Sucedió *de esta manera.*   --

2. *De pronto* notó un objeto extraño. _____

3. Ella me contestó:—*No hay de qué.* _____

4. *Otra vez* llenó el tanque de gasolina. _____

5. *De ese modo* evitó el peligro. _____

B. A la izquierda de cada frase de la lista *A*, escriba Vd. la letra de su traducción que aparece en la lista *B*.

A	*B*
_____ **1.** El accidente ocurrió de este modo.	*a.* The cats go out at night.
_____ **2.** Los chalecos ya no están de moda.	*b.* The employee wrapped the toy willingly.
_____ **3.** De pronto oímos un grito.	*c.* Vests are no longer in style.
_____ **4.** El empleado envolvió el juguete de buena gana.	*d.* The accident occurred in this way.
_____ **5.** De cuando en cuando le falta dinero.	*e.* Suddenly we heard a shout.
_____ **6.** Desapareció de repente.	*f.* He disappeared suddenly.
_____ **7.** Los gatos salen de noche.	*g.* He eats the vegetables unwillingly.
_____ **8.** A mediodía tenía hambre de nuevo.	*h.* At noon he was hungry again.
_____ **9.** Es inútil aprenderlo de memoria.	*i.* From time to time he needs money.
_____ **10.** Come las legumbres de mala gana.	*j.* It's useless to learn it by heart.

C. Conteste Vd. en español en frases completas.

1. En febrero, ¿se pone Vd. el abrigo de mala gana? _____

_____

2. ¿Están de moda las faldas largas o cortas? _____

_____

3. ¿Asiste Vd. a la escuela de día o de noche? _____

_____

4. ¿Sabe Vd. de memoria las reglas de gramática? _____

_____

5. ¿Hace Vd. sus tareas de buena gana? _____

_____

6. ¿A qué hora de la mañana tiene Vd. su segunda clase? _____

_____

7. ¿Qué debe Vd. contestar cuando alguien le dice "Gracias"? _____

_____

8. ¿Se acuerda Vd. de los días de su niñez de cuando en cuando? _____

_____

9. ¿Qué baile está de moda hoy día? _____

_____

10. ¿A qué hora de la noche se acuesta Vd.? _____

_____

D. Traduzca Vd. al español las expresiones en inglés.

1. *Suddenly* vimos un fuego. _____

2. Desgraciadamente, cayó enfermo *again*. _____

3. Muchas gracias. *You're welcome.* _____

4. Aprendió la poesía *by heart*. _____

5. Lea Vd. el capítulo *in this way*. _____

6. La fábrica está abierta *in the daytime*. _____

7. Luis tomó la medicina *willingly*. _____

8. Jamás sale *at night*. _____

9. Los guantes de cuero están *in style*. _____

10. Comió el huevo *unwillingly*. _____

E. Traduzca Vd. al español.

1. I paid the bill unwillingly. _____

_____

2. Mexican dances are in style here. _____

_____

3. He suddenly decided to get dressed. _____

_____

4. The maid arrived at 9 A.M. _____

_____

5. By day his daughter works in a bakery. _____

_____

6. He learned the eighth lesson by heart. _____

_____

7. They want to see England again in the spring. _____

_____

8. The pupil erased the blackboard willingly. _____

_____

9. From time to time he goes out at night. _____

_____

10. He studied, and in that way he learned French. _____

_____

11. IDIOMS WITH *EN*

en casa, at home

    Felipe está *en casa.*   Philip is at home.

en casa de, at the house (home) of

    Pasó la tarde *en casa de* su amiga.   She spent the afternoon at her friend's home.

en cuanto, as soon as

    En cuanto llegó, fuimos a verle.   As soon as he arrived, we went to see him.

en cuanto a, as for, as regards

    En cuanto a su padre, era un abogado famoso.   As for his father, he was a famous lawyer.

en frente de, in front of, opposite

    En frente del edificio hay una estatua.   In front of the building there is a statue.

en lugar de, instead of, in place of

    Fue al cine *en lugar de* estudiar.   He went to the movies instead of studying.

en medio de, in the middle of

    En medio del cuarto había una mesa grande.   In the middle of the room there was a large table.

en punto, exactly, on the dot

    Son las diez *en punto.*   It is exactly ten o'clock.

en seguida, at once, immediately

    Salga Vd. *en seguida.*   Leave at once.

en vano, in vain

    Trabajó *en vano.*   He worked in vain.

en voz alta, aloud, in a loud voice

    Lo anunció *en voz alta.*   He announced it aloud.

en voz baja, in a low voice

    Habla *en voz baja.*   He speaks in a low voice.

EJERCICIOS

A. Complete Vd. cada frase con una de las expresiones siguientes:

en casa	en medio de
en cuanto	en punto
en cuanto a	en seguida
en frente	en vano
en lugar de	en voz baja

1. Consultó el diccionario _____, sin éxito.

2. Vengan Vds. _____.

3. _____ entró el héroe, todos aplaudieron.

4. _____ del palacio, observó un objeto rojo.

5. Se perdió _____ la selva.

6. El avión sale a la una _____.

7. _____ su edad, no se la confiesa a nadie.

8. Quiero oír; no hablen Vds. _____.

9. Pasa demasiado tiempo _____.

10. _____ vender el cuadro, se lo regaló a su novio.

B. Escriba Vd. un sinónimo de cada expresión en letra cursiva, escogiéndolo de la lista siguiente:

> **en frente de**
> **en lugar del**
> **en medio de**
> **en seguida**
> **en vano**

1. *En vez del* gabán se puso la chaqueta. _____

2. Trató de atravesar la montaña, pero *sin éxito*. _____

3. *Delante de* la fábrica había una fuente. _____

4. *En el centro de* la plaza había un parque. _____

5. *Inmediatamente* se echó al lago para salvar a la niña. _____

C. Escriba Vd. un antónimo de cada expresión en letra cursiva, escogiéndolo de la lista siguiente:

> **en casa**
> **en frente de**
> **en medio de**
> **en seguida**
> **en voz baja**

1. *Más tarde* sirvieron refrescos. _____

2. El cura estaba *fuera de* la catedral. _____

3. *Detrás de* la sastrería se sentó para dar de comer a las palomas. _____

4. En octubre me gusta pasar los días *al aire libre*. _____

5. Los pasajeros conversaban *en voz alta*. _____

D. Conteste Vd. en español en frases completas.

1. ¿Habla Vd. en voz alta o baja cuando tiene dolor de garganta? _____
_____

2. En cuanto a los ceros, ¿recibe Vd. muchos? _____
_____

3. ¿Da Vd. un beso a sus hermanos(-as) en cuanto Vd. entra en casa? _____
_____

4. ¿Pasa Vd. mucho tiempo en casa de sus amigos? _____
_____

5. En esta clase, ¿habla el maestro en vano? _____
_____

6. ¿Llega el correo a su casa a las nueve en punto? _____

_____

7. Cuando tiene fiebre, ¿toma Vd. medicina en seguida? _____

_____

8. ¿Juega Vd. a la pelota en medio del camino? _____

_____

9. Para hacer té o café, ¿usa Vd. agua fría o caliente? _____

_____

10. ¿Hay un parque en frente de su casa? _____

_____

E. Traduzca Vd. al español las palabras en inglés.

1. *Instead of* comprar peras compró uvas. _____

2. Puedo estar *at Charles' house* a las tres. _____

3. *As for* su marido, es periodista. _____

4. Pasa sus horas libres *at home.* _____

5. Buscó un remedio *at once.* _____

6. Es la una *exactly.* _____

7. Su casa está situada *opposite* la nuestra. _____

8. Habló *aloud.* _____

9. *As soon as* me vio, me saludó. _____

10. Hay una estatua *in the middle of* la plaza. _____

F. Traduzca Vd. al español.

1. Generally she spent the afternoon at home. _____

_____

2. As soon as he got up he saw his gifts. _____

_____

3. The explorers looked for gold, but in vain. _____

_____

4. The guide stopped in the middle of the park. _____

_____

5. He put on his hat at once, and left the room. _____

_____

6. The man announced the news in a loud voice. _____

_____

7. We spent the holiday at the home of my aunt. _____

_____

8. "Give me the jewels," the thief said in a low voice. _____

_____

9. The lawyer promised to be here at one o'clock sharp. _____

_____

10. Opposite the library there is a museum. _____

_____

Muchos siglos antes de la llegada de los españoles, los mayas habían establecido en la península de Yucatán una civilización avanzada. Hoy se ven, en la ciudad de Chichén-Itzá, las antiguas pirámides y las ruinas de los templos que construyeron.

12. IDIOMS WITH *POR*

por consiguiente, consequently, therefore

    Por consiguiente decidí comprarlo.   Consequently I decided to buy it.

por ejemplo, for example

    Por ejemplo, la palabra "rodeo" es de origen   For example, the word "rodeo" is of Spanish
        español.   origin.

por eso, therefore

    Por eso, era imposible traerlo.   Therefore, it was impossible to bring it.

por favor, please

    Déme Vd. la tinta, *por favor.*   Give me the ink, please.

por fin, finally, at last

    Por fin llegó el tren.   Finally the train arrived.

por la mañana (tarde, noche), in the morning (afternoon, evening)

    Trabajo *por la mañana* y descanso *por la*   I work in the morning and rest in the evening.
        noche.

mañana por la mañana, tomorrow morning

    Saldrán de la ciudad *mañana por la mañana.*   They shall leave the city tomorrow morning.

ayer por la tarde, yesterday afternoon

    Vino *ayer por la tarde.*   He came yesterday afternoon.

por lo general, generally, in general, usually

    Por lo general me acuesto a las diez.   I generally go to bed at ten.

por lo menos, at least

    Por lo menos vale cinco pesos.   It is worth at least five pesos.

por lo visto, apparently

    Por lo visto, Juan está ausente hoy.   Apparently, John is absent today.

por supuesto, of course

    Por supuesto lo haré.   Of course I shall do it.

por todas partes, everywhere

    Había banderas *por todas partes.*   There were flags everywhere.

EJERCICIOS

A. Escriba Vd. un sinónimo de cada expresión en letra cursiva, escogiéndolo de la lista siguiente:

        por eso
        por favor
        por fin
        por lo general
        por lo visto

1. No le gusta el autobús; *por consiguiente* viajó por ferrocarril. ------------------------------

2. *Finalmente* llegó el plomero. ------------------------------

3. *Generalmente* lleva gabán en febrero. ------------------------------

4. *Parece que* el sobre no tiene la dirección correcta. ----------------------------

5. *Haga Vd. el favor de servirme* un par de huevos. ----------------------------

B. Conteste Vd. en español en frases completas.

1. ¿Toma Vd jugo de naranja o de toronja por la mañana? ----------------------------
----

2. ¿Mira Vd. los programas de televisión por la noche? ----------------------------
----

3. Por lo general, ¿lleva Vd. paraguas cuando hay sol? ----------------------------
----

4. ¿Pasó Vd. mucho tiempo al aire libre ayer por la tarde? ----------------------------
----

5. ¿Se encuentran dulcerías por todas partes en su ciudad? ----------------------------
----

C. Traduzca Vd. al español las expresiones en inglés.

1. *Please*, ponga Vd. el tocadiscos en el rincón. ----------------------------

2. No estaba satisfecho; *therefore* se quejó. ----------------------------

3. Ellos irán a misa *tomorrow morning*. ----------------------------

4. Ayer dimos un paseo de tres millas *at least*. ----------------------------

5. *Of course*, las nubes son grises cuando llueve. ----------------------------

6. *In the morning* visitaron el mercado y compraron sarapes. ----------------------------

7. *In the afternoon* el zapatero solía dormir la siesta. ----------------------------

8. Hoy día hay mucha ropa de rayón, *for example*, camisas y calcetines. ----------------------------

9. *Finally*, perdió toda su riqueza. ----------------------------

10. *In the evening* vieron la señal que esperaban. ----------------------------

D. Traduzca Vd. al español.

1. There were many people everywhere.
----

2. We will go to the park tomorrow morning.
----

3. Generally we eat at six o'clock.
----

4. Please speak more slowly.
----

5. There are at least twenty chairs in the room.
----

6. At last they finished the work.
----

7. I saw him yesterday afternoon.

---

8. He visited his friend in the evening.

---

9. Of course what (lo que) he says is true.

---

10. Therefore it is necessary to do it now.

Xochimilco, en las afueras (suburbs) de la Ciudad de México, es famoso por su lago y sus jardines flotantes (floating), donde se ve una gran variedad de flores. Es un lugar favorito de los turistas.

13. IDIOMS WITH *VEZ*

a veces, at times, occasionally

    A veces le gusta fumar un cigarro.   At times he likes to smoke a cigar.

algunas (unas) veces, sometimes

    Algunas veces me desayuno en un restaurante.   Sometimes I eat breakfast in a restaurant.

muchas veces, often, many times

    Le veo *muchas veces* en la tienda.   I often see him in the store.

raras veces, seldom, rarely

    La visitan *raras veces.*   They seldom visit her.

varias veces, several times

    Lo repitió *varias veces.*   He repeated it several times.

una vez, once

    Pruébelo *una vez.*   Try it once.

dos veces, twice

    Lo vio *dos veces.*   He saw it twice.

otra vez, again

    Escribió la carta *otra vez.*   He wrote the letter again.

a la vez, at the same time

    Todos hablaron *a la vez.*   All spoke at the same time.

en vez de, instead of

    Pidió leche *en vez de* café.   He ordered milk instead of coffee.

de vez en cuando, from time to time

    Va al campo *de vez en cuando.*   He goes to the country from time to time.

tal vez, perhaps

    Tal vez se olvidó de hacerlo.   Perhaps he forgot to do it.

EJERCICIOS

A. A la izquierda de cada modismo de la lista *A*, escriba Vd. la letra de su traducción que aparece en la lista *B*.

A	B
_____ **1.** dos veces	*a.* once
_____ **2.** muchas veces	*b.* at the same time
_____ **3.** tal vez	*c.* from time to time
_____ **4.** en vez de	*d.* sometimes
_____ **5.** de vez en cuando	*e.* twice
_____ **6.** algunas veces	*f.* instead of
_____ **7.** una vez	*g.* again
_____ **8.** otra vez	*h.* perhaps
_____ **9.** raras veces	*i.* often
_____ **10.** a la vez	*j.* rarely

B. Escriba Vd. un sinónimo de cada expresión en letra cursiva, escogiéndolo de la lista siguiente:

> de vez en cuando
> en vez de
> muchas veces
> otra vez
> tal vez

1. *De cuando en cuando* el paciente movía los labios. _____

2. *En lugar de* continuar sus estudios, se dedicó al comercio. _____

3. *Acaso* las alturas le hagan daño. _____

4. *A menudo* hacíamos un viaje a un pueblo cercano. _____

5. Antes de salir, estudió el mapa *de nuevo*. _____

C. Subraye Vd. la expresión entre paréntesis que complete cada frase correctamente.

1. (Dos veces, A veces) a la semana tuvo que ir a la clínica.

2. (Varias veces, En vez de) sintió un dolor agudo en el hombro.

3. Aunque las tareas generalmente son difíciles, (otra vez, de vez en cuando) puedo hacerlas.

4. Puede estudiar la aritmética y escuchar la conversación (una vez, a la vez).

5. (Algunas veces, En vez de) la vista de las montañas es espléndida.

6. Pasa el tiempo en el juego (a veces, en vez de) la lectura.

7. (Raras veces, Una vez) se ven chaquetas con mangas cortas.

8. (En vez de, De vez en cuando) la señorita echaba una mirada a su novio.

9. (Tal vez, Raras veces) el taxi está esperando en la esquina ahora.

10. (Muchas veces, A la vez) no comprendo la explicación del maestro.

D. Conteste Vd. en español en frases completas.

1. ¿Cuántas veces a la semana va Vd. al cine?

_____

2. ¿Estudia Vd. a menudo o raras veces?

_____

3. ¿Tiene Vd. deseos de comer varias veces al día?

_____

4. ¿Visita Vd. a su tía de vez en cuando?

_____

5. ¿Duerme Vd. la siesta en la clase algunas veces?

_____

6. ¿Cruzó Colón el mar dos veces o más?

_____

7. ¿Puede Vd. hacer varias cosas a la vez?

_____

8. ¿Tiene Vd. exámenes una vez o varias veces al mes?

_____

9. ¿Prefiere Vd. ir a pescar en vez de estudiar?

---

10. ¿Le gusta a Vd. escuchar la radio a veces?

E. Traduzca Vd. al español las expresiones en inglés.

1. ¡Ojalá se calle ella *again!* ---

2. Puede conversar y comer un emparedado *at the same time.* ---

3. *Perhaps* lo puso en el cajón. ---

4. *Sometimes* lleva abrigo en el otoño. ---

5. Va al cine *instead of* estudiar. ---

6. *At times* no puede respirar. ---

7. El alumno contesta perfectamente *from time to time.* ---

8. El obispo repitió la oración *twice.* ---

9. Leyó el artículo *once.* ---

10. Repita Vd. el proverbio *several times.* ---

F. Traduzca Vd. al español.

1. He often looked at the beautiful painting. ---

2. My parents rarely praise me. ---

3. Instead of pronouncing the word, he wrote it. ---

4. At times the teacher loses his (la) patience. ---

5. Philip once visited Peru. ---

6. Perhaps he received my letter. ---

7. From time to time we listen to the radio programs. ---

8. He can play the piano and speak at the same time. ---

9. Sometimes we went to the park on Sundays. ---

10. Several times she tried to speak to the president. ---

14. MISCELLANEOUS IDIOMATIC EXPRESSIONS—I

acerca de, about (concerning)

    ¿Qué sabe Vd. *acerca de* eso?   What do you know about that?

ahora mismo, right now

    Hágalo Vd. *ahora mismo.*   Do it right now.

alrededor de, around

    Estaban sentados *alrededor de* la mesa.   They were seated around the table.

billete de ida y vuelta, round-trip ticket

    Compré un *billete de ida y vuelta.*   I bought a round-trip ticket.

con frecuencia, frequently, often

    La veo *con frecuencia.*   I see her frequently.

con mucho gusto, gladly, with great pleasure

    Lo haré *con mucho gusto.*   I shall do it gladly.

cuanto antes, as soon as possible

    Vuelva Vd. *cuanto antes.*   Come back as soon as possible.

cuanto más . . . tanto más . . . , the more . . . the more . . .

    Cuanto más gana *tanto más* gasta.   The more he earns the more he spends.

dentro de poco, shortly, presently

    Estará aquí *dentro de poco.*   He will be here shortly.

desde luego, at once, of course

    Vaya Vd. a casa *desde luego.*   Go home at once.
    Desde luego Vd. fue invitado.   Of course you were invited.

es decir, that is to say

    Felipe, *es decir* mi vecino, me lo dio.   Philip, that is to say my neighbor, gave it to me.

está bien, all right

    —¡*Está bien!*—respondió Alberto.   "All right!" answered Albert.

esta noche, tonight

    Voy al cine *esta noche.*   I'm going to the movies tonight.

frente a, facing, in front of

    Hay un parque *frente a* mi casa.   There is a park facing my house.

hasta la vista, goodbye, until I see you again

    Hasta la vista, Dolores.   Goodbye (Until I see you again), Dolores.

hasta luego, goodbye, see you later

    Hasta luego, Jorge.   Goodbye (See you later), George.

hoy día, nowadays

    Hoy día los precios son altos.   Nowadays prices are high.

junto a, next to, beside

    Está sentado *junto a* la profesora.   He is seated next to the teacher.

la mayor parte de, most of, the majority of

> ***La mayor parte de*** la población es alta.   Most of the population is tall.

lo más pronto posible, as soon as possible

> Vinimos ***lo más pronto posible.***   We came as soon as possible.

los (las) dos, both

> ***Los dos*** muchachos son mis primos.   Both boys are my cousins.

EJERCICIOS

A. Complete Vd. cada frase con una de las expresiones siguientes:

acerca de	dentro de poco
alrededor de	está bien
billete de ida y vuelta	hasta la vista
con frecuencia	hoy día
con mucho gusto	la mayor parte de

1. Al separarnos siempre decimos: —_____

2. _____ tiene dolor de estómago.

3. No querían hablar _____ los accidentes.

4. Ganó _____ su fortuna en los negocios.

5. La familia pasó la noche _____ la chimenea, charlando.

6. Aguardó un rato, y _____ llegó su amigo.

7. Aquel día comió las albóndigas _____.

8. Compró un _____, dijo adiós, y subió al tren.

9. Cuando contestamos correctamente el maestro dice: — _____.

10. _____, la situación es distinta.

B. Escriba Vd. un sinónimo de cada expresión en letra cursiva, escogiéndolo de la lista siguiente:

> ahora mismo
> con frecuencia
> cuanto antes
> desde luego
> frente a

1. *Por supuesto* el paño es de la mejor calidad.   _____

2. Paró el coche *en frente de* un hospital.   _____

3. El navegante deseaba llegar al puerto *lo más pronto posible.*   _____

4. *A menudo* vio un relámpago, y oyó el trueno.   _____

5. Vamos a ponerle un telegrama *en este momento.*   _____

C. Escriba Vd. un antónimo de cada expresión en letra cursiva, escogiéndolo de la lista siguiente:

> con frecuencia
> con mucho gusto
> desde luego
> frente al
> junto a

1. El campesino pagó el impuesto *de mala gana.*   _____

2. *Detrás del* colegio había un patio grande.   _____

3. Pasó las vacaciones *lejos de* su familia. _____

4. Estudie Vd. la historia *más tarde*. _____

5. El lechero *raras veces* mezcla agua con la leche. _____

D. A la izquierda de cada modismo de la lista *A*, escriba Vd. la letra de su traducción que aparece en la lista *B*.

	A		*B*
_____	**1.** ahora mismo	*a.*	as soon as possible
_____	**2.** esta noche	*b.*	that is to say
_____	**3.** desde luego	*c.*	both
_____	**4.** hasta luego	*d.*	right now
_____	**5.** los dos	*e.*	about
_____	**6.** cuanto antes	*f.*	the more . . . the more
_____	**7.** junto a	*g.*	goodbye
_____	**8.** es decir	*h.*	of course
_____	**9.** frente a	*i.*	next to
_____	**10.** cuanto más . . . tanto más	*j.*	opposite
		k.	tonight

E. Conteste Vd. en español en frases completas.

1. ¿Le gustaría a Vd. hacer un viaje alrededor del mundo? _____

_____

2. ¿Se apresura Vd. a llegar a la escuela lo más pronto posible por la mañana? _____

_____

3. Si un amigo le pide ayuda, ¿se la da Vd. cuanto antes? _____

_____

4. ¿Va Vd. a tomar el almuerzo dentro de poco? _____

_____

5. ¿Sabe Vd. mucho acerca de la vida hispanoamericana? _____

_____

6. ¿Cuándo dice Vd. "hasta la vista" a un amigo? _____

_____

7. ¿Qué lengua habla la mayor parte de la América del Sur? _____

_____

8. ¿Vive Vd. frente a la escuela? _____

_____

9. ¿Qué piensa Vd. hacer esta noche? _____

_____

10. ¿Es difícil hoy día ir de la América del Norte a la América del Sur? _____

_____

F. Traduzca Vd. al español las expresiones en inglés.

1. Vinieron *at once*. ....

2. *Both* personajes salieron a la vez. ....

3. *The more* estudio, *the more* aprendo. ....

4. Paso *most of* la semana en la oficina. ....

5. Vamos a hacer el baúl *tonight*. ....

6. Ella se puso la blusa nueva *gladly*. ....

7. *See you later*, amigo mío. ....

8. *Nowadays* las cosas cambian rápidamente. ....

9. Hablaré con Carlota *as soon as possible*. ....

10. Llame Vd. al caballero *right now*. ....

11. Pues, vamos a hablar *about* la política. ....

12. El alumno borrará la pizarra *shortly*. ....

13. Están sentados *around the* fuego. ....

14. *"All right,"* contestó la niña. ....

15. *Facing* mi casa hay una panadería. ....

G. Traduzca Vd. al español.

1. Tonight the traveler will speak about South America. ....

2. Goodbye; I'll see you shortly. ....

3. Nowadays most of the pupils have vacations in the summer. ....

4. She stopped in front of the theater, beside the door. ....

5. He promised to buy a round-trip ticket as soon as possible. ....

6. The more I travel, the more I spend. ....

7. In the winter they frequently sit around the fire. ....

8. I must go home right now; goodbye. ....

9. Of course we gave the waiter a tip, and he accepted it gladly. ....

10. My mother said, "All right." That is to say, she consented. ....

15. MISCELLANEOUS IDIOMATIC EXPRESSIONS—II

más tarde, later

    Prometió venir *más tarde.*　　　　　She promised to come later.

mucho tiempo, a long time

    Hace *mucho tiempo* que no le veo.　　　I have not seen him for a long time.

¿no es verdad? or **¿verdad?,** aren't you? isn't he? don't they?, etc.

    Vd. viene con nosotros, *¿no es verdad?*　　You are coming with us, aren't you?

no obstante, notwithstanding, in spite of

    Salió de la casa *no obstante* su enfermedad.　He left the house in spite of his illness.

ocho días, a week; **quince días,** two weeks

    ¿Piensa Vd. quedarse *ocho días* o *quince días?*　Do you intend to remain a week or two weeks?

(el año) pasado, (la semana) pasada, last (year, week)

    El año pasado hice un viaje a México.　　Last year I took a trip to Mexico.

poco a poco, little by little

    Poco a poco se va lejos.　　　　　　Little by little one goes far.

que lo pase Vd. bien
que le vaya bien } good luck to you

    Adiós y *¡que lo pase Vd. bien!*　　　　Goodbye and good luck to you!

(el año) que viene, next (year)

    Vamos a Europa *el año que viene.*　　　We are going to Europe next year.

sin duda, no doubt, without doubt

    Sin duda llegará tarde.　　　　　　No doubt he will arrive late.

sin embargo, however, nevertheless

    Sin embargo, es verdad.　　　　　　However, it is true.

sobre todo, especially, above all

    Me gusta nadar, *sobre todo* en una piscina.　I like to swim, especially in a swimming pool.

todavía no, not yet

    ¿Ha venido? *Todavía no.*　　　　　Has he come? Not yet.

todo el mundo, everybody, everyone

    Todo el mundo aplaudió.　　　　　Everybody applauded.

todos los (todas las), every

    Trabaja *todos los* días.　　　　　　He works every day.

un poco de, a little (of)

    Déme Vd. *un poco de* agua, por favor.　Give me a little water, please.

unos(-as) cuantos(-as), a few, several

    Unos cuantos trabajadores escucharon la　A few workers listened to the speech.
    conferencia.

¡Ya lo creo!, Yes, indeed! I should say so!

    —¿Está Vd. listo?—*¡Ya lo creo!*　　　"Are you ready?" "Yes, indeed!"

ya no, no longer

> *Ya no* recuerda el incidente.   He no longer remembers the incident.

EJERCICIOS

A. Complete Vd. cada frase con una de las expresiones siguientes:

> la semana que viene   sobre todo
> mucho tiempo   todavía no
> no es verdad   todos los
> ocho días   un poco de
> que lo pase Vd. bien   ya lo creo

1. _____ recuerdos de la vieja son tristes.

2. ¿Es linda su novia? —¡_____!

3. Pasó solamente _____ en la República Argentina.

4. Se cortó el dedo y perdió _____ sangre.

5. Al partir me dijo: —_____.

6. Las rocas durarán _____.

7. Me gustan los idiomas extranjeros, _____ el castellano.

8. ¿Ha cesado de nevar? _____.

9. El circo llegará a nuestro pueblo _____.

10. El paciente tiene un catarro, ¿_____?

B. Escriba Vd. un sinónimo de cada expresión en letra cursiva, escogiéndolo de la lista siguiente:

> que lo pase Vd. bien
> quince días
> sin duda
> sobre todo
> unos cuantos

1. *Seguramente* el maestro me dará buenos consejos.   _____

2. Pasó solamente *dos semanas* en el campo.   _____

3. Adiós; *que le vaya bien.*   _____

4. *Varios* soldados tomaron parte en el combate.   _____

5. Me interesan los espectáculos, *especialmente* la corrida de toros.   _____

C. Escriba Vd. un antónimo de cada expresión en letra cursiva, escogiéndolo de la lista siguiente:

> más tarde
> poco a poco
> todo el mundo
> un poco de
> ya no

1. Su esposo *todavía* se dedica a los deportes.   _____

2. Con el cuchillo cortó *un gran pedazo de* queso.   _____

3. *Rápidamente* el paciente perdió la esperanza.   _____

4. Cuando la dama entró, *nadie* la saludó.   _____

5. *Ahora mismo* van a dividir el pastel.   _____

D. Subraye Vd. la expresión entre paréntesis que complete cada frase correctamente.

1. (Todo el mundo, Todos los) debe evitar lo malo.

2. (Un poco de, Poco a poco) aprendió una lengua extranjera.

3. Es perezoso; (sin duda, sin embargo) estudia con frecuencia.

4. (Un poco de, Unos cuantos) guardias andaban por la calle.

5. (Sin duda, Sobre todo) la lucha durará mucho tiempo.

6. (No obstante, Ya no) su enfermedad, el niño se negó a quedarse en la cama.

7. Durante casi medio mes, eso es, (quince días, ocho días), tenía fiebre.

8. Algo extraordinario ocurrió (el año que viene, el año pasado).

9. Descansé un rato, y (ya lo creo, ya no) estoy cansado.

10. Le encontré (más tarde, la semana que viene), comiendo fresas.

E. Conteste Vd. en español en frases completas.

1. ¿Cuándo dice Vd. a un amigo "que lo pase Vd. bien"? _____

2. ¿Prefiere Vd. vacaciones de quince días o de dos meses? _____

3. ¿Debe pagar todo el mundo los impuestos? _____

4. ¿Todavía no ha leído Vd. el periódico de hoy? _____

5. ¿Fue Vd. al campo el año pasado? _____

6. ¿Desea Vd. ser médico, no obstante los muchos años de estudio? _____

7. Por la mañana, ¿se levanta Vd. más tarde que su mamá? _____

8. El mundo es redondo, ¿no es verdad? _____

9. ¿Piensa Vd. visitar un país hispanoamericano el año que viene? _____

10. ¿Dura mucho tiempo un partido de fútbol? _____

F. Traduzca Vd. al español las expresiones en inglés.

1. Hace *a long time* que le espero. _____

2. Tiene mala memoria; *nevertheless*, recuerda aquel día. _____

3. Pasaron las nubes y *later* salió el sol. _____

4. *Everyone* se reunió en la oficina. _____

5. Hay que añadir a la ensalada *a little* vinagre. _____

6. *A few* personas vieron la tragedia. _____

7. *Doubtless* Vd. me debe medio dólar. _____

8. ¿Comprende Vd. el sistema? *Not yet.* _____

9. *Notwithstanding* su terror, se lanzó sobre el ladrón. _____

10. *Last year* la familia pasó sus vacaciones en las montañas. _____

11. Ramón deseaba visitar a Buenos Aires *especially*. _____

12. Me dio la mano y me dijo: *"Good luck to you!"* _____

13. ¿Desea Vd. visitar la América Central? *I should say so!* _____

14. *Every* miércoles el veterano cobraba su pensión. _____

15. Su nieto *no longer* viene a visitarla. _____

16. Pasaron *two weeks* viajando por Francia. _____

17. *Little by little* Luisa logró llenar el saco. _____

18. Aquel mapa es incorrecto, *isn't it?* _____

19. Harán las tareas, *won't they?* _____

20. Roberto llegará *next month*. _____

G. Traduzca Vd. al español.

1. No doubt they will announce the news later. _____
_____

2. Last year we had a dog, but we no longer have it. _____
_____

3. He winds the clock every week; nevertheless, it stopped yesterday. _____
_____

4. You (*pl.*) study every day, don't you? _____
_____

5. Do you want a little milk with your coffee? I should say so! _____
_____

6. Next year I will spend much time in Europe. _____
_____

7. Everybody celebrates Christmas, especially the children. _____
_____

8. I'm leaving for (por) two weeks. Good luck to you! _____
_____

9. Little by little a few brave soldiers approached the city. _____
_____

10. In spite of her illness, she has not yet called the doctor. _____
_____

16. MASTERY EXERCISES

A. Traduzca Vd. al inglés las frases siguientes:

1. No le gustaba el vino, y se negó a beberlo. _____

2. Escribió acerca de los conquistadores que llevaron a cabo la conquista de América. _____

3. Al dar con el león, el explorador su puso pálido. _____

4. Se burlaba de las costumbres de los madrileños, sobre todo la siesta. _____

5. Ella acaba de casarse con su novio. _____

6. Nunca tengo bastante; es decir, cuanto más tengo, tanto más deseo. _____

7. Cuando el pintor tenía cuarenta años, ya gozaba de fama. _____

8. Al levantarse por la mañana, dio cuerda a su reloj. _____

9. Se aprovechó de sus oportunidades, y llegó a ser rico. _____

10. La madre se ocupa de dar de comer a la familia. _____

11. A las tres en punto de la tarde todavía no había vuelto. _____

12. Aunque hacía viento, salió a echar la carta al correo. _____

13. Muchas veces Colón soñó con el descubrimiento de una ruta diferente. _____

14. Los dos célebres autores se dieron la mano. _____

15. En cuanto a Isabel, es diligente y aprende de memoria las lecciones. _____

16. Se echó a volver a casa a pie, con paso rápido. _____

17. Me quedan solamente diez dólares y me toca pagar las entradas. _____

18. Asiste a la escuela, y generalmente llega allí a eso de las nueve. _ _ _ _ _ _ _ _ _ _ _ _ _ _

_ _

19. Se sirven del diccionario para ver lo que quieren decir las palabras. _ _ _ _ _ _ _ _ _ _ _ _ _

_ _

20. Hoy día las medias largas están de moda. _

_ _

21. El reloj dio las tres, y dentro de poco los alumnos salieron de la escuela. _ _ _ _ _ _ _ _ _ _

_ _

22. El comerciante ha de salir esta noche. _

_ _

23. El agricultor se puso en camino la semana pasada. _

_ _

24. No deje Vd. de llegar a tiempo. _

_ _

25. Cuando no está en casa, Dorotea echa de menos su radio. _ _ _ _ _ _ _ _ _ _ _ _ _ _ _ _ _

_ _

26. El chico tenía prisa, y en cuanto cobró el dinero, se fue. _ _ _ _ _ _ _ _ _ _ _ _ _ _ _ _ _

_ _

27. Por lo general, servían refrescos por la tarde. _

_ _

28. La mayor parte de los curas se dedican a ayudar a la raza humana. _ _ _ _ _ _ _ _ _ _ _ _

_ _

29. El jueves se enamoró de ella y decidió casarse, pero al día siguiente cambió de opinión. _ _ _ _ _ _ _ _

_ _

30. Mientras ponía la mesa, dejó caer dos platos y una cuchara. _ _ _ _ _ _ _ _ _ _ _ _ _ _ _ _

_ _

    B. Escriba Vd. un sinónimo de cada expresión en letra cursiva, escogiéndolo de la lista siguiente:

ahora mismo	hacerse
a pesar del	Hasta luego.
con mucho gusto	junto a
de pronto	lo más pronto posible
de vez en cuando	por eso
en lugar de	por supuesto
estaba a punto de	Que le vaya bien.
frente a	seguramente
hace sol	semana
le hace falta	tenga Vd. la bondad de

1. El jefe *de buena gana* le dio permiso para salir. _

2. Cada *ocho días*, la clase tiene que escribir al dictado. _ _ _ _ _ _ _ _ _ _ _ _ _ _ _ _ _ _

3. Estudió para *llegar a ser* periodista. _

4. Cuando salí del restaurante, el propietario me dijo: —*Que lo pase Vd. bien.* _ _ _ _ _ _ _ _ _

5. *De repente* el cantor se calló. ---------------------------------

6. Al despedirme de Rosa, le dije: —*Hasta la vista*. -----------------

7. *No obstante* el polvo, me gustaría vivir en esa ciudad. -----------

8. Es necesario ir ahí *cuanto antes*. --------------------------------

9. *En vez de* leer rápidamente, el alumno leyó despacio. -------------

10. *Al lado de* la joya había una tarjeta con el precio. --------------

11. *De cuando en cuando* el piloto estudiaba el mapa. -----------------

12. *En frente de* la plaza central había un palacio grande. -----------

13. El cocido contiene bastante sal, pero *le falta* pimienta. ---------

14. *Sin duda*, el maestro sabe pronunciar bien las palabras. ----------

15. *Desde luego*, el sol se pone en el oeste. ------------------------

16. Cuando las nubes pasan, *hay sol*. -------------------------------

17. Cayó poca lluvia; *por consiguiente* la cosecha fue pobre. --------

18. *Haga Vd. el favor de* pasarme el pan. ---------------------------

19. Ramón, ven acá *en seguida*. -----------------------------------

20. El vapor *estaba para* partir. ----------------------------------

C. Escriba Vd. un antónimo de cada expresión en letra cursiva, escogiéndolo de la lista siguiente:

a causa de	mucho
a la izquierda	rápidamente
bajó del	raras veces
de buena gana	salí mal
de noche	se pondrá
de pie	se puso
entró en	se puso a
hacía calor	tenía calor
hacía mal tiempo	todo el mundo
más tarde	ya no

1. Se apresuró a marcharse cuando *salió* el sol. -------------------

2. *Salí bien* en el examen de ayer. -------------------------------

3. Cada persona necesita *un poco de* cariño. -----------------------

4. *Nadie* comprende las obras de ese artista. ----------------------

5. El alcalde de la aldea asistió *de mala gana*. -------------------

6. En la estación el viajero *subió al* tren. -----------------------

7. *Se quitará* el sombrero de paja. -------------------------------

8. Estaba *sentada*, esperando la vuelta de su marido. --------------

9. Andando por las calles, el turista *tenía frío*. -----------------

10. El aduanero *dejó de* examinar los artículos. -------------------

11. *En seguida* se puso serio. ------------------------------------

12. Su esposa *todavía* es tan bella como antes. --------------------

13. *A la derecha* del anciano estaba su nieto. ---------------------

14. *Salió de* la casa, llevando el abrigo. -------------------------

15. *A menudo* tomaba el almuerzo en casa. _____

16. *Poco a poco* terminó la bebida. _____

17. Siempre *hacía buen tiempo* en el sur de aquel país. _____

18. *Hacía frío* en el templo aquel día. _____

19. *De día* atravesaron el río. _____

20. *A pesar de* su temor, no se movió. _____

D. Complete Vd. cada frase con una de las expresiones siguientes: (Cada expresión debe usarse solamente una vez.)

a caballo	que sí
a veces	subieron la escalera
billete de ida y vuelta	tal vez
de esta manera	tengo sueño
dio un paseo	todos los días
en voz alta	trató de
por todas partes	ya lo creo
prestó atención	

1. En la estación compró un _____.

2. Anunciaron _____ el resultado.

3. _____ quebrar una rama del árbol.

4. _____ a lo que dijo el sabio.

5. No sé si esos retratos valen mucho, pero creo _____.

6. _____ corriendo, para salvar a la señora.

7. _____ suelen pasar el día.

8. _____ esas uvas todavía están verdes.

9. _____ y quiero acostarme.

10. _____ de siete u ocho minutos.

11. ¿Es importante el estudio del español? ¡_____!

12. _____ la tierra está muy seca cuando no hay lluvia.

13. Vio acercarse la tropa, unos sesenta hombres, montados _____

14. Se hallan teléfonos _____.

15. _____ la zapatería se cierra a las cinco.

E. Subraye Vd. la forma correcta de **haber** o **hacer**.

1. El maestro interrumpió el discurso para (haber, hacer) una pregunta.

2. (Hubo, Hizo) un viaje a España porque sabía el idioma.

3. El guía nos dijo que (había, hacía) polvo en la calle.

4. ¿Qué tiempo (hay, hace) en Inglaterra en la primavera?

5. (Hubo, Hizo) una visita al mercado para comprar un regalo.

6. (Hay, Hace) fresco en mi dormitorio.

7. Se sentía sin fuerzas para (haber, hacer) el baúl.

8. (Hay, Hace) que dividir el pastel en partes iguales.

9. Se (había, hacía) tarde, y el niño metió los juguetes en la caja.

10. Detrás del monte (había, hacía) neblina.

11. De noche, cuando (hay, hace) luna, la naturaleza parece tranquila.

12. Durante la ausencia del rey, el ministro (había, hacía) de gobernador.

13. (Había, Hacía) pinturas interesantes en la pared.

14. (Hay, Hace) media hora que el empleado distribuyó los billetes.

15. Aunque (había, hacía) frío estábamos cómodos alrededor del fuego.

F. Traduzca Vd. al español las expresiones en inglés, empleando la forma correcta del verbo **gustar.**

1. *I like* los colores blanco y azul. _____

2. *Mary and Ann like* la corrida de toros. _____

3. *The teacher doesn't like* oír un ruido continuo en la clase. _____

4. *My brother doesn't like* cruzar las calles solo. _____

5. *We like* el trabajo de aquel carpintero. _____

6. *He likes* los alimentos típicos de Francia. _____

7. *You* (fam. sing.) *will like* el nuevo apartamiento. _____

8. *The children like* las cerezas frescas. _____

9. *He liked* el clima húmedo de aquel lugar. _____

10. *We like* escuchar las ideas del filósofo. _____

11. *They like* la España actual. _____

12. *She likes* los calcetines de nilón. _____

13. *I like* el mes de abril. _____

14. ¿*Would you like* (conditional) visitar la América del Sur? _____

15. *Arthur likes* los asientos de la primera fila. _____

G. Conteste Vd. en español en frases completas.

1. ¿Es posible leer y dormir a la vez? _____
_____

2. ¿Qué hace Vd. cuando tiene hambre? ¿Cuando tiene sed? _____
_____

3. Por lo general, ¿hay luna de día? _____

4. ¿Cuándo responde Vd. "de nada"? _____
_____

5. Al encontrarse con un conocido, ¿le da Vd. los buenos días? _____
_____

6. ¿Tiene Vd. miedo de viajar sin guía? _____
_____

7. ¿Come Vd. varias veces al día? _____

8. Para llegar al piso alto, ¿baja Vd. la escalera? _____
_____

9. ¿Siempre tiene Vd. razón? _____

10. ¿Tiene Vd. mucho que hacer en casa? _____

_____

11. ¿Cuándo cumplió Vd. catorce años? _____

_____

12. Cuando Vd. pide dinero a su papá, ¿pide Vd. en vano? _____

_____

13. ¿Hace Vd. preguntas al maestro si no comprende la lección? _____

_____

14. ¿Contesta Vd. a estas preguntas en voz baja? _____

_____

15. ¿Juega Vd. al béisbol en el mes de febrero? _____

_____

16. ¿Se ríe Vd. de los errores de sus compañeros? _____

_____

17. ¿Le gusta a Vd. dar un paseo en automóvil? _____

_____

18. Si una persona le habla a Vd. con cortesía, ¿contesta Vd. de ese modo también? _____

_____

19. ¿Se graduará Vd. el año que viene? _____

20. ¿Qué se pone Vd. cuando tiene las manos frías? _____

_____

H. Traduzca Vd. al español las expresiones en inglés.

1. Su sobrino *delayed in* abrir la puerta. _____

2. Entre risas y lágrimas *he took leave of* sus padres. _____

3. Estoy seguro de que *you will like* la comedia. _____

4. El representante *fulfilled* su promesa. _____

5. *What's the matter with you?* —preguntó la enfermera. _____

6. *I don't like* seguir los consejos de mis amigos. _____

7. Después que pasó el huracán, todos se sentaron *in the open air.* _____

8. *In the middle of the* bosque se encontraron con un lobo. _____

9. Cuando *the weather is good* estoy de buen humor. _____

10. Compre Vd. para ella algo precioso; *for example*, un diamante. _____

11. En agosto *she likes* ir viajando por muchos países. _____

12. *Again* tropezó con el vendedor de tortillas. _____

13. *Around* la casa había violetas y otras flores. _____

14. La reina se quejó de *having a headache.* _____

15. Cada persona nace sólo *once.* _____

16. *He relies on* la ayuda de su secretaria. _____

17. En *two weeks* recibió su pasaporte. _____

18. Siéntese Vd. en ese sillón, *please.* _____

19. Al verse libres, *they thanked the* libertador. _____

20. ¿Qué *do you think of* las novelas de ese escritor? _____

21. *At last* se atrevió a declarar su amor. _____

22. *I have to* firmar el acuerdo el miércoles. _____

23. Por la tarde *they like* pasar una hora agradable jugando al ajedrez. _____

24. El médico esperaba que el paciente pudiera mover la pierna, *at least.* _____

25. Comió mucho y *in this way* se puso gordo. _____

26. *A few* personas se paseaban por la avenida. _____

27. *There will be* fiesta el martes. _____

28. Aquella señora *is glad to* dar una limosna al pordiosero. _____

29. Llamaron *again* al médico. _____

30. *In the morning*, el director nos habló. _____

31. *Sometimes* pongo un disco en el tocadiscos. _____

32. Es menester *to be careful* cuando hay peligro. _____

33. *The artist likes* crear obras maestras. _____

34. *He hasn't been successful* como médico. _____

35. *Apparently*, los deportes no te interesan. _____

I. Traduzca Vd. al español.

1. Last year my uncle visited the capital twice. _____

_____

2. I always shake hands with my friends. _____

_____

3. When I invited her to the movies, she said: "All right." _____

_____

4. In this lesson there are many exercises to write. _____

_____

5. The maid packed the lady's trunk unwillingly. _____

_____

6. Study every day; in that way you'll learn much. _____

_____

7. I don't like the months of September and October. _____

_____

8. She was tired; nevertheless, she listened attentively. _____

_____

9. In the evening the family usually watches (the) television. _____

_____

10. George is not in favor of inviting Louis to the party. _____

_____

11. There were many wars in the nineteenth century. _____

_____

12. Paul and Rose like to play the piano. _____

_____

13. They announced that there would be a dance on Saturday. _____

_____

14. Do you know any famous people? I think not. _____

_____

15. Everyone knows that Robert loves his fiancée. _____

_____

16. They frequently spent the afternoon in the garden. _____

_____

17. In Madrid we often visited the Prado Museum. _____

_____

18. Yesterday afternoon he accompanied his mother to the doctor. _____

_____

19. In May the pupils think of the summer vacation. _____

_____

20. We enjoyed ourselves at Thomas' house. _____

_____

21. His neighbor was hungry and he fed him. _____

_____

22. She likes to eat oranges and apples. _____

_____

23. The judge thought [for] a long time. _____

_____

24. We like the chicken salad in that restaurant. _____

_____

25. The library is open today, isn't it? _____

_____

Part IV—*Vocabulary Building*

1. SYNONYMS

GROUP I

Synonyms	*Meanings*
acabar, terminar, concluir (y)	to finish, to end, to conclude
acaso, tal vez	perhaps
acordarse (ue) de, recordar (ue)	to remember
afecto, cariño, amor	affection, love
aguardar, esperar	to wait (for)
alegre, feliz, contento	happy, merry, gay
alumno, estudiante	pupil, student
alzar (c), elevar, levantar	to raise
amo, dueño, propietario	master, owner, boss
andar, caminar	to walk
antiguo, viejo	old, ancient
aplicado, diligente, trabajador	industrious, diligent, hard-working
asustar, espantar	to frighten, to scare
atravesar (ie), cruzar (c)	to cross
aún, todavía	still, yet
bastante, suficiente	enough, sufficient
batalla, combate, lucha	battle, fight, struggle
bello, hermoso	beautiful
bonito, lindo	pretty
broma, chiste	joke
buque, barco, vapor	ship, boat
cabello, pelo	hair
cara, rostro	face
célebre, famoso, ilustre	famous
colocar (qu), poner (g)	to put, to place
comprender, entender (ie)	to understand
conseguir (i, gu), obtener (ie, g)	to get, to obtain
contestar, responder	to answer, to reply
corto, breve	short
cuarto, habitación	room
cura, sacerdote	priest
dejar, permitir	to let, to allow, to permit
delgado, flaco	thin, slender

EJERCICIOS

A. Subraye Vd. el sinónimo de la palabra en letra cursiva.

1. *trabajador:* feliz, elevar, diligente

2. *broma:* barco, sacerdote, chiste

3. *alzar:* cruzar, levantar, caminar

4. *todavía:* corto, aún, acaso

5. *lucha:* combate, vapor, amor

6. *bastante:* suficiente, cabello, batalla

7. *cariño:* rostro, feliz, afecto

8. *terminar:* recordar, atravesar, concluir

9. *corto:* cabello, breve, antiguo

10. *conseguir:* obtener, esperar, continuar

B. A la izquierda de cada palabra de la lista *A*, escriba Vd. la letra de su sinónimo que aparece en la lista *B*.

	A	*B*
_ _ _ _ _	**1.** aguardar	*a.* cara
_ _ _ _ _	**2.** antiguo	*b.* esperar
_ _ _ _ _	**3.** diligente	*c.* habitación
_ _ _ _ _	**4.** cuarto	*d.* acaso
_ _ _ _ _	**5.** barco	*e.* aplicado
_ _ _ _ _	**6.** acabar	*f.* buque
_ _ _ _ _	**7.** tal vez	*g.* viejo
_ _ _ _ _	**8.** rostro	*h.* cura
_ _ _ _ _	**9.** hermoso	*i.* terminar
_ _ _ _ _	**10.** sacerdote	*j.* bello

C. Escoja Vd. de la lista siguiente un sinónimo de cada palabra en letra cursiva, y escríbalo en la forma correcta.

acordarse de	contestar	estudiante
alegre	cruzar	flaco
andar	dueño	pelo
bonito	entender	permitir
célebre	espantar	poner

1. El aduanero no nos *dejó* pasar. _____

2. José es el *propietario* de la tienda. _____

3. Las *colocó* en la mesa. _____

4. *Atraviesa* la calle. _____

5. El perro *asustó* al niño. _____

6. No sabía qué *responder*. _____

7. *Camina* rápidamente. _____

8. No *recuerdo* su nombre. _____

9. Ella *comprende* bien la aritmética. _____

10. Los indios son *delgados*. _____

11. Llegaron a una *linda* aldea. _____

12. Tenía el *cabello* rubio. _____

13. Quedó *contento* con el resultado. _____

14. Las espadas de Toledo son *famosas*. _____

15. El *alumno* aprendió el alfabeto. _____

D. Traduzca Vd. al español *de dos maneras* las palabras siguientes:

1. beautiful	_____	**9.** to walk	_____
2. master	_____	**10.** famous	_____
3. to wait for	_____	**11.** to finish	_____
4. perhaps	_____	**12.** thin	_____
5. pupil	_____	**13.** to answer	_____
6. happy	_____	**14.** face	_____
7. to understand	_____	**15.** to obtain	_____
8. enough	_____		

GROUP II

Synonyms	Meanings
demonio, diablo	devil
desear, querer (ie)	to want, to wish
despacio, lentamente	slowly
detenerse (ie, g), pararse	to stop
diferente, distinto	different
echar, arro ar, lanzar (c), tirar	to throw
empezar (ie), principiar, comenzar (ie)	to begin
enfadarse, enojarse	to become angry
enviar (í), mandar	to send
error, falta	error, mistake
esposo, marido	husband
grave, serio	serious
hallar, encontrar (ue)	to find
idioma, lengua	language
igual, semejante	similar, alike
invitar, convidar	to invite
irse, marcharse	to go away
jamás, nunca	never
lugar, sitio	place
maestro, profesor	teacher
miedo, temor	fear
mostrar (ue), enseñar	to show
país, nación	country, nation
pájaro, ave	bird
quedarse, permanecer (zc)	to remain
rogar (ue, gu), suplicar (qu)	to beg, to implore
romper, quebrar (ie)	to break
seguir (i, gu), continuar (ú)	to continue
sólo, solamente	only
sorprender, asombrar	to surprise
suceder, ocurrir	to happen, to occur
sufrir, padecer (zc)	to suffer
tonto, necio	foolish, stupid
volver (ue), regresar	to return

EJERCICIOS

A. Subraye Vd. el sinónimo de la palabra en letra cursiva.

1. *volver:*   lanzar, irse, regresar
2. *demonio:*   diablo, marido, lengua
3. *asombrar:*   padecer, sorprender, regresar
4. *suceder:*   marcharse, ocurrir, convidar
5. *suplicar:*   principiar, mandar, rogar
6. *despacio:*   sólo, lentamente, jamás
7. *marcharse:*   irse, seguir, volver
8. *país:*   ave, idioma, nación
9. *esposo:*   necio, marido, maestro
10. *continuar:*   echar, volver, seguir

B. A la izquierda de cada palabra de la lista *A*, escriba Vd. la letra de su sinónimo que aparece en la lista *B*.

	A	B
_____	1. mostrar	a. padecer
_____	2. sufrir	b. quebrar
_____	3. lugar	c. temor
_____	4. tonto	d. serio
_____	5. romper	e. pájaro
_____	6. grave	f. necio
_____	7. diferente	g. permanecer
_____	8. ave	h. distinto
_____	9. miedo	i. sitio
_____	10. quedarse	j. enseñar

C. Escoja Vd. de la lista siguiente un sinónimo de cada palabra en letra cursiva, y escríbalo en la forma correcta.

arrojar	hallar	pararse
comenzar	el idioma	profesor
convidar	igual	querer
enojarse	jamás	seguir
el error	mandar	sólo

1. Mi padre *se enfadó* conmigo. _____

2. Para el almuerzo tomó *solamente* queso y pan. _____

3. ¿Qué *desea* Vd.? _____

4. Se aprovecha de *las faltas* de los otros. _____

5. *Nunca* come en un restaurante. _____

6. *Tiró* el periódico al suelo. _____

7. *Empezaron* a cultivar la tierra. _____

8. Su amistad *continúa* como antes. _____

9. El nuevo *maestro* es de Alemania. _____

10. *Envió* la carta. _____

11. *Se detuvo* en el camino. _____

12. Le *invité* a tomar una copa de vino. _____

13. Arturo sabe hablar tres *lenguas*. _____

14. Estos artículos son *semejantes*. _____

15. No lo *encontró*. _____

D. Traduzca Vd. al español *de dos maneras* las palabras siguientes:

1. to invite	_____	9. the language	_____
2. the nation	_____	10. husband	_____
3. teacher	_____	11. to want	_____
4. slowly	_____	12. different	_____
5. to continue	_____	13. to throw	_____
6. only	_____	14. serious	_____
7. to go away	_____	15. to happen	_____
8. to return	_____		

2. ANTONYMS

GROUP I

abajo, below, downstairs — arriba, above, upstairs
abrir, to open — cerrar (ie), to close
acercarse (qu) (a), to approach — alejarse (de), to move away (from)
acordarse (ue) de, to remember — olvidarse de, to forget
alegre, happy, gay — triste, sad
algo, something — nada, nothing
alguien, someone, somebody — nadie, no one, nobody
alguno, some — ninguno, none
alto, high, tall — bajo, low, short
allí, there — aquí, here
amar, to love — odiar, to hate
amargo, bitter — dulce, sweet
amigo, friend — enemigo, enemy
amo, master — esclavo, slave
amor, love — odio, hate
ancho, wide — estrecho, narrow
anoche, last night — esta noche, tonight
antes (de), before — después (de), after
antiguo, old, ancient — moderno, modern
aparecer (zc), to appear — desaparecer (zc), to disappear
aprisa, quickly — despacio, slowly
ausente, absent — presente, present
bajar, to go down — subir, to go up
barato, cheap — caro, dear, expensive
bien, well — mal, badly, poorly
blanco, white — negro, black
bueno, good — malo, bad
caballero, gentleman — dama, lady
callarse, to keep quiet — hablar, to speak
cerca de, near — lejos de, far from
cielo, heaven, sky — tierra, earth, ground
comprar, to buy — vender, to sell
común, common — raro, rare
con, with — { sin, without / contra, against
contestar, to answer — preguntar, to ask
corto, short — largo, long

EJERCICIOS

A. Subraye Vd. el antónimo de la palabra en letra cursiva.

1. *amargo:*   bajo, caro, dulce

2. *tierra:*   alto, cielo, abajo

3. *nada:*   algo, alguno, alguien

4. *largo:*   pequeño, ancho, corto

5. *subir:*   aparecer, bajar, odiar

6. *amigo:*   malo, enemigo, bueno

7. *bajo:*   alto, triste, antiguo

8. *anoche:*   esta noche, ayer, antiguo

9. *comprar:*   subir, bajar, vender

10. *alguien:*   nada, nadie, algo

B. A la izquierda de cada palabra de la lista *A*, escriba Vd. la letra de su antónimo que aparece en la lista *B*.

	A		B
_____	1. amo	*a.*	dama
_____	2. despacio	*b.*	odio
_____	3. caballero	*c.*	raro
_____	4. común	*d.*	estrecho
_____	5. bien	*e.*	ninguno
_____	6. amor	*f.*	esclavo
_____	7. ancho	*g.*	caro
_____	8. barato	*h.*	contra
_____	9. con	*i.*	aprisa
_____	10. alguno	*j.*	mal

C. Escoja Vd. de la lista siguiente un antónimo de cada expresión en letra cursiva, y escríbalo en la forma correcta.

acercarse a	aquí	cerrar
acordarse de	arriba	desaparecer
alegre	ausente	después
amar	bueno	lejos
antiguo	callarse	negro

1. *Allí* se fabrica mucho hierro. _____

2. ¿Por qué estás tan *triste?* _____

3. El chófer vive *cerca* del doctor. _____

4. *Se olvidó de* atarlo. _____

5. El público no *habló.* _____

6. *Se alejaron de* la catedral. _____

7. El dueño *abrió* la habitación. _____

8. De pronto *apareció* el guardia. _____

9. Llevaba un impermeable *blanco.* _____

10. Tiene un humor *malo.* _____

11. *Antes* del huracán brilló el sol. _____

12. El alumno está *presente* frecuentemente. _____

13. Las botellas están *abajo.* _____

14. Ella *odia* el mes de febrero. _____

15. El hotel era *moderno.* _____

D. Conteste Vd. en sentido negativo, empleando en cada respuesta un antónimo de la palabra en letra cursiva.

EJEMPLOS: ¿Es *pequeña* la casa?   No, la casa es *grande*.

¿Siempre *se olvida* Vd. *de*   No, siempre *me acuerdo*
traer sus libros?   *de* traer mis libros.

1. ¿Es *amargo* el jugo de naranja? _____

2. ¿*Contesta* Vd. en español? _____

3. ¿Le gustan a Vd. las modas *antiguas?* _____

4. ¿Se lava Vd. *sin* jabón? _____

5. ¿Estuvo Vd. *ausente* el jueves pasado? _____

6. ¿Son *cortas* las vacaciones? _____

7. ¿Son *baratas* las legumbres? _____

8. ¿Es *blanco* el carbón? _____

9. ¿Tiene Vd. muchos *enemigos?* _____

10. ¿*Sube* Vd. la escalera para llegar al piso bajo? _____

_____

Acapulco es un lugar de recreo (vacation spot) en la costa occidental de
México. Es famoso por sus playas anchas y sus hoteles lujosos (luxurious).
Cada año miles de turistas se escapan (escape) del frío del invierno para
pasar las vacaciones aquí.

GROUP II

dar, to give	{ tomar, to take { recibir, to receive
debajo (de), under	encima (de), on top
débil, weak	fuerte, strong
delante de, in front of	detrás de, in back of, behind
despertarse (ie), to wake up	dormirse (ue, u), to fall asleep
día, day	noche, night
difícil, difficult	fácil, easy
duro, hard	blando, soft
empezar (ie, c), to begin	acabar, terminar, to end
encender (ie), to light, to ignite	apagar (gu), to put out, to extinguish
entrada, entrance	salida, exit
este, east	oeste, west
éxito, success	fracaso, failure
feliz, happy	triste, sad
fin, end	principio, beginning
flaco, thin	gordo, fat
frío, cold	caliente, hot
fuera, outside	dentro, inside
grande, large	pequeño, small
guerra, war	paz, peace
hermoso, beautiful	feo, ugly
héroe, hero	heroína, heroine
hombre, man	mujer, woman
hoy, today	{ mañana, tomorrow { ayer, yesterday
inteligente, intelligent	estúpido, stupid
ir, to go	venir (ie, g), to come
levantarse, to get up	{ sentarse (ie), to sit down { acostarse (ue), to go to bed
ligero, light	pesado, heavy
limpio, clean	sucio, dirty
lleno, full	vacío, empty
llorar, to cry	reír (i), to laugh
madre, mother	padre, father
marido, husband	esposa, wife
más, more	menos, less

EJERCICIOS

A. Subraye Vd. el antónimo de la palabra en letra cursiva.

1. *blando:*   feliz, duro, pesado

2. *débil:*   triste, ángel, fuerte

3. *levantarse:*   despertarse, sentarse, callarse

4. *delante:*   debajo, detrás, después

5. *empezar:*   acabar, recibir, reír

6. *éxito:*   pasado, entrada, fracaso

7. *limpio:*   vacío, principio, sucio

8. *día:*   ayer, noche, mañana

9. *entrada:*   salida, llegada, fin

10. *madre:*   mujer, heroína, padre

B. A la izquierda de cada palabra de la lista *A*, escriba Vd. la letra de su antónimo que aparece en la lista *B*.

	A	B
_ _ _ _ _	1. gordo	*a.* paz
_ _ _ _ _	2. guerra	*b.* flaco
_ _ _ _ _	3. fin	*c.* feo
_ _ _ _ _	4. ir	*d.* fuera
_ _ _ _ _	5. ligero	*e.* esposa
_ _ _ _ _	6. hermoso	*f.* venir
_ _ _ _ _	7. dentro	*g.* hombre
_ _ _ _ _	8. mujer	*h.* triste
_ _ _ _ _	9. marido	*i.* pesado
_ _ _ _ _	10. feliz	*j.* principio

C. Escoja Vd. de la lista siguiente un antónimo de cada palabra en letra cursiva, y escríbalo en la forma correcta.

ayer	encima	llorar
dar	este	mañana
difícil	frío	menos
dormirse	la heroína	pequeño
encender	levantarse	vacío

1. *Tomó* noventa dólares por la obra. --

2. Su plato está *lleno.* --

3. La oficina era muy *grande.* --

4. Hay *más* nieve ahora que había el año pasado. --

5. *Se acuesta* temprano. --

6. El piloto dice que llegaremos *hoy.* --

7. Es *fácil* entrar en el palacio. --

8. El lago está ochenta millas al *oeste.* --

9. *El héroe* se paseaba por la calle. --

10. La mujer *ríe.* --

11. *Apagaron* la luz. --

12. El niño *se despierta.* --

13. Algo extraordinario ocurrió *hoy.* --

14. Está *debajo* de la mesa. --

15. No me gustan los panecillos *calientes.* --

D. Conteste Vd. en sentido negativo, empleando en cada respuesta un antónimo de la palabra en letra cursiva.

EJEMPLO: ¿Se ve el sol durante *la noche?*

No, el sol se ve durante *el día.*

1. ¿Le gusta a Vd. *dar* regalos? _____

_____

2. ¿Son *calientes* las aguas de los ríos? _____

_____

3. ¿Son *blandas* las rocas? _____

_____

4. ¿Está *sucio* el suelo de su casa? _____

_____

5. ¿Se siente Vd. *fuerte* cuando tiene un resfriado? _____

_____

6. ¿Están los sótanos *encima de* las casas? _____

_____

7. ¿Son *estúpidos* sus compañeros de clase? _____

_____

8. ¿Se pone el sol en el *este?* _____

_____

9. ¿Es *pequeño* un rascacielos? _____

_____

10. ¿Lleva Vd. sobretodo *dentro de* la casa? _____

_____

GROUP III

mayor, older

mejor, better

mentir (ie, i), to lie

meter, to put (in)

mismo, same

morir (ue, u), to die

mucho(-s), much (many)

muerte, death

no, no

norte, north

obscuro, dark

perder (ie), to lose

perezoso, lazy

permitir, to permit

pobre, poor

ponerse (g), to put on

posible, possible

prestar, to lend

primero, first

príncipe, prince

recoger (j), to pick up

respuesta, answer

rey, king

rubio, blond

ruido, noise

sabio, wise

salir (g) (de), to leave

siempre, always

tarde, late

valiente, brave

verano, summer

verdad, truth

vicio, vice

viejo, old

vivo, alive

menor, younger

peor, worse

decir (i, g) la verdad, to tell the truth

sacar (qu), to take out

diferente, different

vivir, to live

poco(-s), little (few)

vida, life

sí, yes

sur, south

claro, light

{ hallar, to find
{ ganar, to win

trabajador, aplicado, hard-working

prohibir, to prohibit

rico, rich

quitarse, to take off

imposible, impossible

pedir (i) prestado, to borrow

último, last

princesa, princess

dejar caer, to drop

pregunta, question

reina, queen

moreno, brunette

silencio, silence

tonto, foolish

entrar (en), to enter

nunca, never

temprano, early

cobarde, cowardly

invierno, winter

mentira, lie

virtud, virtue

{ joven, young
{ nuevo, new

muerto, dead

EJERCICIOS

A. Subraye Vd. el antónimo de la palabra en letra cursiva.

1. *último:*   primero, vicio, perezoso

2. *ruido:*   vida, moreno, silencio

3. *tonto:*   temprano, sabio, poco

4. *peor:*   mayor, mejor, menor

5. *ganar:*   prestar, morir, perder

6. *mucho:*   poco, grande, pequeño

7. *muerte:*   virtud, vivo, vida

8. *rubio:*   moreno, rico, nuevo

9. *siempre:*   tarde, nunca, temprano

10. *menor:*   más, mejor, mayor

B. A la izquierda de cada palabra de la lista *A*, escriba Vd. la letra de su antónimo que aparece en la lista *B*.

	A	B
_ _ _ _ _	**1.** morir	*a.* invierno
_ _ _ _ _	**2.** respuesta	*b.* diferente
_ _ _ _ _	**3.** obscuro	*c.* vivo
_ _ _ _ _	**4.** valiente	*d.* temprano
_ _ _ _ _	**5.** mismo	*e.* cobarde
_ _ _ _ _	**6.** muerto	*f.* claro
_ _ _ _ _	**7.** perezoso	*g.* vivir
_ _ _ _ _	**8.** viejo	*h.* pregunta
_ _ _ _ _	**9.** tarde	*i.* trabajador
_ _ _ _ _	**10.** verano	*j.* joven

C. Escoja Vd. de la lista siguiente un antónimo de cada palabra en letra cursiva, y escríbalo en la forma correcta.

dejar caer	**mentir**	**posible**
entrar en	**meter en**	**prestar**
hallar	**norte**	**prohibir**
la princesa	**nuevo**	**quitarse**
la reina	**poco**	**mentiras**

1. *El rey* alabó a Colón.   _

2. El aduanero *perdió* el tabaco.   _

3. Aquel tranvía va hacia el *sur*.   _

4. *Muchos* agricultores son ricos.   _

5. La botica está llena de medicinas *viejas*.   _

6. Siempre *dice la verdad*.   _

7. ¿Quién lo *sacó de* la caja?   _

8. *Se puso* el suéter.   _

9. Emplea la boca para decir solamente *la verdad*.   _

10. Se *permite* fumar.   _

11. *Recogió* los papeles.   _

12. Dice que es *imposible* hacerlo.   _

13. *El príncipe* vivió en la torre.   _

14. El cocinero *salió de* la cocina.   _

15. Me *pidió prestados* diez dólares.   _

D. Conteste Vd. en sentido negativo, empleando en cada respuesta un antónimo de la palabra o expresión en letra cursiva.

EJEMPLO: ¿*Se pone* Vd. el sombrero al entrar en casa?

No, *me quito* el sombrero al entrar en casa.

1. ¿Prefiere Vd. ropa *obscura?* _____

   _____

2. ¿*Siempre* toma Vd. el desayuno tarde? _____

   _____

3. ¿Es Vd. *mayor* que su padre? _____

   _____

4. ¿Toca Vd. muchos discos *viejos* durante el día? _____

   _____

5. ¿Es Vd. *perezoso(-a)*? _____

   _____

6. ¿Tienen muchos *vicios* sus amigos? _____

   _____

7. ¿Tienen muchos diamantes los *pobres?* _____

   _____

8. ¿Iría Vd. hacia el *norte* para llegar a México? _____

   _____

9. ¿*Deja* Vd. *caer* papeles *al* suelo? _____

   _____

10. ¿Le gusta a Vd. el *ruido?* _____

   _____

3. WORDS FREQUENTLY CONFUSED

salir (de), to leave, to go out (of)
    Sale de la casa.   He leaves the house
dejar, to leave (something behind)
    Dejó el sombrero en la mesa.   He left the hat on the table.

volver, to return, to come back
    Vuelve a la escuela.   He is returning to school.
devolver, to return, to give back
    Devuelve la pluma.   He is returning the pen.

conocer, to know (a person)
    ¿Conoce Vd. a Juan Pérez?   Do you know John Pérez?
saber, to know (a fact), to know how to
    Sabe la respuesta.   He knows the answer.
    No *sé* nadar.   I don't know how to swim.

preguntar, to ask (a question, for information, etc.)
    —¿Qué hora es?—*preguntó* Juan.   "What time is it?" asked John.
pedir, to ask for, to request
    Pide la cuenta.   He asks for the check.

pasar, to spend (time)
    Pasa una semana en el campo.   He spends a week in the country.
gastar, to spend (money)
    Gasta mucho dinero.   He spends a great deal of money.

jugar, to play (a game)
    Juega al tenis.   He plays tennis.
tocar, to play (an instrument)
    Toca la guitarra.   He plays the guitar.

pensar en, to think of (to direct one's thoughts to)
    Piensa en su hermano.   He is thinking of his brother.
pensar de, to think of (to have an opinion about)
    ¿Qué *piensa* Vd. *de* su hermano?   What do you think of his brother?

poder, can (to be able physically)
    No *puede* caminar.   He can't walk.
saber, can (to know how to)
    No *sabe* bailar.   He can't (= doesn't know how to) dance.

haber, to have (followed by past participle)
    Ha escrito la lección.   She has written the lesson.
tener, to have (to possess)
    Tiene un perro.   She has a dog.

ponerse, to become (generally followed by an adjective indicating temporary change)
    Se pone enfermo (triste, pálido, serio).   He becomes sick (sad, pale, serious).
llegar a ser, to become (generally followed by a noun indicating effort toward a goal)
    Llegó a ser médico (abogado).   He became a doctor (lawyer).

tomar, to take
    Tomó la pluma.   He took the pen.
    Tomó el tranvía.   He took the streetcar.
llevar, to take (from one place to another)
    Llevó la carta al correo.   He took the letter to the post office.
    Me *llevó* al cine.   He took me to the movies.

país, country (nation)
    España es un *país.*   Spain is a country.
campo, country (as contrasted with city)
    Voy al *campo* durante las vacaciones.   I'm going to the country during the vacation.

pequeño, little (size)
    Luisa es una niña *pequeña.*   Louise is a little girl.
poco, little (quantity)
    Tengo *poco* dinero.   I have little money.

hora, time (hour of day)
    ¿Qué *hora* es?   What time is it?
vez, time (part of a series)
    Lo hace muchas *veces.*   He does it many times (often).
tiempo, time (duration of time)
    Pasa mucho *tiempo* en casa.   She spends a lot of time at home.

pero, but
    La silla es bonita, *pero* no es cómoda.   The chair is pretty, but it's not comfortable.
sino, but (meaning *but on the contrary,* after a negative clause)
    No es verde, *sino* azul.   It's not green but blue.

EJERCICIOS

A. Subraye Vd. la palabra entre paréntesis que correctamente complete la frase.

1. No tomé té (pero, sino) café.
2. Todos los días (pienso de, pienso en) ti.
3. ¿Dónde (dejó, salió) Vd. la aguja?
4. ¿Cuánto dinero (gastó, pasó) Vd.?
5. ¿(Conoce, Sabe) Vd. al alcalde?
6. Le (pidió, preguntó) cómo estaba.
7. (Juega, Toca) el piano muy bien.
8. (Llegó a ser, Se puso) pálido.
9. En el (campo, país), lejos de la ciudad, estaba contenta.
10. ¿Le gusta a Vd. (jugar, tocar) al ajedrez?
11. Tengo que (llevar, tomar) el libro a la biblioteca.
12. Él me (devolvió, volvió) la botella.
13. Hace mucho (hora, tiempo, vez) que estoy aquí.
14. ¿A quién (ha, tiene) consultado Vd.?
15. Tiene (pequeña, poca) inteligencia.

16. El cura es viejo (pero, sino) muy fuerte.

17. Voy a (gastar, pasar) un mes en un país europeo.

18. (Llegó a ser, Se puso) capitán.

19. ¿Qué (piensas de, piensas en) la nueva maestra?

20. ¿Qué (hora, tiempo) es?

B. Traduzca Vd. al español las expresiones en inglés.

1. *I left* del laboratorio a las ocho. --

2. Tengo un gato *little*. --

3. ¿Quién *took* el diccionario? --

4. *He asked for* una habitación grande. --

5. *She returned* en julio. --

6. ¿*Do you know* su dirección? --

7. *Leave* Vd. el libro sobre el escritorio. --

8. Nos va a *to take* al circo. --

9. *He has* sus juguetes. --

10. ¿A qué *time* llegó Vd. al despacho? --

11. *They can* leer en alemán. --

12. Estoy enfermo, y *I cannot* montar a caballo. --

13. ¿*How many times* se paseó él delante del balcón? --

14. Es de un *country* extranjero. --

15. No llegará hoy *but* mañana. --

C. Traduzca Vd. al español.

1. Return the pencil to Alfred. --

2. I often think of my friend Charles. --

3. It isn't easy, but difficult. --

4. He became a famous actor. --

5. Can you play the violin? --

6. At what time do they eat lunch? --

7. I know his sister Carmen. --

8. The child became very ill. --

9. I spent nine dollars yesterday. --

10. Where did you leave the umbrella? --

4. WORD BUILDING

A. Some nouns drop their final vowel and add **-ero** to indicate the person associated with the noun; for example:

    la aventura, the adventure   **el aventurero,** the adventurer
    la cocina, the kitchen   **el cocinero,** the cook

In each blank, write the correct Spanish noun.

1. **la carta,** the letter   _____, the letter carrier
2. **la marina,** the navy   _____, the sailor
3. **el mensaje,** the message   _____, the messenger
4. **la obra,** the work   _____, the worker
5. **el tesoro,** the treasure   _____, the treasurer
6. **el viaje,** the trip   _____, the traveler
7. **la guerra,** the war   _____, the warrior
8. **la aduana,** the custom house   _____, the customs inspector
9. **el zapato,** the shoe   _____, the shoemaker
10. **el coche,** the car, coach   _____, the driver, coachman

B. Some nouns ending in **-ero** change to **-ería** to indicate the shop or store in which the person works; for example:

    el barbero, the barber   **la barbería,** the barber shop
    el librero, the book seller   **la librería,** the book store

In each blank, write the correct Spanish noun.

1. **el carnicero,** the butcher   _____, the butcher shop
2. **el joyero,** the jeweler   _____, the jewelry shop
3. **el lechero,** the milkman   _____, the dairy
4. **el panadero,** the baker   _____, the bakery shop
5. **el peluquero,** the hairdresser   _____, the beauty parlor
6. **el zapatero,** the shoemaker   _____, the shoe store
7. **el pastelero,** the pastry baker   _____, the pastry shop
8. **el sombrerero,** the hat seller   _____, the hat store
9. **el florero,** the florist   _____, the flower shop
10. **el relojero,** the watchmaker   _____, the watchmaker's shop

C. Some nouns are derived from the past participle of the verb; for example:

    resultar, to result   **el resultado,** the result
    oír, to hear   **el oído,** the ear
    decir, to say   **el dicho,** the saying

In each blank, write the correct Spanish noun.

1. **emplear,** to employ   _____, the employee
2. **pescar,** to fish   _____, the fish

  3. cuidar, to take care of _____, the care

  4. vestir, to dress _____, the dress

  5. hacer, to do _____, the deed

  6. aparecer, to appear _____, the apparition

  7. asar, to roast _____, the roast

  8. cocer, to cook _____, the stew

  9. conocer, to know _____, the acquaintance

10. contener, to contain _____, the contents

D. Some feminine nouns are formed from past participles by changing the **-o** ending to **-a;** for example:

        entrar, to enter   **la entrada,** the entrance
        beber, to drink   **la bebida,** the drink
        ver, to see   **la vista,** the sight, view

In each blank, write the correct Spanish noun.

  1. nevar, to snow _____, the snowfall

  2. caer, to fall _____, the fall

  3. comer, to eat _____, the meal

  4. herir, to wound _____, the wound

  5. salir, to leave _____, the exit

  6. llegar, to arrive _____, the arrival

  7. parar, to stop _____, the stop

  8. mirar, to look at _____, the look, glance

  9. volver, to return _____, the return

10. huir, to flee _____, the flight

E. Some radical changing verbs have a corresponding noun with a radical change; for example:

        el almuerzo, the lunch   **almorzar,** to lunch
        la lluvia, the rain   **llover,** to rain

In each blank, write the correct Spanish verb.

  1. el encuentro, the meeting _____, to meet

  2. el juego, the game _____, to play

  3. la nieve, the snow _____, to snow

  4. el comienzo, the beginning _____, to begin

  5. el cuento, the story _____, to relate

  6. el sueño, the dream _____, to dream

  7. el vuelo, the flight _____, to fly

  8. la prueba, the proof _____, to prove

  9. el recuerdo, the remembrance _____, to remember

10. el gobierno, the government _____, to govern

F. Some nouns are formed from verbs by dropping the **-ar** ending of the verb and adding **-amiento**, or dropping the **-er** or **-ir** ending of the verb and adding **-imiento**; for example:

casar, to marry   **el casamiento,** the marriage
establecer, to establish **el establecimiento,** the establishment

In each blank, write the correct Spanish noun.

1. **descubrir,** to discover _____, the discovery

2. **mover,** to move _____, the movement

3. **nacer,** to be born _____, the birth

4. **pensar,** to think _____, the thought

5. **sentir,** to feel _____, the feeling

6. **consentir,** to consent _____, the consent

7. **nombrar,** to name _____, the naming, nomination

8. **entender,** to understand _____, the understanding

9. **conocer,** to know _____, the knowledge

10. **ofrecer,** to offer _____, the offer

G. Some nouns are derived from verbs by dropping the **-r** of the infinitive and adding **-ador** to the stems of **-ar** verbs, **-edor** to the stems of **-er** verbs, and **-idor** to those of **-ir** verbs; for example:

trabajar, to work   **el trabajador,** the worker
comer, to eat   **el comedor,** the dining room
servir, to serve   **el servidor,** the servant

In each blank, write the correct Spanish noun.

1. **conquistar,** to conquer _____, the conqueror

2. **gobernar,** to govern _____, the governor

3. **beber,** to drink _____, the drinker

4. **hablar,** to speak _____, the speaker

5. **pensar,** to think _____, the thinker

6. **fundar,** to found _____, the founder

7. **pescar,** to fish _____, the fisherman

8. **vencer,** to conquer _____, the conqueror

9. **descubrir,** to discover _____, the discoverer

10. **explorar,** to explore _____, the explorer

H. Some nouns are formed from adjectives by dropping the final vowel of the adjective and adding **-eza**; for example:

bello, beautiful   **la belleza,** the beauty
limpio, clean   **la limpieza,** the cleanliness

Note. Adjectives ending in **-co** change **c** to **qu** before adding **-eza**; for example:

flaco, thin   **la flaqueza,** the thinness

In each blank, write the correct Spanish noun.

1. **pobre,** poor _____, the poverty

2. **triste,** sad _____, the sadness

3. **rico,** rich _____, the wealth

4. **franco,** frank _____, the frankness

5. **noble,** noble _____, the nobility

6. **agudo,** sharp _____, the sharpness

7. **puro,** pure _____, the purity

8. **vivo,** lively _____, the liveliness

9. **grande,** great _____, the greatness

10. **ligero,** light _____, the lightness

I. Some English nouns ending in *-ty* are translated into Spanish by changing *-ty* to **-dad;** for example:

> brutality, **la brutalidad**
> capacity, **la capacidad**

Translate the following English nouns into Spanish:

1. cruelty _____   6. society _____

2. curiosity _____   7. unity _____

3. generosity _____   8. university _____

4. humanity _____   9. activity _____

5. reality _____   10. prosperity _____

J. Some English nouns ending in *-tion* are translated into Spanish by changing *-tion* to **-ción;** for example:

> invention, **la invención**
> section, **la sección**

Translate the following English nouns into Spanish:

1. nation _____   6. civilization _____

2. conversation _____   7. action _____

3. description _____   8. direction _____

4. invitation _____   9. construction _____

5. intention _____   10. operation _____

K. A number of adjectives are formed from nouns by adding **-oso** (English *-ous*) to the stem of the noun; for example:

> **número,** number   **numeroso,** numerous
> **religión,** religion   **religioso,** religious

In each blank, write the correct form of the adjective.

1. **furia,** fury _____, furious   6. **delicia,** delight _____, delightful

2. **fama,** fame _____, famous   7. **poder,** power _____, powerful

3. **maravilla,** marvel _____, marvelous   8. **roca,** rock _____, rocky

4. **peligro,** danger _____, dangerous   9. **silencio,** silence _____, silent

5. **precio,** price _____, precious   10. **amor,** love _____, amorous

5. CLASSIFIED VOCABULARY

GROUP I

La familia, family

el padre, father
la madre, mother
el hijo, son
la hija, daughter
el hermano, brother
la hermana, sister
el primo, cousin
la prima, cousin
mamá, mother
papá, dad

el abuelo, grandfather
la abuela, grandmother
el tío, uncle
la tía, aunt
el sobrino, nephew
la sobrina, niece
los padres, parents
los parientes, relatives
el nieto, grandson
la nieta, granddaughter

La casa, home

la casa particular, private house
el piso, floor, story, apartment
el apartamiento, apartment
la habitación, room, bedroom
la alcoba ⎫
el dormitorio ⎭ bedroom
el comedor, dining room
la cocina, kitchen
la sala, living room
el cuarto de baño, bathroom
la puerta, door

la ventana, window
la escalera, stairs
el armario ⎫
el ropero ⎭ closet
el techo, ceiling, roof
el suelo, floor
la pared, wall
el sótano, cellar
el patio, patio
el jardín, garden
el garaje, garage

Los muebles, furniture

la mesa, table
la silla, chair
la butaca ⎫
el sillón ⎭ armchair
la cama, bed
la lámpara, lamp
la cortina, curtain
el sofá, sofa
el escritorio, desk

el espejo, mirror
la cómoda, bureau
el tocador, dresser
la alfombra, carpet
el cuadro, picture
la estufa, stove
la nevera ⎫
el refrigerador ⎭ refrigerator

Los alimentos, foods

el huevo, egg
el queso, cheese
el pan, bread
la mantequilla, butter
la carne, meat
el pescado, fish
la sopa, soup
el arroz, rice
la albóndiga, meat ball
la papa ⎫
la patata ⎭ potato

el pollo, chicken
el postre, dessert
la ensalada, salad
la legumbre, vegetable
el helado, ice cream
el pastel, pie, cake
la sal, salt
la pimienta, pepper
el azúcar, sugar

Las bebidas, beverages

el **café,** coffee
el **té,** tea
la **leche,** milk
la **crema,** cream
el **jugo (de naranja),** (orange) juice

la **gaseosa,** soda pop
el **agua,** water
el **vino,** wine
el **chocolate,** chocolate
la **cerveza,** beer

EJERCICIOS

A. En cada grupo, subraye Vd. la palabra que no tiene relación con las otras palabras.

1. mesa, sal, cama, silla, alfombra, espejo

2. leche, crema, vino, agua, té, sofá

3. carne, alcoba, sala, cocina, comedor, ventana

4. abuelo, suelo, hijo, hermano, sobrino, primo

5. queso, pan, mantequilla, sótano, azúcar, legumbre

6. tío, ropero, padre, hermana, pariente, prima

7. pared, patio, garaje, sopa, puerta, armario

8. arroz, pollo, pimienta, pastel, huevo, cuadro

9. café, nevera, escritorio, butaca, lámpara, estufa

10. jugo, chocolate, cerveza, gaseosa, patata, vino

B. Indique Vd. si las frases siguientes son *verdad* o *mentira*. Si la frase es verdad, escriba la palabra *verdad;* si la frase es mentira, corríjala Vd. cambiando las palabras en letra cursiva.

1. La alfombra cubre *el techo*. _____

2. El azúcar es *amargo*. _____

3. La leche es *una bebida*. _____

4. Dormimos en *una cama*. _____

5. El hermano de mi madre es *mi tío*. _____

6. Hay legumbres en *una ensalada*. _____

7. Hay *tres* paredes en un cuarto. _____

8. Una abuela tiene *nietos*. _____

9. Una casa particular tiene *muchos pisos*. _____

10. Los helados se guardan en *una estufa caliente*. _____

C. Complete Vd. cada frase, subrayando la palabra correcta.

1. Si Juana es mi tía, yo soy su (*a*) primo (*b*) sobrino (*c*) hijo.

2. Mi madre prepara la comida en (*a*) el comedor (*b*) el dormitorio (*c*) la cocina.

3. Me lavo la cara en (*a*) el cuarto de baño (*b*) el jardín (*c*) el tocador.

4. Pongo sal y (*a*) postre (*b*) pimienta (*c*) pescado   en la carne.

5. Nos miramos en (*a*) una lámpara (*b*) un espejo (*c*) un sillón.

6. Para llegar al piso alto, subo (*a*) la pared (*b*) la escalera (*c*) el vestíbulo.

7. Generalmente descanso en (*a*) el sillón (*b*) el refrigerador (*c*) el queso.

8. Se entra en una casa por (*a*) la ventana (*b*) el suelo (*c*) la puerta.

9. Guardamos la ropa en (*a*) la alfombra (*b*) la estufa (*c*) la cómoda.

10. En la pared cuelgo (*a*) una cama (*b*) una albóndiga (*c*) un cuadro.

D. Complete Vd. cada frase.

1. Tres cosas que generalmente se toman en el desayuno son --------------------------------
----

2. Tres parientes que viven en mi casa son --------------------------------
----

3. Tres muebles que se hallan en la sala son --------------------------------
----

4. Tres palabras que indican un cuarto de dormir son --------------------------------
----

5. Tres cosas que me gusta tomar cuando tengo sed son --------------------------------
----

6. Tres alimentos que no contienen azúcar son --------------------------------
----

7. Tres parientes míos que no son hijos de mis padres son --------------------------------
----

8. Tres cosas que forman parte de la cena son --------------------------------
----

9. Tres muebles que se hallan en la alcoba son --------------------------------
----

10. Tres muebles en que una persona puede sentarse son --------------------------------
----

GROUP II

Las frutas, fruits

la **manzana,** apple
la **pera,** pear
la **banana,** banana
la **naranja,** orange
la **piña,** pineapple
el **melón,** melon
la **uva,** grape
la **sandía,** watermelon

la **cereza,** cherry
el **melocotón,** peach
la **fresa,** strawberry
la **nuez,** nut
la **toronja,** grapefruit
la **ciruela,** plum
el **limón,** lemon

El servicio de mesa, tableware

la **taza,** cup
el **vaso,** glass
la **copa,** (wine) glass
el **tenedor,** fork
la **cuchara,** spoon

el **cuchillo,** knife
el **plato,** plate
la **servilleta,** napkin
el **mantel,** tablecloth

El cuerpo, body

la **cara,** face
la **cabeza,** head
el **pelo**
el **cabello** } hair
el **ojo,** eye
la **boca,** mouth
la **oreja,** ear
el **oído,** (inner) ear
la **nariz,** nose
el **labio,** lip
el **diente,** tooth
la **mano,** hand
la **uña,** fingernail

el **dedo,** finger, toe
el **brazo,** arm
el **pie,** foot
la **pierna,** leg
el **cuello,** neck
el **estómago,** stomach
la **lengua,** tongue
el **corazón,** heart
el **pecho,** chest
el **hombro,** shoulder
la **espalda,** back
la **sangre,** blood

La ropa, clothing

el **traje,** suit
el **calcetín,** sock
la **camisa,** shirt
los **pantalones,** trousers
la **corbata,** tie
el **sombrero,** hat
el **pañuelo,** handkerchief
el **abrigo**
el **gabán** } overcoat
el **sobretodo**
el **impermeable,** raincoat
la **chaqueta,** jacket
el **vestido,** dress

la **media,** stocking
la **blusa,** blouse
la **falda,** skirt
la **bolsa,** purse
el **zapato,** shoe
el **guante,** glove
el **cinturón,** belt
el **suéter,** sweater
la **gorra,** cap
el **bolsillo,** pocket
prenda de vestir, garment, article of clothing

Los colores, colors

negro, black
blanco, white
rojo, red
verde, green

amarillo, yellow
azul, blue
gris, gray
pardo, brown

EJERCICIOS

A. En cada grupo, subraye Vd. la palabra que no tiene relación con las otras palabras.

1. azul, rojo, amarillo, boca, verde, gris

2. cuchillo, tenedor, pardo, taza, cuchara, servilleta

3. zapato, corbata, falda, traje, labio, camisa

4. oreja, corazón, calcetín, nariz, cuello, ojo

5. naranja, manzana, pecho, piña, uva, melón

6. melocotón, hombro, uña, sangre, lengua, estómago

7. toronja, ciruela, banana, pera, fresa, abrigo

8. sobretodo, blusa, blanca, pantalones, media, cinturón

9. oído, cara, nariz, vaso, espalda, pelo

10. impermeable, nuez, suéter, sombrero, gabán, chaqueta

B. Indique Vd. si las frases siguientes son *verdad* o *mentira*. Si la frase es verdad, escriba la palabra *verdad;* si la frase es mentira, corríjala Vd. cambiando las palabras en letra cursiva.

1. *La cabeza* es una parte del cuerpo humano. --

2. *El pañuelo* es una fruta. --

3. *El mantel* sirve para cubrir la mesa. --

4. Cortamos la carne con *una cuchara.* --

5. Hablamos con *la boca.* --

6. La gorra se lleva en *los pies.* --

7. Una copa se usa para beber *vino.* --

8. Las bananas son *negras.* --

9. La sandía y la cereza son *partes del cuerpo.* --

10. Las mujeres llevan *vestidos.* --

C. Complete Vd. cada frase, subrayando la palabra correcta.

1. La ciruela es (*a*) azul (*b*) roja (*c*) amarilla.

2. Tenemos cinco (*a*) dedos (*b*) pies (*c*) dientes   en cada mano.

3. Usamos (*a*) las orejas (*b*) las piernas (*c*) los brazos   para andar.

4. Me pongo los guantes en (*a*) los cabellos (*b*) los labios (*c*) las manos.

5. Tomamos el café en (*a*) la espalda (*b*) una taza (*c*) un plato.

6. Para mascar uso (*a*) la nariz (*b*) la bolsa (*c*) los dientes.

7. El niño no se atrevió a abrir (*a*) la boca (*b*) la taza (*c*) la oreja.

8. Se hace vino de (*a*) las uñas (*b*) los limones (*c*) las uvas.

9. Bajo el sobretodo se lleva (*a*) el sombrero (*b*) la chaqueta (*c*) los guantes.

10. Llevo mi dinero en (*a*) el pelo (*b*) los ojos (*c*) el bolsillo.

D. Complete Vd. cada frase.

1. Tres prendas de vestir femeninas son _____

_____

2. Tres frutas rojas son _____

_____

3. Tres artículos de metal que se emplean para comer son _____

_____

4. Tres partes del cuerpo encima del cuello son _____

_____

5. Tres colores son _____

_____

6. Tres cosas que una persona puede llevar para protegerse del frío son _____

_____

7. Tres cosas que se emplean para beber son _____

_____

8. Tres frutas amarillas son _____

_____

9. Tres partes del cuerpo que se encuentran en la boca son _____

_____

10. Tres prendas de vestir masculinas son _____

_____

GROUP III

Las profesiones, professions

el abogado, lawyer
el médico, doctor
el dentista, dentist
el ingeniero, engineer
el (la) profesor(-a) ⎫
el (la) maestro(-a) ⎭ teacher
el artista, artist
el científico, scientist

el escritor, writer
el poeta, poet
el cura, priest
el contador, accountant
el periodista, journalist
la enfermera, nurse
el juez, judge
el boticario, druggist

Los oficios, trades, occupations

el barbero, barber
el peluquero, hairdresser
el carnicero, butcher
el carpintero, carpenter
el comerciante, merchant
el criado, servant
la criada, maid
el dependiente, clerk (in a store)
el chófer, chauffeur
el empleado, employee
el piloto, pilot

el agricultor, farmer
la modista, dressmaker
el mozo, waiter
el panadero, baker
el pescador, fisherman
el plomero, plumber
el sastre, tailor
el zapatero, shoemaker
la secretaria, secretary
la taquígrafa, stenographer
el vendedor, seller

Los materiales, materials

el oro, gold
la plata, silver
el hierro, iron
el cobre, copper
la piedra, stone
la madera, wood
el vidrio, glass
el diamante, diamond
el aluminio, aluminum
el nilón, nylon

el acero, steel
el carbón, coal
el paño, cloth
la lana, wool
el algodón, cotton
la seda, silk
el cuero, leather
la piel, fur
el caucho, rubber
el rayón, rayon

Los medios de transporte, means of transportation

el automóvil, automobile
el avión, airplane
el tren, train
el ferrocarril, railroad
el vapor, steamship

el tranvía, streetcar
el autobús, bus
el taxi, taxi
el subterráneo, subway
la bicicleta, bicycle

EJERCICIOS

A. En cada grupo, subraye Vd. la palabra que no tiene relación con las otras palabras.

1. oro, empleado, madera, hierro, piedra, vidrio

2. tren, tranvía, juez, autobús, avión, ferrocarril

3. abogado, cobre, médico, ingeniero, enfermera, cura

4. piloto, algodón, seda, lana, cuero, caucho

5. peluquero, carnicero, piel, sastre, dependiente, panadero

6. taxi, subterráneo, automóvil, tranvía, acero, tren

7. nilón, carbón, diamante, aluminio, plata, criada

8. mozo, poeta, artista, maestro, médico, madera

9. taquígrafa, pescador, vendedor, vapor, secretaria, chófer

10. dentista, periodista, rayón, científico, pintor, escritor

B. Indique Vd. si las frases siguientes son *verdad* o *mentira*. Si la frase es verdad, escriba la palabra *verdad;* si la frase es mentira, corríjala Vd. cambiando las palabras en letra cursiva.

1. El hierro es *un metal duro.* _____

2. *El cura* es un hombre religioso. _____

3. Podemos ir de los Estados Unidos a Sud América en *tranvía.* _____

4. *La modista* hace vestidos para las mujeres. _____

5. Muchas máquinas se fabrican de *lana.* _____

6. *El médico* vende medicinas en una botica. _____

7. La mayor parte de nuestras monedas son o de *plata* o de *cobre.* _____

8. Fui al *plomero* para cortarme el pelo. _____

9. El taxi es el modo más *barato* de viajar. _____

10. *El carbón* y *los diamantes* se sacan de la tierra. _____

C. Complete Vd. cada frase, subrayando la palabra correcta.

1. Si estamos enfermos llamamos al (*a*) médico (*b*) abogado (*c*) contador.

2. El (*a*) sastre (*b*) zapatero (*c*) carpintero   hace trajes.

3. El (*a*) barbero (*b*) dependiente (*c*) agricultor   cultiva la tierra.

4. Va a la escuela en (*a*) vapor (*b*) bicicleta (*c*) avión.

5. El (*a*) comerciante (*b*) plomero (*c*) criado   compra y vende.

6. Los espejos son de (*a*) vidrio (*b*) madera (*c*) piel.

7. El viajar en (*a*) bicicleta (*b*) autobús (*c*) avión   es caro.

8. El (*a*) sastre (*b*) ingeniero (*c*) contador   construye puentes.

9. Del (*a*) pescador (*b*) carnicero (*c*) panadero   obtenemos alimentos del mar.

10. En el verano prefiero ropa de (*a*) lana (*b*) piel (*c*) algodón.

D. Complete Vd. cada frase.

1. Tres personas que deben escribir mucho en sus oficios son _____

2. Tres medios de ir al centro son _____

3. Tres metales son _____

4. Tres personas que trabajan al aire libre son _____

5. Tres materiales que se obtienen de los animales son _____

6. Tres personas que hacen prendas de vestir son _____

7. Tres paños son _____

8. Tres personas que se ocupan de cuidar a los enfermos son _____

9. Tres personas que trabajan en una tienda son _____

10. Tres personas que trabajan en una oficina son _____

GROUP IV

La naturaleza, nature

el cielo, sky
la tierra, earth
el sol, sun
la luna, moon
la estrella, star
la montaña ⎫
el monte ⎭ mountain
la colina, hill
el río, river

el mar, sea
el océano, ocean
el lago, lake
la isla, island
el bosque, forest, woods
la selva, jungle
el valle, valley
el paisaje, countryside

Los animales, animals

el caballo, horse
la vaca, cow
el toro, bull
el león, lion
el tigre, tiger
el oso, bear
el burro, donkey
el perro, dog
el gato, cat
el pájaro, bird

el lobo, wolf
el águila (*f.*), eagle
el pollo, chicken
la gallina, hen
el pavo, turkey
el elefante, elephant
el ratón, mouse
la oveja, sheep
el mono, monkey
la llama, llama

Países, habitantes, e idiomas, countries, inhabitants, and languages

España, Spain	los españoles, Spaniards	el español
los Estados Unidos, the United States	los norteamericanos, Americans	el inglés
Francia, France	los franceses, French	el francés
Italia, Italy	los italianos, Italians	el italiano
Alemania, Germany	los alemanes, Germans	el alemán
Inglaterra, England	los ingleses, English	el inglés
México, Mexico	los mexicanos, Mexicans	el español
la Argentina, Argentina	los argentinos, Argentinians	el español
el Brasil, Brazil	los brasileños, Brazilians	el portugués
Chile, Chile	los chilenos, Chileans	el español
el Canadá, Canada	los canadienses, Canadians	el inglés, el francés
China, China	los chinos, Chinese	el chino
Rusia, Russia	los rusos, Russians	el ruso

Los días de la semana, days of the week

lunes, Monday
martes, Tuesday
miércoles, Wednesday
jueves, Thursday

viernes, Friday
sábado, Saturday
domingo, Sunday

Los meses del año, months of the year

enero, January
febrero, February
marzo, March
abril, April
mayo, May
junio, June

julio, July
agosto, August
septiembre, September
octubre, October
noviembre, November
diciembre, December

Las estaciones del año, seasons of the year

la primavera, spring
el verano, summer

el otoño, autumn, fall
el invierno, winter

El tiempo, time

el segundo, second
el minuto, minute
la hora, hour
el día, day

la semana, week
el mes, month
el año, year
el siglo, century

EJERCICIOS

A. En cada grupo, subraye Vd. la palabra que no tiene relación con las otras palabras.

1. día, semana, vaca, siglo, año, mes

2. toro, selva, gato, perro, oso, águila

3. canal, río, lago, mar, océano, verano

4. colina, paisaje, primavera, bosque, valle, montaña

5. cielo, luna, estrella, tierra, oveja, sol

6. Italia, Rusia, Chile, Rosa, España, Francia

7. viernes, miércoles, sábado, otoño, jueves, lunes

8. invierno, mayo, julio, septiembre, agosto, junio

9. alemán, español, chileno, italiano, norteamericano, domingo

10. octubre, martes, febrero, noviembre, abril, enero

B. Indique Vd. si las frases siguientes son *verdad* o *mentira.* Si la frase es verdad, escriba la palabra *verdad;* si la frase es mentira, corríjala cambiando las palabras en letra cursiva.

1. Hace *calor* en el invierno.   _____

2. Hay estrellas en el *suelo.*   _____

3. *Enero* es el primer mes del año.   _____

4. Hay agua en *el mar.*   _____

5. *Viernes* es un día de la semana.   _____

6. *Los pájaros* vuelan.   _____

7. No hay árboles en *un bosque.*   _____

8. El Brasil está en *Asia*.   `------------------------------`

9. Hay *noventa* segundos en un minuto.   `------------------------------`

10. El león y el tigre son *animales feroces*.   `------------------------------`

C. Complete Vd. cada frase, subrayando la palabra correcta.

1. Inglaterra y Alemania son países de (*a*) Sud América (*b*) Europa (*c*) Asia.

2. La primavera es (*a*) un día (*b*) una estación (*c*) un mes   del año.

3. Hay cien años en (*a*) un mes (*b*) una semana (*c*) un siglo.

4. (*a*) La gallina (*b*) El burro (*c*) La llama   da huevos.

5. El gato coge (*a*) ratones (*b*) lobos (*c*) monos.

6. En México y la Argentina se habla (*a*) chino (*b*) portugués (*c*) español.

7. Marzo y diciembre son (*a*) días de la semana (*b*) meses (*c*) estaciones.

8. Un animal doméstico es el (*a*) elefante (*b*) lobo (*c*) caballo.

9. Los ingleses y los franceses viven en (*a*) Europa (*b*) Asia (*c*) la América del Sur.

10. Hay (*a*) sesenta (*b*) siete (*c*) veinte y cuatro   horas en un día.

D. Complete Vd. cada frase.

1. Tres países sudamericanos, con sus habitantes, son `----------------------------`

`------------------------------------------------------------------`

2. Tres animales que viven en el bosque son `----------------------------`

`------------------------------------------------------------------`

3. Tres formaciones geográficas que contienen agua son `-------------------`

`------------------------------------------------------------------`

4. Tres animales domésticos que tienen solamente dos patas (legs) son `------`

`------------------------------------------------------------------`

5. Tres meses que no tienen la letra "r" son `--------------------------`

`------------------------------------------------------------------`

6. Las tres estaciones del año en que no hace mucho frío son `--------------`

`------------------------------------------------------------------`

7. Tres países europeos, con sus habitantes, son `-------------------------`

`------------------------------------------------------------------`

8. Tres palabras que indican tierra alta son `---------------------------`

`------------------------------------------------------------------`

9. Tres países que forman parte de la América del Norte son `-------------`

`------------------------------------------------------------------`

10. Tres palabras que indican tiempo más largo que un día son `-----------`

`------------------------------------------------------------------`

6. MASTERY EXERCISES

A. Escriba Vd. los sustantivos que se forman de los adjetivos siguientes:

EJEMPLO: limpio—limpieza

silencioso—silencio

1. amoroso _____   9. numeroso _____
2. bello _____   10. peligroso _____
3. famoso _____   11. precioso _____
4. franco _____   12. religioso _____
5. furioso _____   13. rico _____
6. grande _____   14. triste _____
7. maravilloso _____   15. vivo _____
8. noble _____

B. Por cada cosa, indique Vd. la tienda y el tendero (storekeeper).

EJEMPLO: barba—barbería—barbero

1. carne _____   6. pan _____
2. flor _____   7. pastel _____
3. joya _____   8. reloj _____
4. leche _____   9. sombrero _____
5. libro _____   10. zapato _____

C. Escriba Vd. un sustantivo relacionado con cada verbo, y al lado del sustantivo escriba su significado.

EJEMPLO: oír—el oído, the ear

1. almorzar: _____   _____
2. asar: _____   _____
3. beber: _____   _____
4. cocer: _____   _____
5. comer: _____   _____
6. conquistar: _____   _____
7. contener: _____   _____
8. cuidar: _____   _____
9. emplear: _____   _____
10. explorar: _____   _____
11. fundar: _____   _____
12. gobernar: _____   _____
13. herir: _____   _____
14. llover: _____   _____

313

15. mover: ------------------------------ ------------------------------

16. nombrar: ------------------------------ ------------------------------

17. ofrecer: ------------------------------ ------------------------------

18. pescar: ------------------------------ ------------------------------

19. vestir: ------------------------------ ------------------------------

20. viajar: ------------------------------ ------------------------------

D. Escriba Vd. el verbo relacionado con cada sustantivo, y al lado del verbo escriba su significado.

EJEMPLO: la entrada—entrar, to enter

1. la bebida: ------------------------------ ------------------------------

2. el casamiento: ------------------------------ ------------------------------

3. el comedor: ------------------------------ ------------------------------

4. el comienzo: ------------------------------ ------------------------------

5. el descubrimiento: ------------------------------ ------------------------------

6. el empleado: ------------------------------ ------------------------------

7. el gobierno: ------------------------------ ------------------------------

8. la huida: ------------------------------ ------------------------------

9. el juego: ------------------------------ ------------------------------

10. la mirada: ------------------------------ ------------------------------

11. el nacimiento: ------------------------------ ------------------------------

12. la nieve: ------------------------------ ------------------------------

13. el pensamiento: ------------------------------ ------------------------------

14. la prueba: ------------------------------ ------------------------------

15. el recuerdo: ------------------------------ ------------------------------

16. el sentimiento: ------------------------------ ------------------------------

17. el sueño: ------------------------------ ------------------------------

18. la vista: ------------------------------ ------------------------------

19. el vuelo: ------------------------------ ------------------------------

20. la vuelta: ------------------------------ ------------------------------

E. En cada grupo, subraye Vd. las dos palabras del mismo significado.

1. cariño, pájaro, sitio, lugar, lucha

2. tirar, entender, colocar, asustar, echar

3. afecto, amor, marido, amo, cara

4. padecer, suplicar, invitar, rogar, enojarse

5. sufrir, asombrar, mandar, quebrar, enviar

6. levantar, elevar, conseguir, atravesar, suceder

7. suficiente, diligente, diferente, semejante, distinto

8. aguardar, esperar, lanzar, mostrar, enfadar

9. serio, error, temor, miedo, demonio

10. responder, volver, recordar, regresar, acabar
11. delgado, despacio, bello, célebre, hermoso
12. corto, lindo, alegre, necio, feliz
13. hallar, principiar, encontrar, parar, permitir
14. país, habitación, cuarto, dueño, maestro
15. caminar, cruzar, alzar, andar, empezar
16. vapor, broma, breve, chiste, bastante
17. antiguo, sacerdote, viejo, grave, flaco
18. aún, nunca, acaso, solamente, todavía
19. romper, concluir, poner, terminar, espantar
20. pelo, nación, batalla, cabello, falta

F. En cada grupo, subraye Vd. las dos palabras de significado contrario.

1. poco, reina, común, rubio, moreno
2. abrir, callarse, bajar, reír, cerrar
3. odio, hermoso, feo, pequeña, guerra
4. odiar, subir, permitir, amar, hablar
5. esclavo, enemigo, amigo, vicio, héroe
6. bueno, inteligente, limpio, fácil, estúpido
7. con, no, sin, dentro, algo
8. fuera, gordo, negro, blando, flaco
9. encender, mentir, sacar, meter, llorar
10. último, antiguo, fuerte, vacío, lleno
11. cobarde, triste, duro, hermoso, feliz
12. bien, mal, menor, nada, más
13. nadie, muerte, vida, invierno, fracaso
14. mayor, mejor, peor, menos, ninguno
15. hallar, prestar, prohibir, quitar, perder
16. abajo, antes, detrás, después, debajo
17. débil, alto, bajo, pesado, valiente
18. dulce, rico, nuevo, caro, barato
19. entrada, príncipe, fin, cielo, principio
20. delante, estrecho, arriba, salida, ancho

G. Subraye Vd. la palabra en español que correctamente traduzca la palabra en inglés.

1. new: nueve, nieve, nuevo, nuez
2. short: cortés, cortina, corto, corte
3. room: cuarto, cuadro, cuatro, cuadrado
4. care: ciudad, cuento, cuero, cuidado
5. cry: llevar, llegar, llorar, llover

6. put: matar, merecer, mentir, meter

7. month: menos, mes, mesa, misa

8. but: para, peral, pero, perro

9. go to bed: olvidar, adelantar, acordarse, acostarse

10. cross: atravesar, atreverse, alcanzar, aprovecharse

11. steel: cero, acero, acera, acerca

12. hair: caballo, caballero, cabeza, cabello

13. sky: cielo, suelo, ciego, cierto

14. shoulder: hombro, hombre, hambre, hierro

15. play: juzgar, ganar, jugar, jugo

16. nothing: naranja, nariz, nada, nadie

17. feel: sentarse, servirse, sentirse, asegurar

18. foolish: tonto, tesoro, tanto, todo

19. trip: viento, viaje, viejo, traje

20. dream: dormir, sonar, sonreír, soñar

21. fear: tirar, terminar, tener, temer

22. master: año, amor, amargo, amo

23. expensive: caro, barato, cada, carrera

24. long: grande, lago, ancho, largo

25. occupation: oficina, oficial, oficio, odio

26. clothing: rojo, paño, ropa, rubio

27. clean: linda, limpia, clara, lámpara

28. strong: fuerza, fuera, fuerte, fuego

29. struggle: lluvia, lucha, luego, lugar

30. beautiful: bello, hermano, hierro, heroína

31. summer: verano, verde, vano, invierno

32. century: sillón, sello, sitio, siglo

33. dining room: cocina, comida, sala, comedor

34. extinguish: alabar, pagar, apagar, aguardar

35. lend: preguntar, prestar, presentar, apresurar

36. weak: dedo, desagradable, débil, diablo

37. invite: convidar, contar, conseguir, consultar

38. egg: pan, pastel, huevo, queso

39. apple: manzana, toronja, naranja, fresa

40. coat: calcetín, abrigo, corbata, pañuelo

Part V—*Hispanic Civilization*

1. LA GEOGRAFÍA DE ESPAÑA

A. Situación:

1. España está situada en el sudoeste de Europa.

2. Ocupa casi toda la Península Ibérica (menos Portugal).

B. Extensión y Población:

1. Su extensión (area) es de unas 200,000 millas cuadradas, o cuatro veces más grande que la del Estado de Nueva York.

2. Tiene más de 37,000,000 (treinta y siete millones) de habitantes.

C. Sierras y Montañas:

1. Los **Pirineos** (en el nordeste, entre España y Francia).

2. Los **Cantábricos** (noroeste).

3. La **Sierra de Guadarrama** (centro).

4. La **Sierra Morena** (sur).

5. La **Sierra Nevada** (sur).

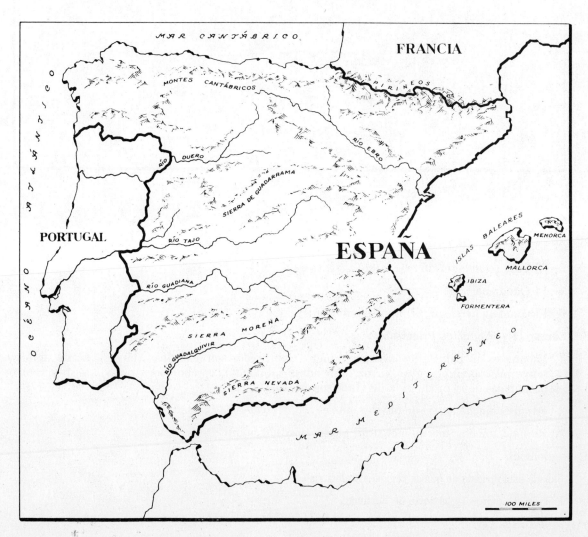

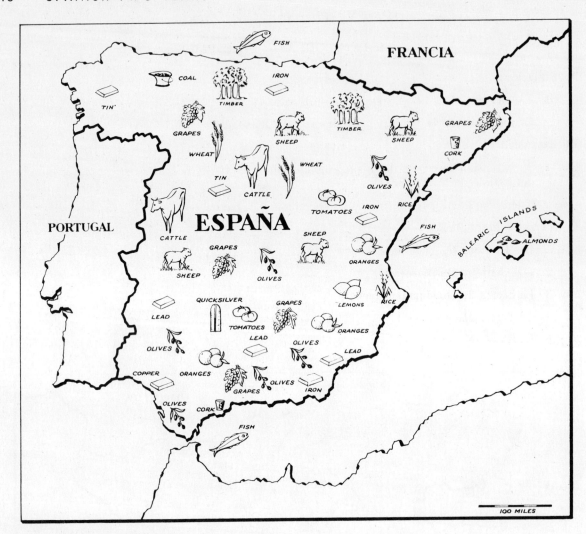

D. Ríos:

    1. El **Ebro** (norte).

    2. El **Duero** (norte).

    3. El **Tajo** (centro; el río más largo).

    4. El **Guadiana** (sur).

    5. El **Guadalquivir** (sur; el río más navegable).

E. Industrias y Productos Principales:

    1. España es un país agrícola. Sus productos principales son aceitunas (olives), aceite de oliva (olive oil), naranjas, uvas, arroz, almendras (almonds), corcho (cork), y vinos. Los centros principales de la producción de vinos son Málaga y Jerez.

    2. Exporta mucho aceite de oliva y vino.

    3. Riqueza minera: hierro, mercurio, plomo (lead), y cobre.

F. Regiones:

España está dividida en quince regiones tradicionales.

    1. **Galicia** (noroeste; al norte de Portugal).

    2. **Asturias** (norte).

3. **Cantabria** (norte).

4. **País Vasco** (norte; en los Pirineos).

5. **Navarra** (norte).

6. **Aragón** (nordeste).

7. **Cataluña** (nordeste).

8. **La Rioja** (centro).

9. **Castilla y León** (noroeste y centro).

10. **Castilla - La Mancha** (centro; al sur de Castilla y León).

11. **Madrid** (centro).

12. **Valencia** (este).

13. **Extremadura** (oeste).

14. **Murcia** (sudeste).

15. **Andalucía** (sur).

G. Idiomas:

1. El **español** (llamado también el **castellano**) es el idioma principal.

2. El **gallego** es un dialecto hablado en Galicia.

3. El **catalán** es la lengua de Cataluña.

4. El **vascuence** es la lengua de los vascos (Basques), que viven en el País Vasco.

H. Ciudades Importantes:

1. **Madrid** es la capital y la ciudad más grande (unos 4,000,000 de habitantes). Lugares de interés:

   a. El **Retiro** es un parque famoso.

   b. La **Puerta del Sol** es la plaza principal de Madrid.

   c. El **Museo del Prado** es un museo de bellas artes.

   d. El **Escorial,** cerca de Madrid, es un enorme monasterio, palacio, y mausoleo (burial place) construido por el rey Felipe II.

   e. El **Valle de los Caídos** (Fallen), cerca de Madrid, es un monumento dedicado a la memoria de los soldados que murieron en la Guerra Civil española (1936–39).

2. **Barcelona,** en Cataluña, es el puerto principal y la ciudad más industrial de España. Tiene unos 2,000,000 de habitantes. Cerca de la ciudad está el famoso monasterio de **Montserrat.**

3. **Sevilla,** en Andalucía, es la ciudad más pintoresca y romántica. Lugares de interés:

   a. La **Catedral de Sevilla** es la catedral más grande de España.

   b. La **Giralda,** una torre de la catedral, es un admirable ejemplo de la arquitectura árabe.

   c. El **Alcázar** es un famoso palacio moro.

4. **Valencia** es la ciudad principal de la provincia del mismo nombre. Esta región se llama "la huerta de España" y es famosa por las naranjas que produce.

5. **Bilbao,** el "Pittsburgh de España," es famosa por su producción de hierro y acero.

6. **Toledo,** ciudad antigua, es famosa por sus productos de acero y de metales preciosos.

7. **Granada** tiene la famosa **Alhambra,** y también otro palacio moro, el **Generalife.**

8. **Córdoba,** en Andalucía, tiene la famosa **Mezquita** (Mosque), un templo antiguo de la época de los moros.

9. **Burgos,** en Castilla y León, es la ciudad donde nació el Cid, héroe nacional de España. Su tumba (tomb) está en la Catedral de Burgos.

10. **Salamanca** tiene **la Universidad de Salamanca,** la universidad más antigua de España.

I. Posesiones Ultramarinas (Overseas):

1. Las **Islas Baleares,** en el Mediterráneo. La más grande de las islas es **Mallorca.**

2. Las **Islas Canarias,** en el Atlántico, cerca de la costa de África.

3. En África: **Ceuta** y **Melilla,** dos ciudades en la costa de Marruecos (Morocco).

EJERCICIOS

A. En cada grupo, subraye Vd. la palabra que no tiene relación con las otras palabras del grupo.

1. Pirineos, Cantábricos, Sierra de Guadarrama, Sierra Morena, Sierra Nevada, Giralda

2. Ebro, Generalife, Duero, Guadalquivir, Guadiana, Tajo

3. Galicia, Castilla - La Mancha, Cataluña, Andalucía, Asturias, Montserrat

4. catalán, vascuence, castellano, gallego, moreno, español

5. Alcázar, Murcia, Alhambra, Generalife, Mezquita, Giralda

B. Subraye Vd. la palabra o expresión que complete correctamente cada frase.

1. Una región del norte de España es (a) Valencia (b) Extremadura (c) Galicia.

2. En la ciudad de Salamanca se halla (a) una torre famosa (b) una universidad antigua (c) un palacio moro.

3. El famoso templo moro de la ciudad de Córdoba se llama (*a*) la Mezquita (*b*) la Alhambra (*c*) el Generalife.

4. Andalucía es (*a*) una ciudad (*b*) un río (*c*) una región   de España.

5. La famosa torre de Sevilla se llama (*a*) el Escorial (*b*) la Giralda (*c*) el Prado.

6. La catedral más grande de España está situada en la ciudad de (*a*) Sevilla (*b*) Córdoba (*c*) Madrid.

7. Las ciudades de Málaga y de Jerez son famosas por sus (*a*) espadas (*b*) vinos (*c*) naranjas.

8. La famosa plaza de Madrid se llama (*a*) el Escorial (*b*) el Retiro (*c*) la Puerta del Sol.

9. Mallorca es una de (*a*) las Islas Baleares (*b*) las Islas Canarias (*c*) los Cantábricos.

10. La población de España es aproximadamente (*a*) 42,000,000 (*b*) 25,000,000 (*c*) 37,000,000   de habitantes.

C. Complete Vd. cada frase con una de las expresiones siguientes: Francia, Guadalquivir, huerta de España, El Retiro, Galicia, Felipe II, África, Castilla, vascuence, Península Ibérica, "Pittsburgh de España," Barcelona, Granada, Tajo, Burgos.

1. Valencia se llama la _____.

2. Los gallegos son los habitantes de _____.

3. En _____, hay dos ciudades españolas en la costa de Marruecos.

4. Los vascos hablan _____ además del español.

5. Los Pirineos separan a España de _____.

6. _____ es un puerto grande de España.

7. _____ es un parque famoso en Madrid.

8. El río más grande de España es el _____.

9. La región central de España se llama _____.

10. El río más navegable de España es el _____.

11. El Escorial es un palacio, monasterio, y mausoleo construido por _____.

12. España ocupa la mayor parte de la _____.

13. El Cid nació en _____.

14. La Alhambra es un palacio moro en _____.

15. Bilbao se llama el _____.

D. En inglés, identifique Vd. cada uno de los siguientes:

1. el Generalife _____

2. el Escorial _____

3. el Prado _____

4. Asturias _____

5. las Islas Canarias _____

6. Montserrat _____

7. Toledo _____

8. el Alcázar de Sevilla _____

9. el vascuence _____

10. el Valle de los Caídos _____

2. LA HISTORIA DE ESPAÑA

A. Primitivos (Earliest) Habitantes:

1. Los **iberos.** Fueron los primeros habitantes de España.

2. Los **celtas** (Celts). De la unión de iberos y celtas se formó la raza **celtíbera** (Celtiberian), precursor (forerunner) de los españoles de hoy.

3. Los **fenicios** (Phoenicians). Fueron una nación de marineros. Fundaron la ciudad de Cádiz.

4. Los **griegos.** Fundaron colonias en la costa oriental (eastern) de España.

5. Los **cartagineses** (Carthaginians). Fueron una nación guerrera (warlike). Vencieron a los celtíberos en la **batalla de Sagunto.**

6. Los **romanos** (Romans).

   a. Vencieron a las otras naciones, y reinaron en España durante seis siglos.

   b. Influencia romana: Dieron a España la religión cristiana, las leyes romanas, y su lengua (el castellano se deriva del latín).

   c. Construyeron acueductos, puentes, y muchos caminos. Todavía existen hoy día el **acueducto de Segovia** y el **puente de Alcántara.**

7. Los **visigodos** (Visigoths). Vencieron a los romanos y reinaron hasta la invasión de los moros.

8. Los **moros.**

   a. Invadieron a España y vencieron a los visigodos en 711. Se quedaron en España ocho siglos, y dominaron el país durante gran parte del tiempo.

   b. Influencia morisca (Moorish).

   (1) Introdujeron la **noria** (waterwheel) para regar (irrigate) los campos.

   (2) Introdujeron las ciencias (matemáticas, medicina, astronomía, filosofía, etc.).

   (3) Construyeron palacios (como la Alhambra), alcázares (fortresses), y mezquitas (mosques).

   (4) Introdujeron nuevas palabras en el idioma español, sobre todo palabras que comienzan con **al-** (algodón, alcalde, álgebra, etc.).

B. Reconquista de España:

1. **Pelayo** venció a los moros en la **batalla de Covadonga** en 718.

2. **El Cid** (Rodrigo Díaz de Vivar), el héroe nacional de España, capturó la ciudad de Valencia de los moros en 1094.

3. En 1492, después de más de siete siglos de lucha, los españoles bajo **Fernando** e **Isabel** (los **Reyes Católicos**) finalmente vencieron a los últimos moros, en Granada. Así terminó la Reconquista.

C. España un País Poderoso (1516–1598):

1. **Carlos V** fue el más poderoso de los reyes de España.

2. **Felipe II** fue hijo de Carlos V. Durante su época, España tomó parte en muchas guerras. Venció a los turcos en la **batalla de Lepanto** (1571). Su "Armada Invencible" fue vencida por Inglaterra en 1588.

D. Decadencia de España (Siglo 18):

La decadencia se debía a (was due to) muchas guerras, muchos impuestos, reyes débiles, y la expulsión de los judíos y los moros, que formaban la mayor parte de los científicos y comerciantes de España.

E. Los Siglos 19 y 20:

1. **Guerra de la Independencia** (1808–1814).

   a. Rebelión contra los franceses (Napoleón) el 2 de mayo de 1808. Esta fecha llegó a ser la fiesta nacional del país.

   b. Las fuerzas francesas fueron expulsadas en 1814.

2. **Guerras Carlistas** (1833–39; 1872–76). Largas guerras civiles en las cuales Carlos, hermano de Fernando VII, trató de quitar el trono del país a (from) Isabel, hija de Fernando VII.

3. **Guerra con los Estados Unidos** (1898). España fue vencida por los Estados Unidos, y perdió a Cuba, Guam, Puerto Rico, y las Islas Filipinas.

4. **Las Dos Repúblicas.**

   a. La primera república fue establecida en 1873; duró solamente un año.

   b. **Alfonso XII** estableció otra vez la monarquía. Su hijo, **Alfonso XIII**, fue rey de España hasta 1931. Durante su reinado, estableció una dictadura bajo **Primo de Rivera.**

   c. La segunda república fue establecida el 14 de abril de 1931.

5. La **Guerra Civil** (1936–39). El general **Francisco Franco** venció a las fuerzas de la república y estableció una dictadura.

6. Franco rigió (ruled) el país hasta su muerte en 1975. El gobierno actual es una monarquía constitucional.

7. **España hoy día.** En 1975, Juan Carlos I fue proclamado rey por las Cortes. En 1982, Felipe González Márquez llegó a ser presidente del Gobierno. A partir de 1986, España es miembro de la Comunidad Económica Europea (C.E.E.).

EJERCICIOS

A. A la izquierda de cada expresión de la lista *A*, escriba Vd. la letra de la expresión correspondiente de la lista *B*.

A	B
_____ 1. Pelayo	*a.* el Cid
_____ 2. los Reyes Católicos	*b.* Napoleón
_____ 3. Rodrigo Díaz de Vivar	*c.* rey de España hasta 1931
_____ 4. Felipe II	*d.* los Estados Unidos
_____ 5. Dos de Mayo	*e.* Fernando e Isabel
_____ 6. Alfonso XIII	*f.* Armada Invencible
_____ 7. guerra que ocurrió al fin del siglo 19	*g.* monumento romano
_____ 8. puente de Alcántara	*h.* April 14, 1931
_____ 9. la segunda república	*i.* dictador español
_____ 10. Francisco Franco	*j.* principió la Reconquista

B. Subraye Vd. la palabra o expresión que complete correctamente cada frase.

1. Los primeros habitantes de España fueron los (*a*) iberos (*b*) celtas (*c*) romanos.

2. La segunda república española se estableció en el año (*a*) 718 (*b*) 1931 (*c*) 1808.

3. El acueducto de Segovia fue construido por los (*a*) fenicios (*b*) romanos (*c*) moros.

4. Muchas palabras españolas que principian con "al-" son de origen (*a*) romano (*b*) árabe (*c*) ibero.

5. Las guerras entre los moros y los españoles se llaman (*a*) las Guerras Civiles (*b*) las Guerras Carlistas (*c*) la Reconquista.

6. España perdió a Cuba, Puerto Rico, y las Filipinas en (*a*) la guerra civil (*b*) la guerra con los Estados Unidos (*c*) la guerra de la independencia.

7. Pelayo venció a los moros en la batalla de (*a*) Covadonga (*b*) Lepanto (*c*) Sagunto.

8. Los visigodos vencieron a los (*a*) moros (*b*) romanos (*c*) fenicios.

9. El dictador de España bajo Alfonso XIII fue (*a*) Francisco Franco (*b*) Primo de Rivera (*c*) Pelayo.

10. El hijo de Carlos V fue (*a*) Fernando VII (*b*) Felipe II (*c*) Alfonso XIII.

C. Complete Vd. cada frase con una de las expresiones siguientes: los Reyes Católicos, Cádiz, las Guerras Carlistas, diez y ocho, Sagunto, latín, el dos de mayo, la noria, el Cid, Lepanto.

1. El español se deriva del _____.

2. El día de la independencia española se celebra _____.

3. Los cartagineses vencieron a los celtíberos en la batalla de _____.

4. La Reconquista fue terminada por _____.

5. Los moros introdujeron _____ en España.

6. España sufrió una decadencia completa en el siglo _____.

7. Los fenicios fundaron la ciudad de _____.

8. Los españoles vencieron a los turcos en la batalla de _____.

9. El héroe nacional de España es _____.

10. Las guerras entre la reina Isabel y Carlos se llaman _____.

3. LA LITERATURA ESPAÑOLA

A. Antes del Siglo de Oro:

1. *Poema del Cid.* Poema épico, de autor anónimo (anonymous). Celebra la vida y las hazañas (heroic deeds) del Cid. Fue escrito en el siglo 12, y es la primera obra importante de la literatura española.

2. **Alfonso X, El Sabio** (siglo 13). Compiló una colección de leyes y costumbres, *Las siete partidas.* También escribió varias obras de poesía.

3. **Jorge Manrique** (siglo 15). Autor de las *Coplas,* una bella poesía escrita en memoria de la muerte de su padre. Esta poesía fue traducida al inglés por el poeta norteamericano Henry Wadsworth Longfellow.

4. Antonio de **Nebrija.** Autor del primer libro de gramática española, escrito en 1492.

B. El Siglo de Oro (1535–1680):

1. **La Novela Picaresca.**

   a. Las aventuras de un **pícaro,** una persona que trata de vivir sin trabajar. Es una sátira de la vida y la sociedad de la época.
   b. La primera y la más famosa de las novelas picarescas es *Lazarillo de Tormes,* escrita en el siglo 16.

2. Miguel de **Cervantes** (1547–1616) fue el novelista principal de España.

   a. Autor de *Don Quijote de la Mancha,* que se considera tal vez la mejor novela del mundo. Los personajes principales son don Quijote y Sancho Panza, su escudero y criado.
   b. También escribió una colección de cuentos, las *Novelas ejemplares.*

3. **Lope de Vega** fue el dramaturgo más importante del Siglo de Oro. Escribió centenares (hundreds) de obras de teatro. Se le considera el padre del teatro español.

4. **Tirso de Molina.** Creó el personaje de don Juan en su obra *El burlador de Sevilla.*

5. **Calderón** fue el último de los grandes dramaturgos del Siglo de Oro. Fue autor de *La vida es sueño.* Con su muerte, en 1681, se considera terminado el Siglo de Oro.

C. Los Siglos 19 y 20:

1. José **Zorrilla.** Escribió obras de teatro inspiradas en (inspired by) las leyendas de España. Su obra principal, *Don Juan Tenorio,* se representa (is performed) en los teatros de todo el mundo hispánico el 2 de noviembre, el Día de los Difuntos (All Souls' Day).

2. **Pérez Galdós** fue el novelista principal de los siglos 19 y 20. Fue gran enemigo de la intolerancia religiosa. Una de sus mejores novelas, *Doña Perfecta,* ataca el fanatismo (fanaticism).

3. **Palacio Valdés** fue un novelista muy popular. Entre sus obras debe mencionarse *José.*

4. Vicente **Blasco Ibáñez** escribió novelas sobre la vida de los campesinos de Valencia. Su obra principal es *La barraca.* También escribió *Los cuatro jinetes del Apocalipsis* (The Four Horsemen of the Apocalypse), sobre la primera Guerra Mundial, y *Sangre y arena* (Blood and Sand), sobre la corrida de toros.

5. La **"Generación del '98."** La guerra contra los Estados Unidos, en 1898, resultó un desastre (disaster) para España. Como resultado de la guerra, muchos escritores y filósofos se dedicaron a examinar y modernizar (modernize) la cultura del país. Estos escritores se conocen hoy con el título de la "Generación del '98."

6. Algunos escritores de la "Generación del '98":

   a. Miguel de **Unamuno,** filósofo y ensayista (essayist).
   b. **Azorín,** novelista y ensayista.
   c. **Pío Baroja,** novelista.
   d. Jacinto **Benavente,** dramaturgo; ganó el Premio Nobel de Literatura en 1922.
   e. Antonio **Machado,** poeta.
   f. Ramón **Menéndez Pidal,** erudito (scholar) famoso.

7. Otros Autores Modernos:

    a. José **Ortega y Gasset,** filósofo y ensayista; autor de *La rebelión de las masas.*

    b. Juan Ramón **Jiménez,** poeta. También escribió en prosa *Platero y yo.* Ganó el Premio Nobel de Literatura en 1956.

    c. Gregorio **Martínez Sierra,** dramaturgo. Escribió *Canción de cuna* (Cradle Song).

    d. Federico **García Lorca,** poeta y dramaturgo. Escribió *Bodas de sangre* y *La casa de Bernarda Alba.*

    e. Vicente **Aleixandre,** poeta. Escribió *Pasión de la tierra.* Ganó el Premio Nobel de Literatura en 1977.

    f. Camilo José **Cela,** novelista. Escribió *La familia de Pascual Duarte.* Ganó el Premio Nobel de Literatura en 1989.

EJERCICIOS

A. Identifique Vd. cada escritor como *novelista, dramaturgo, poeta, o ensayista.*

1. Cervantes -----------------	**6.** Lope de Vega -----------------
2. Benavente -----------------	**7.** Martínez Sierra -----------------
3. Ortega y Gasset -----------------	**8.** Unamuno -----------------
4. Pío Baroja -----------------	**9.** Calderón -----------------
5. Antonio Machado -----------------	**10.** Juan Ramón Jiménez -----------------

B. A la izquierda de cada nombre de autor en la lista *A,* escriba Vd. la letra del título de una obra del autor que aparece en la lista *B.*

A

----- **1.** García Lorca	----- **6.** José Zorrilla
----- **2.** Blasco Ibáñez	----- **7.** Jorge Manrique
----- **3.** Tirso de Molina	----- **8.** Calderón
----- **4.** Alfonso X	----- **9.** Antonio de Nebrija
----- **5.** Cervantes	----- **10.** Pérez Galdós

B

a. Don Quijote de la Mancha
b. El burlador de Sevilla
c. Bodas de sangre
d. Doña Perfecta
e. Sangre y arena
f. La vida es sueño
g. Las siete partidas
h. Don Juan Tenorio
i. gramática de la lengua castellana
j. Coplas

C. Complete Vd. las frases siguientes:

1. El escudero de don Quijote se llamaba ----------------------------------.

2. La novela *José* fue escrita por ----------------------------.

3. Un dramaturgo que ganó el Premio Nobel fue ------------------------------------.

4. La más famosa de las novelas picarescas es ------------------------------------.

5. El fundador del drama nacional español fue --------------------------------.

6. La primera obra importante de la literatura española fue un poema épico, --------------------.

7. El último de los grandes escritores del Siglo de Oro fue ----------------------.

8. ------------------------ fue un rey español que complió una colección de leyes.

9. ------------------------------ creó el personaje de don Juan.

10. Un drama que se representa el Día de los Difuntos en todos los países hispánicos es ----------

------------------------------.

4. ARTE, MÚSICA, Y CIENCIAS

A. Pintores:

1. **El Greco** (Doménico Theotocópuli). Pintor de origen griego que vivió en Toledo en el siglo 16.

    a. Sus obras tienen un profundo tono religioso.

    b. Su obra maestra es *El entierro* (burial) *del conde de Orgaz.*

2. Diego **Velázquez.** Se le considera el más importante de los pintores españoles.

    a. Fue pintor de cámara (court painter) del rey Felipe IV, y pintó muchos retratos de la familia real.

    b. Su obra maestra es *Las meninas.* También pintó *La rendición de Bredá*, llamada también *Las lanzas.*

3. Francisco **Goya** fue el pintor español más importante de los siglos 18 y 19. Fue pintor de cámara del rey Carlos IV.

    a. En sus obras ataca la decadencia social y política de España.

    b. Entre sus obras principales deben mencionarse *Los fusilamientos* (shootings) *del dos de mayo* y *Los caprichos.*

4. Joaquín **Sorolla** es el pintor de "sol y color." Pintó las costumbres y los trajes de las varias regiones. Muchos de sus cuadros se encuentran en el Museo de la Sociedad Hispánica, en Nueva York.

5. José María **Sert.** Pintor de murales, muchos de los cuales se encuentran en el Rockefeller Center y en el Salón Sert del Hotel Waldorf-Astoria, en Nueva York.

6. Pablo **Picasso.** Fundador del **cubismo,** estilo de pintura en que figuras geométricas representan figuras humanas.

7. Salvador **Dalí.** Uno de los fundadores del **surrealismo** en la pintura. El artista trató de pintar los pensamientos y los sueños.

B. Músicos y Compositores:

1. Isaac **Albéniz** compuso música para el piano. Dos de sus composiciones más conocidas son *Iberia* y *El Albaicín.*

2. Enrique **Granados** también compuso música para el piano. Escribió la ópera *Goyescas*, basada en las obras de Goya.

3. Manuel **de Falla** fue el más importante de los compositores españoles. Compuso *La vida breve* y *El amor brujo.*

4. José **Iturbi** fue un pianista y compositor famoso.

5. Andrés **Segovia** fue el guitarrista más famoso del mundo.

6. Pablo **Casals** fue el mejor violoncelista (cellist) del mundo.

C. Baile:

Vicente **Escudero,** que murió en 1980, fue el más famoso de los bailarines españoles. Fue un gran intérprete (interpreter) de los bailes gitanos.

D. Bailes e Instrumentos Típicos:

1. **Bailes.** De Andalucía viene un gran número de bailes, tales como el **bolero,** el **fandango,** el **jaleo,** y el **flamenco.** De otras regiones vienen la **jota** (Aragón), la **sardana** (Cataluña), y la **muñeira** (Galicia).

2. **Instrumentos.** El instrumento típico de España es la **guitarra.** Además, en Galicia se emplea la **gaita** (bagpipe). La **pandereta** (tambourine) y las **castañuelas** (castanets) se emplean para acompañar la música.

E. Científicos:

1. Santiago **Ramón y Cajal.** Recibió el Premio Nobel de Medicina por sus estudios acerca del sistema nervioso.

2. Juan **de la Cierva** inventó el autogiro (autogyro), precursor (forerunner) del helicóptero.

3. Severo **Ochoa.** Recibió el Premio Nobel de Medicina en 1959 por sus estudios sobre la herencia (heredity).

EJERCICIOS

A. Identifique Vd. las siguientes personas como *bailarín, pintor, científico,* o *músico:*

1. El Greco	_____	9. Pablo Casals	_____
2. Ramón y Cajal	_____	10. Albéniz	_____
3. Severo Ochoa	_____	11. Sorolla	_____
4. Vicente Escudero	_____	12. Andrés Segovia	_____
5. José Iturbi	_____	13. Dalí	_____
6. Manuel de Falla	_____	14. Granados	_____
7. Juan de la Cierva	_____	15. Velázquez	_____
8. Goya	_____		

B. A la izquierda de cada nombre de la lista *A*, escriba Vd. la letra de la expresión de la lista *B* que tenga relación con él.

	A	B
_____	1. Goya	a. *Las meninas*
_____	2. El Greco	b. pintor de murales
_____	3. Velázquez	c. Doménico Theotocópuli
_____	4. Juan de la Cierva	d. guitarrista
_____	5. Manuel de Falla	e. violoncelista
_____	6. Albéniz	f. *La vida breve*
_____	7. Picasso	g. autogiro
_____	8. Pablo Casals	h. *Iberia*
_____	9. Andrés Segovia	i. cubismo
_____	10. Sert	j. *Los fusilamientos del dos de mayo*

C. Complete Vd. cada frase, escogiendo un nombre o una palabra de la lista siguiente: Manuel de Falla, castañuelas, bolero, jota, El Greco, Felipe IV, médico, *Las lanzas,* gaita, Granados, Goya, Sert, Sorolla, Dalí, sardana.

1. Velázquez fue el pintor de cámara de _____.

2. El _____ es un baile de Andalucía.

3. Ramón y Cajal fue un gran _____ español.

4. *La rendición de Bredá* se llama también _____.

5. _____ compuso música basada en las obras de un gran pintor.

6. Para acompañar la música se emplean las _____.

7. _____ fue un gran compositor español.

8. _____ pintó *El entierro del conde de Orgaz*.

9. El baile regional de Cataluña es la _____.

10. _____ fue el pintor de cámara de Carlos IV.

11. Muchas de las obras de _____ se hallan en el Waldorf-Astoria y el Rockefeller Center.

12. Los aragoneses bailan mucho la _____.

13. _____ fue un famoso pintor surrealista.

14. _____ pintó el "sol y color" de España.

15. En Galicia se oye mucha música producida en la _____.

5. LA VIDA Y LAS COSTUMBRES ESPAÑOLAS

A. Casa:

En los pueblos de España, las casas generalmente son de un solo piso. Cada casa tiene su **patio** (inner courtyard), donde la familia pasa las tardes. Hay **rejas** (iron gratings) en las ventanas. En muchas casas las paredes están cubiertas de **azulejos** (glazed tiles).

B. Nombres (Given Names) **y Apellidos** (Family Names):

1. Cada español tiene dos apellidos, el apellido del padre seguido del apellido de la madre. Ejemplo: Juan **López Carranza.** Muchas veces se pone **y entre** los dos apellidos: Juan López **y** Carranza.

2. A veces se omite el apellido de la madre: Juan **López.**

3. Al casarse una mujer, añade a su propio apellido el apellido de su marido, con la preposición **de.** Ejemplo: María Gómez **de González.**

4. La mayor parte de los niños españoles tienen el nombre de un santo, y en vez de celebrar su cumpleaños, celebran **el día del santo.**

C. Tipos Pintorescos:

1. El **sereno** guarda las calles y las casas de noche.

2. El **pordiosero** es un mendigo (beggar) que pide limosna "por Dios."

3. Los **gitanos** viven en el sur de España, sobre todo en Sevilla y Granada.

4. El **aguador** es un vendedor de agua. Es común en las regiones secas.

D. Vida Social y Costumbres:

1. Por la tarde la gente tiene la costumbre de ir al **café** para tomar la **merienda** (afternoon snack), una comida que generalmente consiste en un ligero refresco.

2. Muchos hombres van al **casino** (club) después del trabajo para pasar una hora o dos.

3. En muchas ciudades hay un **ateneo** (club literario y científico).

4. La **tertulia** es una reunión, generalmente en casa, donde la gente pasa el tiempo charlando.

5. **Pelando la pava** es una costumbre que se observa en muchas partes. El novio, que está fuera de la casa, habla a través de la **reja** con su novia, que está dentro.

6. Frecuentemente hay una **lotería** dirigida por el gobierno. El primer premio vale mucho dinero, y se llama el **premio gordo.**

7. Después del almuerzo, y durante el calor de la tarde, la gente duerme la **siesta.**

E. Fiestas Religiosas:

1. La **Navidad,** que cae el 25 de diciembre, es la fiesta más importante del año. Desde principios de diciembre en cada casa se preparan los **nacimientos** (grupos de figuras que representan el nacimiento de Jesucristo). En México, la Navidad se celebra desde el 16 de diciembre con las **Posadas,** unas reuniones en casa, en que se rompe la **piñata,** una jarra que está llena de dulces. La **Nochebuena** (Christmas Eve) la gente asiste a la **misa del gallo** (midnight mass) en las iglesias. Grupos de personas andan por las calles cantando **villancicos** (Christmas carols). Los niños reciben regalos el 6 de enero, que se llama el **Día de los Reyes Magos.** Los Reyes Magos corresponden a nuestro Santa Claus.

2. El **Carnaval** es un período de tres días de diversión antes de la **Cuaresma** (Lent).

3. La **Pascua Florida** (Easter) se celebra en toda España. Es famosa la celebración de **Semana Santa** (Holy Week) en Sevilla.

4. El día del **santo patrón** (patron saint). Cada pueblo tiene su santo patrón, cuyo día se celebra con una fiesta. La noche anterior se celebra una **verbena** (evening festival). El día del santo hay **romerías** (religious picnics) a la tumba (tomb) del santo.

5. El **Día de los Difuntos** (All Souls' Day) se celebra el 2 de noviembre, en memoria de los muertos.

F. Fiestas Nacionales:

1. El **Dos de Mayo** es la fiesta nacional de España.

2. El **Día de la Raza** corresponde a nuestro *Columbus Day*, el 12 de octubre.

G. Deportes y Diversiones (Amusements):

1. La **corrida de toros** (bullfight) tiene lugar en la **plaza de toros.** Hay toreros de varias clases:
   a. Los **picadores** van montados a caballo. Llevan lanzas largas, con las cuales resisten el toro.

   b. Los **banderilleros,** que ponen **banderillas** en el cuello del toro.

   c. El **matador** es el torero principal, que al fin mata el toro.

2. **Jai-alai** es un juego de pelota, de origen vasco, que se juega en un gran **frontón** (court) de tres paredes. Es algo semejante al *handball*, aunque el jugador (player) usa una **cesta** para coger la pelota, y no la mano.

3. Se juega mucho al **fútbol,** que en los Estados Unidos se llama *soccer*.

H. Prendas de Vestir:

   La ropa de los españoles es semejante a la ropa que llevamos nosotros. Sin embargo, en muchas partes la gente todavía lleva ropa tradicional.

1. La **mantilla** es un pañuelo grande de seda y encajes (lace) que la mujer lleva en la cabeza.

2. Los días de fiesta, las mujeres todavía llevan en la cabeza un peine (comb) alto, llamado la **peineta.**

3. El **mantón** es un chal (shawl) de seda, bordado (embroidered) de flores de muchos colores.

4. La **boina** es una gorra al estilo del "beret."

5. Los trabajadores en muchas partes llevan **alpargatas,** una especie (kind) de sandalia (sandal) hecha de lona (canvas).

I. Alimentos:

1. El **cocido** (stew), que también se llama **puchero,** es el alimento diario (daily) de los campesinos y trabajadores.

2. El **arroz con pollo** es muy popular.

3. La **paella** es el arroz con pollo mezclado con mariscos (seafood). Es popular en Valencia.

J. Bebidas:

1. El **chocolate** caliente se toma en el desayuno, con panecillos o bizcochos (biscuits).

2. La **horchata** es una bebida fría de almendras (almonds), agua, y azúcar.

EJERCICIOS

A. Identifique Vd. cada uno de los siguientes como *alimento, bebida, prenda de vestir, fiesta religiosa,* o *costumbre social:*

1. boina	_____	9. alpargatas	_____
2. verbena	_____	10. arroz con pollo	_____
3. paella	_____	11. mantilla	_____
4. tertulia	_____	12. Carnaval	_____
5. cocido	_____	13. merienda	_____
6. romería	_____	14. peineta	_____
7. horchata	_____	15. chocolate	_____
8. Día de los Difuntos	_____		

B. A la izquierda de cada expresión de la lista *A*, escriba Vd. la letra de la palabra o expresión de la lista *B* que tenga relación con ella.

	A	*B*
_____	**1.** apellido	*a.* premio gordo
_____	**2.** pelando la pava	*b.* frontón
_____	**3.** lotería	*c.* limosna
_____	**4.** Nochebuena	*d.* verbena
_____	**5.** sereno	*e.* reja
_____	**6.** banderillero	*f.* nombre
_____	**7.** jai-alai	*g.* alimento
_____	**8.** día del santo patrón	*h.* Navidad
_____	**9.** puchero	*i.* corrida de toros
_____	**10.** pordiosero	*j.* guardia

C. Complete Vd. las frases siguientes:

1. Para evitar el calor de la tarde, los españoles duermen la _____.

2. Antonio Moreno y Villa está casado con Luisa Gómez y Vega, y tienen un hijo, Juan. El nombre completo del hijo es Juan _____ y _____.

3. Un alimento popular en Valencia, hecho de arroz, pollo, y mariscos, se llama _____.

4. La fiesta nacional de España se celebra _____.

5. El vendedor de agua se llama un _____.

6. _____ se celebra el 12 de octubre.

7. Los niños españoles reciben regalos el 6 de enero, el Día de los _____.

8. El torero que va montado a caballo se llama el _____.

9. _____ es el nombre que se da a un club científico y literario.

10. En vez de celebrar su cumpleaños, los niños españoles celebran su _____.

D. En inglés, identifique Vd. los siguientes:

1. Día de los Difuntos _____

2. matador _____

3. Semana Santa _____

4. las Posadas _____

5. azulejos _____

6. verbena _____

7. Pascua Florida _____

8. romería _____

9. villancicos _____

10. nacimiento _____

6. MASTERY EXERCISES ON SPAIN

A. Complete Vd. cada frase, subrayando la palabra o expresión correcta.

1. Don Juan es un personaje de (a) *La vida es sueño* (b) *La barraca* (c) *Doña Perfecta* (d) *El burlador de Sevilla.*

2. Manuel de Falla fue un célebre (a) compositor (b) pintor (c) cantor (d) bailarín moderno español.

3. Un baile regional de Cataluña es (a) el jaleo (b) la muñeira (c) el bolero (d) la sardana.

4. Lope de Vega escribió (a) dramas (b) ensayos (c) gramáticas (d) enciclopedias.

5. El Día de la Raza se celebra el (a) 14 de abril (b) 2 de mayo (c) 12 de octubre (d) 6 de enero.

6. Sancho Panza fue (a) un poeta español (b) el escudero de don Quijote (c) el Cid (d) un héroe español.

7. El río más navegable de España es el (a) Guadalquivir (b) Duero (c) Tajo (d) Ebro.

8. El jai-alai es un (a) baile (b) juego (c) torero (d) autor.

9. La Alhambra de Granada fue construida por (a) los iberos (b) Felipe II (c) los moros (d) los griegos.

10. El Greco fue un célebre (a) escritor (b) actor (c) libertador (d) pintor   español.

11. El refresco que los españoles toman por la tarde es la (a) lotería (b) merienda (c) reja (d) tertulia.

12. Un alimento español es (a) la Navidad (b) el pordiosero (c) la guerra (d) el cocido.

13. Barcelona está en (a) Galicia (b) Cataluña (c) Aragón (d) Castilla y León.

14. El Escorial está cerca de (a) Madrid (b) Vigo (c) Valencia (d) Sevilla.

15. En el noroeste de España está la región de (a) Aragón (b) Galicia (c) Castilla - La Mancha (d) Murcia.

16. Una prenda de vestir es (a) la cesta (b) la boina (c) el villancico (d) la horchata.

17. Los Reyes Católicos eran (a) Carlos y María (b) Felipe y Cristina (c) Alfonso y Victoria (d) Fernando e Isabel.

18. El que pide limosna es el (a) sereno (b) matador (c) trabajador (d) pordiosero.

19. La noria se emplea (a) en la construcción de edificios (b) en el teatro (c) para regar los campos (d) para fabricar ropa.

20. El día anterior a la Navidad se llama (a) la Nochebuena (b) las Posadas (c) la Cuaresma (d) el Día de la Raza.

B. A la izquierda de cada expresión de la lista *A*, escriba Vd. la letra de la palabra o expresión de la lista *B* que tenga relación con ella.

GRUPO I

	A	*B*
_ _ _ _ _	1. Cervantes	*a.* nacimiento
_ _ _ _ _	2. Nochebuena	*b.* matador
_ _ _ _ _	3. los Reyes Magos	*c.* pícaro
_ _ _ _ _	4. gaita	*d.* baile
_ _ _ _ _	5. corrida de toros	*e.* 6 de enero
_ _ _ _ _	6. fandango	*f.* dramaturgo
_ _ _ _ _	7. día del santo	*g.* limosna
_ _ _ _ _	8. *Lazarillo de Tormes*	*h.* cumpleaños
_ _ _ _ _	9. Calderón	*i.* *Don Quijote*
_ _ _ _ _	10. pordiosero	*j.* Galicia

GRUPO II

A	B
_____ 1. Aragón	a. héroe nacional de España
_____ 2. jai-alai	b. las Posadas
_____ 3. el Cid	c. montañas
_____ 4. Tirso de Molina	d. museo
_____ 5. pelar la pava	e. torero
_____ 6. Pirineos	f. don Juan
_____ 7. banderillero	g. región de España
_____ 8. el Prado	h. Covadonga
_____ 9. piñata	i. frontón
_____ 10. Pelayo	j. reja

C. Complete Vd. las frases siguientes:

1. La jota es un _____ de Aragón.

2. Dos sierras del sur de España son _____ y _____
_____.

3. El premio principal en la lotería se llama el _____.

4. La región del sur de España es _____.

5. La Reconquista terminó en el año _____.

6. El torero que va montado a caballo es el _____.

7. _____ fue un poeta de la "Generación del '98."

8. La obra maestra de Velázquez es _____.

9. La fiesta nacional de España ocurre _____.

10. Una bebida española es _____.

11. El compositor que compuso la ópera *Goyescas* es _____.

12. El dramaturgo español que escribió *Canción de cuna* es _____.

13. El inventor del autogiro fue _____.

14. La catedral más grande de España está en la ciudad de _____.

15. El pintor español más importante de los siglos 18 y 19 fue _____.

16. Un escritor del Siglo de Oro fue _____.

17. El pintor español que fundó el cubismo es _____.

18. El idioma español se deriva del _____.

19. Un alimento muy popular en Valencia es _____.

20. Dos novelistas de la "Generación del '98" son _____ y _____.

21. La primera gramática de la lengua española fue escrita por _____.

22. Una novela de Blasco Ibáñez que trata de (deals with) la vida de los campesinos de Valencia es
_____.

23. Un escritor español que ganó el Premio Nobel fue _____.

24. Las montañas de la parte central de España son la sierra de _____.

25. El catalán es el idioma de la región de _____.

26. Los niños españoles reciben sus regalos de Navidad el Día de _____.

27. La segunda república española fue establecida en el año _____.

28. La más famosa de las novelas picarescas es _____.

29. El Cid capturó la ciudad de Valencia de los _____.

30. La Alhambra está en la ciudad de _____.

31. Sorolla fue un famoso _____ español.

32. El fútbol, deporte muy popular en España, se llama _____ en los Estados Unidos.

33. _____ fue dictador de España entre los años 1939–1975.

34. Dos ríos de España son _____ y _____.

35. Los moros invadieron a España en el año _____.

36. Las montañas que separan a España de Francia son _____.

37. Si Pedro Ortega y Carlota Rivera se casan, el nombre completo de Carlota será _____

_____.

38. Los primeros habitantes de España fueron _____.

39. _____ es la capital de España.

40. El instrumento músico típico de Galicia es la _____.

D. Conteste Vd. en español en frases completas.

1. ¿Quién fue el dramaturgo más importante del Siglo de Oro? _____

_____

2. ¿Dónde está la universidad más antigua de España? _____

_____

3. ¿En cuántas regiones tradicionales está dividida España? _____

_____

4. ¿Cuáles son los dos países que forman la Península Ibérica? _____

_____

5. ¿En qué ciudad se encuentra la Giralda? _____

_____

6. ¿Quiénes introdujeron en España las ciencias? _____

_____

7. ¿En qué fecha cae la Navidad? _____

_____

8. ¿Qué ciudad fundaron los fenicios? _____

_____

9. ¿Quién pintó *El entierro del conde de Orgaz*? _____

_____

10. ¿Cuál es el instrumento músico típico de España? _____

_____

7. LA GEOGRAFÍA DE LA AMÉRICA HISPANA

MÉXICO

México está al sur de los Estados Unidos. El **Río Grande** (que los mexicanos llaman el **Río Bravo del Norte**) separa a México del estado de Tejas. Al oeste de Tejas hay frontera (frontier) con los estados de Nuevo México, Arizona, y California.

A. Extensión y Población:

México tiene la cuarta parte (1/4) de la extensión de los Estados Unidos. Tiene más de 76,000,000 de habitantes.

B. Montañas y Volcanes:

Hay dos sierras que cruzan el país de norte a sur: la **Sierra Madre Oriental** (Eastern) y la **Sierra Madre Occidental** (Western). También hay varios volcanes, tales como el **Orizaba, Popocatépetl, Ixtaccíhuatl,** y **Paricutín.**

C. Productos:

Son importantes la agricultura y la industria minera (mining). Se producen mucha plata, petróleo, trigo, maíz, y ganado (cattle). En la península de **Yucatán** se produce el henequén (hemp).

D. Ciudades Principales:

1. La **Ciudad de México** (México, D. F.) está situada en una meseta (plateau), a unos 7,000 pies de altura. Fue la antigua capital de los **aztecas,** quienes la llamaban **Tenochtitlán.**

   Hay mucho que ver en la capital:

   a. el **Castillo de Chapultepec,** que es hoy un museo de historia colonial.

b. el **Palacio de Bellas Artes,** teatro y museo muy grande y hermoso.

c. la **Ciudad Universitaria.**

d. la **Basílica de Guadalupe,** iglesia fundada en honor de la **Virgen de Guadalupe,** santa patrona del país.

e. el **Zócalo,** la plaza principal de la ciudad. A un lado de la plaza está la **Catedral de México,** la catedral más grande y más vieja del continente.

f. Cerca de la capital se ven los famosos **jardines flotantes** (floating) de **Xochimilco.**

2. **Guadalajara,** la segunda ciudad de México, es un centro industrial.

3. **Tampico** y **Veracruz** son puertos del Golfo (Gulf) de México. Tampico es el centro de la industria de petróleo.

4. **Acapulco** es una playa famosa de la costa occidental.

5. **Taxco** es una ciudad antigua, la más pintoresca de México.

6. **Chichén-Itzá,** en Yucatán, es famosa por las ruinas de la cultura maya que se encuentran allí.

EJERCICIOS

A. Complete Vd. las frases siguientes:

1. El nombre antiguo de la Ciudad de México fue _____.

2. Un producto importante de México es _____.

3. Una sierra del este de México es _____.

4. El Orizaba y el Paricutín son _____.

5. La segunda ciudad de México es _____.

6. Dos puertos del Golfo de México son _____ y _____.

7. El Río Bravo del Norte se llama el _____ en los Estados Unidos.

8. Una ciudad industrial de México es _____.

9. El _____ es un hermoso teatro y museo en la Ciudad de México.

10. La Virgen de _____ es la santa patrona de México.

B. A la izquierda de cada nombre de lugar en la lista *A*, escriba Vd. la letra de la palabra o expresión de la lista *B* que tenga relación con él.

	A		B
_____	1. Zócalo	*a.*	museo histórico
_____	2. Taxco	*b.*	petróleo
_____	3. Xochimilco	*c.*	ruinas
_____	4. Popocatépetl	*d.*	plaza principal
_____	5. Chapultepec	*e.*	henequén
_____	6. Tenochtitlán	*f.*	ciudad pintoresca
_____	7. Acapulco	*g.*	jardines flotantes
_____	8. Chichén-Itzá	*h.*	capital azteca
_____	9. Tampico	*i.*	playa
_____	10. Yucatán	*j.*	volcán

LA AMÉRICA CENTRAL

A. **Guatemala** produce bananas, café, y chicle. El chicle se usa para fabricar la goma de mascar (chewing gum). Su capital es la **Ciudad de Guatemala.**

B. **El Salvador** es el país más pequeño de la América Central. Su capital es **San Salvador.**

C. **Honduras** exporta bananas y café. Su capital es **Tegucigalpa.**

D. **Nicaragua** es la república más grande de la América Central. **Managua** es su capital.

E. **Costa Rica** exporta mucho café y plátanos (bananas). Su capital es **San José.**

F. **Panamá** es un istmo (isthmus) que junta (joins) las dos Américas. El **Canal de Panamá** cruza el país. Su capital también se llama **Panamá.**

LAS ANTILLAS

Las Antillas Mayores son un grupo de tres islas al sudeste de la costa de la Florida.

A. **Cuba** es la isla más grande e importante de las tres islas. Se llama "la perla (pearl) de las Antillas." Su capital es **La Habana.** Produce mucho azúcar y tabaco.

B. **Puerto Rico** produce mucho café y azúcar. Antes fue una posesión de los Estados Unidos. Hoy está asociado (associated) a los Estados Unidos como estado libre. Su capital es **San Juan.**

C. **La República Dominicana** comparte (shares) con Haití la isla llamada La Española. Su capital es **Santo Domingo.**

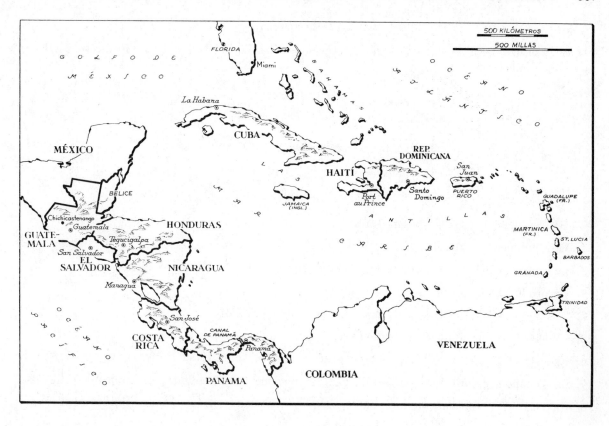

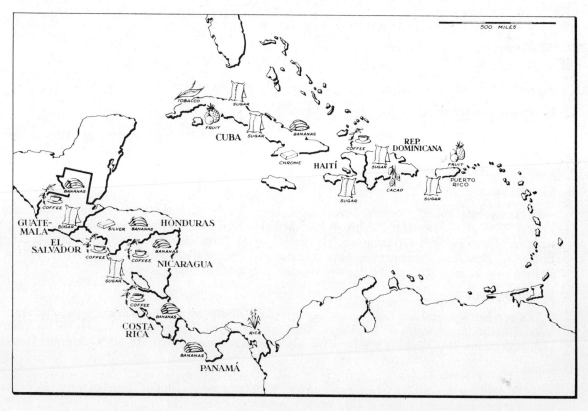

EJERCICIOS

A. A la izquierda de cada país de la lista *A*, escriba Vd. la letra del nombre de su capital que aparece en la lista *B*.

	A	B
_____	1. Nicaragua	*a.* San José
_____	2. Cuba	*b.* Santo Domingo
_____	3. República Dominicana	*c.* Managua
_____	4. Honduras	*d.* La Habana
_____	5. Costa Rica	*e.* Tegucigalpa

B. Complete Vd. las frases siguientes:

1. La república más grande de la América Central es _____.

2. La república más pequeña de la América Central es _____.

3. Un producto importante de Guatemala es _____.

4. "La perla de las Antillas" es un nombre que se da a _____.

5. El plátano es un producto importante de _____.

6. El _____ es el país que junta (joins) la América del Norte con la América del Sur.

7. La Española es una isla compartida por dos naciones: la República Dominicana y _____.

8. Una isla de las Antillas que forma un estado libre asociado con los Estados Unidos es _____.

9. Para fabricar la goma de mascar se usa el _____.

10. El azúcar y el tabaco son productos importantes de _____.

LA AMÉRICA DEL SUR

A. Montañas y Picos:

Los **Andes** cruzan el continente de norte a sur, a lo largo de (along) la costa occidental. **Chimborazo** y **Cotopaxi** son dos volcanes de los Andes. Los dos están situados en el Ecuador. **Aconcagua,** el pico más alto de los Andes, y de toda la América del Sur, está situado en la Argentina.

B. Ríos y Lagos:

El **Amazonas,** que atraviesa el Brasil, es el segundo río del mundo en longitud (the second longest river in the world). En los países de habla española los ríos principales son el **Magdalena** (en Colombia), el **Orinoco** (en Venezuela), y el **Plata** (en la Argentina). Entre la Argentina y el Brasil se encuentra la famosa **catarata** (waterfalls) **del Iguazú.** Entre Bolivia y el Perú está el **lago Titicaca,** el lago navegable más alto del mundo.

C. Llanuras (Plains):

Las **pampas** son grandes llanuras en la Argentina, donde se producen trigo y ganado. Aquí se halla el **ombú,** árbol típico de la pampa. Aquí también vive el **gaucho.** En Venezuela las llanuras se llaman **llanos.** En Colombia y el Brasil se encuentran las **selvas,** densos bosques de gran extensión.

D. Clima:

En la América del Sur las estaciones ocurren en orden opuesto (opposite) a las nuestras. Cuando nosotros tenemos el verano aquí, allí tienen el invierno, y viceversa.

E. Población:

Hay gran variedad (variety) de razas en la América del Sur:

1. La raza **blanca** que, en su mayor parte, consiste en **inmigrados** (immigrants) de Europa y **criollos.** Los criollos son personas nacidas en América de padres españoles.

2. La raza **india.** El grupo más numeroso son los **incas.** También hay muchos **mestizos,** personas que tienen sangre india y blanca.

3. La raza **negra.** Los negros fueron importados como esclavos durante la época colonial.

EJERCICIOS

A. Subraye Vd. la palabra o expresión que complete correctamente cada frase.

1. El ombú es un (a) animal (b) producto importante (c) árbol.

2. El río más largo de Sudamérica es el (a) Amazonas (b) Orinoco (c) Magdalena.

3. Una persona de sangre blanca e india es un (a) criollo (b) inmigrado (c) mestizo.

4. Entre Bolivia y el Perú está el lago (a) Chimborazo (b) Titicaca (c) Plata.

5. Las llanuras de la Argentina se llaman (a) llanos (b) pampas (c) selvas.

B. Complete Vd. las frases siguientes:

1. Una catarata famosa entre la Argentina y el Brasil es _____.

2. El río principal de Venezuela es el _____.

3. Una persona nacida en América de padres españoles se llama un _____.

4. El pico más alto de la América del Sur es _____.

5. Un volcán de los Andes, situado en el Ecuador, es _____.

6. Los bosques extensos de la América del Sur se llaman _____.

7. Cuando en la Argentina tienen el invierno, aquí tenemos el _____.

8. La raza india más numerosa de la América del Sur es la de los _____.

9. El río más importante de la Argentina es el _____.

10. El habitante típico de la pampa es el _____.

PAÍSES DEL ESTE

A. **La Argentina** se extiende desde el Chaco, en el norte, hasta el extremo sur del continente. Está separada de Chile por los Andes. En la frontera entre Chile y la Argentina hay una estatua grande, llamada el **Cristo de los Andes,** que conmemora (commemorates) el arreglo pacífico (peaceful settlement) de una disputa entre los dos países. Los productos principales de la Argentina son carne, lana, y trigo. Su capital, **Buenos Aires,** es la ciudad hispánica más grande de Sudamérica. Los habitantes de la capital se llaman **porteños.**

B. **El Uruguay** es el país hispano más pequeño de Sudamérica. Como la Argentina, sus productos principales son carne, lana, y cereales. Su capital es **Montevideo.**

C. **El Paraguay** no tiene puerto de mar, pero puede comunicarse con la costa por medio del **río Paraná.** Produce yerba mate, un té que se usa mucho allí, y quebracho, una madera muy dura que se usa para fabricar el cuero. Su capital es **Asunción.**

Países de los Andes

D. **Chile** se encuentra entre los Andes y el Océano Pacífico. De norte a sur se extiende unas 3,000 millas. Es el país más largo y más estrecho del continente. Sus productos principales son el cobre y el salitre (nitrates). Las ciudades principales son **Santiago,** la capital, y **Valparaíso,** el puerto principal.

E. **Bolivia** es el único país de Sudamérica que no tiene contacto con el mar. Para exportar sus productos depende de los países vecinos. Produce mucho estaño (tin). Su capital, **La Paz,** es la capital más alta del mundo (a unos 12,000 pies).

F. **El Perú** fue el centro del gobierno de los **incas,** que establecieron su capital en **Cuzco.** Hoy día, la capital y ciudad principal es **Lima.** En Lima se encuentra la universidad más antigua de la América del Sur, la de **San Marcos,** fundada en 1551. **El Callao,** cerca de Lima, es el puerto principal. El Perú tiene mucha riqueza minera. También exporta lana (de la alpaca) y guano (a fertilizer), que se usa en la agricultura.

G. **El Ecuador** está en el centro de la Zona Tórrida. La línea geográfica llamada *el ecuador* cruza el país. Aquí se producen los *sombreros de jipijapa,* que nosotros llamamos "Panama hats." También se produce mucho cacao, del cual se hace chocolate. Las ciudades principales son **Quito,** la capital, y **Guayaquil,** el puerto principal.

H. **Colombia** está en el noroeste del continente. Tiene puertos en los dos mares: el mar Caribe y el Océano Pací..co. Su capital es **Bogotá. Medellín,** en la costa, es el centro de la industria de café. Los productos principales del país son café, petróleo, platino (platinum), y esmeraldas (emeralds).

I. **Venezuela,** patria del Libertador, Bolívar, está en el norte. Exporta mucho petróleo. Su capital es **Caracas,** y su puerto principal, **La Guaira.**

EJERCICIOS

A. A la izquierda de cada país de la lista *A,* escriba Vd. la letra del nombre de su capital que aparece en la lista *B.*

A	B
_____ **1.** Chile	*a.* La Paz
_____ **2.** Venezuela	*b.* Bogotá
_____ **3.** el Perú	*c.* Quito
_____ **4.** el Ecuador	*d.* Asunción
_____ **5.** Colombia	*e.* Santiago
_____ **6.** Bolivia	*f.* Lima
_____ **7.** el Uruguay	*g.* Buenos Aires
_____ **8.** el Paraguay	*h.* Montevideo
_____ **9.** la Argentina	*i.* Caracas

B. Identifique Vd. los productos de cada país de la lista *A* escribiendo a la izquierda de su nombre la letra correspondiente de la lista *B*. (Cada letra de la lista *B* debe usarse una vez solamente.)

	A	*B*
_____	**1.** Venezuela	*a.* salitre, cobre
_____	**2.** Bólivia	*b.* petróleo
_____	**3.** el Ecuador	*c.* esmeraldas, platino, café
_____	**4.** Chile	*d.* sombreros de jipijapa
_____	**5.** el Paraguay	*e.* estaño
_____	**6.** Colombia	*f.* carne, trigo, lana
_____	**7.** la Argentina	*g.* yerba mate

C. Complete Vd. las frases siguientes:

1. Los habitantes de Buenos Aires se llaman _____.

2. _____ es un país sudamericano con puertos en dos mares.

3. La ciudad hispana más grande de Sudamérica es _____

4. Cuzco fue la capital antigua de los _____.

5. _____ es el país más estrecho de la América del Sur.

6. _____ es una estatua en los Andes entre Chile y la Argentina.

7. El país hispano más pequeño de la América del Sur es _____.

8. San Marcos es el nombre de una _____ antigua del Perú.

9. Del cacao se hace _____.

10. El único país sudamericano que no tiene contacto con el mar es _____

8. LA HISTORIA DE HISPANOAMÉRICA

A. Descubrimiento, Exploración, y Conquista:

1. Cristóbal **Colón** salió de España con tres barcos, la Niña, la Pinta, y la Santa María. El 12 de octubre de 1492 descubrió la isla de San Salvador (que hoy se llama *Watlings Island*). La fecha de este descubrimiento se celebra en todo el mundo hispánico como el "Día de la Raza."

2. Vasco Núñez de **Balboa** cruzó el istmo de Panamá y descubrió el Océano Pacífico, que él llamó "Mar del Sur."

3. Hernando **de Soto** descubrió el río Misisipí.

4. Juan **Ponce de León** descubrió la Florida.

5. Francisco Vázquez de **Coronado** exploró el sudoeste de los Estados Unidos, y descubrió el Gran Cañón (Grand Canyon).

6. Álvar Núñez **Cabeza de Vaca** exploró Nuevo México, Tejas, y parte de Kansas.

7. Fernando de **Magallanes** (Magellan), un navegante portugués, trató de dar la vuelta (circumnavigate) al mundo. Descubrió y pasó por el **Estrecho** (Strait) **de Magallanes.** Magallanes murió durante el viaje, y Juan Sebastián **del Cano,** un español, llevó a cabo el viaje.

8. Hernán **Cortés** conquistó a México, venciendo a los aztecas y a su rey, **Moctezuma.**

9. Francisco **Pizarro** conquistó el Perú. Venció a los incas, matando a su rey, **Atahualpa.** Fundó la ciudad de Lima, que él llamó "Ciudad de los Reyes."

10. Pedro de **Valdivia** conquistó a Chile, luchando con los araucanos, una tribu (tribe) de indios muy feroces.

B. Gobierno de las Colonias:

Las colonias eran gobernadas por el **Consejo** (Council) **de Indias,** un grupo de hombres nombrados por el rey. La **Casa de Contratación** dirigió el comercio colonial. Las colonias estaban divididas en cuatro **virreinatos** (viceroyalties), cada uno gobernado por un **virrey** (viceroy). Los virreinatos eran:

1. **Nueva España** (México, Antillas, y la América Central).

2. **Nueva Granada** (Colombia, Panamá, Venezuela, y el Ecuador).

3. **El Perú** (el Perú, Bolivia, y Chile).

4. **La Plata** (la Argentina, el Uruguay, y el Paraguay).

C. Misioneros (Missionaries):

1. Fray Junípero **Serra** estableció misiones en California.

2. Fray Bartolomé de **las Casas,** el "apóstol (apostle) de los indios," luchó en favor de los indios.

D. La Independencia (Revolución Contra España):

1. Francisco **Miranda,** de Venezuela, fue el primero de los revolucionarios.

2. Simón **Bolívar,** llamado "El Libertador," es la figura principal de la revolución. Ganó la libertad de Venezuela, Colombia, y el Ecuador.

3. José de **San Martín** ganó la libertad de la Argentina, Chile, y el Perú.

4. Bernardo **O'Higgins,** un general chileno, ayudó a San Martín en la lucha en Chile.

5. Antonio José de **Sucre** venció a los españoles en la batalla de **Ayacucho,** en 1824, la última batalla de la revolución.

6. El padre Miguel **Hidalgo,** cura del pueblo mexicano de Dolores, inició el movimiento por la independencia en México con el "Grito (battle cry) de Dolores."

7. El padre José **Morelos,** también sacerdote, continuó el trabajo comenzado en México por Hidalgo.

8. José **Martí** fue un patriota y poeta cubano que luchó por la independencia de Cuba.

E. Dictadores:

Las guerras de independencia fueron seguidas de una época de dictaduras en muchos países:

1. Agustín de **Iturbide** se declaró emperador (Agustín I) de México en 1822. La monarquía fue derribada (overthrown) un año después, en 1823.

2. **Maximiliano** (1864-1867), de Austria, fue enviado por Napoleón III a ser emperador de México. Fue matado por las fuerzas republicanas de Benito **Juárez,** un patriota mexicano. Los mexicanos consideran a Juárez el "Abrahán Lincoln de México."

   Otros dictadores:

3. Porfirio **Díaz,** México, 1877–1880, 1884–1911.

4. Juan Manuel de **Rosas,** la Argentina, 1829–1852.

5. Juan **Perón,** la Argentina, 1943–1955.

6. José Gaspar de **Francia,** el Paraguay, 1814–1840.

7. Vicente **Gómez,** Venezuela, 1908–1935.

8. Marcos **Pérez Jiménez,** Venezuela, 1953–1958.

9. Fulgencio **Batista,** Cuba, 1934–1944; 1952–1958.

10. Fidel **Castro,** Cuba, 1959—.

F. Relaciones Interamericanas:

1. **El Panamericanismo:** un movimiento que trata de fomentar (promote) la paz, el comercio. y la ayuda mutua (mutual) entre los Estados Unidos y las repúblicas de la América Latina,

   a. La **Unión Panamericana** fue establecida en 1910 para realizar los ideales del panamericanismo. En 1948 se cambió el nombre a la **Organización de Estados Americanos** (O.E.A.; en inglés, O.A.S.).

   b. El **Día Panamericano** se celebra cada año el 14 de abril.

2. La **Política** (Policy) **del Buen Vecino:** una política de amistad hacia los otros países americanos, iniciada por el presidente Franklin D. Roosevelt.

3. El **Cuerpo de Paz** (Peace Corps) y la **Alianza Para el Progreso** (Alliance for Progress) fueron iniciados por el presidente Kennedy. El Cuerpo de Paz envía maestros y técnicos (technicians) a otros países para ayudar a los habitantes a mejorar su condición. La Alianza Para el Progreso ofrece dinero y ayuda técnica a los países latinoamericanos que quieran hacer más democrático su gobierno.

EJERCICIOS

A. Subraye Vd. la palabra o expresión que correctamente complete cada frase.

1. Atahualpa fue el rey de (a) los incas (b) los mayas (c) los aztecas (d) los araucanos.

2. Colombia formaba parte del virreinato de (a) Nueva España (b) Nueva Granada (c) Perú (d) La Plata.

3. Ciudad de los Reyes es el nombre que Pizarro dio a la ciudad de (a) México (b) Buenos Aires (c) Caracas (d) Lima.

4. El libertador de la Argentina, de Chile, y del Perú fue (a) Miranda (b) Martí (c) San Martín (d) Morelos.

5. El jefe de las fuerzas que vencieron a Maximiliano fue (a) Benito Juárez (b) Porfirio Díaz (c) Hidalgo (d) O'Higgins.

6. El Día Panamericano se celebra (*a*) el dos de mayo (*b*) el catorce de abril (*c*) el doce de octubre (*d*) el cinco de mayo.

7. La Política del Buen Vecino fue iniciada por (*a*) Perón (*b*) Roosevelt (*c*) Castro (*d*) Batista.

8. El patriota que luchó por la independencia de Cuba fue (*a*) Martí (*b*) Batista (*c*) O'Higgins (*d*) Sucre.

9. Los Estados Unidos trata de ayudar el desarrollo (development) de la democracia en la América Latina por medio de (*a*) la Unión Panamericana (*b*) la Política del Buen Vecino (*c*) las conferencias panamericanas (*d*) la Alianza Para el Progreso.

10. El navegante español que completó el primer viaje alrededor del mundo fue (*a*) Sebastián del Cano (*b*) Magallanes (*c*) Valdivia (*d*) Cabeza de Vaca.

B. Identifique Vd. la persona que descubrió, exploró, o conquistó cada lugar de la lista *A* escribiendo la letra correspondiente de la lista *B*.

A	B
_____ 1. Chile	*a*. Balboa
_____ 2. San Salvador	*b*. de Soto
_____ 3. el Perú	*c*. Ponce de León
_____ 4. México	*d*. Coronado
_____ 5. Estrecho de Magallanes	*e*. Cabeza de Vaca
_____ 6. la Florida	*f*. Cortés
_____ 7. Nuevo México, Tejas, y Kansas	*g*. Valdivia
_____ 8. Océano Pacífico	*h*. Magallanes
_____ 9. río Misisipí	*i*. Colón
_____ 10. el Gran Cañón	*j*. Pizarro

C. A la izquierda de cada nombre de la lista *A*, escriba Vd. la letra de la expresión de la lista *B* que tenga relación con él.

A	B
_____ 1. Bartolomé de las Casas	*a*. el Libertador
_____ 2. Bolívar	*b*. Maximiliano
_____ 3. Hidalgo	*c*. dictador mexicano
_____ 4. Napoleón III	*d*. apóstol de los indios
_____ 5. Rosas	*e*. dictador cubano
_____ 6. Fray Junípero Serra	*f*. batalla de Ayacucho
_____ 7. Colón	*g*. misiones en California
_____ 8. Castro	*h*. la Pinta
_____ 9. Porfirio Díaz	*i*. dictador argentino
_____ 10. Sucre	*j*. Grito de Dolores

9. LA LITERATURA, EL ARTE, Y LA MÚSICA
DE HISPANOAMÉRICA

A. Poetas:

1. Alonso de **Ercilla** (siglo 16) escribió *La araucana*, un poema épico acerca de las luchas entre los conquistadores españoles y los indios araucanos de Chile. Fue la primera obra literaria importante escrita en el Nuevo Mundo.

2. Sor **Juana Inés de la Cruz** (siglo 17), de México, escribió la mejor poesía de la época colonial.

3. José **Hernández** (siglo 19) escribió *Martín Fierro*, un poema épico que describe la vida del gaucho. Es el mejor ejemplo de la literatura gauchesca.

4. José **Martí** (siglo 19) fue un poeta y patriota cubano.

5. Rubén **Darío** (siglos 19 y 20), de Nicaragua, fue el mejor poeta de la América Hispana. Fundó un nuevo movimiento en la poesía llamado el *modernismo*. Sus obras principales son *Prosas profanas* y *Cantos de vida y esperanza*.

6. Gabriela **Mistral** (siglo 20), poetisa de Chile, ganó el Premio Nobel de Literatura en 1945.

7. Jorge Luis **Borges** (siglo 20), argentino, fue uno de los poetas más importantes de Hispanoamérica.

8. Pablo **Neruda** (siglo 20), poeta chileno, ganó el Premio Nobel de Literatura en 1971.

9. Octavio **Paz** (siglo 20), poeta de México, ganó el Premio Nobel de Literatura en 1990.

B. Ensayistas y Novelistas:

1. José Enrique **Rodó** (siglo 20), del Uruguay, fue el ensayista más famoso de Hispanoamérica. Su obra maestra es *Ariel*, un libro de ensayos.

2. Ricardo **Palma** (siglos 19 y 20), del Perú, fue el autor de *Tradiciones peruanas*, cuentos de la época colonial.

3. Jorge **Isaacs** (siglo 19), de Colombia, escribió *María*, una novela romántica.

4. Ricardo **Güiraldes** (siglo 20), de la Argentina, escribió *Don Segundo Sombra*, una novela del gaucho.

5. Rómulo **Gallegos** (siglo 20), de Venezuela, escribió *Doña Bárbara*, una novela de los llanos de Venezuela.

6. Mariano **Azuela** (siglo 20), de México, escribió una novela de la revolución mexicana, *Los de abajo*.

7. Ciro **Alegría** (siglo 20), del Perú, escribió de los indios de su país en su novela *El mundo es ancho y ajeno* (alien).

8. Gabriel **García Márquez** (siglo 20), de Colombia, escribió la novela *Cien años de soledad*, que cuenta la historia de un pueblo colombiano ficticio (fictitious). García Márquez ganó el Premio Nobel de Literatura en 1982.

C. Educadores:
1. Andrés **Bello** (siglo 19), de Venezuela, fue poeta, crítico (critic), y erudito (scholar). Su *Gramática castellana*, escrita hace más de cien años, todavía se considera una de las mejores.
2. Domingo Faustino **Sarmiento** (siglo 19), de la Argentina, fue profesor y también presidente de su país. Escribió *Facundo*, biografía de un jefe gaucho.

D. Pintores:
1. Los tres pintores principales de México, Diego **Rivera**, José **Orozco**, y David **Siqueiros**, son todos del siglo 20, todos pintaron murales, y todos trataron temas (topics) sociales y políticos.
2. Cesáreo Bernaldo de **Quirós** (siglo 20), de la Argentina, pintó la vida pintoresca del gaucho.
3. Tito **Salas** (siglo 20), de Venezuela, pintó muchos cuadros sobre la lucha por la independencia.

E. Músicos y Compositores:
1. Carlos **Chávez** fue el compositor más famoso de México. También fue director de orquesta.
2. Agustín **Lara,** mexicano, compuso canciones populares, por ejemplo, *Granada*.
3. Ernesto **Lecuona,** cubano, también compuso canciones. Entre las más populares son *Siboney* y *Malagueña*.
4. Claudio **Arrau,** de Chile, fue un gran pianista.

F. Cantantes (Singers) y Actores:
1. Ramón **Vinay,** de Chile, fue famoso tenor de ópera.
2. Yma **Sumac,** peruana, fue una de las cantantes mejores y más conocidas del mundo.
3. **Cantinflas,** actor mexicano, fue un famoso cómico (comedian) de cine.

G. Bailes:
1. El **jarabe tapatío** es el baile típico de México. En los Estados Unidos se conoce como *The Mexican Hat Dance*.
2. La **rumba,** el **mambo,** y el **cha-cha-chá** son bailes de Cuba.
3. El **tango** es un baile de la Argentina.
4. La **zamacueca,** generalmente llamada la **cueca,** es un baile de Chile.
5. El **merengue** es un baile de la República Dominicana.

H. Instrumentos Músicos:
1. La **guitarra** es tan popular en la América Hispana como en España.
2. La **quena** es una flauta (flute) usada por los indios del Perú.
3. La **marimba** es semejante al *xylophone*. Es muy popular en México y en Guatemala.
4. Tres instrumentos que se usan mucho en Cuba para acompañar la música y marcar el ritmo (beat time) son:

   a. las **maracas** (made of gourds filled with pebbles)
   b. las **claves** (two round sticks that are struck against one another)
   c. el **güiro** (dried gourd scraped with a rod)

EJERCICIOS

A. Subraye Vd. la palabra o expresión que correctamente complete cada frase.

1. Una novela de la vida de los gauchos fue escrita por (*a*) Rodó (*b*) Güiraldes (*c*) Ercilla.

2. Una cantora del Perú que tuvo fama mundial fue (*a*) Tito Salas (*b*) Yma Sumac (*c*) Carlos Chávez.

3. *Los de abajo* fue escrito por (*a*) Rómulo Gallegos (*b*) Siqueiros (*c*) Mariano Azuela.

4. El padre del modernismo en la poesía es (*a*) Rubén Darío (*b*) Gabriela Mistral (*c*) Agustín Lara.

5. Andrés Bello y Domingo Sarmiento eran dos (*a*) pintores (*b*) educadores (*c*) compositores.

6. Una famosa poetisa mexicana de la época colonial fue (*a*) Yma Sumac (*b*) Gabriela Mistral (*c*) Sor Juana Inés de la Cruz.

7. Un célebre pintor de Venezuela fue (*a*) Orozco (*b*) Siqueiros (*c*) Salas.

8. Un baile típico de México es (*a*) el jarabe tapatío (*b*) la rumba (*c*) la quena.

9. Un pianista famoso de Chile fue (*a*) Lecuona (*b*) Cantinflas (*c*) Arrau.

10. *El mundo es ancho y ajeno* describe la vida y los problemas de los (*a*) indios (*b*) gauchos (*c*) actores.

B. A la izquierda de cada nombre de la lista *A*, escriba Vd. la letra de una expresión de la lista *B* que tenga relación con él.

A	B
_____ 1. José Martí	*a.* poeta argentino
_____ 2. marimba	*b.* *Doña Bárbara*
_____ 3. Diego Rivera	*c.* poeta cubano
_____ 4. Cantinflas	*d.* ensayista
_____ 5. José Enrique Rodó	*e.* xylophone
_____ 6. Jorge Luis Borges	*f.* compositor mexicano
_____ 7. Quirós	*g.* *María*
_____ 8. Carlos Chávez	*h.* pintor argentino
_____ 9. Jorge Isaacs	*i.* pintor mexicano
_____ 10. Rómulo Gallegos	*j.* cómico mexicano

C. Complete Vd. las frases siguientes:

1. En Chile el baile típico es la _____.

2. *Don Segundo Sombra, Facundo,* y *Martín Fierro* tratan de (deal with) la vida de los _____.

3. La primera obra literaria de importancia escrita en el Nuevo Mundo fue _____.

4. _____ es el autor de una famosa gramática española.

5. El mejor ejemplo de la literatura gauchesca es _____.

6. Para acompañar la música se usan las _____.

7. _____ fue una poetisa chilena.

8. Un pintor argentino fue _____.

9. El tango tuvo su origen en _____.

10. El instrumento más popular de los países hispánicos es la _____.

11. _____ fue un famoso autor peruano que escribió cuentos de la época colonial.

12. Dos bailes típicos de Cuba son _____ y _____.

13. _____ es el autor de *Cien años de soledad.*

14. Orozco fue un célebre _____ mexicano.

15. La flauta de los indios del Perú se llama _____.

10. LA VIDA Y LAS COSTUMBRES DE HISPANOAMÉRICA

A. Tipos Pintorescos:

1. El **charro** es el vaquero (cowboy) mexicano. Generalmente va montado a caballo. La **china poblana** es la compañera del charro.

2. En la Argentina el vaquero de las pampas se llama el **gaucho.** En los llanos de Venezuela se llama el **llanero.**

3. Los **mariachis** son grupos de cantantes mexicanos que andan por las calles cantando y pidiendo dinero.

B. Alimentos Mexicanos:

La **tortilla** es un *pancake* hecho de maíz. Las tortillas muchas veces vienen arrolladas (rolled) y contienen carne y salsa de ají (chili sauce). En estas formas se llaman **tacos** o **enchiladas.** Se comen también **chile con carne** y **tamales,** que consisten en maíz, carne picada (chopped meat), pimientos (peppers), etc.

C. Bebidas:

Además del café, que se bebe en todas partes, en la Argentina y el Paraguay también se bebe **mate,** que se hace de la planta *yerba mate.* Se bebe de una **calabaza** (gourd) por medio de un tubo llamado **bombilla.**

En México se producen el **pulque** y la **tequila,** bebidas intoxicantes hechas del *maguey.*

D. Ropa Típica:

1. Los **sombreros de jipijapa** (Panama hats) no se fabrican en Panamá, sino en el Ecuador.

2. El **poncho** es una capa que usa el gaucho para protegerse del frío y de la lluvia.

3. El **sarape** es una manta (blanket) que el mexicano lleva en el hombro.

4. Los **huaraches** son sandalias (sandals) que llevan los mexicanos.

5. El **rebozo** es un chal (shawl) que la mujer mexicana lleva en los hombros.

E. Fiestas:

Las fiestas religiosas son generalmente las mismas que en España. De las demás fiestas, hay dos que se celebran en toda la América Española:

1. El **Día de la Raza,** que corresponde a *Columbus Day* (el 12 de octubre), y que se celebra también en España.

2. El **Día Panamericano** (el 14 de abril), que se celebra en todos los países americanos.

En México se observan dos fiestas públicas:

3. El **16 de septiembre,** la fiesta nacional, conmemora (commemorates) el principio de la rebelión contra España.

4. El **5 de mayo** conmemora la lucha contra Francia y Maximiliano.

EJERCICIOS

A. Complete Vd. las frases siguientes:

1. _____ es un alimento mexicano.

2. Los sombreros de jipijapa se fabrican en _____.

3. La calabaza y la bombilla se usan para beber _____.

4. La mujer mexicana lleva en los hombros un _____.

5. Las _____ y las _____ se hacen de maíz.

6. Dos licores hechos del maguey son _____ y _____.

7. En Venezuela el *cowboy* se llama _____.

8. En los pies los mexicanos llevan _____.

9. Los mexicanos celebran el 5 de mayo para conmemorar su independencia de _____

10. Para protegerse de la lluvia, el gaucho lleva un _____

B. A la izquierda de cada expresión de la lista *A*, escriba Vd. la letra de la expresión de la lista *B* que tenga relación con ella.

	A		B
_____	1. taco	*a.*	cantante
_____	2. 16 de septiembre	*b.*	manta
_____	3. mariachi	*c.*	Columbus Day
_____	4. sarape	*d.*	alimento mexicano
_____	5. china poblana	*e.*	té
_____	6. 14 de abril	*f.*	Día Panamericano
_____	7. Día de la Raza	*g.*	maguey
_____	8. yerba mate	*h.*	Panama hat
_____	9. sombrero de jipijapa	*i.*	charro
_____	10. pulque	*j.*	día de la independencia mexicana

11. MASTERY EXERCISES ON SPANISH AMERICA

A. A la izquierda de cada expresión de la lista *A*, escriba Vd. la letra de la expresión de la lista *B* que tenga relación con ella.

GRUPO I

A	*B*
_____ 1. Cuba	*a.* iglesia famosa
_____ 2. charro	*b.* gramática
_____ 3. Basílica de Guadalupe	*c.* patriota mexicano
_____ 4. Bolívar	*d.* ciudad mexicana
_____ 5. Junípero Serra	*e.* pampas
_____ 6. Andrés Bello	*f.* instrumento músico
_____ 7. Hidalgo	*g.* azúcar
_____ 8. Tampico	*h.* misiones
_____ 9. gaucho	*i.* china poblana
_____ 10. marimba	*j.* el Libertador

GRUPO II

A	*B*
_____ 1. Benito Juárez	*a.* volcán en México
_____ 2. Cabeza de Vaca	*b.* patriota cubano
_____ 3. Ixtaccíhuatl	*c.* general chileno
_____ 4. el Cristo de los Andes	*d.* país pequeño
_____ 5. José Martí	*e.* presidente mexicano
_____ 6. El Salvador	*f.* montañas de Sudamérica
_____ 7. Orinoco	*g.* educador argentino
_____ 8. los Andes	*h.* monumento a la paz
_____ 9. O'Higgins	*i.* río de Venezuela
_____ 10. Sarmiento	*j.* explorador

B. Subraye Vd. la palabra o expresión que correctamente complete cada frase.

1. Uno de los lagos más altos del mundo se llama (*a*) Amazonas (*b*) Titicaca (*c*) el Zócalo (*d*) Iguazú.

2. Buenos Aires está en (*a*) Chile (*b*) el Perú (*c*) Cuba (*d*) la Argentina.

3. Una novela famosa de la revolución mexicana es (*a*) *Los de abajo* (*b*) *Facundo* (*c*) *Prosas profanas* (*d*) *Don Segundo Sombra*.

4. Antes de la conquista española, los aztecas reinaron en (*a*) México (*b*) el Perú (*c*) el Ecuador (*d*) la América Central.

5. Los incas fueron conquistados por (*a*) Coronado (*b*) Pizarro (*c*) Cortés (*d*) Balboa.

6. Un volcán del Ecuador es (*a*) Paricutín (*b*) Aconcagua (*c*) Cotopaxi (*d*) Popocatépetl.

7. El (*a*) Río Grande (*b*) Orinoco (*c*) Amazonas (*d*) Magdalena   separa a México de los Estados Unidos.

8. (a) Ernesto Lecuona (b) Carlos Chávez (c) Hernando de Soto (d) Cabeza de Vaca   fue un famoso compositor y director mexicano.

9. Un alimento mexicano es (a) mate (b) poncho (c) pulque (d) tortilla.

10. (a) El gaucho (b) El mexicano (c) El inca (d) El llanero   usa el sarape.

11. Un país de la América del Sur que no tiene costa de mar es (a) el Uruguay (b) Bolivia (c) Venezuela (d) el Perú.

12. Un gran poeta hispanoamericano es (a) Ciro Alegría (b) Sarmiento (c) Rubén Darío (d) Rodó.

13. La capital de Chile es (a) Asunción (b) Córdoba (c) Santiago (d) Valparaíso.

14. Se produce mucho petróleo en (a) Cuba (b) Venezuela (c) el Uruguay (d) el Perú.

15. El Castillo de Chapultepec se halla en (a) Buenos Aires (b) La Habana (c) Lima (d) la Ciudad de México.

16. La bombilla y la calabaza se usan para beber (a) café (b) pulque (c) mate (d) tequila.

17. Diego Rivera fue un famoso (a) músico (b) novelista (c) pintor (d) filósofo.

18. San Martín ganó la independencia (a) de Colombia (b) del Uruguay (c) de México (d) de la Argentina.

19. Un baile típico de Chile es (a) la cueca (b) la rumba (c) el tango (d) el jarabe tapatío.

20. Uno de los mejores ejemplos de la literatura gauchesca es (a) *Doña Bárbara* (b) *Martín Fierro* (c) *María* (d) *El mundo es ancho y ajeno*.

C. Complete Vd. las frases siguientes:

1. Una playa famosa de México es _____.

2. El salitre es un producto importante de _____.

3. Valdivia conquistó a _____.

4. La universidad más antigua de la América del Sur es la de _____.

5. Quirós pintó la vida del _____.

6. _____ fue una poetisa chilena que ganó el Premio Nobel.

7. La rebelión de México contra España fue iniciada por el padre _____.

8. Una poetisa de la época colonial fue _____.

9. Atahualpa fue el jefe de los _____.

10. El Día Panamericano se celebra el _____.

11. _____ es la capital del Uruguay.

12. _____ se considera el "Abrahán Líncoln de México."

13. _____ y _____ son dos famosos novelistas hispanoamericanos.

14. La capital de Venezuela es _____.

15. México celebra dos fiestas nacionales: el 5 de mayo y _____.

16. El pico más alto de los Andes es _____.

17. Las personas nacidas en el Nuevo Mundo de padres españoles se llaman _____.

18. _____ es el río principal de la Argentina.

19. El "apóstol de los indios" fue _____.

20. El país hispánico más pequeño de Sudamérica es _____.

21. El emperador de los aztecas fue _____.

22. La capital de Costa Rica es ------------------------.

23. El general ------------- venció a los españoles en la batalla de Ayacucho.

24. --------------------------- exporta mucho cacao.

25. La ciudad de ----------------------, en México, es famosa por sus jardines flotantes.

26. El Día de la Raza se celebra el ----------------------------------.

27. La Paz es la capital de ----------------------.

28. El jarabe tapatío es un baile de --------------------.

29. La capital del Perú es --------------.

30. Asunción es la capital del ----------------------

Part VI—*Auditory Comprehension*
A. COMPLETION OF ORAL SENTENCES

Directions to the Pupil: The teacher will read aloud a sentence, in Spanish, and will repeat it. After the *second* reading of the sentence, *circle* the letter of the answer that best completes the sentence.

1.	*a*	*b*	*c*	*d*	26.	*a*	*b*	*c*	*d*
2.	*a*	*b*	*c*	*d*	27.	*a*	*b*	*c*	*d*
3.	*a*	*b*	*c*	*d*	28.	*a*	*b*	*c*	*d*
4.	*a*	*b*	*c*	*d*	29.	*a*	*b*	*c*	*d*
5.	*a*	*b*	*c*	*d*	30.	*a*	*b*	*c*	*d*
6.	*a*	*b*	*c*	*d*	31.	*a*	*b*	*c*	*d*
7.	*a*	*b*	*c*	*d*	32.	*a*	*b*	*c*	*d*
8.	*a*	*b*	*c*	*d*	33.	*a*	*b*	*c*	*d*
9.	*a*	*b*	*c*	*d*	34.	*a*	*b*	*c*	*d*
10.	*a*	*b*	*c*	*d*	35.	*a*	*b*	*c*	*d*
11.	*a*	*b*	*c*	*d*	36.	*a*	*b*	*c*	*d*
12.	*a*	*b*	*c*	*d*	37.	*a*	*b*	*c*	*d*
13.	*a*	*b*	*c*	*d*	38.	*a*	*b*	*c*	*d*
14.	*a*	*b*	*c*	*d*	39.	*a*	*b*	*c*	*d*
15.	*a*	*b*	*c*	*d*	40.	*a*	*b*	*c*	*d*
16.	*a*	*b*	*c*	*d*	41.	*a*	*b*	*c*	*d*
17.	*a*	*b*	*c*	*d*	42.	*a*	*b*	*c*	*d*
18.	*a*	*b*	*c*	*d*	43.	*a*	*b*	*c*	*d*
19.	*a*	*b*	*c*	*d*	44.	*a*	*b*	*c*	*d*
20.	*a*	*b*	*c*	*d*	45.	*a*	*b*	*c*	*d*
21.	*a*	*b*	*c*	*d*	46.	*a*	*b*	*c*	*d*
22.	*a*	*b*	*c*	*d*	47.	*a*	*b*	*c*	*d*
23.	*a*	*b*	*c*	*d*	48.	*a*	*b*	*c*	*d*
24.	*a*	*b*	*c*	*d*	49.	*a*	*b*	*c*	*d*
25.	*a*	*b*	*c*	*d*	50.	*a*	*b*	*c*	*d*

B. SUITABLE RESPONSES TO QUESTIONS OR STATEMENTS

Directions to the Pupil: The teacher will read aloud a question or statement, in Spanish, and will repeat it. After the *second* reading of the question or statement, *circle* the letter of the alternative which is the most suitable response to the oral question or statement.

1. *a.* Es de mi padre y mi madre.
   b. Cae el mes próximo.
   c. Este regalo es para ellos.
   d. Es su aniversario quinientos.

2. *a.* Está en el gabinete.
   b. Cuesta mucho.
   c. Pertenece al muchacho.
   d. Debes colgarla en el ropero.

3. *a.* Di con mi amigo el joyero.
   b. Le regalé una joya preciosa.
   c. La casa daba al parque.
   d. Me dio un libro.

4. *a.* Busco una moneda que perdí.
   b. Espero la llegada del tren.
   c. El vestíbulo está oscuro.
   d. Asistí a una tertulia.

5. *a.* Hay dos sellos en el sobre.
   b. El cartero llegó tarde.
   c. Mi cartera está en casa.
   d. No comprendo algunos párrafos.

6. *a.* Sí, llegué a las nueve en punto.
   b. Sí, hacía buen tiempo.
   c. Sí, voy a la escuela todos los días.
   d. Sí, paso mucho tiempo allí.

7. *a.* No es muy modesta.
   b. Celebró su boda recientemente.
   c. Es muy bondadosa.
   d. Pintó aquel cuadro bonito.

8. *a.* Sí, porque estoy en la ciudad.
   b. Sí, comenzó al anochecer.
   c. Sí, comenzó al amanecer.
   d. Sí, me acosté tarde anoche.

9. *a.* Hay mucho que hacer en el centro.
   b. Mi amigo sale en media hora.
   c. Me gusta viajar por ferrocarril.
   d. Las tiendas se cierran a las cinco.

10. *a.* No pude comer.
   b. No me gusta bailar.
   c. La ópera terminó a las once.
   d. Sí, y vi una película interesante.

11. *a.* Es de noche.
   b. Es el mes de junio.
   c. Hace frío.
   d. Es peligroso salir.

12. *a.* Limpió los sillones.
   b. Compró una almohada.
   c. Se bañó en la fuente.
   d. Abrió la nevera.

13. *a.* Llegará pronto.
   b. Hay que correr a la estación.
   c. Va a llover dentro de poco.
   d. Brilla el sol.

14. *a.* Es agradable visitar el campo.
   b. Hay una buena película.
   c. Voy a comprar huevos.
   d. Hay noticias de gran importancia.

15. *a.* Sueña con príncipes y princesas.
   b. Es bastante rica ahora.
   c. Son las dos de la madrugada.
   d. Tiene una belleza encantadora.

16. *a.* Salí hace una hora.
   b. No estoy por salir.
   c. Hice una visita al sacerdote.
   d. No estoy listo todavía.

17. *a* No, porque el relojero está muy lejos.
   b. Me lo dio mi padre.
   c. No doy mi reloj a nadie.
   d. Sí, por eso anda bien.

18. *a.* El agua corre lentamente.
   b. Hay mucho lodo.
   c. Hay numerosos pescadores.
   d. Todo el mundo está patinando.

19. *a.* Tiene un lugar conveniente.
   b. en el mes de septiembre
   c. Ocurre en muchos sitios.
   d. Todavía buscan un lugar.

20. *a.* Vuelven inmediatamente.
   b. No salen del nido.
   c. Mueren en seguida.
   d. Se echan a volar.

21. *a.* Tuvo mucha suerte en la lotería.
   b. Pasó la noche en su alcoba.
   c. Salió en compañía de su cuñado.
   d. Se encontró con un antiguo amigo.

22. *a.* Sí, porque nuestro equipo siempre gana.
   b. No, porque siempre pierdo.
   c. Sí, porque es semejante al tenis.
   d. Sí, cuando hace sol.

23. *a.* Se hizo daño en la cabeza.
   b. Se quebró la pierna izquierda.
   c. Se rompió en mil pedazos.
   d. Pepe lo recogió.

24. *a.* Hable Vd. con él.
   b. Póngalo Vd. en la mesa.
   c. Una carta llega más pronto.
   d. Allí está la oficina de la compañía.

25. *a.* Se usa en un partido de fútbol.
   b. Es enorme.
   c. Es redonda.
   d. Es bastante pequeña.

26. *a.* Ella está muy ocupada ahora.
   b. Ella está leyéndoles un cuento.
   c. La lección no es interesante.
   d. No prestan atención.

27. *a.* Es la una y media.
   b. Hace sol.
   c. No hago nada.
   d. Trabajo todo el día.

28. *a.* La recibirán mañana.
    b. El carretero vendrá tarde.
    c. Espero recibirla en dos días.
    d. Me enviaron una tarjeta.

29. *a.* Di una peseta al niño.
    b. Tengo diez centavos en la bolsa.
    c. Acabo de gastar un dólar.
    d. Mi papá me dio diez dólares.

30. *a.* Produce música muy bonita.
    b. La orquesta es muy buena.
    c. Juega muy bien.
    d. Recibió una buena nota.

31. *a.* Tiene el pelo rubio.
    b. Las boinas están de moda.
    c. Es una boina negra.
    d. Las boinas deben llevarse en los pies.

32. *a.* Nadie lleva paraguas hoy.
    b. El cielo está claro.
    c. Se ven nubes grises.
    d. Llovió ayer.

33. *a.* Ella prefiere un alfiler.
    b. Ella quería venderlo.
    c. Ella me lo devolvió.
    d. Sí, y la noticia le gustó.

34. *a.* La tierra está seca.
    b. El florero es muy hábil.
    c. Llueve bastante aquí.
    d. Debe ser roja.

35. *a.* ¿Le traigo la cuenta, señor?
    b. ¿Dónde está el lechero?
    c. Vamos a comer.
    d. Tiene buen apetito.

36. *a.* Visito al dentista a menudo.
    b. Compro objetos raros.
    c. Compro solamente las cosas necesarias.
    d. No me gusta hacerlo.

37. *a.* Mire Vd. estos calcetines.
    b. Se fue ayer.
    c. Tome Vd. un vaso de agua.
    d. ¿Cómo le gusta este color?

38. *a.* Irá en un buque grande.
    b. El teléfono está en la pared.
    c. Compró un billete de ida y vuelta.
    d. Hará un viaje a Italia.

39. *a.* Juan la abrió.
    b. Quiero aprovecharme del sol.
    c. Hace mucho viento.
    d. Me gusta el aire fresco.

40. *a.* Siempre pierdo.
    b. No gano nada estudiando.
    c. Es posible ganar mucho.
    d. Me gusta estudiar.

41. *a.* Vamos a subir para ver.
    b. Es un edificio alto.
    c. Voy a tomar el ascensor.
    d. Por lo visto, el árbol es demasiado alto.

42. *a.* La librería está bastante lejos.
    b. Deseo hacer ejercicios.
    c. Tengo que ponerme el abrigo.
    d. Me molesta el sol.

43. *a.* Se usa para cortar la hierba.
    b. Busco un empleo.
    c. No tiene gasolina.
    d. Es un rascacielos.

44. *a.* Están de buen humor.
    b. Dejó de fumar.
    c. El fuego es muy grande.
    d. Se prohibe fumar aquí.

45. *a.* Sirven a las cinco de la tarde.
    b. Tomaban la merienda.
    c. El propietario del restaurante lo sirvió.
    d. Sirvieron una taza a aquella dama.

46. *a.* Nos da frutas.
    b. Es muy útil.
    c. Se puede comer.
    d. Se sirve con té y limón.

47. *a.* Daremos un paseo largo mañana.
    b. El comité se reunió a las diez.
    c. Nadie va a pasar por aquí hoy.
    d. Es un asunto muy serio.

48. *a.* Tengo más amigos que él.
    b. Están muy lejos de aquí.
    c. Tiene pensamientos muy alegres.
    d. Son muy crueles.

49. *a.* No, tú ya tienes mucho.
    b. Sí, es imposible estudiar aquí.
    c. Sí, tu mamá sabe cocinar bien.
    d. La música suena mejor en la mía.

50. *a.* Borro la pizarra.
    b. Meto el pie en la cesta.
    c. Vuelvo la espalda al maestro.
    d. Salgo de la escuela.

C. AUDITORY COMPREHENSION PASSAGES

Directions to the Pupil: The teacher will read aloud, in Spanish, a question followed by a passage, and will repeat the reading of both the question and the passage. After the *second* reading, *circle* the letter of the alternative that best answers the question. Base your answers only on the content of the passage.

1. ¿Cuántas cosas tomó Alfonso en el almuerzo?
   a. doce   b. cuatro   c. dos   d. tres

2. ¿Qué estación se describe aquí?
   a. el invierno   c. el verano
   b. la primavera   d. el otoño

3. ¿De qué color tenía los ojos?
   a. pardo   b. gris   c. azul·   d. negro

4. ¿Qué hacen los niños?
   a. Se arrojan al agua.   c. Se divierten con la nieve.
   b. Se dedican a estudiar.   d. Nadan en los ríos.

5. ¿Qué son las selvas?
   a. bosques   c. ríos largos
   b. plantas tropicales   d. animales enormes

6. ¿Quién fue Juárez?
   a. emperador de México   c. soldado del ejército
   b. amigo de Maximiliano   d. presidente de México

7. ¿Por qué no hago viajes?
   a. Tengo miedo de cruzar el mar. c. Los libros son mejores.
   b. Cuestan mucho.   d. No quiero viajar.

8. ¿Para quiénes es el club español?
   a. para todos los alumnos   c. para los alumnos avanzados
   b. para los alumnos del primer año d. para los que no hablan español

9. ¿Quién descubrió el Nuevo Mundo?
   a. muchos hombres   c. un hombre serio
   b. solamente Colón   d. cuatro hombres europeos

10. ¿Dónde está Bogotá?
    a. en España   c. cerca de Colombia
    b. en las plazas y calles   d. en una llanura alta

11. ¿Cuántos ríos hay en el Brasil?
    a. muchos   c. uno solamente
    b. menos que en los otros países d. ningunos

12. ¿Qué hicieron primero al entrar en la casa?
    a. Se sentaron a comer.   c. Regresaron a la casita.
    b. Discutieron las noticias del día. d. Tomaron el aire fresco.

13. ¿Qué tiempo hacía cuando Juan salió de casa?
    a. Hacía buen tiempo.   c. Llovía.
    b. No hacía sol.   d. Hacía mucho fresco.

14. ¿Por qué hay poco progreso en la América del Sur?
    a. No se emplean los burros.   c. No hay bastantes ferrocarriles.
    b. Son abundantes los caminos.   d. El progreso es muy lento.

15. ¿Qué es la Alhambra?
    a. un hotel para turistas   c. un palacio
    b. una calle de Granada   d. una época romántica

16. ¿Por qué es famoso Montevideo?
    a. por su playa de mar   c. Es más grande que Buenos Aires.
    b. Está en el Uruguay.   d. Está cerca de Buenos Aires.

17. ¿Quiénes asisten al mercado?
    a. los que quieren comprar algo   *c.* todo el mundo
    b. los que no quieren comprar   *d.* los que quieren hablar

18. ¿Quién fue Ojeda?
    a. un conquistador español   *c.* el compañero íntimo de Colón
    b. un personaje imaginario   *d.* un escritor de leyendas

19. ¿Por qué era noble el conde?
    a. Vivía en el campo.   *c.* Sus vecinos le ayudaban.
    b. Le gustaba trabajar.   *d.* Hacía cosas buenas.

20. ¿Cuándo fue construido el acueducto de Segovia?
    a. en el siglo diez y ocho   *c.* hace mil años
    b. en el siglo primero   *d.* hace nueve siglos

21. ¿Qué estación era?
    a. el otoño   *c.* el verano
    b. el invierno   *d.* la primavera

22. ¿De qué están hablando estas personas?
    a. de la vida de campo   *c.* de una rebelión
    b. de la cárcel   *d.* de la guerra

23. ¿Cómo están viajando?
    a. a caballo   *c.* por tren
    b. en autobús   *d.* en automóvil

24. ¿Cómo está la madre?
    a. triste   *b.* sentada   *c.* alegre   *d.* tranquila

25. ¿Qué se aprende de este párrafo?
    a. Teresa escribía para un diario.   *c.* Su padre no mencionaba el casamiento.
    b. Teresa cuidaba a su padre.   *d.* Teresa estaba enferma.

26. ¿Qué se sabe de este joven?
    a. Sabe bailar.   *c.* Baila muy mal.
    b. No desea bailar con Elena.   *d.* Sale a menudo.

27. ¿Por qué dice Luis que es la segunda visita?
    a. Está enfermo.   *c.* El médico no es bueno.
    b. No desea pagar diez dólares.   *d.* Le gusta la medicina que toma.

28. ¿Por qué quería el muchacho dar dinero al hombre?
    a. Era un niño bueno.   *c.* El hombre era viejo.
    b. Quería comprar algo.   *d.* Le gustaba ayudar a los pobres.

29. ¿Qué desea el hombre?
    a. Desea conocer a la familia del joyero.   *c.* Desea hablar español.
    b. Desea comprar una joya.   *d.* Desea ver una tarjeta.

30. ¿Qué no le gustaba al chófer?
    a. parar el autobús   *c.* tomar un asiento
    b. cobrar dinero   *d.* contestar a las personas

31. ¿Qué se prepara a hacer la gente?
    a. escuchar la voz de la madre   *c.* comer
    b. poner las luces   *d.* hacer ruido

32. ¿Qué se puede ver hoy día en Toledo?
    a. solamente piedras   *c.* moros y cristianos
    b. la cultura de varias razas   *d.* una ciudad moderna

33. ¿Cuándo llegaron al teatro?
    a. antes de las ocho y media   *c.* al principio de la función
    b. después de comenzar la función   *d.* después del segundo acto

34. ¿Por qué celebraban las personas?
    a. Habían ganado una victoria.
    b. El enemigo entró en la capital.
    c. Su ejército había sido destruido.
    d. Comenzó la guerra.

35. ¿Cuánto vino se exporta de España?
    a. menos de la mitad
    b. todo el vino
    c. ningún vino
    d. más de la mitad

36. ¿Cuánto territorio ocuparon los incas?
    a. las montañas del Perú
    b. todo el continente
    c. solamente la capital
    d. gran parte del continente

37. ¿Qué se encuentra en Buenos Aires?
    a. unas pampas extensas
    b. el centro del gobierno
    c. muchos gauchos
    d. lo más típico de la Argentina

38. ¿Por qué no lloró Juanito?
    a. Buscó a su madre.
    b. Tenía solamente seis años.
    c. Se cayó.
    d. Nadie estaba con él.

39. ¿Por qué no sabía Ricardo hablar español?
    a. Era inteligente.
    b. Deseaba aprender mucho.
    c. No estudiaba.
    d. Era mexicano.

40. ¿Por qué abandonó el hombre su casa?
    a. Fue un desertor.
    b. Fue a ver al juez.
    c. El juez conocía a su esposa.
    d. Su esposa le trataba mal.

41. ¿Por qué era loca la muchacha?
    a. No sabía elegir un buen esposo.
    b. No quería al joven.
    c. El padre le decía que debía casarse.
    d. No deseaba casarse.

42. ¿Cuántos países libertó Bolívar?
    a. cinco
    b. menos de cinco
    c. toda la América del Sur
    d. No se sabe.

43. ¿Por qué fue el hombre a casa de su amigo?
    a. Tenía mucho dinero.
    b. Se encontraba sin dinero.
    c. Quería dormir.
    d. Quería hablar con el criado.

44. ¿Cuándo se ven las nubes?
    a. de noche
    b. cuando el avión vuela muy alto
    c. cuando el cielo está claro
    d. cuando hay mucha luz

45. ¿Qué costumbre tenía este muchacho?
    a. Estudiaba mucho.
    b. Tenía sueño en las clases.
    c. Luchaba con los amigos.
    d. Se divertía todas las noches.

46. ¿Qué sabían hacer los mayas?
    a. luchar contra los aztecas
    b. construir edificios grandes
    c. vencer a los españoles
    d. leer libros de arquitectura

47. ¿Qué son las "casas colgadas"?
    a. piedras muy grandes
    b. unas montañas
    c. edificios antiguos
    d. casas formadas por la naturaleza

48. ¿Cuánto tiempo habían caminado?
    a. por la tarde
    b. todo el día
    c. cuatro horas
    d. por la mañana

49. ¿Qué se aprende de este párrafo?
    a. Las personas ven las cosas con ojos distintos.
    b. Las fábricas de Bilbao son grandes.
    c. Todo el mundo tiene las mismas ideas.
    d. Los pintores no saben nada.

50. ¿Qué palabra describe al criado?
    a. perezoso   *b.* alto   *c.* inteligente   *d.* estúpido

Part VII—*Passages for Reading Comprehension*

A. BRIEF PASSAGES FOR COMPREHENSION

Lea Vd. los pasajes siguientes. Al fin de cada pasaje hay una pregunta, con varias respuestas posibles. Subraye Vd. la respuesta correcta, según el sentido del pasaje.

1. Una tarde primaveral mis amigos y yo pescábamos en el río. Nos encantó la esperanza de comer pescado fresco aquella noche. Pasamos allí un par de horas, sin éxito, pues no se acercó ni un solo pez. Cansados de aquel ejercicio, nos decidimos a regresar al pueblo.

   ¿Por qué volvieron al pueblo?

   a. Hacía fresco.
   b. Les gustaban los ejercicios.
   c. No cogieron nada.
   d. La noche se acercaba.

2. En España casi nadie, cuando sale de noche, lleva consigo la llave de su casa. Si una persona vuelve tarde y quiere entrar, da unas palmadas, y pronto llega un individuo que se llama el sereno. Lleva en la mano unas llaves. Con una de éstas deja abierta la puerta.

   ¿Qué hace el sereno?

   a. Le da a uno la llave.
   b. Entra en la casa.
   c. Le da la mano.
   d. Le permite a uno entrar.

3. El viejo y su sobrina, seguidos del criado, entraron en el comedor, una sala tan vasta que había lugar allí para cien personas más. Se sentaron a una mesa enorme, que tenía bastante comida para una compañía de soldados. Solos se pusieron a comer, aunque sin apetito.

   ¿Cuántas personas estaban en la sala?

   a. cien personas
   b. muchos soldados
   c. tres personas
   d. dos personas

4. En Madrid casi todo el mundo asiste al café por la tarde. Allí van grupos de estudiantes, de políticos, de hombres de negocios, personas de todas clases. Toman cerveza o café, con algo de comer, no porque tienen hambre, sino para pasar un par de horas charlando con amigos, lo cual es la razón principal para reunirse.

   ¿Por qué van las personas al café?

   a. Tienen hambre.
   b. Les gusta hablar.
   c. Desean estudiar.
   d. Están en Madrid.

5. La primera casa por donde pasábamos era tan hermosa que parecía un palacio. Sus dueños eran los más ricos del pueblo, y no tenían hijos. Esto último les debía causar mucha pena, porque eran muy aficionados a los niños. Su mayor gusto, siempre que íbamos a la escuela o volvíamos a casa para almorzar, era asomarse al balcón que daba sobre el camino. De allí hablaban con nosotros y nos echaban regalitos.

   ¿Qué solían hacer los niños?

   a. tomar el almuerzo en el camino
   b. pasar por la casa
   c. hacer llorar a los dueños de la casa
   d. mirar desde el balcón

6. El pequeño Ricardito ayudaba a su madre una noche a lavar los platos. La madre notó que su hijo trabajaba despacio, sin entusiasmo. Para animarle un poco, le dijo: —Debes trabajar más rápido. No debes dejar para mañana lo que puedes terminar hoy.
   —En ese caso—contestó el niño—debemos terminar hoy el pastel que está en la mesa, y no dejarlo para mañana.

   ¿Por qué contestó Ricardo a su madre?

   a. Deseaba ayudar a su madre.
   b. Siempre pensaba en mañana.
   c. Le gustó el pastel.
   d. Le gustaba trabajar.

7. En México la tierra tiene muchos aspectos distintos: llanuras fértiles y extensas cubiertas de magníficas plantas; cadenas de montañas cubiertas de nieve; ríos, grandes y pequeños, que con sus aguas hacen posible la agricultura; y a los dos lados de los ríos, valles hermosos.

¿Cómo es la tierra de México?

a. muy montañosa
b. Hay nieve por todas partes.

c. cubierta de agua
d. variada

8. En el siglo XVI los mares del mundo estaban llenos de buques hispanos, tanto comerciales como de guerra. En esos tiempos los españoles amaban el mar, porque el mar había dado a España una dimensión mayor, un nuevo horizonte. Por medio del mar, el comercio español llegó a ser el más importante del mundo, y España la primera entre las naciones de Europa.

¿Por qué era importante el mar?

a. a causa del comercio

b. Estaba lleno de buques españoles.

c. Los españoles eran los mejores navegantes del mundo.
d. Todos los españoles salían de España.

9. Había unas veinte y cinco casas blancas, con balcones, situadas en calles estrechas y tortuosas al pie de una colina. Alrededor, se extendía un hermoso prado, cortado por un pequeño río. De este río sacaban agua para el trigo y el maíz. De las casas salían los campesinos todos los días a trabajar en los campos.

¿De qué se habla aquí?

a. de una montaña
b. de un pueblo rural

c. de un museo
d. de una ciudad moderna

10. Al fin de tantos años de trabajo, yo todavía tengo que ganar hoy lo que he de comer mañana. Es decir, que en mi casa no hay abundancia de pesetas, y antes de comprar algo tengo que pensarlo bien.

¿Qué se sabe de este hombre?

a. Es rico.
b. Tiene hambre.

c. Todavía trabaja.
d. Está acostumbrado a gastar mucho dinero.

11. Yo tuve un tío que era conocido y respetado de todo el mundo por hombre serio. Sus palabras, su estilo, sus pasos, sus gestos, su ropa, su barba, todos sus actos, iban acompañados de una terrible severidad. Muy raras veces se le veía reír.

¿Cómo era el tío?

a. Tenía un carácter grave.
b. Se reía mucho.

c. Era actor.
d. Le gustaba la buena compañía.

12. Al llegar al puerto de La Coruña, en Galicia, la cosa más notable que se ve es una torre muy alta que sirve de faro para guiar a los marineros. Tan antigua es esta torre, que su verdadero origen está perdido en la tradición. No se sabe ni cuándo, ni cómo, ni por quién fue construida. Lo que sí se sabe es que tiene una base tan firme que ni los siglos ni las tempestades han bastado para destruirla.

¿Qué se sabe de la torre?

a. su origen
b. Es muy fuerte y sólida.

c. Fue construida recientemente.
d. No sirve para nada.

13. En el año 1769, por orden del rey Carlos III, salió de México una compañía de militares españoles a explorar la tierra de lo que es hoy California. Pasaron varios años en esta obra, avanzando desde el sur hacia el norte. Iban acompañados de varios sacerdotes, entre ellos el padre Junípero Serra. En aquel mismo año fundó éste la misión de San Diego, primera de las veinte y una que estableció.

¿Quién estableció las misiones en California?

a. el padre Junípero Serra
b. San Diego

c. los soldados
d. el rey

14. Castilla y Aragón, los dos viejos reinos (kingdoms) más grandes e importantes de España, se unieron en el siglo XV con el casamiento de Isabel de Castilla y Fernando de Aragón. Castilla contribuyó más que ningún otro reino a la formación de una España unida. Esta unidad se logró por fin en el año 1492 con la conquista de Granada, el último reino de los moros en España.

¿Cuál de éstos fue el más importante para la formación de España?

a. los moros　　　　　　　　　　　*c.* Aragón
b. Granada　　　　　　　　　　　　*d.* Castilla

15. En una aldea vivía un hombre pobre que tenía un hijo, un joven bueno y simpático. En la misma aldea había otro hombre, que era muy rico. Este hombre tenía una hija cuyo carácter era todo lo contrario del carácter del muchacho. Era ella de naturaleza violenta, dispuesta a cada momento a gritar o a dar golpes a cualquier persona. Por ser rica la muchacha, el muchacho quería casarse con ella, y se arregló el casamiento.

Los dos novios eran

a. de carácter distinto　　　　　　　*c.* de carácter semejante
b. simpáticos　　　　　　　　　　　*d.* ricos

16. Ganada la independencia de la Argentina, el general San Martín quería libertar a Chile. Para esto era necesario vencer a los españoles que ocupaban aquel país. San Martín se vio obligado a cruzar las montañas con todo su ejército, entrar en Chile, y allí luchar con los españoles. Esta marcha a través de los Andes, desde la Argentina a Chile, es la obra suprema de San Martín, y le hace brillar como un genio militar de primer orden. En veinte días pudo llevar a cabo una obra que debía ocupar meses enteros.

¿Dónde estaban los españoles?

a. con San Martín　　　　　　　　　*c.* en Chile
b. en la Argentina　　　　　　　　　*d.* en las montañas

17. Entre los pintores españoles, el que se distingue por la luz y alegría de sus obras es Sorolla. A diferencia de las obras religiosas de Ribera y Murillo, o del duro realismo de Velázquez y Goya (que pintan la alta sociedad tanto como la clase baja), en Sorolla se ven escenas alegres: las flores, los jardines, los pescadores, los niños corriendo por la playa o nadando en las aguas del mar, todo esto bañado en un sol espléndido que parece más real que el sol mismo.

¿Qué se ve en las obras de Sorolla?

a. escenas al aire libre　　　　　　　*c.* la clase alta
b. temas religiosos　　　　　　　　　*d.* la gente dentro de sus casas

18. Andando por la calle un día, Juan Perezoso vio a un hombre que no conocía. Se acercó a él y le dijo:
　　—Buenos días, caballero. ¿Cómo está Vd.?
　　—Bien, gracias.
　　—Quiero pedirle—dijo Juan—que me preste dinero; necesito doscientos dólares.
　　—Eso es imposible. ¿Habla Vd. en serio? No tengo el honor de conocerle.
　　—Es mucho mejor así. Las personas que me conocen no quieren prestarme ni un centavo.

¿Por qué pidió dinero a una persona que no conocía?

a. Era rico.　　　　　　　　　　　　*c.* Sus amigos le conocían.
b. Le conocía bien.　　　　　　　　　*d.* Sus amigos eran pobres.

19. Alrededor todo estaba quieto. No se oía ni el más leve ruido de animal ni persona. Nuestros ojos, ya acostumbrados a la oscuridad, podían ver las formas negras de los árboles. Allá arriba en el cielo se veía la línea curva de la luna creciente, que echaba reflejos en las aguas del lago.

¿Cuándo tiene lugar esto?

a. a medianoche　　　　　　　　　　*c.* por la mañana
b. a mediodía　　　　　　　　　　　*d.* por la tarde

20. Pasando por la calle, un caballero de aspecto simpático vio a un chiquillo que lloraba mucho. El amable caballero le preguntó por qué lloraba. El niño respondió:
    —Mi mamá me dio una moneda de diez centavos, y la he perdido.
    Y siguió llorando amargamente.
    —No llores, niño. Aquí tienes otros diez centavos.
    Los ojos del niño brillaron un momento de alegría; pero de pronto volvió a llorar.
    —¿Por qué lloras ahora? ¿No tienes diez centavos?
    —Sí, pero si no hubiera perdido mis diez centavos, ahora tendría veinte.

    ¿Cómo quedó el niño?

    a. rico   *b.* Tenía diez centavos.   *c.* sin dinero   *d.* satisfecho

21. En el coche seguimos la orilla del río, y cuando era ya de noche entramos en Entralgo, donde pensábamos pasar el verano. Yo estaba medio dormido. Sólo recuerdo que delante de mí había unas montañas muy altas, muchos árboles, un río, una casa grande con balcones de madera, y delante de ella, esperándonos, unos cuantos aldeanos que nos saludaron con alegría.

    Esta escena tuvo lugar en

    a. la casa   *b.* el río   *c.* una gran ciudad   *d.* el campo

22. En una tertulia un hombre joven, rico y muy guapo, fue presentado a una señorita hermosa, pero muy fría y egoísta (selfish). Se habló de varias cosas aquella noche, especialmente las diferencias de opinión entre marido y mujer. Dijo el joven:
    —Yo creo que desde el principio el marido debe comenzar de la manera que piensa continuar. Por ejemplo, el fumar. Yo, el primer día fumaría un cigarro; de esta manera daría a entender a mi esposa que pensaba continuar fumando cigarros.
    —¡Y yo le quitaría de la boca ese cigarro!—exclamó la señorita.
    —¿De veras? (Really?)—contestó el joven. —Estoy seguro de que Vd. no estaría allí.

    ¿Qué piensa hacer el joven?

    a. seguir la opinión de la señorita   *c.* seguir con sus costumbres
    b. casarse con la señorita   *d.* no fumar más

23. La noche estaba tan oscura que le era difícil ver la cabeza del caballo en que iba montado. Tenía que pasar por un llano muy extenso y cruzar un río, pero no tenía la menor idea qué dirección tomar para llegar al río. Para colmo de su mala suerte comenzó a llover con fuerza. "Aquí estoy en esta tierra desierta," dijo para sí. "No se ve ni aldea, ni casa, ni luz, ni persona. Y lo peor es que mi caballo no ha comido ni bebido en siete horas, desde las dos de la tarde."

    El viajero

    a. está perdido   *b.* tiene sed   *c.* sabe dónde debe ir   *d.* tiene hambre

24. Las señoritas Pérez eran hijas de un médico, ya viejo, que había gozado de fama en Sevilla en otro tiempo. Por su edad avanzada y porque habían llegado otros médicos, es lo cierto que poco a poco había ido perdiendo sus clientes, hasta perder la mayor parte de ellos. Las niñas no sabían dirigir su propia casa. Mientras duró el éxito del padre, gastaron mucho y vivieron bien. Nadie pensó en mañana. Pero los tiempos habían cambiado.

    ¿Cuántos pacientes tenía el médico en esta época?

    a. pocos   *b.* muchos   *c.* ningunos   *d.* más que ningún otro médico de Sevilla

25. En la América del Sur, en las anchas llanuras del río Amazonas, se hallan las selvas, bosques muy densos, de una extensión mayor que cualquier otro bosque del mundo. Contienen una variedad de plantas, animales, y pájaros tropicales; una variedad más grande que la de ninguna otra parte del mundo. Además de miles de especies de flores, hay más de trescientas variedades de la palma, muchos árboles frutales, y muchos otros, tales como la caoba y el caucho, útiles para el comercio. Los animales de la selva son casi tan numerosos y variados como la vegetación.

    En la selva hay más de mil especies de

    a. árboles frutales   *b.* flores   *c.* llanuras   *d.* la palma

B. LONGER PASSAGES FOR COMPREHENSION

1. Lea Vd. el pasaje siguiente. Después, escriba *verdad* o *mentira* por cada frase basada en el pasaje.

Puerto Rico es el nombre de la isla, y quien se lo dio tenía razón. Descubierta por Cristóbal Colón en su segundo viaje, y nombrada por él "San Juan Bautista," no fue hasta el año 1521 que recibió el nombre que lleva ahora. Pero antes, en el año 1508, el conquistador Ponce de León había fundado una colonia en lo que es hoy día San Juan, la capital. Este paraíso tropical, la más oriental y la más pequeña de las Antillas Mayores, fue una de las colonias favoritas de España en el Nuevo Mundo, hasta el año 1898, cuando España la perdió.

En Puerto Rico hay riqueza por todas partes. Pero no es una riqueza de dinero, de oro. Es la riqueza de su clima, de su paisaje, de su espíritu, y de sus tradiciones, españolas éstas en su mayor parte. Pero al lado de las antiguas casas y costumbres, se ven hoy día hoteles elegantes, altos rascacielos, grandes casas comerciales, y otras evidencias de la influencia norteamericana.

a. El nombre de Puerto Rico se debe a un error.   ---------------

b. La isla fue descubierta por San Juan Bautista.   ---------------

c. La capital de Puerto Rico es San Juan.   ---------------

d. Puerto Rico recibió su nombre actual en 1508.   ---------------

e. Puerto Rico es más grande que las demás islas de las Antillas Mayores.   ---------------

f. Puerto Rico está en el este de las Antillas Mayores.   ---------------

g. España perdió la isla al fin del siglo 19.   ---------------

h. Ponce de León encontró mucho oro en Puerto Rico.   ---------------

i. No hay ningunos edificios altos en San Juan.   ---------------

j. En Puerto Rico se mezclan las influencias de España y de los Estados Unidos.   ---------------

2. Lea Vd. el pasaje siguiente. Después, subraye Vd. la expresión entre paréntesis que correctamente complete cada una de las frases que siguen.

El deseo de volver a mi pueblo se hizo tan fuerte que no dejó lugar en mi cabeza para ninguna otra idea. Hubo días enteros cuando, en vez de estudiar, pensaba en la manera de salir de esa casa miserable.

Un martes por la noche escondí mi maleta, con parte de mi ropa, en el fondo del jardín, en un rincón donde podría sacarla fácilmente sin ser visto. Me acosté en seguida, sin decir nada a nadie, pero no me fue posible dormir aquella noche. Me consideraba libre ya, lejos de aquella casa, que más bien me parecía una cárcel. Ahora mis pensamientos volvieron a la Sra. Gómez, y busqué en mi imaginación la manera de hacerla pagar todo lo que me había hecho sufrir. ¿Qué daño podría yo hacer a esa vieja sin matarla? Al principio no pude pensar en nada. Pero no quería abandonar la casa sin encontrar algún castigo. Este pensamiento me consumía como un fuego. Al amanecer me levanté y comencé a vestirme.

a. Mientras vivía en aquella casa, el autor (salía a menudo, no era feliz, estaba contento).

b. El autor era (criminal, prisionero, estudiante).

c. Deseaba (escaparse de la casa, perder la maleta, pasar la noche en el jardín).

d. Antes de salir de la casa, se determinó a (prender fuego a la casa, matar a la vieja, castigar a la vieja).

e. Cuando se levantó, (todavía era de noche, vio la primera luz del día, buscó a la vieja).

3. Lea Vd. el pasaje siguiente. Después, conteste Vd. *en inglés*, en frases completas, a las preguntas que siguen.

Un joven sacerdote una vez tenía que dar un sermón en su iglesia. Fue la primera vez que hablaba en público, y había estudiado mucho su sermón, hasta aprenderlo de memoria. Pero estaba tan nervioso que, en el momento de comenzar a hablar, lo olvidó por completo.

Allí estaba en el púlpito el pobre cura, cara a cara con la gente, sin saber qué decir. Así permaneció largo rato. La gente le miraba, esperando el sermón. El silencio se hizo intolerable. Al fin el pobre cura dijo:

—Vds. ya saben lo que quiero decir, lo que está en mi corazón.

Un hombre que estaba sentado allí se levantó y le contestó: —Puede ser, padre, que algunos saben lo que Vd. quiere decir. Pero mejor es que Vd. lo diga, porque hay otros que no lo saben.

A lo que respondió el cura: —Pues, los que saben lo que quiero decir, hagan Vds. el favor de decírselo a los que no lo saben.

Y bajó del púlpito y salió de la iglesia.

a. ¿Por qué olvidó el cura su sermón? _____

_____

b. ¿Cuánto tiempo se quedó sin decir nada? _____

_____

c. ¿Qué dijo al fin? _____

_____

d. ¿Por qué dijo el hombre que el cura debía hablar? _____

_____

e. ¿Qué respondió el cura? _____

_____

4. Lea Vd. el pasaje siguiente. Después, conteste Vd. *en inglés*, en frases completas, a las preguntas que siguen.

En cierto pueblo vivía un hombre que estaba casado con una mujer muy contraria. Si él decía que un color era negro, decía ella que era blanco; si él decía que era de noche, decía ella que era de día; si él decía que sí, ella decía que no.

Un día salieron a dar un paseo por el campo, cerca del río. Ella comenzó a argüir con su esposo. Tanto hablaba que no miró dónde andaba. Se cayó en el río, y desapareció en seguida.

El marido corrió al pueblo, y algunos de sus amigos volvieron con él para ayudarle a buscar a su mujer. Todos los amigos la buscaron río abajo, en la dirección en que iba la corriente, pero el marido la buscó río arriba. Los amigos, creyéndole loco, le preguntaron:

—Pero, hombre, ¿por qué busca Vd. a su esposa río arriba?

—Mi mujer era tan contraria que aun muerta va en contra de la corriente—contestó él.

a. ¿Cómo era la mujer con quién estaba casado el hombre? _____

_____

b. ¿Por qué se cayó la mujer en el río? _____

_____

c. ¿Qué hizo el hombre cuando su mujer cayó en el río? _____

_____

d. ¿Quiénes ayudaron al hombre a buscar a su mujer? _____

_____

e. ¿Por qué buscó el hombre a su mujer río arriba? _____

_____

5. Lea Vd. el pasaje siguiente. Después, conteste Vd. *en inglés*, en frases completas, a las preguntas que siguen.

Paseándose por las calles de San Francisco un día, el Sr. Hernández entró en una tienda para comprar una corbata. Escogió una corbata bonita, de color azul, que valía un dólar. Pagó al dueño de la tienda, y salió muy contento.

Poco después, al abrir la cartera, notó que le faltaba un billete de diez dólares. Recordó entonces que en vez de dar al dueño un dólar, le había dado un billete de diez dólares. Volvió en seguida y preguntó al dueño:

—¿Le he dado a Vd. un billete de diez dólares en vez de un dólar?

—No, señor—contestó el comerciante, sin dudar un instante.

El Sr. Hernández no sabía qué hacer. Evidentemente el dueño de la tienda no quería abrir el cajón para devolverle el billete de diez dólares. Al fin pensó en un plan. Dijo:

—El caso es que yo tenía en la cartera un billete falso de diez dólares, y ahora no puedo encontrarlo.

—Oh—dijo el dueño. —Espere Vd. un momento. Seguramente está en el cajón.

a. ¿Para qué entró en la tienda el Sr. Hernández? ----------------------------------

----

b. ¿Qué error había hecho? ---

----

c. ¿Por qué no quería el dueño abrir el cajón? --------------------------------

----

d. ¿Qué respondió el dueño cuando el Sr. Hernández le dijo que el billete era falso? ----------

----

e. ¿Era falso el billete? ---

----

6. Lea Vd. el pasaje siguiente. Después, conteste Vd. *en inglés*, en frases completas, a las preguntas que siguen.

Un hombre mal vestido se acercó un día a una señora, y le pidió de limosna un billete de diez dólares. La mujer, sorprendida, le dijo:

—¡Diez dólares! Así no se pide la caridad. Vd. debe pedir diez centavos o veinte y cinco. Pero diez dólares, ¡no, señor!

—Señora—respondió el pordiosero—he pedido diez dólares a varias personas hoy, porque es la cantidad que necesito. Todo el mundo me dice lo mismo, que no. No voy a pedir a ninguna otra persona. Ahora voy a salir a hacer una cosa de desesperación, una cosa terrible.

La pobre señora no sabía qué decir. ¿Qué cosa terrible iba a hacer aquel hombre? ¿Tal vez robar, o matar? Y todo porque ella no le había dado diez dólares. De pronto le dijo:

—Si yo le doy diez dólares, prométame Vd. que no hará esa cosa terrible que piensa.

—Yo prometo, señora.

—Pues, aquí tiene Vd. diez dólares—dijo. Y luego preguntó: —¿Cuál era la cosa terrible que Vd. iba a hacer?

—Señora, estuve a punto de ir a trabajar.

a. What did the beggar want? --

b. Why did the lady refuse to give it to him? -------------------------------

----

c. What did the beggar threaten to do? -------------------------------------

d. On what condition did she give him the money? ----------------------------

----

e. What had the beggar planned to do? -------------------------------------

7. Lea Vd. el pasaje siguiente. Después, conteste Vd. *en inglés*, en frases completas, a las preguntas que siguen.

Pasé días y días arreglando mi baúl, preparándome para la primera gran aventura de mi vida. Vi en la imaginación una multitud de escenas, de la infancia que acababa de terminar, y otras, imaginarias, de la vida futura. Esperaba impaciente el día de salir de mi pueblo.

Por fin llegó el momento de la partida. Era, si no recuerdo mal, el día primero de octubre, cuatro días después de cumplir yo los diez y siete años. Mi padre me acompañó hasta Oviedo, de donde salía el tren para Madrid. El reloj de la torre, cuya voz me había llamado al estudio tantas veces, dio al fin diez solemnes campanadas. El tren empezó a moverse, avanzando despacio hacia las montañas. Los árboles y las colinas se veían indistintamente, aunque la noche era clara, con luna y estrellas. Cerré los ojos, tratando de dormir, pero no pude. Pensé en la vida universitaria que iba a comenzar.

a. ¿Qué pensamientos tenía el joven mientras se preparaba para su viaje? _____

_____

b. ¿Cuántos años tenía? _____

_____

c. ¿A qué hora salió el tren? _____

_____

d. ¿Qué vio el muchacho desde la ventanilla del tren? _____

_____

e. ¿Para qué iba a la ciudad? _____

_____

8. Lea Vd. el pasaje siguiente. Después, conteste Vd. *en inglés*, en frases completas, a las preguntas que siguen.

Un campesino, al ir un día al establo a buscar su caballo, descubrió que el caballo ya no estaba allí, que alguien lo había robado. Corrió por el camino, dando gritos. Llegó al pueblo, y allí vio a un hombre que no conocía, un viajero que andaba montado en el caballo robado.

Fue al juez, que mandó comparecer ante él al viajero, con el caballo. Allí el nuevo dueño del caballo dijo que el caballo era suyo, que lo había criado desde que nació, y que el campesino decía mentiras. Puesto que el campesino no tenía ningunas pruebas, el juez estaba a punto de decidir en favor del otro. De pronto exclamó el campesino:

—El caballo es mío y voy a probarlo.

Se quitó la chaqueta, la echó sobre la cabeza del animal, y dijo:

—Si este hombre es el dueño del animal, sin duda sabrá decir de qué ojo es ciego.

El viajero tuvo que contestar algo, y dijo: —Del ojo derecho.

—Pues—dijo el campesino—el caballo no es ciego ni del ojo derecho ni del izquierdo.

El juez decidió en su favor, y echó al viajero en la cárcel, por ladrón.

a. ¿Qué es la primera cosa que hizo el campesino al descubrir el robo? _____

_____

b. ¿Dónde vio su caballo? _____

_____

c. ¿Qué dijo el viajero al juez? _____

_____

d. ¿Qué preguntó el campesino al viajero? _____

_____

e. ¿De qué ojo era ciego el caballo? _____

_____

9. Lea Vd. el pasaje siguiente. Después, conteste Vd. *en inglés*, en frases completas, a las preguntas que siguen.

Un campesino español fue un día a ver al maestro de escuela de su pueblo, llevando consigo a su único hijo, un muchacho de doce años.

—Señor maestro, éste es mi hijo. Quiere asistir a su escuela de Vd.

—Sabe leer?—preguntó el maestro.

—No, señor, ni una palabra.

—Sabe escribir su nombre?

—No, no sabe nada; absolutamente nada.

—Pues—dijo el maestro—en ese caso será necesario enseñarle todo. Es mucho trabajo.

Pensó un momento, y luego dijo: —Esto le va a costar cien duros.

—¡Cien duros! ¡Imposible! Por cien duros puedo comprar un burro.

—Pues, señor—le contestó el maestro—compre Vd. su burro. Entonces, con el burro que Vd. compre, y con este niño, tendrá Vd. dos burros.

a. ¿Por qué fue el campesino a ver al maestro? _____

_____

b. ¿Qué sabía el niño? _____

_____

c. ¿Por qué costaría mucho educar al muchacho? _____

_____

d. ¿Por qué no deseaba el campesino pagar tanto dinero? _____

_____

e. ¿Por qué tendría dos burros? _____

_____

10. Lea Vd. el pasaje siguiente. Después, subraye Vd. la frase o expresión que correctamente conteste la pregunta o complete la frase.

Un sacerdote estaba acostumbrado a recibir cada semana una cesta llena de frutas, que le mandaba un amigo suyo. El amigo, que era dueño de una frutería, generalmente mandaba la cesta con un criado suyo que tenía un automóvil.

El criado, que nunca había recibido ninguna propina del sacerdote, siempre hacía este encargo de mala gana. Una vez entró, sin llamar a la puerta, en la sala donde estaba el cura, puso la cesta en la mesa sin decir palabra, y se volvió para salir. Pero el cura, que quería darle una lección de cortesía, le llamó y le dijo:

—Ven acá, joven. Debes saber que así no se entregan los regalos. Permíteme enseñarte un poco de cortesía. Siéntate en esta silla. Tú estarás en mi lugar, y yo en el tuyo.

El muchacho se sentó. El cura fue a la puerta, volvió a entrar con la cesta, avanzó hacia la mesa, y, haciendo una profunda reverencia, dijo: —Señor, mi amo le saluda a Vd., y ruega que Vd. acepte este pobre regalo.

—¡De veras! (Really!) —replicó el muchacho. —Dígale a su amo que le doy las gracias por su generosidad, y tome Vd. este dólar como propina.

El cura se rió mucho, y le dio al muchacho el doble del dólar, en pago de la lección que el muchacho le había dado.

(1) ¿Qué recibía el sacerdote de regalo?
    a. un criado
    b. la frutería
    c. algo de comer
    d. un automóvil

(2) El criado era
    a. rudo
    b. cortés
    c. hablador
    d. alegre

(3) ¿Qué quería hacer el sacerdote?
    a. ir a otro lugar
    b. sentarse en la silla
    c. dar una lección al muchacho
    d. entregar la cesta al amo

(4) ¿Qué hizo el muchacho?
    a. Ofreció una propina al cura.   *c.* Salió por la puerta.
    b. Saludó a su amo.   *d.* Dio una fruta al cura.

(5) ¿Por qué le dio dos dólares el cura al muchacho?
    a. Quería agradecer al frutero.   *c.* No le gustaban las frutas.
    b. Había aprendido algo.   *d.* Aceptó el regalo.

11. Lea Vd. el pasaje siguiente. Después, escoja Vd. la frase o expresión que correctamente conteste la pregunta o complete la frase.

El coronel y su esposa acababan de cenar, y ahora estaban en el salón. El coronel leía un periódico mientras fumaba un cigarro. Su mujer miraba unas fotos.

Alguien llamó a la puerta. La criada no estaba en casa, y la esposa del coronel fue a abrirla. Volvió pronto, diciendo:

—Un caballero que desea verte. ¿Le digo que entre?

—¿Quién es?

—No quiere decir su nombre, pero parece una persona distinguida, y creo que es extranjero.

—Que pase. Le veré aquí en el salón.

Entró el desconocido, un hombre alto y delgado. Cerró la puerta del salón con aire misterioso, y se acercó al coronel.

—¿Sabe Vd. quién soy?—preguntó en voz baja. —¿No reconoce Vd. a su antiguo amigo, Pablo Gómez?

—¡Gómez! ¿Es posible? Yo creí que Gómez había muerto—dijo la señora.

—No. Me escapé en compañía de otros dos hombres, uno inglés y el otro francés. Pasé años allá en Inglaterra, sufriendo hambre y frío. Acabo de volver a España. Ahora deseo ver a mis amigos, y también a mis enemigos.

(1) ¿Qué hacían el coronel y su esposa?
    a. Acababan de salir.   *c.* Discutían las noticias.
    b. Estaban descansando.   *d.* Estaban comiendo.

(2) ¿Quién llamó a la puerta?
    a. un hombre que no tenía nombre   *c.* el coronel
    b. la criada   *d.* un hombre desconocido

(3) ¿Quién fue el hombre?
    a. un muerto   *c.* un amigo del coronel
    b. un enemigo del coronel   *d.* un criado

(4) Gómez deseaba ver
    a. a un inglés
    b. a otros hombres desconocidos   *c.* a sus enemigos solamente
                               d. a las personas que había conocido antes

(5) ¿Cuántas personas aparecen en esta escena?
    a. tres   *c.* cuatro
    b. dos   *d.* una

12. Lea Vd. el pasaje siguiente. Después, escoja Vd. la frase o expresión que correctamente conteste la pregunta.

Llegué a la ciudad de Guatemala a las dos de la tarde. Después de almorzar y descansar un rato, salí a dar un paseo. Era una ciudad de calles largas y amplias, paseos anchos y elegantes, iglesias imponentes, y casas grandes, de buena construcción. Pero mi primera impresión no fue completamente favorable. Sentí cierto miedo que no podía describir, como de algo terrible que iba a ocurrir.

Aquella noche, poco antes de medianoche, me desperté bruscamente de un sueño profundo. Algo había ocurrido, algo extraño y violento. Me parecía que el hotel se movía, que toda la ciudad se movía. Abrí los ojos, y vi que por la ventana entraba la luz de un fuego. Súbitamente la luz eléctrica se encendió por sí sola.

No pude creer mis ojos. "Estoy soñando," pensé.

Después de esperar algunos momentos, traté de acostarme otra vez, pero sin cerrar los ojos. Escuché atentamente, y me pareció oír el ruido de hombres y mujeres que hablaban y gritaban mientras corrían hacia la calle. Me levanté y me vestí rápidamente.

"No puedo quedarme aquí," me dije.

(1) ¿Cuál de estas palabras describe la ciudad de Guatemala?
    a. sucia   *c.* hermosa
    b. pequeña   *d.* estrecha

(2) ¿Cómo se sintió el viajero?
    a. Tenía hambre.   *c.* cansado
    b. Temía algo.   *d.* enfermo

(3) ¿A qué hora se acostó aquella noche?
    a. antes de las doce   *c.* a las dos de la tarde
    b. a las doce   *d.* después de medianoche

(4) ¿Qué le despertó?
    a. una luz   *c.* el fuego
    b. Estaba soñando.   *d.* el movimiento de la tierra

(5) ¿Qué se decidió a hacer?
    a. cerrar los ojos   *c.* quedarse en el hotel
    b. salir a la calle   *d.* encender la luz

13. Lea Vd. el pasaje siguiente. Después, escoja Vd. la frase o expresión que correctamente conteste la pregunta.

El señor Gómez quiso arreglar el casamiento de su hijo Pedro. Fue difícil encontrar novia para él, porque ninguna muchacha que le conocía quería casarse con él. La triste verdad es que Pedro, aunque rico, era el más estúpido de todos los estúpidos que hay en el mundo.

Por fin, el padre pudo encontrar a una muchacha bastante amable para su hijo en otro pueblo, donde nadie conocía al muchacho. Llegó el día en que la familia de Pedro había de visitar por primera vez a la familia de la novia. El padre de Pedro le dijo que no debía hablar en toda la tarde, para no mostrar su estupidez.

Llegaron a casa de la novia, y el padre presentó a Pedro. El muchacho, que era bastante guapo, gustó a la novia. Las dos familias se sentaron a comer. Un tío de la novia, que estaba sentado cerca de Pedro, le hizo varias preguntas. Pedro, que recordaba las instrucciones de su padre, no contestó nada. Al fin el tío dijo en voz baja a otro pariente:

—¿Sabes, Tomás, que el nuevo sobrino me parece un grandísimo burro?

Pedro, al oír esto, dijo a su padre: —Papá, ahora que me conocen aquí, puedo hablar, ¿verdad?

(1) ¿Por qué era difícil encontrar esposa para Pedro?
    a. Pedro era pobre.   *c.* Pedro no quería casarse.
    b. Pedro tenía muy poca inteligencia.   *d.* Pedro era rico.

(2) ¿Por qué consintió la muchacha en casarse con él?
    a. Estaba triste.   *c.* No era amable.
    b. Le conocía bien.   *d.* No le conocía.

(3) ¿Qué debía hacer Pedro?
    a. Debía tener cerrada la boca.   *c.* Debía confesar que era estúpido.
    b. Debía hablar mucho.   *d.* Debía quedarse en casa.

(4) ¿Quién trató de conversar con Pedro?
    a. un pariente de la novia   *c.* el padre de Pedro
    b. el padre de la novia   *d.* la novia

(5) ¿Por qué quería hablar Pedro?
    a. para mostrar su inteligencia   *c.* para saludar a su tío
    b. porque ya le conocían   *d.* para decir la verdad a su padre

14. Lea·Vd. el pasaje siguiente. Después, escoja Vd. la frase o expresión que correctamente conteste la pregunta.

—Ven conmigo, muchacho—dijo el doctor Sangredo. —No te daré salario, pero vivirás bien. Yo te enseñaré a ser médico, como yo. Más que criado, serás mi discípulo.

Acepté la proposición del doctor, esperando, bajo su dirección, llegar a ser un médico famoso y sabio.

Yo tenía que escribir el nombre, la calle, y la casa donde vivían los enfermos que le llamaban. Para esto tenía un libro. Si se podría poner un título a aquel libro, con razón debía llamarse "Libro de Muertos," porque murieron casi todos los enfermos mencionados allí.

Un día me dijo: —Estoy muy contento contigo, y voy a enseñarte a ser médico. Mi arte no necesita mucho estudio; simplemente consiste en sangrar a los enfermos, porque tienen demasiada sangre. De hoy en adelante yo visitaré solamente a los nobles y los ricos. Tú, muchacho, visitarás a los otros.

Todos los días tuve que visitar a ocho o diez enfermos. No sé por qué, pero nunca tuve que hacer una segunda visita a ningún paciente. Una visita era bastante para enviar al paciente al otro mundo.

(1) ¿Qué le ofreció el médico?
   a. pagarle con dinero
   b. hacerle médico
   c. comidas malas
   d. curar sus enfermedades

(2) ¿Qué tenía que hacer el muchacho?
   a. matar a los enfermos
   b. estudiar en un libro
   c. servir la comida al médico
   d. escribir la dirección de cada paciente

(3) ¿Cómo curaba el médico a los enfermos?
   a. Les daba medicinas baratas.
   b. Estudiaba mucho.
   c. Sabía bien su profesión.
   d. Les quitaba la sangre.

(4) ¿A quiénes debía visitar el muchacho?
   a. a todos los pacientes
   b. a los ricos
   c. a la gente pobre
   d. a los nobles

(5) ¿Qué les pasó a los pacientes?
   a. No estaban enfermos.
   b. Se murieron.
   c. Se quedaban enfermos.
   d. Salieron curados.

15. Lea Vd. el pasaje siguiente. Después, escoja Vd. la frase o expresión que correctamente conteste la pregunta o complete la frase.

Los mexicanos siempre tendrán en grata memoria al padre Miguel Hidalgo, el primer jefe de la lucha por la independencia.

México entonces era una colonia española. Los mexicanos no podían tomar parte en el gobierno. Los gobernadores eran todos españoles, nombrados por el rey de España. Muchos aceptaron puestos solamente para hacerse ricos, a costa de los mexicanos.

El deseo de libertar a su patria inflamaba el corazón de Hidalgo, que entonces era sacerdote de la pequeña aldea de Dolores. En 1810 organizó un partido patriótico cuyo objeto era trabajar y luchar por la independencia. Formaron un ejército y avanzaron sobre Guanajuato, una ciudad grande y rica, fortificada y defendida por los españoles. Por el heroísmo de Hidalgo, los revolucionarios pudieron vencer a los españoles.

Hidalgo fortificó la ciudad y la hizo centro de la revolución. En seguida empezaron a llegar miles de mexicanos, que querían juntarse a las fuerzas patrióticas. Con la ayuda de éstos, Hidalgo pudo continuar la lucha.

(1) ¿Quién fue Hidalgo?
   a. un jefe del gobierno
   b. un español
   c. un soldado
   d. un cura mexicano

(2) ¿Qué hicieron los gobernadores?
   a. Perdieron dinero.
   b. Robaron a los mexicanos.
   c. Vivieron en la costa.
   d. Gobernaron bien.

(3) ¿Cuál fue el objeto del grupo que Hidalgo organizó?
   a. ganar la libertad
   b. luchar contra los mexicanos
   c. poner fuego al pueblo de Dolores
   d. hacerse rico

(4) ¿Por qué atacaron a Guanajuato?
   a. La ciudad era independiente.
   b. Eran patriotas.
   c. Muchos españoles estaban allí.
   d. Era fácil vencerla.

(5) Después de tomar la ciudad de Guanajuato,
   a. Hidalgo continuó la revolución desde allí
   b. Hidalgo mató a miles de soldados
   c. la revolución se acabó
   d. era difícil encontrar soldados

16. Lea Vd. el pasaje siguiente. Después, escoja Vd. la frase o expresión que correctamente conteste la pregunta o complete la frase.

Vasco Núñez de Balboa era un hombre que no sabía estar parado; siempre buscaba nuevos territorios. Había oído hablar del mar del Sur (Océano Pacífico), que los indios dijeron quedaba hacia el oeste. Determinó ir a buscar·el mar. Si no él, otro explorador lo descubriría y le quitaría la gloria del descubrimiento. Pues, partió de Darién una mañana con ciento noventa soldados, a fines de agosto del año 1513.

Llegaron por fin a un pueblo indio. El jefe salió con mucha gente para averiguar qué querían. Cuando le dijeron que iban al mar del Sur, que traían una nueva religión, y que buscaban oro, el jefe les impidió el paso libre, y les mandó volver atrás. Pero los españoles insistieron en seguir adelante, y en la lucha que siguió el jefe indio fue muerto. Los demás indios huyeron, porque creían que las armas de los españoles eran rayos del cielo. Balboa y los suyos pudieron entrar en el pueblo. Vieron a algunos habitantes, los viejos y los enfermos, pero nada de lo que buscaban.

(1) ¿Cómo era Balboa?
    a. estudioso   *c.* perezoso
    b. activo   *d.* cruel

(2) ¿Por qué quería ir en busca del mar del Sur?
    a. Buscaba una ruta a las Indias.   *c.* Quería la gloria.
    b. Tenía miedo a los indios.   *d.* Estaba al oeste.

(3) Salió de Darién en
    a. el verano   *c.* el otoño
    b. el invierno   *d.* la primavera

(4) ¿Qué hizo el jefe de los indios?
    a. Les prohibió el paso.   *c.* Les permitió pasar.
    b. Aceptó la religión de los españoles.   *d.* Les dio mucho oro.

(5) ¿Qué encontraron los españoles en el pueblo?
    a. mucho oro   *c.* unas armas
    b. un rayo del cielo   *d.* algunos indios

17. Lea Vd. el pasaje siguiente. Después, escoja Vd. la frase o expresión que correctamente conteste la pregunta.

Dos amigos, Juan y Pedro, caminaban por el bosque un día. De repente apareció delante de ellos un oso enorme. Juan, lleno de terror, se puso a correr. Rápidamente subió a un árbol alto, dejando solo a su amigo Pedro. Éste, que se vio sin defensa y abandonado de su amigo, se cayó al suelo, y se quedó allí sin moverse. Pareció muerto.

El oso se acercó a él, le miró, y con la nariz le tocó la cara y las orejas. Al fin se fue sin hacerle daño, porque se dice que los osos nunca comen carne muerta.

Juan, el amigo cobarde, que había visto la escena desde las ramas del árbol, bajó y corrió a su amigo. Le abrazó, y le dijo qué alegre se sentía de verle vivo y sin daño. Terminó diciendo:

—Desde el árbol me pareció ver que el oso te decía algo. ¿Es verdad?

—Sí—respondió Pedro. —Me dijo que el amigo que me abandona cuando estoy en peligro es mal amigo.

(1) ¿Qué vieron los dos amigos?
    a. nada   *c.* un camino
    b. un animal feroz   *d.* un árbol alto

(2) ¿Qué hizo Juan?
    a. Se acercó a su amigo.   *c.* Se escapó.
    b. Corrió a buscar ayuda.   *d.* Ayudó a su amigo.

(3) ¿Por qué se fue el oso sin hacer daño a Pedro?
    a. Creyó que estaba muerto.   *c.* Le gustó.
    b. No tenía hambre.   *d.* Vio al amigo en el árbol.

(4) ¿Qué hizo Juan después?
    a. Subió al árbol.   *c.* No hizo nada.
    b. Se alejó de su amigo.   *d.* Bajó del árbol.

(5) Según Pedro, ¿qué le había dicho el oso?
    a. que debía correr
    b. que su amigo estaba en peligro
    c. que debía abandonar a su amigo
    d. que Juan no era buen amigo

18. Lea Vd. el pasaje siguiente. Después, escoja Vd. la frase o expresión que correctamente conteste la pregunta o complete la frase.

Un señor muy rico tenía una hija que estaba casada con un abogado. El abogado era bastante avaro, y no le gustaba sacar el dinero del bolsillo. Su mujer, en cambio, tenía la costumbre de gastar libremente el dinero en cosas frívolas e innecesarias. Su marido trabajaba mucho, pero cuanto más ganaba él, tanto más gastaba ella.

Cada vez que el abogado se encontraba con el padre de su esposa, le contaba, con todos los detalles cómo y cuánto su mujer gastaba. El padre, después de tolerar estas historias mucho tiempo, dijo a su yerno (son-in-law):

—Dígale Vd. a su esposa que ya estoy cansado de su frivolidad. Si yo oigo que ella continúa gastando tanto dinero, no voy a dejar para ella ni un centavo cuando me muera. Voy a desheredarla por completo.

El resultado fue que el abogado nunca más le habló del dinero que su mujer gastaba.

(1) ¿Cómo era el abogado?
    a. liberal
    b. perezoso
    c. generoso
    d. trabajador

(2) ¿Qué hacía la mujer?
    a. Hacía cosas buenas.
    b. Gastaba mucho.
    c. Ganaba dinero.
    d. Guardaba el dinero en la bolsa.

(3) El abogado decía que su mujer
    a. gastaba dinero sin pensar
    b. era innecesaria
    c. era buena
    d. contaba el dinero

(4) El padre dijo que
    a. el abogado ganaba mucho
    b. iba a dejar todo su dinero a su hija
    c. su hija estaba cansada
    d. no dejaría nada a su hija si ella seguía gastando dinero

(5) ¿Por qué no volvió el abogado a hablar del dinero?
    a. Su mujer ya no gastaba mucho dinero.
    b. No le gustaba el dinero.
    c. No quería perder el dinero del padre.
    d. El padre desheredó a su hija.

19. Lea Vd. el pasaje siguiente. Después, escoja Vd. la frase o expresión que correctamente conteste la pregunta.

Vivió en el pueblo un joven que el señor cura había recogido cuando todavía era niño, porque tuvo la desgracia de perder a sus padres. Lo había criado, dándole la educación que pudo, pues el señor cura era tan bueno que solía privarse de lo necesario para que los desgraciados pudiesen comer. El resultado fue que su bolsa estaba tan limpia de dinero como su alma de pecados.

Pedro González, que así se llamaba el niño, creció teniendo siempre por delante el santo ejemplo del cura. Como tenía una naturaleza buena, de niño bueno llegó a ser joven honrado, el más honrado del pueblo. Como su protector, estaba siempre dispuesto a sacar del bolsillo su última peseta y ofrecerla al que tuviera necesidad. Además, andaba por la ciudad buscando pobres que ayudar. No había función pública sin que Pedro tomara parte en los preparativos, haciendo más que ningún otro. Muchas veces la gente del pueblo, o el alcalde mismo, le buscaba para pedir su ayuda en arreglar alguna fiesta.

(1) ¿Por qué ayudó el cura al niño?
    a. Vivía en el pueblo.
    b. Era su vecino.
    c. Era su criado.
    d. No tenía ni padre ni madre.

(2) ¿Cuál de estas palabras describe al cura?
    a. desgraciado
    b. rico
    c. pobre
    d. privado

(3) ¿Por qué era Pedro honrado?
    a. Era un santo.
    b. Protegió al cura.
    c. Seguía el ejemplo del cura.
    d. Robaba dinero a los demás.

(4) ¿Cómo ayudó a los pobres?
    a. Les dio dinero.
    b. Fue su protector.
    c. Los buscaba.
    d. Andaba por las calles.

(5) ¿Quién buscaba su ayuda?
    a. solamente el alcalde
    b. todo el pueblo
    c. los niños
    d. el cura

20. Lea Vd. el pasaje siguiente. Después, escoja Vd. la frase o expresión que correctamente conteste la pregunta.

En cierto país vivió un rey muy cruel, y además, supersticioso. Toda la gente le odiaba y le temía. Su diversión favorita era llamar a la corte a cualquier persona, hablar con él un rato, y después, matar al infeliz con quien hablaba. También pasaba muchas horas estudiando las estrellas. Creía que así podría saber el futuro.

Un día sus soldados llevaron a su presencia a un hombre viejo, que era astrólogo. El rey pensaba hablar con él, como era su costumbre, y después matarle. El astrólogo, que sabía la intención del rey, tenía un plan.

Después de dos o tres preguntas de poca importancia, el rey le preguntó:

—¿Sabes tú cuándo vas a morir?

Y el astrólogo contestó: —He consultado las estrellas. No me dicen el día exacto, pero me dicen que voy a morir el mismo día que Vd.

Al oír esto el rey quedó muy asustado. En vez de matarle, le dio una buena casa, con pensión, y los mejores médicos del país para cuidar de su salud.

(1) ¿Cuál de estas palabras describe al rey?
    a. justo
    b. bondadoso
    c. cobarde
    d. malo

(2) ¿Por qué estudiaba el rey las estrellas?
    a. Se interesaba por las ciencias.
    b. Era infeliz.
    c. Le gustaba estudiar.
    d. Era supersticioso.

(3) ¿Qué pensaba el rey hacer?
    a. decirle unas cosas al astrólogo
    b. dar la muerte al astrólogo
    c. llamar a sus soldados
    d. contestar a las preguntas del astrólogo

(4) ¿Qué sabía el astrólogo?
    a. Sabía lo que el rey pensaba hacer.
    b. Sabía todo el futuro.
    c. Sabía el día en que el rey iba a morir.
    d. Sabía que el rey era viejo.

(5) Según el astrólogo, ¿qué le dijeron las estrellas?
    a. El rey debía consultar un médico.
    b. Debía tener un plan.
    c. Él viviría tanto como el rey.
    d. El rey viviría muchos años.

Part VIII—*Practice in Directed Composition*

Write a composition of at least five sentences, in Spanish, for each of the following topics. Each sentence should contain the information asked for in the suggested outline. Following each outline are several suggested vocabulary items, which you may use as you wish.

1. Write a composition about your birthday. Mention the following:

   a. the date of your birthday
   b. how old you were on your last birthday
   c. how you celebrated your last birthday
   d. what gifts you received
   e. what you hope to get for your next birthday

   Vocabulary

   birthday, **el cumpleaños**
   to celebrate, **celebrar**
   gift, **el regalo**
   party, **la tertulia, la fiesta**

2. Write a composition about your plans for next Saturday. Say that:

   a. You are going to study in the morning.
   b. In the afternoon you will attend a baseball game.
   c. You are going to have supper at home.
   d. After supper you will visit a friend.
   e. You and your friend are going to the movies together.

   Vocabulary

   to attend, **asistir a**
   baseball game, **el partido de béisbol**
   to have supper, **cenar**
   movies, **el cine**
   together, **juntos (-as)**

3. Write about a day's shopping trip. Mention:

   a. that you went shopping with your mother
   b. what you had to buy (two things)
   c. what your mother bought (two things)
   d. that you and she had lunch in a restaurant
   e. that you returned home at 5 o'clock

   Vocabulary

   to go shopping, **ir de compras**
   to have lunch, **almorzar**
   to return home, **volver a casa**

4. You are writing a composition on "My Family." Tell:

   a. in what year you were born
   b. how many brothers and sisters you have
   c. how old your parents are
   d. what your father does
   e. in what city you live

   Vocabulary

   to be born, **nacer**
   to be . . . years old, **tener . . . años**
   parents, **los padres**

378

5. Write about your plans for a picnic. Say that:

  a. Your friends are going on a picnic.
  b. You want to go also.
  c. It won't cost much.
  d. One of your friends will bring the lunch.
  e. You will return home early.

Vocabulary

to cost, **costar**
to go on a picnic, **ir de jira**

6. Write about your mark in a recent test. Say that:

  a. You received your mark in Spanish.
  b. It was not as good as you wished.
  c. You did not pay attention in class.
  d. You intend to study more.
  e. You will get an excellent mark next month.

Vocabulary

to intend, **pensar**
mark, **la nota**
next month, **el mes que viene**
to pay attention, **prestar atención**

7. You are at the railroad station waiting to meet a friend. Tell:

  a. where you are
  b. for whom you are waiting
  c. that the train will arrive in half an hour
  d. that he (she) will spend the Christmas vacation with you
  e. that you will go to many parties together

Vocabulary

party, **la tertulia, la fiesta**
railroad, **el ferrocarril**
to spend (time), **pasar**
to wait (for), **esperar**

8. Write about the Spanish Club in your school. Tell:

  a. that you are a member of the Spanish Club
  b. on what day the club meets
  c. how many pupils attend the meetings
  d. that the members speak only Spanish at the meetings
  e. that you have learned many pretty Spanish songs

Vocabulary

to attend, **asistir a**
to meet, **reunirse**
meeting, **la reunión**
member, **el socio, la socia**
Spanish Club, **el Círculo Español**

9. Write about a party you attended recently. Tell:

  a. that the party took place last Saturday
  b. who gave the party
  c. with whom you went
  d. what you did at the party
  e. what was served

Vocabulary

last Saturday, **el sábado pasado**
party, **la tertulia, la fiesta**
refreshments, **los refrescos**
to take place, **tener lugar**

10. A pen pal from Spain asks you what foreign language you are studying. Write him that:

    a. You have been studying Spanish for two years.
    b. Your Spanish class is very interesting.
    c. You are learning to speak and write in Spanish.
    d. You will continue studying it in college.
    e. Some day you will visit Spain.

Vocabulary

college, **la universidad**
to continue, **seguir, continuar** (+ present participle)
to have been, **hace** + time + **que** + present tense
Spanish class, **la clase de español**

11. You are walking in the street. It is January. Tell that:

    a. You are returning from a friend's house.
    b. It is very cold.
    c. You are wearing an overcoat and gloves.
    d. You are hungry and tired.
    e. After supper you have to study.

Vocabulary

to be (very) cold (weather), **hacer (mucho) frío**
to be hungry, **tener hambre**
glove, **el guante**
to have to, **tener que** + infinitive
overcoat, **el sobretodo**
tired, **cansado**
to wear, **llevar**

12. Write a note to your teacher telling why you failed to do your homework for today. Explain that:

    a. You fell while returning home yesterday.
    b. You hurt your hand.
    c. You went to the doctor.
    d. He said that you needed to rest.
    e. You are better today.

Vocabulary

to hurt oneself (in), **hacerse daño (en)**
to need, **necesitar**
to rest, **descansar**
to return home, **volver a casa**

13. Write about your after-school activities. Give the following information:

    a. Your classes end at half past three.
    b. After returning home you study.
    c. You speak on the telephone till suppertime.
    d. Afterwards you help your mother wash the dishes.
    e. You watch television for two hours and then go to bed.

Vocabulary

to end, **terminar**
to go to bed, **acostarse**
suppertime, **la hora de cenar**
to speak on the telephone, **hablar por teléfono**
television, **la televisión**
to wash, **lavar**
to watch, **mirar**

14. Write about a visit to the library. Tell that:

a. In the library you met a friend.
b. He was returning a book.
c. You asked him if it was interesting.
d. He said that he liked it very much.
e. You are going to read it next week.

Vocabulary

to like (to be pleasing), **gustar**
next week, **la semana que viene**
to return (to give back), **devolver**
very much, **muchísimo**

15. In your Spanish class you are writing on "How I Spent the Summer." Say that:

a. Last summer you went to the country.
b. In the morning you used to play tennis.
c. After lunch you had an hour of rest.
d. Later you generally swam in the lake (or river).
e. In the evening you either danced (used to dance) or went to the movies (used to go).

Vocabulary

in the morning (evening), **por la mañana (noche)**
lake, **el lago**
last summer, **el verano pasado**
movies, **el cine**
to play, **jugar (a)**
rest, **el descanso**
to swim, **nadar**

16. Write about a meeting with an old friend. Say that:

a. You were walking in the street near your home.
b. You suddenly saw your friend Paul.
c. You didn't recognize him because he was wearing eyeglasses.
d. He said that his family was well.
e. He promised to pay you a visit soon.

Vocabulary

eyeglasses, **las gafas**
to pay a visit (to), **hacer una visita (a)**
to recognize, **reconocer**
suddenly, **de pronto**
to wear, **llevar**

17. Write to a friend telling him (or her):

a. at what time you get up on Sunday
b. what you have for breakfast
c. what you do after breakfast (read the newspaper, go to church, etc.)
d. that in the afternoon you visit friends or relatives
e. that in the evening you study or watch a television program

Vocabulary

in the afternoon (evening), **por la tarde (noche)**
relative, **el pariente**
television program, **el programa de televisión**
to watch, **mirar**

18. Write about meeting another passenger on a plane going to Mexico.

    a. Tell him your name and where you come from.
    b. Ask him if he likes to travel.
    c. Tell him that this is your first trip to Mexico.
    d. Tell him the things you want to see in Mexico (mention two).
    e. Ask him how long he intends to stay in Mexico.

Vocabulary

to intend, **pensar** + infinitive
to like (to be pleasing), **gustar**
to stay, **quedarse**

19. Write about the following incident:

    a. Last night a neighbor knocked at your door.
    b. She wanted to ask for some sugar.
    c. You told her your mother was not at home.
    d. You found some sugar and gave it to her.
    e. She promised to return it the next day.

Vocabulary

to ask for, **pedir**
to knock at the door, **llamar a la puerta**
last night, **anoche**
neighbor, **el vecino, la vecina**
the next day, **al día siguiente**
to return (give back), **devolver**

20. You are writing about shopping in a large food store. You approach the clerk.

    a. Ask him how much the milk costs.
    b. Ask him where you can find the meat.
    c. You also want to buy a pound of butter.
    d. Tell him what kinds of fruit you need (mention two).
    e. Ask him how much you owe him.

Vocabulary

butter, **la mantequilla**
to cost, **costar**
to find, **hallar**
to owe, **deber**
pound, **la libra**

21. You came late to school today. Write a note explaining that:

    a. You were ready to leave the house.
    b. You could not find your Spanish book.
    c. You spent fifteen minutes looking for it.
    d. You found it under the table.
    e. You ran, but you missed the bus.

Vocabulary

bus, **el autobús**
to be ready (to), **estar listo(-a) (para)**
to leave, **salir (de)**

to look for, **buscar**
to miss, **perder**
Spanish book, **libro de español**
to spend (time), **pasar**
under, **debajo de**

22. You are writing to a pen pal.

   a. Tell him (her) that you think of him (her) often.
   b. Tell him (her) that you hope to go to the seashore this year.
   c. Ask him (her) where he (she) traveled last summer.
   d. Ask him (her) when he (she) will visit the United States.
   e. Tell him (her) to answer this letter soon.

Vocabulary

last summer, **el verano pasado**
seashore, **la playa**
to think of, **pensar en**

23. Write about a visit to a sick friend.

   a. Ask him how he is today.
   b. Ask him when he became ill.
   c. Ask him if the doctor was there.
   d. Ask him when he will be well again.
   e. Tell him you have to be home at 5 o'clock, and say goodbye.

Vocabulary

to be (health), **estar**
to become, **ponerse**
to have to, **tener que** + infinitive

24. You are planning a trip to Europe. Write to a friend telling him (or her) that:

   a. You have always dreamed of traveling.
   b. You are going to Europe next week.
   c. You will travel by steamship.
   d. You will spend the whole summer there.
   e. You will visit many interesting cities.

Vocabulary

to dream of, **soñar con**
next week, **la semana que viene**
to spend (time), **pasar**
steamship, **el vapor**

25. Imagine that you are in Madrid. You approach a policeman.

   a. Tell him that you have just arrived from the United States.
   b. Tell him how long you have been studying Spanish.
   c. Ask him where you can find a good restaurant.
   d. Ask him on what days the bullfights take place.
   e. Thank him, and tell him he is very kind.

Vocabulary

bullfight, **la corrida de toros**
to have been, **hace** + time + **que** + present tense
to have just, **acabar de** + infinitive
kind, **amable**
to take place, **tener lugar**

Irregular Verb Forms

Note. (1) Verbs that are similar in structure to the verbs in the following chart are listed alphabetically at the end of the chart.

(2) The only verbs that are irregular in the imperfect indicative are:

ir : iba, ibas, iba, íbamos, ibais, iban
ser : era, eras, era, éramos, erais, eran
ver : veía, veías, veía, veíamos, veíais, veían

Infinitive, Present Part., Past Part.	Present Indicative	Preterite	Future	Present Subjunctive	Imperfect Subjunctive	Familiar Command (tú)
1. abrazar		abracé abrazaste abrazó etc.		abrace abraces abrace abracemos abracéis abracen		
2. abrir abriendo **abierto**						
3. almorzar	**almuerzo** **almuerzas** **almuerza** almorzamos almorzáis **almuerzan**	almorcé almorzaste almorzó etc.		almuerce almuerces almuerce almorcemos almorcéis almuercen		**almuerza**
4. andar		anduve anduviste anduvo anduvimos anduvisteis anduvieron			anduviera (-se) anduvieras (-ses) anduviera (-se) anduviéramos (-'semos) anduvierais (-seis) anduvieran (-sen)	
5. averiguar		averigüé averiguaste averiguó etc.		averigüe averigües averigüe averigüemos averigüéis averigüen		
6. buscar		busqué buscaste buscó etc.		busque busques busque busquemos busquéis busquen		
7. caber	quepo cabes cabe etc.	cupe cupiste cupo cupimos cupisteis cupieron	cabré cabrás cabrá cabremos cabréis cabrán	quepa quepas quepa quepamos quepáis quepan	cupiera (-se) cupieras (-ses) cupiera (-se) cupiéramos (-'semos) cupierais (-seis) cupieran (-sen)	
8. caer cayendo caído	caigo caes cae etc.	caí caíste cayó caímos caísteis cayeron		caiga caigas caiga caigamos caigáis caigan	cayera (-se) cayeras (-ses) cayera (-se) cayéramos (-'semos) cayerais (-seis) cayeran (-sen)	
9. conocer	**conozco** conoces conoce etc.			conozca conozcas conozca conozcamos conozcáis conozcan		

Infinitive, Present Part., Past Part.	Present Indicative	Preterite	Future	Present Subjunctive	Imperfect Subjunctive	Familiar Command (tú)
10. continuar	continúo			continúe		continúa
	continúas			continúes		
	continúa			continúe		
	continuamos			continuemos		
	continuáis			continuéis		
	continúan			continúen		
11. creer		creí			creyera(-se)	
creyendo		creíste			creyeras(-ses)	
creído		creyó			creyera(-se)	
		creímos			creyéramos(-'semos)	
		creísteis			creyerais(-seis)	
		creyeron			creyeran(-sen)	
12. dar	doy	di		dé	diera(-se)	
	das	diste		des	dieras(-ses)	
	da	dio		dé	diera(-se)	
	damos	dimos		demos	diéramos(-'semos)	
	dais	disteis		deis	dierais(-seis)	
	dan	dieron		den	dieran(-sen)	
13. decir	digo	dije	diré	diga	dijera(-se)	di
diciendo	dices	dijiste	dirás	digas	dijeras(-ses)	
dicho	dice	dijo	dirá	diga	dijera(-se)	
	decimos	dijimos	diremos	digamos	dijéramos(-'semos)	
	decís	dijisteis	diréis	digáis	dijerais(-seis)	
	dicen	dijeron	dirán	digan	dijeran(-sen)	
14. dirigir	dirijo			dirija		
	diriges			dirijas		
	dirige			dirija		
	etc.			dirijamos		
				dirijáis		
				dirijan		
15. distinguir	distingo			distinga	distinguiera(-se)	
	distingues			distingas	distinguieras(-ses)	
	distingue			distinga	distinguiera(-se)	
	etc.			distingamos	distinguiéramos(-'semos)	
				distingáis	distinguierais(-seis)	
				distingan	distinguieran(-sen)	
16. dormir	duermo	dormí		duerma	durmiera(-se)	duerme
durmiendo	duermes	dormiste		duermas	durmieras(-ses)	
dormido	duerme	durmió		duerma	durmiera(-se)	
	dormimos	dormimos		durmamos	durmiéramos(-'semos)	
	dormís	dormisteis		durmáis	durmierais(-seis)	
	duermen	durmieron		duerman	durmieran(-sen)	
17. elegir	elijo	elegí		elija	eligiera(-se)	elige
eligiendo	eliges	elegiste		elijas	eligieras(-ses)	
elegido	elige	eligió		elija	eligiera(-se)	
	elegimos	elegimos		elijamos	eligiéramos(-'semos)	
	elegís	elegisteis		elijáis	eligierais(-seis)	
	eligen	eligieron		elijan	eligieran(-sen)	
18. empezar	empiezo	empecé		empiece		empieza
	empiezas	empezaste		empieces		
	empieza	empezó		empiece		
	empezamos	etc.		empecemos		
	empezáis			empecéis		
	empiezan			empiecen		
19. enviar	envío			envíe		envía
	envías			envíes		
	envía			envíe		
	enviamos			enviemos		
	enviáis			enviéis		
	envían			envíen		

Infinitive, Present Part., Past Part.	Present Indicative	Preterite	Future	Present Subjunctive	Imperfect Subjunctive	Familiar Command (tú)
20. escribir escribiendo **escrito**						
21. estar	estoy estás está estamos estáis están	estuve estuviste estuvo estuvimos estuvisteis estuvieron		esté estés esté estemos estéis estén	estuviera (-se) estuvieras (-ses) estuviera (-se) estuviéramos (-'semos) estuvierais (-seis) estuvieran (-sen)	está
22. haber	he has ha hemos habéis han	hube hubiste hubo hubimos hubisteis hubieron	habré habrás habrá habremos habréis habrán	haya hayas haya hayamos hayáis hayan	hubiera (-se) hubieras (-ses) hubiera (-se) hubiéramos (-'semos) hubierais (-seis) hubieran (-sen)	
23. hacer haciendo **hecho**	hago haces hace etc.	hice hiciste hizo hicimos hicisteis hicieron	haré harás hará haremos haréis harán	haga hagas haga hagamos hagáis hagan	hiciera (-se) hicieras (-ses) hiciera (-se) hiciéramos (-'semos) hicierais (-seis) hicieran (-sen)	haz
24. huir **huyendo** huido	huyo huyes huye huimos huís huyen	huí huiste huyó huimos huisteis huyeron		huya huyas huya huyamos huyáis huyan	huyera (-se) huyeras (-ses) huyera (-se) huyéramos (-'semos) huyerais (-seis) huyeran (-sen)	huye
25. ir **yendo** ido	voy vas va vamos vais van	fui fuiste fue fuimos fuisteis fueron		vaya vayas vaya vayamos vayáis vayan	fuera (-se) fueras (-ses) fuera (-se) fuéramos (-'semos) fuerais (-seis) fueran (-sen)	ve
26. jugar	juego juegas juega jugamos jugáis juegan	jugué jugaste jugó etc.		juegue juegues juegue juguemos juguéis jueguen		juega
27. llegar		llegué llegaste llegó etc.		llegue llegues llegue lleguemos lleguéis lleguen		
28. morir muriendo muerto	muero mueres muere morimos morís mueren	morí moriste murió morimos moristeis murieron		muera mueras muera muramos muráis mueran	muriera (-se) murieras (-ses) muriera (-se) muriéramos (-'semos) murierais (-seis) murieran (-sen)	muere
29. mostrar	muestro muestras muestra mostramos mostráis muestran			muestre muestres muestre mostremos mostréis muestren		muestra
30. mover	muevo mueves mueve movemos movéis mueven			mueva muevas mueva movamos mováis muevan		mueve

Infinitive, Present Part., Past Part.	Present Indicative	Preterite	Future	Present Subjunctive	Imperfect Subjunctive	Familiar Command (tú)
31. negar	niego	negué		niegue		niega
	niegas	negaste		niegues		
	niega	negó		niegue		
	negamos	etc.		neguemos		
	negáis			neguéis		
	niegan			nieguen		
32. oír	oigo	oí	oiré	oiga	oyera (-se)	oye
oyendo	oyes	oíste	oirás	oigas	oyeras (-ses)	
oído	oye	oyó	oirá	oiga	oyera (-se)	
	oímos	oímos	oiremos	oigamos	oyéramos (-'semos)	
	oís	oísteis	oiréis	oigáis	oyerais (-seis)	
	oyen	oyeron	oirán	oigan	oyeran (-sen)	
33. oler	huelo			huela		huele
	hueles			huelas		
	huele			huela		
	olemos			olamos		
	oléis			oláis		
	huelen			huelan		
34. pedir	pido	pedí		pida	pidiera (-se)	pide
pidiendo	pides	pediste		pidas	pidieras (-ses)	
pedido	pide	pidió		pida	pidiera (-se)	
	pedimos	pedimos		pidamos	pidiéramos (-'semos)	
	pedís	pedisteis		pidáis	pidierais (-seis)	
	piden	pidieron		pidan	pidieran (-sen)	
35. pensar	pienso			piense		piensa
	piensas			pienses		
	piensa			piense		
	pensamos			pensemos		
	pensáis			penséis		
	piensan			piensen		
36. perder	pierdo			pierda		pierde
	pierdes			pierdas		
	pierde			pierda		
	perdemos			perdamos		
	perdéis			perdáis		
	pierden			pierdan		
37. poder	puedo	pude	podré	pueda	pudiera (-se)	puede
pudiendo	puedes	pudiste	podrás	puedas	pudieras (-ses)	
podido	puede	pudo	podrá	pueda	pudiera (-se)	
	podemos	pudimos	podremos	podamos	pudiéramos (-'semos)	
	podéis	pudisteis	podréis	podáis	pudierais (-seis)	
	pueden	pudieron	podrán	puedan	pudieran (-sen)	
38. poner	pongo	puse	pondré	ponga	pusiera (-se)	pon
poniendo	pones	pusiste	pondrás	pongas	pusieras (-ses)	
puesto	pone	puso	pondrá	ponga	pusiera (-se)	
	etc.	pusimos	pondremos	pongamos	pusiéramos (-'semos)	
		pusisteis	pondréis	pongáis	pusierais (-seis)	
		pusieron	pondrán	pongan	pusieran (-sen)	
39. querer	quiero	quise	querré	quiera	quisiera (-se)	quiere
	quieres	quisiste	querrás	quieras	quisieras (-ses)	
	quiere	quiso	querrá	quiera	quisiera (-se)	
	queremos	quisimos	querremos	queramos	quisiéramos (-'semos)	
	queréis	quisisteis	querréis	queráis	quisierais (-seis)	
	quieren	quisieron	querrán	quieran	quisieran (-sen)	
40. reír	río	reí	reiré	ría	riera (-se)	ríe
riendo	ríes	reíste	reirás	rías	rieras (-ses)	
reído	ríe	rió	reirá	ría	riera (-se)	
	reímos	reímos	reiremos	riamos	riéramos (-'semos)	
	reís	reísteis	reiréis	riáis	rierais (-seis)	
	ríen	rieron	reirán	rían	rieran (-sen)	

Infinitive, Present Part., Past Part.	Present Indicative	Preterite	Future	Present Subjunctive	Imperfect Subjunctive	Familiar Command (tú)
41. reunir	reúno reúnes reúne reunimos reunís reúnen			reúna reúnas reúna reunamos reunáis reúnan		reúne
42. rogar	ruego ruegas ruega rogamos rogáis ruegan	rogué rogaste rogó etc.		ruegue ruegues ruegue roguemos roguéis rueguen		ruega
43. romper rompiendo roto						
44. saber	sé sabes sabe etc.	supe supiste supo supimos supisteis supieron	sabré sabrás sabrá sabremos sabréis sabrán	sepa sepas sepa sepamos sepáis sepan	supiera (-se) supieras (-ses) supiera (-se) supiéramos (-'semos) supierais (-seis) supieran (-sen)	
45. salir	salgo sales sale etc.		saldré saldrás saldrá saldremos saldréis saldrán	salga salgas salga salgamos salgáis salgan		sal
46. seguir siguiendo seguido	sigo sigues sigue seguimos seguís siguen	seguí seguiste siguió seguimos seguisteis siguieron		siga sigas siga sigamos sigáis sigan	siguiera (-se) siguieras (-ses) siguiera (-se) siguiéramos (-'semos) siguierais (-seis) siguieran (-sen)	sigue
47. sentir sintiendo sentido	siento sientes siente sentimos sentís sienten	sentí sentiste sintió sentimos sentisteis sintieron		sienta sientas sienta sintamos sintáis sientan	sintiera (-se) sintieras (-ses) sintiera (-se) sintiéramos (-'semos) sintierais (-seis) sintieran (-sen)	siente
48. ser	soy eres es somos sois son	fui fuiste fue fuimos fuisteis fueron		sea seas sea seamos seáis sean	fuera (-se) fueras (-ses) fuera (-se) fuéramos (-'semos) fuerais (-seis) fueran (-sen)	sé
49. tener	tengo tienes tiene tenemos tenéis tienen	tuve tuviste tuvo tuvimos tuvisteis tuvieron	tendré tendrás tendrá tendremos tendréis tendrán	tenga tengas tenga tengamos tengáis tengan	tuviera (-se) tuvieras (-ses) tuviera (-se) tuviéramos (-'semos) tuvierais (-seis) tuvieran (-sen)	ten
50. traducir	traduzco traduces traduce etc.	traduje tradujiste tradujo tradujimos tradujisteis tradujeron		traduzca traduzcas traduzca traduzcamos traduzcáis traduzcan	tradujera (-se) tradujeras (-ses) tradujera (-se) tradujéramos (-'semos) tradujerais (-seis) tradujeran (-sen)	
51. traer trayendo traído	traigo traes trae etc.	traje trajiste trajo trajimos trajisteis trajeron		traiga traigas traiga traigamos traigáis traigan	trajera (-se) trajeras (-ses) trajera (-se) trajéramos (-'semos) trajerais (-seis) trajeran (-sen)	

Infinitive, Present Part., Past Part.	Present Indicative	Preterite	Future	Present Subjunctive	Imperfect Subjunctive	Familiar Command (tú)
52. vencer	**venzo** vences vence etc.			**venza** **venzas** **venza** **venzamos** **venzáis** **venzan**		
53. venir **viniendo** venido	**vengo** **vienes** **viene** venimos venís **vienen**	**vine** viniste vino vinimos vinisteis vinieron	vendré vendrás vendrá vendremos vendréis vendrán	**venga** **vengas** **venga** **vengamos** **vengáis** **vengan**	viniera (-se) vinieras (-ses) viniera (-se) viniéramos (-'semos) vinierais (-seis) vinieran (-sen)	ven
54. ver viendo **visto**	veo ves ve etc.			**vea** **veas** **vea** **veamos** **veáis** **vean**		
55. volver volviendo **vuelto**	**vuelvo** **vuelves** **vuelve** volvemos volvéis **vuelven**			**vuelva** **vuelvas** **vuelva** volvamos volváis **vuelvan**		**vuelve**

OTHER VERBS WITH IRREGULAR FORMS

acercarse (*See* buscar)
acordarse (*See* mostrar)
acostarse (*See* mostrar)
agradecer (*See* conocer)
alcanzar (*See* abrazar)
alzar (*See* abrazar)
apagar (*See* llegar)
aparecer (*See* conocer)
atacar (*See* buscar)
atender (*See* perder)
atravesar (*See* pensar)
avanzar (*See* abrazar)
calentar (*See* pensar)
cargar (*See* llegar)
castigar (*See* llegar)
cerrar (*See* pensar)
coger (*See* dirigir)
colgar (*See* rogar)
colocar (*See* buscar)
comenzar (*See* empezar)
componer (*See* poner)
comunicarse (*See* buscar)
concluir (*See* huir)
conducir (*See* traducir)
confesar (*See* pensar)
conseguir (*See* seguir)
consentir (*See* sentir)
construir (*See* huir)
contar (*See* mostrar)
contener (*See* tener)
contribuir (*See* huir)
convencer (*See* vencer)

corregir (*See* elegir)
costar (*See* mostrar)
crecer (*See* conocer)
cruzar (*See* abrazar)
cubrir (*See* abrir)
dedicar (*See* buscar)
defender (*See* perder)
demostrar (*See* mostrar)
desaparecer (*See* conocer)
describir (*See* escribir)
descubrir (*See* abrir)
despedirse (*See* pedir)
despertarse (*See* pensar)
destruir (*See* huir)
detener (*See* tener)
devolver (*See* volver)
distribuir (*See* huir)
divertirse (*See* sentir)
encender (*See* perder)
encontrar (*See* mostrar)
entender (*See* perder)
entregar (*See* llegar)
envolver (*See* volver)
equivocarse (*See* buscar)
escoger (*See* dirigir)
establecer (*See* conocer)
explicar (*See* buscar)
extender (*See* perder)
fabricar (*See* buscar)
gobernar (*See* pensar)
gozar (*See* abrazar)
graduarse (*See* continuar)

guiar (*See* enviar)
herir (*See* sentir)
identificar (*See* buscar)
impedir (*See* pedir)
indicar (*See* buscar)
influir (*See* huir)
introducir (*See* traducir)
juzgar (*See* llegar)
lanzar (*See* abrazar)
leer (*See* creer)
llover (*See* mover)
mantener (*See* tener)
mascar (*See* buscar)
mentir (*See* sentir)
merecer (*See* conocer)
morder (*See* mover)
nacer (*See* conocer)
nevar (*See* pensar)
obedecer (*See* conocer)
obligar (*See* llegar)
obtener (*See* tener)
ofrecer (*See* conocer)
padecer (*See* conocer)
pagar (*See* llegar)
parecer (*See* conocer)
pegar (*See* llegar)
permanecer (*See* conocer)
perseguir (*See* seguir)
pertenecer (*See* conocer)
pescar (*See* buscar)
poseer (*See* creer)
preferir (*See* sentir)

probar (*See* mostrar)
producir (*See* traducir)
proteger (*See* dirigir)
quebrar (*See* pensar)
realizar (*See* abrazar)
recoger (*See* dirigir)
reconocer (*See* conocer)
recordar (*See* mostrar)
reducir (*See* traducir)
repetir (*See* pedir)
rezar (*See* abrazar)
sacar (*See* buscar)
sentarse (*See* pensar)
servir (*See* pedir)
significar (*See* buscar)
situar (*See* continuar)
soler (Present and imperfect tenses only. *See* mover)
soltar (*See* mostrar)
sonar (*See* mostrar)
sonreír (*See* reír)
soñar (*See* mostrar)
suplicar (*See* buscar)
temblar (*See* pensar)
tocar (*See* buscar)
tropezar (*See* empezar)
valer (*See* salir)
vestir (*See* pedir)
volar (*See* mostrar)

a, to, at

abajo, below, down, downstairs

abeja, *f.,* bee

abierto, -a, open

abogado, *m.,* lawyer

abrazar (c), to embrace

abrigo, *m.,* overcoat

abril, *m.,* April

abrir, to open

abuelo, *m.,* grandfather; **abuela,** *f.,* grandmother

acá, here

acabar, to finish, to end; **acabar de** + *inf.,* to have just . . .

acaso, perhaps

accidente, *m.,* accident

acento, *m.,* accent

aceptar, to accept

acera, *f.,* sidewalk

acerca de, about, concerning

acercarse (qu) (a), to approach

acero, *m.,* steel

acompañar, to accompany

aconsejar, to advise

acordarse (ue) (de), to remember

acostarse (ue), to go to bed, to lie down

acto, *m.,* act

actor, *m.,* actor; **actriz,** *f.,* actress

actual, present, present-day

acueducto, *m.,* aqueduct

acuerdo, *m.,* agreement, accord

adelantar (se), to advance, to progress

adelante, ahead, forward

además (de), besides, moreover

adiós, goodbye

adjetivo, *m.,* adjective

admirar, to admire, to wonder

¿adónde?, where?

adondequiera, wherever

aduana, *f.,* custom house

aduanero, *m.,* customs inspector

adverbio, *m.,* adverb

aeropuerto, *m.,* airport

afecto, *m.,* affection

agosto, *m.,* August

agradable, pleasant, agreeable

agradecer (zc), to thank (for)

agrícola, agricultural

agricultor, *m.,* farmer

agua (el), *f.,* water

aguador, *m.,* water-carrier

aguardar, to await, to wait (for)

agudo, -a, sharp

águila (el), *f.,* eagle

aguja, *f.,* needle

ahí, there

ahora, now; **ahora mismo,** right now

aire, *m.,* air; **al aire libre,** in the open air, outdoors

ajedrez, *m.,* chess

al, to the, at the; **al** + *inf.,* on, upon (speaking, etc.)

alabar, to praise

albóndiga, *f.,* meat ball

alcalde, *m.,* mayor

alcanzar (c), to overtake, to reach

alcázar, *m.,* Moorish castle, fortress

alcoba, *f.,* bedroom

aldea, *f.,* village

alegrarse (de), to be glad (to, of)

alegre, merry, gay, happy

alegría, *f.,* joy, merriment

alejarse (de), to move away, to withdraw (from)

alemán, alemana, German; **alemán,** *m.,* German (language)

Alemania, *f.,* Germany

alfabeto, *m.,* alphabet

alfiler, *m.,* pin

alfombra, *f.,* carpet

algo, something, somewhat

algodón, *m.,* cotton

alguien, someone, somebody

alguno, -a (algún), some; **algún día,** some day; **alguna vez,** some time; **algunas veces,** sometimes

alimento, *m.,* food

alma (el), *f.,* soul

almohada, *f.,* pillow

almorzar (ue, c), to lunch, to eat (have) lunch

almuerzo, *m.,* lunch

alrededor (de), around

alto, -a, high, tall; **en voz alta,** aloud, in a loud voice

altura, *f.,* height

alumbrar, to illuminate

aluminio, *m.,* aluminum

alumno, -a, pupil, student

alzar (c), to raise, to lift

allá, allí, there

amable, kind, amiable

amanecer (zc), to dawn, to grow light; **al amanecer,** at daybreak

amar, to love

amargo, -a, bitter

amarillo, -a, yellow

ambos, -as, both

América, *f.,* America; **la América Central,** Central America; **la América del Norte,** North America; **la**

América del Sur, South America; **la América Hispana,** Spanish America

americano, -a, American

amigo, -a, friend

amistad, *f.,* friendship

amo, *m.,* master, owner

amor, *m.,* love

anciano, -a, old man, old woman

ancho, -a, wide

andaluz, -a, Andalusian

andar, to walk, to go

ángel, *m.,* angel

animal, *m.,* animal

aniversario, *m.,* anniversary

anoche, last night

anochecer: al anochecer, at nightfall

ante, before

anteojos, *m., pl.,* eyeglasses

anterior, former, preceding

antes, before, previously; **antes de, antes (de) que,** before; **cuanto antes,** as soon as possible

antiguo, -a, old, ancient

antónimo, *m.,* antonym

anunciar, to announce

añadir, to add

año, *m.,* year; **el año pasado,** last year; **el año que viene,** next year; **hace un año,** a year ago

apagar (gu), to put out, to extinguish

aparecer (zc), to appear

apartamiento, *m.,* apartment

apetito, *m.,* appetite

aplaudir, to applaud

aplicado, -a, studious, industrious, diligent

aprender, to learn

apresurarse (a), to hurry (to), to hasten (to)

aprisa, quickly

aprovecharse (de), to take advantage (of), to profit (by)

aproximadamente, approximately

aquel, aquella, that; **aquél, aquélla,** that one, the former; **aquellos, -as,** those; **aquéllos, -as,** those, the former

aquí, here

árabe, Arab, Arabian, Arabic

árbol, *m.,* tree

argentino, -a, Argentinian

aritmética, *f.,* arithmetic

arma (el), *f.,* weapon, arm

armada, *f.,* navy, fleet; **la Armada Invencible,** the Invincible Armada

armario, *m.,* closet

arquitectura, *f.,* architecture

arreglar, to arrange

arriba, above, up, upstairs

arrojar, to throw

arroz, *m.,* rice

arte, *m.* or *f.,* art; **bellas artes,** fine arts

artículo, *m.,* article

artista, *m.* or *f.,* artist

asado, -a, roasted

asar, to roast

ascensor, *m.,* elevator

asegurar, to assure

así, so, thus

asiento, *m.,* seat

asistir (a), to attend

asno, *m.,* donkey

asombrar, to astonish, to amaze

aspecto, *m.,* aspect, appearance

asunto, *m.,* matter, affair

asustar, to frighten; **asustarse,** to be frightened

atacar (qu), to attack

atar, to tie

atención, *f.,* attention; **con atención,** attentively; **prestar atención,** to pay attention

atender (ie) (a), to attend (to)

atentamente, attentively

atómico, -a, atomic

atravesar (ie), to cross

atreverse (a), to dare (to)

aula (el), *f.,* classroom

aumentar, to increase

aún, even, still, yet

aunque, although

ausencia, *f.,* absence

ausente, absent

autobús, *m.,* bus

automóvil (auto), *m.,* automobile

autor, *m.,* author

avanzar (c), to advance

ave (el), *f.,* bird

avenida, *f.,* avenue

aventura, *f.,* adventure

aventurero, *m.,* adventurer

averiguar (ü), to find out, to verify

avión, *m.,* airplane

ayer, yesterday

ayuda, *f.,* aid, help

ayudar, to help, to aid

azúcar, *m.,* sugar

azul, blue

bailar, to dance

bailarín, -ina, dancer

baile, *m.,* dance

bajar, to go down, to descend; **bajar de**, to get out of (a vehicle)

bajo, -a, low, short; **en voz baja**, in a low voice; **bajo**, *adv.*, under

balcón, *m.*, balcony, porch

banco, *m.*, bench, bank

bandera, *f.*, flag

banderilla, *f.*, banderilla (dart used in the bullfight)

bañar(se), to bathe (oneself)

baño, *m.*, bath; **el cuarto de baño**, bathroom

barato, -a, cheap

barba, *f.*, beard, chin

barbería, *f.*, barber shop

barbero, *m.*, barber

barco, *m.*, ship, boat

basado, -a, based

bastante, enough, quite

batalla, *f.*, battle

baúl, *m.*, trunk; **hacer (g) el baúl**, to pack one's trunk

beber, to drink

bebida, *f.*, beverage, drink

béisbol, *m.*, baseball

belleza, *f.*, beauty

bello, -a, beautiful; **bellas artes**, fine arts

besar, to kiss

beso, *m.*, kiss

biblioteca, *f.*, library

bicicleta, *f.*, bicycle

bien, well; **está bien**, all right; **salir (g) bien**, to pass (an examination); **que le vaya bien**, good luck to you; **que lo pase Vd. bien**, good luck to you

billete, *m.*, ticket, note; **billete de ida y vuelta**, round-trip ticket

bizcocho, *m.*, biscuit

blanco, -a, white

blando, -a, soft

blusa, *f.*, blouse

boca, *f.*, mouth

boda, *f.*, wedding

boina, *f.*, beret

bolsa, *f.*, purse

bolsillo, *m.*, pocket

bomba, *f.*, bomb

bondad, *f.*, goodness, kindness; **con bondad**, kindly; **tenga Vd. la bondad de +** *inf.*, please . . .

bondadoso, -a, kind

bonito, -a, pretty

borrar, to erase

bosque, *m.*, forest, woods

botella, *f.*, bottle

botica, *f.*, drugstore

botón, *m.*, button

(el) Brasil, Brazil

brazo, *m.*, arm

breve, short, brief

brillar, to shine

broma, *f.*, joke, jest

bueno, -a **(buen)**, good; **dar los buenos días (las buenas noches)**, to say good morning (evening); **de buena gana**, willingly; **hace buen tiempo**, the weather is good

buque, *m.*, boat, ship

burlarse **(de)**, to make fun (of), to laugh (at**)**

burro, *m.*, donkey

buscar **(qu)**, to look for, to seek

butaca, *f.*, armchair

caballero, *m.*, gentleman, knight

caballo, *m.*, horse; **a caballo**, on horseback; **dar un paseo a caballo**, to go horseback riding

cabello, *m.*, hair

caber **(quepo)**, to fit

cabeza, *f.*, head; **tener (ie, g) dolor de cabeza**, to have a headache

cabo: **llevar a cabo**, to carry out

cada **(uno, -a)**, each (one)

caer **(g)**, to fall; **caerse**, to fall down; **dejar caer**, to drop

café, *m.*, coffee, café

cafetería, *f.*, cafeteria

caja, *f.*, box

cajón, *m.*, drawer

calcetín, *m.*, sock

calendario, *m.*, calendar

calentar **(ie)**, to heat

calidad, *f.*, quality

caliente, hot, warm

calor, *m.*, heat; **hace calor**, it is warm (weather); **él tiene calor**, he is warm

callarse, to be silent, to keep still

calle, *f.*, street

cama, *f.*, bed

cambiar, to change; **cambiar de**, to change (opinion, trains, etc.)

cambio, *m.*, change; **en cambio**, on the other hand

caminar, to walk

camino, *m.*, road; **ponerse en camino**, to set out, to start out

camisa, *f.*, shirt

campana, *f.*, bell

campesino, *m.*, farmer, peasant

campo, *m.*, country, field

(el) Canadá, Canada

canción, *f.*, song

cansado, -a, tired

cantante, *m.* or *f.*, singer

cantar, to sing

cantidad, *f.*, quantity

cantor, *m.*, singer

cañón, *m.*, canyon; **el Gran Cañón**, the Grand Canyon

capa, *f.*, cape

capital, *f.*, capital (city)

capitán, *m.*, captain

capítulo, *m.*, chapter

capturar, to capture

cara, *f.*, face

carácter, *m.*, character

carbón, *m.*, coal, carbon

cárcel, *f.*, prison

cargar **(gu)**, to load

cariño, *m.*, affection

cariñoso, -a, affectionate

Carnaval, *m.*, Carnival

carne, *f.*, meat

carnicería, *f.*, butcher shop

carnicero, *m.*, butcher

caro, -a, expensive, dear

carpintero, *m.*, carpenter

carrera, *f.*, profession, career, race

carretero, *m.*, truckman

carta, *f.*, letter; **echar (una carta) al correo**, to mail (a letter)

cartera, *f.*, wallet

cartero, *m.*, letter carrier, postman

casa, *f.*, house, home; **la casa particular**, private house; **a casa**, (to) home; **de casa**, (from) home; **en casa**, (at) home

casamiento, *m.*, marriage

casarse **(con)**, to marry, to get married (to)

casi, almost

caso, *m.*, case; **en caso de que**, in case

castellano, -a, Spanish, Castilian

castigar **(gu)**, to punish

castillo, *m.*, castle

catalán,-ana, Catalonian

catarro, *m.*, cold (illness)

catedral, *f.*, cathedral

católico, -a, Catholic

catorce, fourteen

caucho, *m.*, rubber

causa, *f.*, cause; **a causa de**, because of

celebrar, to celebrate

célebre, famous

cena, *f.*, supper

cenar, to eat supper

centavo, *m.*, cent

centro, *m.*, center, downtown

cepillo, *m.*, brush

cerca, near; **cerca de**, near

cercano, -a, nearby, neighboring

cereal, *m.*, cereal

cereza, *f.*, cherry

cerezo, *m.*, cherry tree

cero, *m.*, zero

cerrado, -a, closed

cerrar **(ie)**, to close

cerveza, *f.*, beer

cesar **(de)**, to stop, to cease

cesta, *f.*, basket

ciego, -a, blind

cielo, *m.*, sky, heaven

ciencia, *f.*, science

científico, -a, scientific; *m.*, scientist

ciento **(cien)**, one hundred

cierto, -a, certain, a certain

cinco, five

cincuenta, fifty

cine, *m.*, movies

cinturón, *m.*, belt

circo, *m.*, circus

ciruela, *f.*, plum

ciudad, *f.*, city

claro, -a, light, clear; **claramente**, clearly

clase, *f.*, class, kind

clavel, *m.*, carnation

clima, *m.*, climate

club, *m.*, club (group of people)

cobarde, *m.*, coward

cobrar, to collect, to charge

cobre, *m.*, copper

cocer **(ue, z)**, to cook

cocido, *m.*, stew

cocina, *f.*, kitchen

cocinar, to cook

cocinero, -a, cook

coche, *m.*, coach, car

cochero, *m.*, coachman, driver

coger, **(j)**, to seize, to catch

colección, *f.*, collection

colegio, *m.*, college, boarding school

colgar **(ue, gu)**, to hang

colina, *f.*, hill

colocar **(qu)**, to place, to put

Colón, Columbus

colonia, *f.*, colony

color, *m.*, color

combate, *m.*, fight, combat

comedia, *f.*, comedy, play

comedor, *m.*, dining room

comenzar **(ie, c)**, to begin, to commence

comer, to eat

comerciante, *m.*, merchant

comercio, *m.*, trade, commerce

comida, *f.*, food, dinner, meal

comienzo, *m.*, beginning

comité, *m.*, committee

como, as, like; **tan +** *adj.* or *adv.* **+ como**, as . . . as; **tanto(-a, -os, -as) +** *noun* **+ como**, as much (many) . . . as

¿cómo?, how?, what?

cómoda, *f.*, bureau, dresser

cómodo, -a, comfortable

compañero, -a, companion

compañía, *f.*, company

compilar, to compile

completar, to complete

completo, -a, complete; **completamente**, completely

componer **(g)**, to compose

composición, *f.*, composition

compositor, *m.*, composer

comprar, to buy

comprender, to understand

común, common

comunicarse **(qu) con**, to communicate with

con, with; **con tal que**, provided that

concierto, *m.*, concert

concluir (y), to conclude

conde, *m.*, count

condición, *f.*, condition

conducir (zc), to lead, to drive

confesar (ie), to confess

conmigo, with me

conocer (zc), to know

conocido, -a, acquaintance, known

conquista, *f.*, conquest

conquistador, *m.*, conqueror

conquistar, to conquer

conseguir (i, gu), to get, to obtain, to succeed in

consejo, *m.*, advice

consentir (ie, i), to consent

conservar, to preserve, to save, to conserve

considerar, to consider

consigo, with him(self), with her(self), etc.

consiguiente: por consiguiente, consequently, therefore

consistir en, to consist of

construcción, *f.*, construction

construir (y), to construct, to build

consultar, to consult

contador, *m.*, accountant

contar (ue), to count, to narrate; contar con, to rely on, to count on

contener (ie, g), to contain

contento, -a, content(ed)

contestar, to answer

contigo, with you

continente, *m.*, continent

continuar (ú), to continue

continuo, -a, continuous

contra, against

contrario, -a, contrary, opposite

contribuir (y), to contribute

convencer (z), to convince

conversación, *f.*, conversation

conversar, to converse

convidar, to invite

copa, *f.*, (wine) glass

copiar, to copy

corazón, *m.*, heart

corbata, *f.*, necktie

cordero, *m.*, lamb

coronel, *m.*, colonel

corrección, *f.*, correction

correcto, -a, correct; correctamente, correctly

corregir (i, j), to correct

correo, *m.*, mail, post office; echar (una carta) al correo, to mail (a letter)

correr, to run

corrida (de toros), *f.*, bullfight

cortar, to cut

corte, *f.*, court

cortés, courteous, polite

cortesía, *f.*, courtesy; con cortesía, courteously, politely

cortina, *f.*, curtain

corto, -a, short

cosa, *f.*, thing

cosecha, *f.*, harvest

costa, *f.*, coast, cost; a costa de, at the expense of

costar (ue), to cost

costumbre, *f.*, custom, habit

crear, to create

crecer (zc), to grow, to increase

creer, to believe; creer que sí (no), to think so (not); ¡Ya lo creo!, Yes indeed!, I should say so!

crema, *f.*, cream

criado, *m.*, servant; criada, *f.*, maid, servant

crimen, *m.*, crime

cristiano, -a, Christian

cruz, *f.*, cross

cruzar (c), to cross

cuaderno, *m.*, notebook

cuadrado, -a, square; *m.*, square

cuadro, *m.*, picture

ccuál?, ¿cuáles?, which?

cualquier(a), whatever, any

cuando, when; ¿cuándo?, when?; de cuando en cuando, from time to time; de vez en cuando, from time to time

cuanto, -a, as much as; ¿cuánto, -a?, how much?; ¿cuántos, -as?, how many?; cuanto antes, as soon as possible; cuanto más . . . tanto más, the more . . . the more; ¿cuánto tiempo?, how long?; ¿Cuántos años tiene Vd.?, How old are you?; ¿A cuántos estamos?, What is today's date?; en cuanto, as soon as; en cuanto a, as regards, as for; unos cuantos (unas cuantas), a few, several

cuarenta, forty

cuarto, -a, fourth; *m.*, room, quarter

cuatro, four

cuatrocientos, -as, four hundred

cubano, -a, Cuban

cubierto, -a, covered

cubrir, to cover

cuchara, *f.*, spoon

cuchillo, *m.*, knife

cuello, *m.*, neck, collar

cuenta, *f.*, account, bill

cuento, *m.*, story, tale

cuerda: dar cuerda a, to wind

cuero, *m.*, leather

cuerpo, *m.*, body

cuidado, *m.*, care; con cuidado, carefully; tener (ie, g) cuidado, to be careful

cuidadoso, -a, careful

cuidar (de, a), to take care (of)

cultivar, to cultivate

cultura, *f.*, culture

cumpleaños, *m.*, birthday

cumplir, to fulfill, to keep (a promise); cumplir . . . años, to be . . . years old

cuñado, *m.*, brother-in-law

cura, *m.*, priest

curar, to cure

cursivo, -a: letra cursiva, italics

curso, *m.*, course

cuyo, -a, whose

chaleco, *m.*, vest

chaqueta, *f.*, jacket

charlar, to chat

chico, -a, child, boy, girl

chileno, -a, Chilean

chimenea, *f.*, chimney, fireplace

chino, -a, Chinese

chiste, *m.*, joke

chocolate, *m.*, chocolate

chófer, *m.*, chauffeur

dama, *f.*, lady

daño, *m.*, damage, harm; hacer (g) daño (a), to hurt, to harm

dar, to give; dar a, to face; dar con, to come upon; dar cuerda a, to wind; dar de comer a, to feed; dar la hora (las siete), to strike the hour (seven o'clock); dar la mano (a alguien), to shake hands (with someone); darse la mano, to shake hands with each other; dar las gracias a, to thank; dar las buenas noches (a alguien), to say good evening (to someone); dar los buenos días (a alguien), to say good morning (to someone); dar un paseo, to take a walk; dar un paseo en automóvil (en coche), to take an automobile ride; dar un paseo a caballo, to go horseback riding

de, of, from, by, than, with

debajo de, under

deber, should, ought to, to owe; *m.*, duty

débil, weak

decadencia, *f.*, decay, decline

decidir, to decide; decidirse a + *inf.*, to decide to

décimo, -a, tenth

decir (i, g), to say, to tell; es decir, that is to say; querer (ie) decir, to mean

decisión, *f.*, decision

declarar, to declare

decorar, to decorate

dedicar (qu), to dedicate, to devote; dedicarse a, to devote oneself to

dedo, *m.*, finger, toe

defender (ie), to defend

dejar, to let, to allow, to leave; dejar caer, to drop; dejar de + *inf.*, to stop, to fail to

del, of the, from the

delante de, in front of

delgado, -a, thin, slender

delicia, *f.*, delight

demasiado, -a (demasiados, -as), too much (too many); demasiado, *adv.*, too

democracia, *f.*, democracy

demonio, *m.*, devil

demostrar (ue), to demonstrate

dentista, *m.*, dentist

dentro (de), inside, within; dentro de poco, in a little while, presently

depender (de), to depend (on)

dependiente, *m.*, clerk

deporte, *m.*, sport

derecho, -a, right, straight; a la derecha, at (to) the right

desagradable, disagreeable

desaparecer (zc), to disappear

desayunarse, to eat (have) breakfast

desayuno, *m.*, breakfast

descansar, to rest

descanso, *m.*, rest

describir, to describe

descubrimiento, *m.*, discovery

descubrir, to discover

desde, from, since; desde luego, at once, of course

desear, to wish, to desire

deseo, *m.*, wish

desgraciadamente, unfortunately

despacio, slowly

despacho, *m.*, office

despedirse (i) (de), to take leave (of), to say goodbye (to)

despertarse (ie), to wake up

después, afterward; después de, after

destruir (y), to destroy

detener (ie, g), to stop, to detain; detenerse, to stop (oneself)

detrás (de), in back (of), behind

devolver (ue), to return, to give back

día, *m.*, day; al día siguiente, on the following day; algún día, some day; dar los buenos días (a), to say good morning (to); de día, by day, in the daytime; hoy día, nowadays; ocho días, a week; quince días, two weeks, a fortnight; todos los días, every day

diablo, *m.*, devil

dialecto, *m.*, dialect
diamante, *m.*, diamond
diccionario, *m.*, dictionary
diciembre, *m.*, December
dictado, *m.*, dictation
dictador, *m.*, dictator
dictadura, *f.*, dictatorship
dicho, -a, said; *m.*, saying
diente, *m.*, tooth
diez, ten
diferencia, *f.*, difference; a diferencia de, unlike
diferente, different
difícil, difficult
dificultad, *f.*, difficulty
diligente, diligent
dinamita, *f.*, dynamite
dinero, *m.*, money
Dios, God
dirección, *f.*, address, direction
director, *m.*, director, principal, conductor
dirigir (j), to direct; dirigirse a, to make one's way toward, to address
disco, *m.*, phonograph record
discurso, *m.*, speech, talk
disputa, *f.*, dispute
distancia, *f.*, distance
distinguir (g), to distinguish
distinto, -a, different
distribuir (y), to distribute
diversión, *f.*, amusement
divertirse (ie, i), to enjoy oneself, to have a good time
dividir, to divide
doblar, to fold, to turn
doce, twelve
docena, *f.*, dozen
documento, *m.*, document
dólar, *m.*, dollar
dolor, *m.*, pain, sorrow; tener (ie, g) dolor de cabeza, to have a headache; tener dolor de estómago, to have a stomachache; tener dolor de garganta, to have a sore throat; tener dolor de muelas, to have a toothache
doméstico, -a, domestic
dominar, to dominate
domingo, *m.*, Sunday
don, *m.*, doña, *f.* (title given to a gentleman or a lady, equivalent to *Mr.*, *Mrs.*, or *Miss* in English, but used only before given names)
donde, where; ¿dónde?, where?
dondequiera, wherever
dormir (ue, u), to sleep; dormirse, to fall asleep
dormitorio, *m.*, bedroom
dos, two; dos veces, twice
doscientos, -as, two hundred
drama, *m.*, drama
dramaturgo, *m.*, dramatist
duda, *f.*, doubt; sin duda, no doubt, doubtless

dudar, to doubt
dudoso, -a, doubtful
dueño, *m.*, master, owner
dulce, sweet; dulces, *m. pl.*, candy
dulcería, *f.*, candy shop
durante, during
durar, to last
duro, -a, hard; *m.*, Spanish coin

e, and (used only before a word beginning with i or hi, but not hie)
echar, to throw; echar de menos, to miss; echar (una carta) al correo, to mail (a letter); echarse a + *inf.*, to start to
edad, *f.*, age
edificio, *m.*, building
educador, *m.*, educator, teacher
ejemplo, *m.*, example
ejercicio, *m.*, exercise; hacer (g) ejercicios, to take exercise
ejército, *m.*, army
el, the; el que, the one who, the one that
él, he, it
eléctrico, -a, electric, electrical
elefante, *m.*, elephant
elegir (i, j), to elect
elevar, to raise, to lift
ella, she, her, it
ellos, -as, they, them
embargo: sin embargo, nevertheless, however
emparedado, *m.*, sandwich
emperador, *m.*, emperor
empezar (ie, c), to begin
empleado, *m.*, employee
emplear, to employ, to use
empleo, *m.*, job
en, in, on; en cuanto, as soon as; en cuanto a, as for
enamorarse (de), to fall in love (with)
encantador, -a, charming, enchanting
encantar, to charm, to enchant
encender (ie), to light
encima (de), on top (of), above
encontrar (ue), to meet, to find; encontrarse, to find oneself, to be
encuentro, *m.*, meeting, encounter
enemigo, -a, enemy
enero, *m.*, January
enfadarse, to become angry
enfermedad, *f.*, sickness, illness
enfermera, *f.*, nurse
enfermo, -a, sick, ill
en frente (de), in front (of), opposite

engañar, to deceive, to fool, to cheat
enojarse, to become angry
enorme, enormous
ensalada, *f.*, salad
ensayista, *m.*, essayist
ensayo, *m.*, essay
enseñar, to teach, to show
entender (ie), to understand
entero, -a, entire, whole
entonces, then
entrada, *f.*, entrance, admission ticket
entrar (en), to enter
entre, between, among
entregar (gu), to deliver, to hand over
enviar (í), to send
envolver (ue), to wrap up
época, *f.*, epoch, time, period
equipo, *m.*, team
equivocarse (qu), to be mistaken
error, *m.*, error, mistake
escalera, *f.*, stairs, staircase
escena, *f.*, scene
esclavo, -a, slave
escoger (j), to choose, to select
esconder, to hide
escribir, to write
escrito, -a, written
escritor, -a, writer
escritorio, *m.*, desk
escuchar, to listen (to)
escudero, *m.*, squire, attendant
escuela, *f.*, school
ese, -a, that; ése, -a, that one; eso, that; esos, -as, those; ésos, -as, those; a eso de, at about + *time expression*; de esa manera, de ese modo, in that way; por eso, therefore
espacio, *m.*, space
espada, *f.*, sword
espalda, *f.*, back, shoulder
espantar, to frighten, to scare
España, *f.*, Spain
español, -a, Spanish, Spaniard; español, *m.*, Spanish (language)
especialmente, especially
espectáculo, *m.*, spectacle
espejo, *m.*, mirror
esperanza, *f.*, hope
esperar, to wait for, to await, to hope, to expect
espléndido, -a, splendid
esposo, *m.*, husband; esposa, *f.*, wife
esquina, *f.*, corner
establecer (zc), to establish
estación, *f.*, station, season
estado, *m.*, state; los Estados Unidos, the United States
estante (para libros), *m.*, bookcase
estar, to be; ¿A cuántos estamos?, What is today's date?; estamos a + *date*,

today's date is . . . ; estar a punto de + *inf.*, estar para + *inf.*, to be about to; está bien, all right; estar por + *inf.*, to be in favor of
estatua, *f.*, statue
este, *m.*, east
este, -a, this; éste, -a, this one, the latter; esto, this; estos, -as, these; éstos, -as, these, the latter; esta noche, tonight; de esta manera, de este modo, in this way; en este momento, at this moment
estilo, *m.*, style
estómago, *m.*, stomach; tener (ie, g) dolor de estómago, to have a stomachache
estrecho, -a, narrow
estrella, *f.*, star
estudiante, *m.* or *f.*, student
estudiar, to study
estudio, *m.*, study
estufa, *f.*, stove
estúpido, -a, stupid
Europa, *f.*, Europe
europeo, -a, European
evidente, evident
evitar, to avoid
examen, *m.*, examination
examinar, to examine
excelente, excellent
existir, to exist
éxito, *m.*, success
explicación, *f.*, explanation
explicar (qu), to explain
explorador, *m.*, explorer
explorar, to explore
explosión, *f.*, explosion
exportar, to export
expresar, to express
expresión, *f.*, expression
expulsar, to expel
extenderse (ie), to extend
extenso, -a, extensive, broad
extranjero, -a, foreign, foreigner
extraño, -a, strange
extraordinario, -a, extraordinary

fábrica, *f.*, factory
fabricar (qu), to manufacture
fácil, easy
facilidad: con facilidad, easily
fácilmente, easily
falda, *f.*, skirt
falso, -a, false
falta, *f.*, lack, mistake, error; hacerle (g) falta a alguien, to be lacking (to someone), to lack, to need
faltar, to be lacking, to lack, to need
fama, *f.*, fame, reputation
familia, *f.*, family
famoso, -a, famous
fatigado, -a, tired

favor, *n.*, favor; **haga Vd. el favor de** + *inf.*, please; **por favor**, please

favorito, -a, favorite

febrero, *m.*, February

fecha, *f.*, date

felicidad, *f.*, happiness

feliz, happy

femenino, -a, feminine

feo, -a, ugly

feria, *f.*, fair

feroz, ferocious

ferrocarril, *m.*, railroad

fiebre, *f.*, fever

fiel, faithful

fiesta, *f.*, holiday, party

figura, *f.*, figure, shape

fijar, to fix, to set

fila, *f.*, row

filosofía, *f.*, philosophy

filósofo, *m.*, philosopher

fin, *m.*, end; **al fin**, finally, at last; **por fin**, finally

finalmente, finally

fino, -a, delicate, fine

firmar, to sign

flaco, -a, thin

flor, *f.*, flower

florero, *m.*, florist

fonda, *f.*, inn

forma, *f.*, form

formación, *f.*, formation

formar, to form

fortuna, *f.*, fortune

fósforo, *m.*, match

fracaso, *m.*, failure

francés, francesa, French; francés, *m.*, French (language), Frenchman

Francia, *f.*, France

franco, -a, frank, open

frase, *f.*, sentence, phrase

frecuencia: **con frecuencia**, frequently

frecuentemente, frequently

frente: **en frente de**, in front of, opposite; **frente a**, facing, in front of

fresa, *f.*, strawberry

fresco, -a, cool; **hace fresco**, it is cool

frío, -a, cold; *m.*, cold; **hace frío**, it is cold (weather); **él tiene frío**, he is cold

fruta, *f.*, fruit

fuego, *m.*, fire

fuente, *f.*, fountain

fuera (de), outside (of)

fuerte, strong

fuerza, *f.*, force, strength

fumar, to smoke

fundador, *m.*, founder

fundar, to found, to establish

furia, *f.*, fury

furioso, -a, furious

fútbol, *m.*, football, soccer

futuro, *m.*, future

gabán, *m.*, overcoat

gabinete, *m.*, office

gafas, *f.*, eyeglasses

gallego, -a, Galician

gallina, *f.*, hen

gallo, *m.*, rooster; **la misa del gallo**, midnight mass

gana: **de buena gana**, willingly; **de mala gana**, unwillingly

ganar, to win, to earn

garaje, *m.*, garage

garganta, *f.*, throat; **el dolor de garganta**, sore throat

gaseosa, *f.*, soda pop

gasolina, *f.*, gasoline

gastar, to spend

gasto, *m.*, expense

gato, *m.*, cat

generación, *f.*, generation

general: **por lo general**, generally, in general

generalmente, usually, generally

gente, *f.*, people

geografía, *f.*, geography

geográfico, -a, geographic

gerente, *m.*, manager, boss

gitano, -a, Gypsy

gobernador, *m.*, governor

gobernar (ie), to govern

gobierno, *m.*, government

gordo, -a, fat, stout

gorra, *f.*, cap

gozar (c) de, to enjoy

gracias, *f. pl.*, thanks; **dar las gracias (a)**, to thank

graduarse (ú), to graduate

gramática, *f.*, grammar

grande (gran), large, big, great

grave, serious

griego, -a, Greek

gris, gray

gritar, to shout

grito, *m.*, shout

grupo, *m.*, group

guante, *m.*, glove

guapo, -a, handsome

guardar, to guard, to keep

guardia, *m.*, guard, policeman

guerra, *f.*, war

guía, *m.*, guide; *f.*, guidebook; **la guía de teléfonos**, telephone directory

guiar (í), to guide, to drive (a vehicle)

guisante, *m.*, pea

guitarra, *f.*, guitar

gustar, to be pleasing; **gustarle (a alguien) una cosa**, to like something

gusto, *m.*, pleasure; **con mucho gusto**, gladly; **tener (ie, g) gusto (en)** + *inf.*, to be glad (to)

La Habana, Havana

haber, to have (auxiliary); **hay**, there is, there are; **había, hubo**, there was, there were; **haber de** + *inf.*, to be to, to be sup-

posed to; **hay lodo**, it is muddy; **hay luna**, it is moonlight; **hay neblina**, it is foggy; **hay polvo**, it is dusty; **hay sol**, it is sunny; **no hay de qué**, don't mention it, you're welcome; **hay que** + *inf.*, one must . . . ; **hay** + *noun* + **que** + *inf.* (**hay mucho trabajo que hacer**), there is (are) + *noun* + *inf.* (there is much work to do)

hábil, skillful

habitación, *f.*, room

habitante, *m.* or *f.*, inhabitant

habla: **de habla española**, Spanish-speaking

hablado, -a, spoken

hablador, -a, talkative

hablar, to speak

hacer (g), to do, to make; **hace buen (mal) tiempo**, the weather is good (bad); **hace calor (fresco, frío)**, it is warm (cool, cold); **hace sol**, it is sunny; **hace viento**, it is windy; **hace una semana (un mes, un año)** + *preterite*, a week (a month, a year) ago; **hacer daño (a)**, to harm, to hurt; **hacer de**, to act as; **hacer ejercicios**, to take exercise; **hacer el baúl (la maleta)**, to pack one's trunk (suitcase); **hacer un viaje**, to take a trip; **hacer una pregunta**, to ask a question; **hacer una visita**, to pay a visit; **hacerle falta (a alguien)**, to be lacking, to lack, to need; **no tener (ie, g) nada que hacer**, to have nothing to do; **haga Vd. el favor de** + *inf.*, please . . . ; **¿Qué tiempo hace?**, How is the weather?; **hacerse**, to become (through one's own efforts); **hacerse tarde**, to be getting late

hacia, toward

hacienda, *f.*, estate

hacha (el), *f.*, ax

hallar, to find; **hallarse**, to find oneself, to be

hambre (el), *f.*, hunger; **tener (ie, g) hambre**, to be hungry

hasta, until, to; **hasta la vista**, goodbye, until I see you again; **hasta luego**, goodbye, see you later

hecho, -a, done, made

helado, *m.*, ice cream

herida, *f.*, wound

herido, -a, wounded

herir (ie, i), to wound

hermano, *m.*, brother; hermana, *f.*, sister

hermoso, -a, beautiful

héroe, *m.*, hero; heroína, *f.*, heroine

hierba, *f.*, grass

hierro, *m.*, iron

hijo, *m.*, son; hija, *f.*, daughter; hijos, -as, children

hispánico, -a, hispano, -a, Hispanic, Spanish

Hispanoamérica, *f.*, Spanish America

hispanoamericano, -a, Spanish-American

historia, *f.*, story, history

hoja, *f.*, leaf

hombre, *m.*, man

hombro, *m.*, shoulder

honrar, to honor

hora, *f.*, hour, time; **¿a qué hora?**, at what time?; **dar la hora**, to strike the hour; **¿Qué hora es?**, What time is it?

hospital, *m.*, hospital

hotel, *m.*, hotel

hoy, today; **hoy día**, nowadays

huerta, *f.*, garden

hueso, *m.*, bone

huésped, *m.*, guest, host

huevo, *m.*, egg

huida, *f.*, flight

huir (y), to flee

humano, -a, human

húmedo, -a, humid, damp

humilde, humble

humor, *m.*, humor

huracán, *m.*, hurricane

ibérico, -a, ibero, -a, Iberian

ida: **el billete de ida y vuelta**, round-trip ticket

identificar (qu), to identify

idioma, *m.*, language

iglesia, *f.*, church

igual, equal

imaginarse, to imagine

imitar, to imitate

impedir (i), to hinder, to impede

impermeable, *m.*, raincoat

importancia, *f.*, importance

importante, important

importar, to import, to be important

imposible, impossible

impuesto, *m.*, tax

incorrecto, -a, incorrect

independencia, *f.*, independence

indicar (qu), to indicate

indio, -a, Indian

industria, *f.*, industry

infeliz, unhappy, unfortunate

influencia, influence

influir (y) (en), to influence

ingeniero, *m.*, engineer

Inglaterra, *f.*, England

inglés, inglesa, English; inglés, *m.*, English (language), Englishman

iniciar, to initiate, to begin

inmediatamente, immediately

inocencia, f., innocence; con inocencia, innocently

inocente, innocent

insistir (en), to insist (on)

instrumento, m., instrument

inteligencia, f., intelligence; con inteligencia, intelligently

inteligente, intelligent

interesante, interesting

interesar, to interest

interrumpir, to interrupt

introducir (zc) (en), to bring in, to introduce (into)

inútil, useless

invadir, to invade

inventar, to invent

invierno, m., winter

invitar, to invite

ir, to go; irse, to go away; que le vaya bien, good luck to you

isla, f., island

Italia, f., Italy

italiano, -a, Italian

izquierdo, -a, left; a la izquierda, at (to) the left

jabón, m., soap

jai-alai, m., jai-alai (Basque game somewhat similar to handball)

jamás, never

jamón, ham

jardín, m., garden

jefe, m., chief, boss

joven, young, young person

joya, f., jewel

joyero, m., jeweler

judío, -a, Jewish, Jew

juego, m., game

jueves, m., Thursday

juez, m., judge

jugar (ue, gu), to play

jugo, m., juice

juguete, m., toy

julio, m., July

junio, m., June

junto, -a, joined; pl., together; junto a, next to, beside

justicia, f., justice

juventud, f., youth

juzgar (gu), to judge

la, the, her, it, you

labio, m., lip

laboratorio, m., laboratory

lado, m., side; al lado de, beside, next to

ladrón, m., thief

lago, m., lake

lágrima, f., tear

lámpara, f., lamp

lana, f., wool

lanza, f., lance

lanzar (c), to throw

lápiz, m., pencil

largo, -a, long

lástima, f., pity

latín, m., Latin (language)

lavar, to wash; lavarse, to wash oneself

le, him, to him, to her, you, to you

leal, loyal

lección, f., lesson

lectura, f., reading

leche, f., milk

lechero, m., milkman

leer, to read

legumbre, f., vegetable

lejos (de), far (from); a lo lejos, in the distance

lengua, f., language, tongue

lentamente slowly

lento, -a, slow

león, m., lion

les, to them, to you

letra, f., letter (of the alphabet); letra cursiva, italics

levantar, to raise; levantarse, to get up, to stand up

ley, f., law

leyenda, f., legend

libertad, f., liberty

libertador, m., liberator

libra, f., pound

libre, free; al aire libre, in the open air, outdoors

librería, f., bookstore

librero, m., bookseller

libro, m., book

ligero, -a, light

limitar, to limit

límite, m., limit

limón, m., lemon

limosna, f., charity, alms

limpiar, to clean

limpio, -a, clean

lindo, -a, pretty

línea, f., line

lista, f., list

listo, -a, ready, clever

lo, it, him, the; lo que, what (that which)

lobo, m., wolf

loco, -a, insane, mad, crazy

lodo: hay lodo, it is muddy

lograr, to obtain; lograr + inf., to succeed in

los, las, the, them, you

lotería, f., lottery

lucha, f., fight, struggle

luchar, to fight, to struggle

luego, then; luego que, as soon as; desde luego, of course, at once; hasta luego, goodbye, see you later

lugar, m., place; en lugar de, instead of; tener (ie, g) lugar, to take place

luna, f., moon; hay luna, it is moonlight

lunes, m., Monday

luz, f., light

llama, f., flame, llama

llamar, to call; llamarse, to be called or named

llanos, m. pl., plains

llanura, f., plain

llave, f., key

llegada, f., arrival

llegar (gu), to arrive, to reach; llegar a ser, to become

llenar, to fill

lleno, -a, full

llevar, to carry, to take, to wear; llevar a cabo, to carry out

llorar, to cry

llover (ue), to rain

lluvia, f., rain

madera, f., wood

madre, f., mother

madrileño, -a, Madrilenian (inhabitant of Madrid)

madrugada, f., (early) morning

maestro, -a, teacher; la obra maestra, masterpiece

magnífico, -a, magnificent

maíz, m., corn

mal, badly, poorly, ill; salir (g) mal, to fail (an examination)

maleta, f., suitcase; hacer (g) la maleta, to pack one's suitcase

malo, -a (mal), bad; (with estar) ill; de mala gana, unwillingly

mamá, f., mamma, mother

mandar, to order, to send

manera, f., manner, way; de esta (esa) manera, in this (that) way; de ninguna manera, by no means

manga, f., sleeve

mano, f., hand; dar la mano a, to shake hands with; darse la mano, to shake hands with each other

mantel, m., tablecloth

mantener (ie, g), to maintain, to support

mantequilla, f., butter

manzana, f., apple

manzano, m., apple tree

mañana, tomorrow; f., morning; de la mañana, in the morning, A.M.; por la mañana, in (during) the morning

mapa, m., map

máquina, f., machine

mar, m. or f., sea

maravilla, f., marvel

maravilloso, -a, marvelous

marchar, to march, to walk; marcharse, to go away

marido, m., husband

marina, f., navy

marinero, m., sailor

martes, m., Tuesday

marzo, m., March

más, more; más tarde, later

mascar (qu), to chew

masculino, -a, masculine

matador, m., matador (bullfighter who kills the bull)

matar, to kill

matemáticas, f. pl., mathematics

material, m., material

mayo, m., May

mayor, older, oldest; larger, largest; greater, greatest; la mayor parte de, most of, the majority of

me, me, to me, myself

media, f., stocking

medianoche, midnight; a medianoche, at midnight

medicina, f., medicine

médico, m., doctor

medio, -a, half; y media, half past; en medio de, in the midst of; por medio de, by means of

mediodía, noon; a mediodía, at noon

mejilla, f., cheek

mejor, better, best

mejorar, to improve

melocotón, m., peach

melón, m., melon

memoria, f., memory; de memoria, by heart

mencionar, to mention

menester: es menester, it is necessary

menor, younger, youngest; lesser, least; smaller, smallest

menos, less, minus; a menos que, unless; echar de menos, to miss; por lo menos, at least

mensaje, m., message

mentir (ie, i), to lie

mentira, f., lie

menudo: a menudo, often

mercado, m., market

merecer (zc), to deserve, to merit

merienda, f., (afternoon) snack

mes, m., month; el mes pasado, last month; hace un mes + preterite, a month ago

mesa, f., table; poner (g) la mesa, to set the table

metal, m., metal

meter, to put (in), to insert

mexicano, -a, Mexican

México, m., Mexico

mezclar, to mix

mi, mis, my

mí, me

miedo, m., fear; tener (ie, g) miedo, to be afraid

mientras (que), while

miércoles, m., Wednesday

mil, one thousand

milla, f., mile

millón, m., million

ministro, *m.*, minister

minuto, *m.*, minute

mío, -a, mine, of mine

mirada, *f.*, glance

mirar, to look at; mirarse, to look at oneself.

misa, *f.*, mass (religious); la misa del gallo, midnight mass

mismo, -a, same; ahora mismo, right now; lo mismo, the same

mitad, *f.*, half

moda, *f.*, style; de moda, in style

moderno, -a, modern

modesto, -a, modest

modista, *f.*, dressmaker

modo, *m.*, manner, way; de este (ese) modo, in this (that) way

molestar, to disturb, to annoy, to bother

momento, *m.*, moment; en este momento, at this moment

monarquía, *f.*, monarchy

monasterio, *m.*, monastery

moneda, *f.*, coin

mono, -a, monkey

montado, -a, mounted, riding

montaña, *f.*, mountain

montar, to ride (on horseback)

monte, *m.*, mountain

monumento, *m.*, monument

morder (ue), to bite

moreno, -a, dark-complexioned, brunette

morir (ue, u), to die

moro, -a, Moorish, Moor

mosca, *f.*, fly

mostrar (ue), to show

mover (ue), to move (something); moverse, to move (oneself)

movimiento, *m.*, movement

mozo, *m.*, waiter, porter, servant

muchacho, *m.*, boy; muchacha, *f.*, girl

muchísimo, very much

mucho, -a, much; muchos, -as, many; muchas veces, often; mucho tiempo, a long time

mudo, -a, mute, silent

mueble, *m.*, article of furniture; *pl.*, furniture

muela, *f.*, tooth; tener (ie, g) dolor de muelas, to have a toothache

muerte, *f.*, death

muerto, -a, dead

mujer, *f.*, woman, wife

mundial, worldwide, world (*adj.*)

mundo, *m.*, world; todo el mundo, everybody; el Nuevo Mundo, the New World

museo, *m.*, museum

música, *f.*, music

músico, -a, musical; *m.*, musician

muy, very

nacer (zc), to be born

nacimiento, *m.*, birth, representation of the Nativity scene

nación, *f.*, nation

nacional, national

nada, nothing, not . . . anything; de nada, you are welcome, don't mention it; no tener (ie, g) nada que hacer, to have nothing to do

nadar, to swim

nadie, no one, nobody, not . . . anyone, not . . . anybody

naranja, *f.*, orange

nariz, *f.*, nose

naturaleza, *f.*, nature

navegable, navigable

navegante, *m.*, navigator

Navidad, *f.*, Christmas

neblina, *f.*, fog; hay neblina, it is foggy

necesario, -a, necessary

necesidad, *f.*, necessity, need

necesitar, to need

necio, -a, stupid, foolish

negar (ie, gu), to deny; negarse a + *inf.*, to refuse

negativo, -a, negative

negocio, *m.*, business, business transaction; *pl.*, business

negro, -a, black

nervioso, -a, nervous

nevar (ie), to snow

nevera, *f.*, refrigerator

ni, neither, nor; ni . . . ni, neither . . . nor

nido, *m.*, nest

nieto, *m.*, grandson; nieta, *f.*, granddaughter

nieve, *f.*, snow

nilón, *m.*, nylon

ninguno, -a (ningún), no, none, no one

niñez, *f.*, childhood

niño, -a, child

no, no, not; no obstante, notwithstanding, in spite of

noche, *f.*, night, evening; de noche, at night, in the evening; de la noche, in the evening, P.M.; esta noche, tonight; por la noche, in (during) the evening; dar las buenas noches (a), to say good evening (to)

nombrar, to name, to appoint

nombre, *m.*, name

nordeste, *m.*, northeast

noroeste, *m.*, northwest

norte, north

norteamericano, -a, North American, American

nos, us, to us, ourselves

nosotros, -as, we, us

nota, *f.*, grade, mark, note

notar, to notice, to note

noticia, *f.*, news item; *pl.*, news

novecientos, -as, nine hundred

novela, *f.*, novel

novelista, *m. or f.*, novelist

noveno, -a, ninth

noventa, ninety

noviembre, *m.*, November

novio, *m.*, bridegroom, sweetheart, fiancé; novia, *f.*, bride, sweetheart, fiancée

nube, *f.*, cloud

nuestro, -a, our, ours, of ours

nueve, nine

nuevo, -a, new; de nuevo, again; el Día de Año Nuevo, New Year's Day; el Nuevo Mundo, the New World

nuez, *f.*, nut

número, *m.*, number

numeroso, -a, numerous

nunca, never

o, or

obedecer (zc), to obey

obispo, *m.*, bishop

objeto, *m.*, object

obligar (gu), to obligate, to compel

obra, *f.*, work; obra maestra, masterpiece

obscuro, -a, oscuro, -a, dark

observar, to observe

obstante: no obstante, notwithstanding, in spite of

obtener (ie, g), to obtain

ocasión, *f.*, opportunity

occidental, western

océano, *m.*, ocean

octavo, -a, eighth

octubre, *m.*, October

ocupado, -a, busy

ocupar, to occupy; ocuparse de, to busy oneself with, to concern oneself with

ocurrir, to occur, to happen

ochenta, eighty

ocho, eight; ocho días, a week

ochocientos, -as, eight hundred

odiar, to hate

odio, *m.*, hatred

oeste, *m.*, west

oficial, *m.*, official

oficina, *f.*, office

oficio, *m.*, trade, occupation

ofrecer (zc), to offer

oído, *m.*, (inner) ear, hearing

oír (y, g), to hear

¡ojalá!, God grant . . . !, if only . . . !

ojo, *m.*, eye

oler (hue), to smell

olvidar, to forget; olvidarse (de), to forget

omitir, to omit

ómnibus, *m.*, bus

once, eleven

ópera, *f.*, opera

opinión, *f.*, opinion

oportunidad, *f.*, opportunity

oración, *f.*, prayer, sentence

orden, *f.*, order, command

oreja, *f.*, ear

(la) Organización de Estados Americanos (O.E.A.), Organization of American States (O.A.S.)

oriental, eastern

origen, *m.*, origin

oro, *m.*, gold; el Siglo de Oro, Golden Age

orquesta, *f.*, orchestra

oso, *m.*, bear

otoño, *m.*, autumn, fall

otro, -a, other, another; otra vez, again

oveja, *f.*, sheep

paciencia, *f.*, patience; con paciencia, patiently

paciente, patient

padecer (zc), to suffer

padre, *m.*, father; *pl.*, parents

pagar (gu), to pay

página, *f.*, page

país, *m.*, country, nation

paisaje, *m.*, countryside

paja, *f.*, straw

pájaro, *m.*, bird

palabra, *f.*, word

palacio, *m.*, palace

pálido, -a, pale

paloma, *f.*, dove, pigeon

pan, *m.*, bread

panadería, *f.*, bakery

panadero, *m.*, baker

panecillo, *m.*, roll, bun

pantalones, *m. pl.*, trousers, pants

paño, *m.*, cloth

pañuelo, *m.*, handkerchief

papá, *m.*, papa, dad

papel, *m.*, paper

paquete, *m.*, package

par, *m.*, pair, couple

para, for, in order to; para que, in order that; ¿para qué?, why?, for what purpose?; estar para + *inf.*, to be about to

paraguas, *m.*, umbrella

parar, to stop; pararse, to stop (oneself)

pardo, -a, brown

parecer (zc), to seem, to appear

pared, *f.*, wall

paréntesis, *m. pl.*, parentheses

pariente, -a, relative

parque, *m.*, park

párrafo, *m.*, paragraph

parte, *f.*, part; la mayor parte de, most of, the majority of; por (en) todas partes, everywhere; **tomar parte (en)**, to take part (in)

particular: **la casa particular**, private house

partido, *m.*, game, -party (political)

partir, to depart

pasado, -a, past; **el año (mes) pasado**, last year (month); **la semana pasada**, last week

pasajero, *m.*, passenger

pasaporte, *m.*, passport

pasar, to pass, to spend (time), to happen; **que lo pase Vd. bien**, good luck to you

pasear, to walk, to ride; **pasearse**, to take a walk

paseo, *m.*, walk, drive; **dar un paseo**, to take a walk; **dar un paseo en coche**, to take an automobile ride

paso, *m.*, step, pace, passage

pastel, *m.*, pie, cake

pastelero, *m.*, pastry baker

patata, *f.*, potato

patinar, to skate

patio, *m.*, courtyard, patio

pato, *m.*, duck

patria, *f.*, (native) country, fatherland

patriota, *m.* or *f.*, patriot

patrón: **santo patrón**, patron saint

pavo, *m.*, turkey

paz, *f.*, peace

pecho, *m.*, chest

pedazo, *m.*, piece

pedir (i), to ask for, to request; **pedir prestado, -a**, to borrow

pegar (gu), to stick, to beat

peinarse, to comb one's hair

película, *f.*, film, movie

peligro, *m.*, danger

peligroso, -a, dangerous

pelo, *m.*, hair

pelota, *f.*, ball

peluquería, *f.*, beauty parlor, barber shop

peluquero, *m.*, hairdresser, barber

península, *f.*, peninsula

pensamiento, *m.*, thought

pensar (ie), to think, to intend to; **pensar de**, to think of (have an opinion about); **pensar en**, to think of (direct one's thoughts to)

pensión, *f.*, pension

peor, worse, worst

pequeño, -a, small

pera, *f.*, pear

peral, *m.*, pear tree

perder (ie), to lose; **perderse**, to get lost

perdonar, to pardon, to forgive

perezoso, -a, lazy

perfectamente, perfectly

perfecto, -a, perfect

perfume, *m.*, perfume

periódico, *m.*, newspaper

periodista, *m.*, journalist, newspaperman

período, *m.*, period

permanecer (zc), to remain

permiso, *m.*, permission

permitir, to permit

pero, but

perro, *m.*, dog

perseguir (i, g), to pursue, to persecute

persona, *f.*, person

personaje, *m.*, character (in a play, novel)

pertenecer (zc), to belong

peruano, -a, Peruvian

pesado, -a, heavy

pesar, to weigh; **a pesar de**, in spite of

pescado, *m.*, fish

pescador, *m.*, fisherman

pescar (qu), to fish

peseta, *f.*, peseta (monetary unit of Spain)

peso, *m.*, peso (monetary unit of several Spanish-American countries)

petróleo, *m.*, petroleum

picador, *m.*, picador (bullfighter mounted on horseback, carrying a long spear)

picaresco, -a, picaresque, roguish

pícaro, -a, roguish, rogue, rascal

pico, *m.*, peak

pie, *m.*, foot; **a pie**, on foot; **de pie**, standing

piedra, *f.*, stone

piel, *f.*, fur, hide

pierna, *f.*, leg

piloto, *m.*, pilot

pimienta, *f.*, (black) pepper

pintar, to paint

pintor, *m.*, painter

pintoresco, -a, picturesque

pintura, *f.*, painting

piña, *f.*, pineapple

pirámide, *f.*, pyramid

piso, *m.*, floor, story, apartment; **el piso bajo**, ground floor

pizarra, *f.*, blackboard

placer, *m.*, pleasure

plan, *m.*, plan

planta, *f.*, plant

plata, *f.*, silver

plato, *m.*, plate, dish

playa, *f.*, beach, seashore

plaza, *f.*, square, plaza; **la plaza de toros**, bullring

plomero, *m.*, plumber

pluma, *f.*, pen

población, *f.*, population, town

pobre, poor

poco, -a, little; **poco a poco**, little by little; **dentro de poco**, in a little while; **un**

poco (de), a little bit (of); **pocos, -as**, few

poder (ue), to be able, can; *m.*, power

poderoso, -a, powerful

poema épico, *m.*, epic poem

poesía, *f.*, poem, poetry

poeta, *m.*, poet

poetisa, *f.*, poetess

policía, *f.*, police; *m.*, policeman

político, -a, political, politician; *f.*, policy, politics

polvo, *m.*, dust; **hay polvo**, it is dusty

pollo, *m.*, chicken

poner (g), to put, to set; **poner la mesa**, to set the table; **poner un telegrama**, to send a telegram; **ponerse**, to put on (clothing); **ponerse** + *adj.*, to become (involuntarily); **ponerse a**, to begin to; **ponerse en camino**, to start out, to set out; **el sol se pone**, the sun sets

por, for, by, through, "times"; **por consiguiente**, therefore, consequently; **por eso**, therefore; **por favor**, please; **por fin**, finally; **por la mañana**, in the morning; **por la tarde**, in the afternoon; **por la noche**, in the evening; **por lo general**, generally, in general; **por lo menos**, at least; **por lo visto**, apparently; **por supuesto**, of course; **por todas partes**, everywhere; **estar por** + *inf.*, to be in favor of

pordiosero, *m.*, beggar

porque, because

¿por qué?, why?

portorriqueño, -a, puertorriqueño, -a, Puerto Rican

portugués, portuguesa, Portuguese; **portugués**, *m.*, Portuguese (language)

poseer, to possess

posesión, *f.*, possession

posible, possible; **lo más pronto posible**, as soon as possible

postre(s), *m.*, dessert

preceder, to precede

precio, *m.*, price

precioso, -a, precious

preciso, -a, necessary; **es preciso**, it is necessary

preferible, preferable

preferir (ie, i), to prefer

pregunta, *f.*, question; **hacer (g) una pregunta**, to ask a question

preguntar, to ask

premio, *m.*, prize, reward; **el premio gordo**, grand prize

prenda de vestir, *f.*, article of clothing, garment

preparar, to prepare; **prepararse a**, to get ready to

presentar, to present, to introduce; **presentarse**, to appear, to present oneself

presente, present

prestar, to lend; **pedir prestado, -a**, to borrow; **prestar atención**, to pay attention

primavera, *f.*, spring (season)

primero, -a (primer), first

primo, -a, cousin

princesa, *f.*, princess

principal, main, principal

príncipe, *m.*, prince

principiar, to begin

principio, *m.*, beginning

prisa, *f.*, haste; **tener (ie, g) prisa**, to be in a hurry

probar (ue), to prove, to try, to test

problema, *m.*, problem

producir (zc), to produce

producto, *m.*, product

profesión, *f.*, profession

profesor, -a, teacher

profundo, -a, deep, profound

programa, *m.*, program

prohibir, to prohibit, to forbid

promesa, *f.*, promise

prometer, to promise

pronombre, *m.*, pronoun

pronto, soon; **de pronto**, suddenly; **lo más pronto posible**, as soon as possible; **tan pronto como**, as soon as

pronunciación, *f.*, pronunciation

pronunciar, to pronounce

propietario, *m.*, proprietor

propina, *f.*, tip

propio, -a, proper, own

prosa, *f.*, prose

proteger (j), to protect

proverbio, *m.*, proverb

provincia, *f.*, province

próximo, -a, next

prueba, *f.*, test, proof

público, -a, public; *m.*,' public

pueblo, *m.*, town, people

puente, *m.*, bridge

puerta, *f.*, door

puerto, *m.*, port

pues, then, well

puesta: **la puesta del sol**, sunset

puesto, -a, placed, put; *m.*, position, post, stand; **puesto que**, since

punto, *m.*, point, dot; **en punto**, exactly, on the dot; **estar a punto de** + *inf.*, to be about to

pupitre, *m.*, (pupil's) desk

puro, -a, pure

que, who, whom, which, that, than

¿qué?, what?; **¡qué . . . !**, what a . . . !; **¿Qué hora**

es?, What time is it?; ¿Qué tiempo hace?, How is the weather?; ¿a qué hora?, at what time?; no hay de qué, you're welcome, don't mention it

quebrar (ie), to break

quedar(se), to remain; quedarle una cosa a alguien, to have something left, to remain to someone

quejarse (de), to complain (about)

querer (ie), to want, to wish, to love; querer decir, to mean

queso, m., cheese

quien, who, whom; ¿quién?, ¿quiénes?, who?, whom?; ¿a quién?, whom?; ¿de quién?, whose?

quienquiera, whoever

quince, fifteen; quince días, two weeks, a fortnight

quinientos, -as, five hundred

quinto, -a, fifth

quitar, to take away; quitarse, to take off (clothing)

radio, m. or f., radio (generally f. in Spain; m. in Spanish America)

rama, f., branch

rápidamente, rapidly

rápido, -a, rapid

raro, -a, rare; raras veces, seldom, rarely

rascacielos, m., skyscraper

rato, m., (little) while

ratón, m., mouse

rayón, m., rayon

raza, f., race (of people)

razón, f., reason; tener (ie, g) razón, to be right; no tener razón, to be wrong

real, royal, real

realizar (c), to fulfill, to realize (a profit)

rebelión, f., rebellion

recibir, to receive

recientemente, recently

recoger (j), to gather, to pick up

reconocer (zc), to recognize, to acknowledge

reconquista, f., reconquest

recordar (ue), to remember

recuerdo, m., remembrance, souvenir; pl., regards, memories

redondo, -a, round

reducir (zc), to reduce

refresco, m., refreshment

refrigerador, m., refrigerator

regalar, to give (as a gift)

regalo, m., gift, present

región, f., region

regla, f., rule, ruler

regresar, to return

reina, f., queen

reinar, to reign, to rule

reír (í), to laugh; reírse de, to laugh at

relámpago, m., lightning

religión, f., religion

religioso, -a, religious

reloj, m., watch, clock

relojero, m., watchmaker

remedio, m., remedy, cure

repente: de repente, suddenly, all of a sudden

repetir (i), to repeat

representación, f., performance

representante, m., representative

representar, to represent

república, f., republic

resfriado, m., cold (illness)

resistir, to resist

respetar, to respect

respirar, to breathe

responder, to answer, to respond

respuesta, f., reply, answer

restaurante, m., restaurant

resultado, m., result

resultar, to result

resumen, m., summary

retirarse, to withdraw

retrato, m., portrait

reunión, f., meeting

reunir (ú), to gather, to bring together; reunirse, to meet, to assemble

revista, f., magazine

revolución, f., revolution

rey, m., king

rezar (c), to pray

rico, -a, rich

rincón, m., corner

río, m., river

riqueza, f., wealth, riches

risa, f., laughter

rival, m., rival

robar, to steal

roca, f., rock

rodear, to surround

rogar (ue, gu), to beg, to request

rojo, -a, red

romper, to break, to tear

ropa, f., clothes, clothing

ropero, m., closet

rosa, f., rose

rosbif, m., roast beef

rostro, m., face

roto, -a, broken

rubio, -a, blond

ruido, m., noise

ruina, f., ruin

Rusia, f., Russia

ruta, f., route

sábado, m., Saturday

saber (sé), to know, to know how (to)

sabio, -a, wise, wise man

sacapuntas, m., pencil sharpener

sacar (qu), to take out

sacerdote, m., priest

saco, m., sack, bag

sal, f., salt

sala, f., living room, hall, parlor

salida, f., exit, departure

salir (g) (de), to leave, to go out (of); salir bien (mal), to pass (fail) (an examination); el sol sale, the sun rises

saltar, to jump, to leap

salud, f., health

saludar, to greet, to salute

salvar, to save, to rescue

sandía, f., watermelon

sangre, f., blood

Santo, -a (San), Saint, St.; el santo patrón, patron saint

sarape, m., serape (Mexican blanket)

sastre, m., tailor

sastrería, f., tailor shop

sátira, f., satire

satisfecho, -a, satisfied

se, to him, to her, to you, to them, himself, herself, yourselves, themselves

seco, -a, dry

secretario, -a, secretary

sed, f., thirst; tener (ie, g) sed, to be thirsty

seda, f., silk

seguida: en seguida, immediately, at once

seguir (i, g), to follow, to continue

según, according to

segundo, -a, second

seguramente, surely

seguro, -a, secure, sure, safe

seis, six

seiscientos, -as, six hundred

selva, f., jungle

sello, m., seal, stamp

semana, f., week; la semana pasada, last week; la semana que viene, next week; hace una semana + preterite, a week ago

semejante, similar, alike

senador, m., senator

sencillo, -a, simple

sentado, -a, seated

sentarse (ie), to sit down

sentido, m., meaning, sense

sentimiento, m., sentiment

sentir (ie, i), to regret, to feel; sentirse, to feel

señal, f., signal

señalar, to point out

señor (Sr.), m., master, gentleman, Mr., sir

señora (Sra.), f., lady, madam, Mrs.

señorita (Srta.), f., young lady, Miss

separar, to separate; separarse (de), to withdraw (from)

septiembre, m., September

ser, to be

sereno, m., night watchman

serio, -a, serious; en serio, seriously

servicio, m., service

servilleta, f., napkin

servir (i), to serve; servir para, to be useful for; servirse de, to use, to make use of

sesenta, sixty

setecientos, -as, seven hundred

setenta, seventy

sexto, -a, sixth

si, if

sí, yes, himself, herself, yourself, themselves

siempre, always

sierra, f., mountain range

siesta, f., siesta, afternoon nap

siete, seven

siglo, m., century; el Siglo de Oro, Golden Age

significar (qu), to mean

siguiente, following; el (al) día siguiente, (on) the following day

silencio, m., silence

silenciosamente, silently

silla, f., chair

sillón, m., armchair

simpático, -a, nice, pleasant

sin, without; sin duda, no doubt, doubtless; sin embargo, nevertheless, however

sincero, -a, sincere

sino, but, except

sinónimo, -a, synonymous; m., synonym

sistema, m., system

sitio, m., place, site

situación, f., situation, place

situado, -a, situated

situar (ú), to place, to locate

sobre, m., envelope

sobre, on, upon; sobre todo, especially, above all

sobretodo, m., overcoat

sobrino, m., nephew; sobrina, f., niece

sociedad, f., society

sofá, m., sofa

sol, m., sun; hace (hay) sol, it is sunny; el sol sale (se pone), the sun rises (sets); la puesta del sol, sunset

solamente, only

soldado, m., soldier

soler (ue), to be in the habit of, to be accustomed to

solo, -a, alone

sólo, only

soltar (ue), to loosen, to let go of

sombra, f., shade, shadow

sombrero, m., hat

sombrerero, m., hat seller

sonar (ue), to sound

sonreír (í), to smile

soñar (ue), to dream; soñar con, to dream of

sopa, f., soup

sorprender, to surprise; sorprenderse, to be surprised

sótano, m., cellar, basement

su, sus, his, her, your, their, its

subir, to go up, to ascend, to climb; subir a, to get into (a vehicle)

subjuntivo, m., subjunctive

subrayar, to underline

subterráneo, m., subway

suceder, to happen

suceso, m., event, occurrence

sucio, -a, dirty

Sud América (Sudamérica), f., South America

sudamericano, -a, South American

sudeste, m., southeast

sudoeste, m., southwest

suegro, m., father-in-law; suegra, f., mother-in-law

suelo, m., floor, ground, soil

sueño, m., sleep, dream; tener (ie, g) sueño, to be sleepy

suerte, f., luck; tener (ie, g) suerte, to be lucky

suéter, m., sweater

suficiente, enough, sufficient

sufrir, to suffer, to undergo

sujeto, m., subject

supermercado, m., supermarket

suplicar (qu), to beg, to implore

supuesto: por supuesto, of course

sur, m., south; la América del Sur, South America

sustantivo, m., noun

suyo, -a, his, hers, yours, theirs

tabaco, m., tobacco

tal, such (a); tal vez, perhaps

talento, m., talent

también, also

tampoco, neither; ni yo tampoco, neither do I, nor I either

tan, so; tan + adj. or adv. + como, as . . . as

tanque, m., tank

tanto, -a, so much; tanto (-a, -os, -as) + noun + como, as much (many) . . . as; cuanto más . . . tanto más, the more . . . the more

taquígrafo, -a, stenographer

tardar (en), to delay (in)

tarde, late; f., afternoon; de la tarde, in the afternoon, P.M.; por la tarde, in (during) the afternoon; hacerse tarde, to be getting late; más tarde, later; todas las tardes, every afternoon

tarea, f., task, chore

tarjeta, f., card

taxímetro, taxi, m., taxi

taza, f., cup

te, you, to you, yourself

té, m., tea

teatro, m., theater

techo, m., ceiling, roof

teléfono, m., telephone; la guía de teléfonos, telephone directory

telegrama, m., telegram; poner (g) un telegrama, to send a telegram

televisión, f., television

temblar (ie), to tremble

temer, to fear

temor, m., fear

templo, m., temple

temprano, early

tenedor, m., fork

tener (ie, g), to have; tener . . . años, to be . . . years old; tener calor (frío), to be warm (cold); tener cuidado, to be careful; tener dolor de cabeza (estómago, muelas), to have a headache (stomachache, toothache); tener dolor de garganta, to have a sore throat; tener hambre (sed), to be hungry (thirsty); tener lugar, to take place; tener miedo, to be afraid; tener mucho gusto en + inf., to be very glad to; tener prisa, to be in a hurry; tener que + inf., to have to; tener razón, to be right; no tener razón, to be wrong; tener sueño, to be sleepy; no tener nada que hacer, to have nothing to do; tenga Vd. la bondad de + inf., please; ¿Qué tiene Vd.?, What's the matter with you?; tiene las manos frías (los ojos cansados), his hands are cold (his eyes are tired)

tenis, m., tennis

tercero, -a (tercer), third

terminar, to finish, to end

terror, m., terror

tertulia, f., party, gathering

tesoro, m., treasure

ti, you

tiempo, m., time, weather, tense; a tiempo, on time; al mismo tiempo, at the same time; ¿cuánto tiempo?, how long?; hace buen (mal) tiempo, the weather is good (bad); mucho tiempo, a long time; ¿Qué tiempo hace?, How is the weather?

tienda, f., store

tierra, f., land, earth

tigre, m., tiger

tinta, f., ink

tintero, m., inkwell

tío, m., uncle; tía, f., aunt; los tíos, uncle and aunt, uncles

típico, -a, typical

tipo, m., type

tirar, to throw

título, m., title

tiza, f., chalk

tocadiscos, m., record player

tocador, m., dresser

tocar (qu), to touch, to play (an instrument); tocarle a alguien, to be someone's turn

todavía, still, yet; todavía no, not yet

todo, -a, all; m., everything; todos, -as, everyone; todo el día, all day; todos los, todas las, every; todo el mundo, everybody; sobre todo, especially; por todas partes, everywhere

tomar, to take, to have (food or drink); tomar parte (en), to take part (in)

tono, m., tone

tonto, -a, foolish, stupid

torero, m., bullfighter

toro, m., bull; la corrida de toros, bullfight

toronja, f., grapefruit

torre, f., tower

tortilla, f., omelet, tortilla (Mexican cornmeal pancake)

trabajador, -a, worker, hardworking

trabajar, to work

trabajo, m., work

tradicional, traditional

traducción, f., translation

traducir (zc), to translate

traer (g), to bring

tragedia, f., tragedy

traje, m., suit

tranquilo, -a, tranquil, calm

tranvía, m., streetcar

tras (de), after, behind

tratar, to treat; tratar de + inf., to try to

través: a través de, through, across

trece, thirteen

treinta, thirty

tren, m., train

tres, three

trescientos, -as, three hundred

trigo, m., wheat

triste, sad

tristeza, f., sadness; con tristeza, sadly

trono, m., throne

tropa, f., troop

tropezar (ie, c), to stumble; tropezar con, to come upon

trueno, m., thunder

tu, tus, your

tú, you

tubo, m., tube

turco, -a, Turkish

turista, m. or f., tourist

tuyo, -a, yours

u, or (used only before words beginning with o or ho)

último, -a, last

un, una, a, an, one

único, -a, only

unido, -a, united; los Estados Unidos, the United States

unión, f., union

unir(se) (a), to unite (with), to join (to)

universidad, f., university

uno, -a, one; a la una, at one o'clock

unos, -as, some, about; unos(-as) cuantos(-as), a few, several

uña, f., fingernail

usar, to use

usted (Vd.), ustedes (Vds.), you

útil, useful

uva, f., grape

vaca, f., cow

vacaciones, f. pl., vacation

vacío, -a, empty

valer (g), to be worth

valiente, brave

valle, m., valley

vano, -a, vain; en vano, in vain

vapor, m., steamship, steam

varios, -as, several

vasco, -a, Basque

vascongado, -a, Basque

vascuence, m., Basque (language)

vaso, m., glass

vecino, -a, neighbor

veinte, twenty

vencer (z), to conquer, to defeat

vendedor, m., seller, vendor

vender, to sell

venir (ie, g), to come; el año (la semana) que viene, next year (week)

ventana, f., window

ver, to see

verano, m., summer

verbo, m., verb

verdad, f., truth; ¿no es verdad? or ¿verdad?, aren't you?, isn't he?, don't they?, etc.

verdadero, -a, true, real

verde, green

vestíbulo, m., vestibule

vestido, m., dress

vestir (i), to dress; vestirse (de), to get dressed (in); la prenda de vestir, article of clothing, garment

veterano, m., veteran

vez, f., time; a veces, at

times; **a la vez,** at the same time; **alguna vez,** some time; **algunas veces,** sometimes; **de vez en cuando,** from time to time; **dos veces,** twice; **en vez de,** instead of; **esta vez,** this time; **muchas veces,** often; **otra vez,** again; **raras veces,** seldom; rarely; **tal vez,** perhaps; **una vez,** once; **varias veces,** several times

viajar, to travel

viaje, *m.,* trip; **hacer (g) un viaje,** to take a trip

viajero, *m.,* traveler

vicio, *m.,* vice

vida, *f.,* life

vidrio, *m.,* glass

viejo, -a, old

viento, *m.,* wind; **hace viento,** it is windy

viernes, *m.,* Friday

vinagre, *m.,* vinegar

vino, *m.,* wine

violeta, *f.,* violet

virgen, *f.,* virgin

virtud, *f.,* virtue

visita, *f.,* visit; **hacer (g) una visita (a),** to pay a visit (to)

visitar, to visit

vista, *f.,* sight, view; **hasta la vista,** goodbye, until I see you again

visto : por lo visto, apparently

vivir, to live

vivo, -a, alive, lively

vocabulario, *m.,* vocabulary

volar (ue), to fly

volcán, *m.,* volcano

voluntad, *f.,* will

volver (ue), to return, to go back; **volver a + *inf.,*** to . . . again

vosotros, -as, you

voz, *f.,* voice; **en voz alta (baja),** in a loud (low) voice

vuelo, *m.,* flight

vuelta, *f.,* return; **el billete de ida y vuelta,** roundtrip ticket

vuestro, -a, your

y, and

ya, already; **¡ya lo creo!,** yes indeed!, I should say so!; **ya no,** no longer

yo, I

zapatería, *f.,* shoe store

zapatero, *m.,* shoemaker, shoe dealer

zapato, *m.,* shoe

English-Spanish Vocabulary

a, an, un, una

able: to be able, poder (ue)

about, de, acerca de; **at about,** a eso de; **to be about to,** estar para + *inf.*, estar a punto de + *inf.*

accept, aceptar

accompany, acompañar

account: on account of, a causa de

ache, el dolor; **stomach ache,** el dolor de estómago

acquaintance, el conocido, la conocida

act: to act as, hacer (g) de

action, la acción

activity, la actividad

actor, el actor

address, la dirección; **to address,** dirigirse (j) a

admire, admirar

advance, avanzar (c)

advantage: to take advantage (of), aprovecharse (de)

afraid: to be afraid of, tener (ie, g) miedo de (a)

after, después de; **it is (five) after (nine),** son las (nueve) y (cinco)

afternoon, la tarde; **in the afternoon,** por la tarde; **(at three) in the afternoon,** (a las tres) de la tarde

again, otra vez, de nuevo; **to** (*verb*) **again,** volver a + *inf.*

ago, hace + *time expression* (+ que)

air: in the open air, al aire libre

Alfred, Alfredo

all, todo, -a

all right, está bien

aloud, en voz alta

Alphonse, Alfonso

already, ya

always, siempre

A.M., de la mañana

America: South America, la América del Sur, Sud América

American, americano, -a, norteamericano, -a

amorous, amoroso, -a

amuse (oneself), divertir(se) (ie, i)

and, y, e (before *i* or *hi*)

angel, el ángel

angry: to get angry, enfadarse, enojarse

animal, el animal

Anna, Ann, Ana

announce, anunciar

another, otro, -a

answer, responder, contestar

anyone: not . . . anyone, no . . . nadie

anything: not . . . anything, no . . . nada

apparently, por lo visto

apparition, el aparecido

appear, aparecer (zc)

applaud, aplaudir

apple, la manzana

approach, acercarse (qu) a

April, abril

Argentina, la Argentina

army, el ejército

around, alrededor (de)

arrival, la llegada

arrive, llegar (gu)

art, el arte, *m.* or *f.*

Arthur, Arturo

article, el artículo

artist, el (la) artista

as, como; **as** + *adj.* or *adv.* + **as,** tan + *adj.* or *adv.* + como; **as for,** en cuanto a; **as much** + *noun* + **as,** tanto(-a) + *noun* + como; **as many** + *noun* + **as,** tantos(-as) + *noun* + como; **as soon as,** en cuanto, así que, luego que, tan pronto como; **as soon as possible,** cuanto antes, lo más pronto posible

ask (for information), preguntar; **(request)** pedir (i); **to ask a question,** hacer (g) una pregunta

asleep: to fall asleep, dormirse (ue, u)

at: at about, a eso de; **at home,** en casa; **at last,** al fin, por fin; **at least,** por lo menos; **at night,** de noche; **at once,** en seguida; **at the same time,** a la vez; **at times,** a veces

attack, atacar (qu)

attend, asistir (a)

attention, la atención; **to pay attention,** prestar atención

attentively, atentamente, con atención

August, agosto

aunt, la tía

author, el autor

automobile, el automóvil, el coche; **to take an automobile ride,** dar un paseo en automóvil (coche)

autumn, el otoño

avenue, la avenida

away: to take away, quitar; **to go away,** irse, marcharse

bad, malo, -a (mal); **the bad,** lo malo

badly, mal

baker, el panadero

bakery, la panadería

ball, la pelota

baseball, el béisbol

battle, la batalla

be, estar, ser; **to be able,** poder (ue); **to be about to,** estar para + *inf.*, estar a punto de + *inf.*; **to be afraid to (of),** tener (ie, g) miedo de (a); **to be born,** nacer (zc); **to be careful,** tener cuidado; **to be cold (weather),** hacer (g) frío; **to be cool (weather),** hacer fresco; **to be concerned with,** ocuparse de; **to be dusty,** haber polvo; **to be frightened,** asustarse; **to be glad,** alegrarse; **to be glad to,** tener gusto en + *inf.*, alegrarse de + *inf.*; **to be good (bad) weather,** hacer buen (mal) tiempo; **to be hungry,** tener hambre; **to be in a hurry,** tener prisa; **to be in favor of,** estar por + *inf.*; **to be mistaken,** equivocarse (qu); **to be muddy,** haber lodo; **to be one's turn,** tocarle (qu) a uno; **to be right,** tener razón; **to be silent,** callarse; **to be sleepy,** tener sueño; **to be sorry,** sentir (ie, i); **to be standing,** estar de pie; **to be successful,** tener éxito; **to be sunny,** haber (hacer) sol; **to be thirsty,** tener sed; **to be to (to be supposed to),** haber de + *inf.*; **to be warm (personal),** tener calor; **(weather),** hacer calor; **to be windy,** hacer viento; **to be worth,** valer (g); **to be wrong,** no tener razón; **to be . . . years old,** tener (cumplir) . . . años

bear: to bear, llevar

beautiful, hermoso, -a, bello, -a

beauty parlor, la peluquería

because, porque; **because of,** a causa de

become, llegar (gu) a ser, hacerse (g); **(involuntarily),** ponerse (g)

bed: to go to bed, acostarse (ue)

before, antes de, antes (de) que

beg, rogar (ue, gu), suplicar (qu)

begin, comenzar (ie, c), empezar (ie, c), principiar, echarse a + *inf.*

behind, detrás (de)

believe, creer

belong, pertenecer (zc)

beside, al lado de, junto a

best, el (la) mejor

better, mejor

between, entre

big, grande

bill, la cuenta

birth, el nacimiento

birthday, el cumpleaños

blackboard, la pizarra

blouse, la blusa

book, el libro; **Spanish book,** el libro de español

born: to be born, nacer (zc)

borrow, pedir (i) prestado, -a

both, los (las) dos, ambos, -as

box, la caja; **candy box,** la caja para dulces; **iron box,** la caja de hierro

boy, el muchacho

brave, valiente

bread, el pan

breakfast, el desayuno

bring, traer (g)

brother, el hermano; **brother(s) and sister(s),** los hermanos

build, construir (y)

building, el edificio

business, los negocios

but, pero; *(after neg.)*, sino

butcher, el carnicero

butcher shop, la carnicería

buy, comprar

by, por, de; **by day,** de día; **by heart,** de memoria; **by no means,** de ninguna manera, de ningún modo

call, llamar

can (*to be able*), poder (ue)

Canada, el Canadá

candy, los dulces

cannot (can't), no poder (ue)

capital, la capital

captain, el capitán

capture, capturar, tomar

car, el automóvil, el coche

care, el cuidado

careful: to be careful, tener (ie, g) cuidado

carefully, con cuidado, cuidadosamente

case: in case, en caso de que

catch, coger (j)

Catholic, católico, -a

celebrate, celebrar

cent, el centavo

central, central

Central America, la América Central, Centro América

century, el siglo

certain (a certain), cierto, -a

chair, la silla
change, cambiar
chapter, el capítulo
Charles, Carlos
cheap, barato, -a
check (bill), la cuenta
chicken, el pollo; chicken salad, la ensalada de pollo
child, el niño, la niña; children, los niños, las niñas
chocolate, el chocolate
Christmas, la Navidad
church, la iglesia
city, la ciudad
civilization, la civilización
class, la clase
clean: to clean, limpiar
clearly, claramente
clock, el reloj
close, cerrar (ie)
club, el círculo, el club
coat, el abrigo
coffee, el café
cold, frío, -a; to be cold (weather), hacer (g) frío
colony, la colonia
come, venir (ie, g)
comedy, la comedia
complain (of), quejarse (de)
concerned: to be concerned with, ocuparse de
conclude, concluir (y)
conquer, conquistar, vencer (z)
conqueror, el conquistador, el vencedor
consent, el consentimiento; to consent (to), consentir (ie, i) (en)
construct, construir (y)
construction, la construcción
contents, el contenido
continue, continuar (ú), seguir (i, g)
contribute, contribuir (y)
conversation, la conversación
convince, convencer (z)
cool: to be cool (weather), hacer fresco
copy, copiar
corner, la esquina
correct: to correct, corregir (i, j)
correctly, correctamente
cost, costar (ue)
cotton, el algodón
could, poder (ue) (imperfect or preterite)
country (nation), el país; (in contrast with city), el campo
course: of course, por supuesto, desde luego
courteous, cortés
cousin, el primo, la prima
cover, cubrir
cream: ice cream, el helado
create, crear
cross, cruzar (c), atravesar (ie)
cruel, cruel
cruelty, la crueldad

cry, llorar
cup, la taza
curiosity, la curiosidad
custom, la costumbre
customs inspector, el aduanero

dairy, la lechería
dance, el baile; to dance, bailar
dangerous, peligroso, -a
dare (to), atreverse (a)
date, la fecha
daughter, la hija
day, el día; by day, de día; every day, todos los días; in the daytime, de día; on the following day, al día siguiente
dead, muerto, -a
December, diciembre
decide, decidir
declare, declarar
deed, el hecho
defend, defender (ie)
delay in, tardar en + inf.
delightful, delicioso, -a
deliver, entregar (gu)
deny, negar (ie, gu)
descend, bajar
description, la descripción
deserve, merecer (zc)
desk, el escritorio
destroy, destruir (y)
devote oneself (to), dedicarse (qu) a
diamond, el diamante
die, morir (ue, u)
different, distinto, -a, diferente
difficult, difícil
dinner, la comida
direction, la dirección
dirty, sucio, -a
disappear, desaparecer (zc)
discover, descubrir
discoverer, el descubridor
discovery, el descubrimiento
distribute, distribuir (y)
divide, dividir
do, hacer (g); to have much to do, tener (ie, g) mucho que hacer
doctor, el médico, el doctor
dog, el perro
dollar, el dólar
done, hecho, -a
door, la puerta
doubt: to doubt, dudar; no doubt, doubtless, sin duda
down: to fall down, caerse (g); to go down, bajar; to sit down, sentarse (ie); downtown, el centro
dozen, la docena
drama, el drama
dream (of), soñar (ue) con
dress, el vestido; to dress (oneself), vestir(se) (i)
drink, beber
drinker, el bebedor

drive, conducir (zc)
driver, el cochero
drop, dejar caer
during, durante
dusty: to be dusty, haber polvo

each (one), cada uno, -a
ear, la oreja
early, temprano
earn, ganar
easy, fácil
eat, comer; to eat breakfast, desayunarse; to eat lunch, almorzar (ue, c)
egg, el huevo
eight, ocho; eighteen(th), diez y ocho; eighth, octavo, -a; eight hundred, ochocientos, -as; eighty, ochenta
either (after neg.), tampoco; either . . . or (after neg.), ni . . . ni; nor I either, ni yo tampoco
elect, elegir (i, j)
eleven, once
employ, emplear
employee, el empleado, la empleada
empty, vacío, -a
end, terminar
enemy, el enemigo, la enemiga
England, Inglaterra
English, inglés, inglesa; (language), el inglés; Englishman, el inglés
enjoy, gozar (c) de; to enjoy oneself, divertirse (ie, i)
enough, bastante, suficiente
enter, entrar
erase, borrar
error, el error, la falta
especially, sobre todo
Europe, Europa
evening, la noche; in the evening, por la noche
ever, jamás; (after neg.), nunca
every, todos los, todas las
everybody, everyone, todos, -as, todo el mundo
everywhere, por todas partes
exactly, exactamente, en punto
examination, el examen, la prueba
example, el ejemplo; for example, por ejemplo
exercise, el ejercicio
exit, la salida
expect, esperar
expensive, caro, -a
explain, explicar (qu)
explorer, el explorador
explosion, la explosión
extremely, muy, -ísimo, -a
eye, el ojo

face, la cara, el rostro; to face, dar a; facing, frente a

fail, salir (g) mal (en); to fail to, dejar de + inf.
faithful, fiel
faithfully, fielmente
fall, la caída; to fall, caer (g); to fall asleep, dormirse (ue, u); to fall down, caerse (g); to fall in love with, enamorarse de
family, la familia
famous, famoso, -a, célebre
father, el padre
favor: to be in favor of, estar por + inf.
fear: to fear, temer
February, febrero
feed, dar de comer a
feel, sentirse (ie, i)
feeling, el sentimiento
few, pocos, -as; a few, unos cuantos (unas cuantas)
fiancée, la novia
fifteen(th), quince
fifth, quinto, -a
fifty, cincuenta
fight, luchar
fill, llenar
finally, al fin, por fin, finalmente
find, hallar, encontrar (ue), dar con; to find out, averiguar (ü)
fine: the weather is fine, hace buen tiempo
finish, acabar, terminar
fire, el fuego
first, primero, -a (primer)
fish, el pescado, el pez; fisherman, el pescador
fit, caber (quepo)
five, cinco; five hundred, quinientos, -as
flag, la bandera
flee, huir (y)
flight, la huida
flower, la flor; flower shop, la florería
fly, volar (ue)
follow, seguir (i, g); on the following day, al día siguiente
foot, el pie; on foot, a pie
for, para, por; as for, en cuanto a; for example, por ejemplo
forget, olvidar, olvidarse de
forty, cuarenta
founder, el fundador
four, cuatro; four hundred, cuatrocientos, -as; fourteen (th), catorce; fourth, cuarto, -a
France, Francia
frankness, la franqueza
French, francés, francesa; (language), el francés; Frenchman, el francés
frequently, frecuentemente, con frecuencia, a menudo
Friday, el viernes
friend, el amigo, la amiga

frighten, asustar, espantar; **to be frightened,** asustarse

from, de, desde; **from time to time,** de cuando en cuando de vez en cuando

front: in front of, delante de, enfrente de, frente a

fulfill, cumplir (con)

fun: to make fun of, burlarse de

furniture, los muebles

furious, furioso, -a

Galician, gallego, -a

game, el juego

garden, el jardín

general, el general; **generally,** generalmente, por lo general

generosity, la generosidad

George, Jorge

German, alemán, alemana; (*language*), el alemán

Germany, Alemania

get: to get angry, enfadarse, enojarse; **to get dressed,** vestirse (i); **to get off,** bajar de; **to get on,** subir a; **to get up,** levantarse

gift, el regalo

girl, la muchacha, la chica

give, dar

glad: to be glad (to), alegrarse (de), tener (ie, g) mucho gusto (en); **gladly,** con mucho gusto

glove, el guante

go, ir; **to go away,** irse, marcharse; **to go down (stairs),** bajar (la escalera); **to go home,** ir a casa; **to go horseback riding,** dar un paseo a caballo; **to go out,** salir (g); **to go to bed,** acostarse (ue); **to go up (stairs),** subir (la escalera)

gold, el oro

good, bueno, -a (buen); **the good,** lo bueno; **good luck to you,** que le vaya bien, que lo pase Vd. bien; **good morning,** buenos días

goodbye, adiós, hasta la vista, hasta luego; **to say goodbye (to),** despedirse (i) (de)

govern, gobernar (ie)

government, el gobierno

governor, el gobernador

graduate, graduarse (ú)

great, grande (gran); **greatest,** el (la) mayor; **greatness,** la grandeza

green, verde

ground, el suelo

guide, el guía; **to guide,** guiar (í)

guitar, la guitarra

half, medio, -a; **half past,** . . . y media

hand, la mano; **to shake hands with,** dar la mano a; **to shake hands with each other,** darse la mano

happen, ocurrir, suceder

happy, feliz, contento, -a, alegre

hard-working, trabajador, -a

hat, el sombrero; **hat store,** la sombrerería

hate, odiar

Havana, La Habana

have (possess), tener (ie, g); (*helping verb*), haber; **to have a good time,** divertirse (ie, i); **to have a headache,** tener dolor de cabeza; **to have just . . . ,** acabar de + *inf.*; **to have (something) left,** quedarle (algo) a alguien; **to have much (something) to do,** tener mucho (algo) que hacer; **to have to,** tener que + *inf.*

he, él

headache, el dolor de cabeza

hear, oír (y, g)

heart: by heart, de memoria

Helen, Elena

help, ayudar

Henry, Enrique

her: her book, su libro; **her books,** sus libros; (*prep. + her*), ella; **I see her,** la veo; **I speak to her,** le hablo

here, aquí

hero, el héroe

hers, el suyo, la suya, los suyos, las suyas; el (la, los, las) de ella; **(a friend) of hers,** (un amigo) suyo, (una amiga) suya

herself, se

high, alto, -a

him: for him, para él; **I know him,** le (lo) conozco; **I speak to him,** le hablo

his (*adj.*), su, sus; (*pron.*), el suyo, la suya, los suyos, las suyas; el (la, los, las) de él; **(a friend) of his,** (un amigo) suyo, (una amiga) suya

holiday, la fiesta

home, la casa; **at home,** en casa; **at the home of,** en casa de; **to go home,** ir a casa

hope, esperar

horse, el caballo; **on horseback,** a caballo

hotel, el hotel

hour, la hora

house, la casa; **at Charles' house,** en casa de Carlos

how?, ¿cómo?; **How is the weather?,** ¿Qué tiempo hace?; **how long?,** ¿cuánto tiempo?; **how much?,** ¿cuánto, -a?; **how many?,**

¿cuántos, -as?; **how (good it is),** lo (bueno) que (es)

however: however rich he may be, por rico que sea

humanity, la humanidad

hundred, ciento (cien)

hungry: to be (very) hungry, tener (ie, g) (mucha) hambre

hurry: to be in a hurry, tener (ie, g) prisa

husband, el esposo, el marido

I, yo

ice cream, el helado

idea, la idea

if, si

ill, enfermo, -a

illness, la enfermedad

important, importante

impossible, imposible

in, en; (*after superlative*), de; **in a loud (low) voice,** en voz alta (baja); **in order to,** para; **in order that,** para que; **in spite of,** a pesar de; **in style,** de moda; **in the daytime,** de día; **in the middle of,** en medio de; **in the morning (afternoon, evening),** por la mañana (tarde, noche); **in the open air,** al aire libre; **in this (that) way,** de este (ese) modo, de esta (esa) manera; **in vain,** en vano

information, los informes

inhabitant, el (la) habitante

innocent, inocente

insist (on), insistir (en)

instead of, en vez de, en lugar de

intelligent, inteligente

intention, la intención

interest, interesar

interesting, interesante

invitation, la invitación

invite, invitar, convidar

iron, el hierro

isn't it?, ¿no es verdad?, ¿verdad?

it: for it, para él (ella); **I see it,** lo (la) veo; **its,** su, sus

Italy, Italia

January, enero

Japan, el Japón

jewel, la joya

jewelry shop, la joyería

John, Juan; **Johnny,** Juanito

joke, el chiste

Joseph, José

judge, el juez

Julia, Julia

July, julio

June, junio

just: to have just . . . , acabar de + *inf.*

keep, guardar; **to keep on,** seguir (i, g), continuar (ú); **to keep one's promise,** cumplir la promesa; **to keep still,** callarse

kind, bondadoso, -a

king, el rey; **king and queen,** los reyes

kitchen, la cocina

knife, el cuchillo

know (a person), conocer (zc); **(a fact),** saber (sé); **(how to),** saber

knowledge, el conocimiento, los conocimientos

lady, la dama, la señora

language, la lengua, el idioma

large, grande

last: at last, al fin, por fin, finalmente; **last month,** el mes pasado; **last night,** anoche; **last week,** la semana pasada; **last year,** el año pasado

late, tarde

later, más tarde; **see you later,** hasta luego

laugh, reír (í); **to laugh at,** reírse de

lawyer, el abogado

lazy, perezoso, -a

lead, conducir (zc)

learn, aprender

least, el (la) menor; **at least,** por lo menos

leave, salir (g) (de), dejar; **to take leave (of),** despedirse (i) (de)

left: at (to) the left, a la izquierda; **to have (something) left,** quedarle (algo) a alguien

lend, prestar

less, menos

lesson, la lección

let, dejar, permitir

letter, la carta; **letter carrier,** el cartero; **to mail a letter,** echar una carta al correo

library, la biblioteca

lie, mentir (ie, i)

light, la luz

lightness, la ligereza

like (to be pleasing), gustar

listen (to), escuchar

little (size), pequeño, -a; **(quantity),** poco, -a; **little by little,** poco a poco; **a little (water),** un poco de (agua)

live, vivir

liveliness, la viveza

long, largo, -a; **a long time,** mucho tiempo; **how long?,** ¿cuánto tiempo?; **no longer,** ya no; **to be long (in),** tardar (en)

look, la mirada; **to look at,** mirar; **to look for,** buscar (qu)

lose, perder (ie)

lot: a lot, mucho

loud: in a loud voice, en voz alta

Louis, Luis

love, amar, querer (ie); to fall in love with, enamorarse de

low: in a low voice, en voz baja

luck: good luck to you, que lo pase Vd. bien, que le vaya bien

lunch, el almuerzo; to (eat) lunch, almorzar (ue)

magazine, la revista

maid, la criada

mail (a letter), echar (una carta) al correo

make, hacer (g); to make fun of, burlarse de

man, el hombre

many, muchos, -as; as many . . . as, tantos(-as) . . . como; how many?, ¿cuántos, -as?; very many, muchísimos, -as

map, el mapa

March, marzo

marry, casarse (con)

marvelous, maravilloso, -a

Mary, María

master, el amo, el dueño

masterpiece, la obra maestra

matter: no matter how rich (he may be), por rico (que sea); What's the matter with you?, ¿Qué tiene Vd.?

May, mayo

me: for me, para mí; he sees me, me ve; he speaks to me, me habla; with me, conmigo

meal, la comida

mean, significar (qu), querer (ie) decir

means: by no means, de ningún modo, de ninguna manera

meat, la carne

medicine, la medicina

meet, encontrar (ue); (for the first time), conocer (zc)

mention: don't mention it, no hay de qué, de nada

messenger, el mensajero

Mexican, mexicano, -a

Mexico, México

middle: in the middle of, en medio de

midnight, medianoche

milk, la leche

million, el millón

mine, el mío, la mía, los míos, las mías; (a friend) of mine, (un amigo) mío, (una amiga) mía

minute, el minuto

miss, echar de menos; Miss, (la) señorita, (la) Srta.

mistaken: to be mistaken, equivocarse (qu)

money, el dinero

month, el mes; a month ago, hace un mes; last month, el mes pasado; next month, el mes que viene

moonlight: it is moonlight, hay luna

more, más; the more . . . the more, cuanto(-a) más . . . tanto(-a) más

morning, la mañana; at (six) in the morning, a (las seis) de la mañana; good morning, buenos días; in the morning, por la mañana; tomorrow morning, mañana por la mañana

most, más; most of, la mayor parte de

mother, la madre

mountain, la montaña

movement, el movimiento

movie, la película; movies, el cine

much, mucho, -a; as much . . . as, tanto(-a) . . . como; how much?, ¿cuánto, -a?; so much, tanto, -a; very much, muchísimo, -a

muddy: it is muddy, hay lodo

museum, el museo

music, la música

must, deber, tener (ie, g) que + inf.; one must, hay que + inf.

my, mi, mis

name, el nombre; to be named, llamarse

Napoleon, Napoleón

nation, la nación, el país

national, nacional

near, cerca de

necessary: it is necessary, es necesario, es preciso

need, necesitar, hacer (g) falta a alguien, faltar a alguien

neighbor, el vecino, la vecina

neither . . . nor, ni . . . ni

nephew, el sobrino

never, jamás, nunca

nevertheless, sin embargo

new, nuevo, -a

news, las noticias

newspaper, el periódico, el diario

next: the next day, el (al) día siguiente; next Thursday, el jueves que viene; next to, al lado de, junto a; next week, la semana que viene

night, la noche; at night, de noche; last night, anoche; tonight, esta noche

nine, nueve; nine hundred, novecientos, -as; nineteen (th), diez y nueve; ninety, noventa; ninth, noveno, -a

no, no, ninguno, -a (ningún); no doubt, sin duda; no longer, ya no; by no means, de ningún modo, de ninguna manera; no one, nadie

noble, noble

nobility, la nobleza

nobody, nadie

noise, el ruido

nomination, el nombramiento

none, ninguno, -a

noon, mediodía; at noon, a mediodía

nor: nor I either, ni yo tampoco

North America, la América del Norte, Norte América

not, no; not yet, todavía no

nothing, nada

notice, notar

notwithstanding, no obstante

novel, la novela

November, noviembre

now, ahora; right now, ahora mismo

nowadays, hoy día

obey, obedecer (zc)

obtain, obtener (ie, g), conseguir (i, g)

occur, ocurrir

o'clock: at eight o'clock, a las ocho; it is (two) o'clock, son las (dos)

October, octubre

of, de; of course, por supuesto, desde luego

off: to take off (clothing), quitarse

offer, el ofrecimiento; to offer, ofrecer (zc)

office, la oficina

often, a menudo, muchas veces

old, viejo, -a, antiguo, -a; to be . . . years old, tener (ie, g) . . . años

older, mayor

omit, omitir

on, en, sobre; on account of, a causa de; on foot, a pie; on horseback, a caballo; on (speaking), al (hablar); on the following day, al día siguiente; on time, a tiempo; on Tuesdays, los martes; on Wednesday, el miércoles

once, una vez; at once, en seguida, inmediatamente

one, uno, -a (un); no one, nadie

only, sólo, solamente, no . . . más que

open, abierto, -a; to open, abrir; in the open air, al aire libre

operation, la operación

opportunity, la oportunidad, la ocasión

opposite, en frente de

orange, la naranja

order, mandar; in order to, para; in order that, para que

ought to, deber

our, nuestro(-a, -os, -as); ours, el nuestro, la nuestra, los nuestros, las nuestras

out: to find out, averiguar (ü); to go out, salir (g); to take out, sacar (qu)

outdoors, al aire libre

overtake, alcanzar (c)

pack: to pack one's trunk, hacer (g) el baúl

package, el paquete

page, la página

painting, la pintura

pair, el par

paper, el papel

paragraph, el párrafo

parents, los padres

park, el parque

party, la fiesta, la tertulia

pass, salir (g) bien (en)

past: half past, y media

pastry shop, la pastelería

patience, la paciencia

patiently, con paciencia, pacientemente

Paul, Pablo

pay, pagar (gu); to pay a visit (to), hacer (g) una visita (a); to pay attention (to), prestar atención (a)

pen, la pluma

pencil, el lápiz

people, la gente, las personas

perfect, perfecto, -a

perhaps, tal vez, acaso

person, la persona

Peru, el Perú

Philip, Felipe

piano, el piano

pick up, recoger (j)

picture, el cuadro, la fotografía

pie, el pastel

place, colocar (qu), poner (g)

plan, el plan, el proyecto

plate, el plato

play (a game), jugar (ue, gu); (an instrument), tocar (qu)

pleasant, agradable

please, por favor; haga Vd. el favor de + inf.; tenga Vd. la bondad de + inf.

P.M., de la tarde, de la noche

poet, el poeta

polite, cortés

politely, con cortesía, cortésmente

poor, pobre

popular, popular

port, el puerto

possible, posible; as soon as possible, cuanto antes

potato, la patata, la papa

pound, la libra

poverty, la pobreza

powerful, poderoso, -a

praise, alabar

precious, precioso, -a

prefer, preferir (ie, i)

prepare, preparar

president, el presidente

pretty, bonito, -a, lindo, -a

price, el precio

priest, el cura, el sacerdote

principal (adj.), principal

probable, probable

probably, probablemente (or use future or conditional)

produce, producir (zc)

program, el programa

promise, la promesa; to promise, prometer

pronounce, pronunciar

prosperity, la prosperidad

prove, probar (ue)

punish, castigar (gu)

pupil, el alumno, la alumna, el (la) estudiante

purity, la pureza

put, colocar (qu), poner (g); to put on (clothing), ponerse

quarter, el cuarto

queen, la reina; king and queen, los reyes

question, la pregunta; to ask a question, hacer (g) una pregunta

quickly, rápidamente

radio, el radio, la radio

rain, la lluvia; to rain, llover (ue)

raise, levantar, alzar (c)

rapidly, rápidamente

rarely, raras veces, raramente

reach, alcanzar (c), llegar (gu) a

read, leer

reality, la realidad

receive, recibir

recognize, reconocer (zc)

refuse to, negarse (ie, gu) a

regret, sentir (ie, i)

relate, contar (ue)

remain, quedarse

remember, recordar (ue), acordarse (ue) de

repeat, repetir (i)

reply, la respuesta

respect, respetar

restaurant, el restaurante

return, la vuelta; to return (to come back), volver (ue), regresar; (to give back), devolver (ue)

rich, rico, -a

right, derecho, -a; all right, está bien; at (to) the right, a la derecha; to be right, tener razón; right now, ahora mismo

ring, el anillo

rise: the sun rises, el sol sale

river, el río

road, el camino

roast, el asado

Robert, Roberto

rocky, rocoso, -a

room, el cuarto, la habitación

rose, la rosa; Rose, Rosa

round-trip ticket, el billete de ida y vuelta

row, la fila

ruler, la regla

run, correr

sad, triste

sadness, la tristeza

said, dicho, -a

sailor, el marinero

Saint, Santo, -a (San)

salad: chicken salad, la ensalada de pollo

same, mismo, -a; at the same time, a la vez, al mismo tiempo

Saturday, el sábado

save, salvar

say, decir (i, g); I should say so!, ¡Ya lo creo!; that is to say, es decir; to say goodbye (to), despedirse (i) (de); to say good morning (good night) (to), dar los buenos días (las buenas noches) (a)

school, la escuela

season, la estación

seat, el asiento

seated, sentado, -a

second, segundo, -a

see, ver; he sees me, me ve; see you again, hasta la vista; see you later, hasta luego

seem, parecer (zc)

seize, coger (j)

sell, vender

send, enviar (í), mandar

September, septiembre

serious, serio, -a, grave

serve, servir (i)

set, poner (g); the sun sets, el sol se pone; to set out, ponerse en camino; to set the table, poner la mesa

seven, siete; seven hundred, setecientos, -as; seventeen (th), diez y siete; seventh, séptimo, -a; seventy, setenta

several, varios, -as; several times, varias veces

shake hands (with), dar la mano (a); to shake hands (with each other), darse la mano

sharp (hour), en punto

sharpness, la agudeza

she, ella

shirt, la camisa

shoe, el zapato; shoemaker, el zapatero; shoe store, la zapatería

short, corto, -a, breve

shortly, dentro de poco

should: I should say so!, ¡Ya lo creo!

shout, gritar

show, mostrar (ue), enseñar

sick, enfermo, -a

silent, silencioso, -a; to be silent, callarse

silk, la seda

sing, cantar

sister, la hermana

sit down, sentarse (ie)

six, seis; six hundred, seiscientos, -as; sixteen(th), diez y seis; sixth, sexto, -a; sixty, sesenta

sleep, dormir (ue); to be sleepy, tener (ie, g) sueño

slowly, lentamente, despacio

small, pequeño, -a

smell, oler (hue)

smile, sonreír (í)

smoke, fumar

snow, la nieve; to snow, nevar (ie); snowfall, la nevada

so, tan; so much, tanto, -a; so that, para que; I think so, creo que sí

society, la sociedad

sofa, el sofá

soldier, el soldado

some, alguno, -a (algún); some day, algún día

someone, alguien

something, algo

sometimes, algunas veces

son, el hijo

song, la canción

soon, pronto; as soon as, así que, luego que, en cuanto, tan pronto como; as soon as possible, cuanto antes, lo más pronto posible

sorry: to be sorry, sentir (ie, i)

soup, la sopa; tomato soup, la sopa de tomates

South America, la América del Sur, Sud América

Spain, España

Spaniard, el español, la española

Spanish, español, española; (language), el español

speak, hablar

speaker, el hablador

spend (money), gastar; (time), pasar

spite: in spite of, a pesar de

spring, la primavera

stairs, la escalera

standing, de pie

state: the United States, los Estados Unidos

station, la estación

stay, quedarse

stew, el cocido

still: to keep still, callarse

stomach ache, el dolor de estómago

stop, la parada; to stop, cesar de + inf.; to stop (oneself), detenerse (ie, g), pararse

store, la tienda

story, el cuento, la historia

street, la calle; streetcar, el tranvía

strike (the hour), dar (la hora)

strong, fuerte

student, el alumno, la alumna

studious, aplicado, -a

study, estudiar

stupid, estúpido, -a

style, la moda; in style, de moda

substitute, sustituir (y)

succeed (in), lograr + inf., conseguir (i, g)

successful: to be successful, tener (ie, g) éxito

such (a), tal

suddenly, de pronto, de repente

suffer, sufrir

suit, el traje

summer, el verano

sun, el sol; the sun rises (sets), el sol sale (se pone)

Sunday, el domingo

sunny: it is sunny, hace sol, hay sol

sweet, dulce

swim, nadar

table, la mesa

tailor, el sastre

take, tomar, llevar; to take a trip, hacer (g) un viaje; to take a walk, dar un paseo; to take advantage (of), aprovecharse (de); to take an automobile ride, dar un paseo en coche; to take away, quitar; to take leave (of), despedirse (i) (de); to take off (clothing), quitarse; to take out, sacar (qu)

talk, hablar

tall, alto, -a

tea, el té

teach, enseñar

teacher, el profesor, la profesora, el maestro, la maestra

television, la televisión

tell, decir (i, g)

ten, diez; tenth, décimo, -a

test, el examen

than, que, de

thank, dar las gracias (a); to thank for, agradecer (zc); thanks, gracias

that (adj.), ese, esa, aquel, aquella; that (one) (pron.), ése, ésa, eso, aquél, aquélla, aquello; that is to say, es decir; (the book) that (I bought), (el libro) que (compré)

the, el, la, los, las

theater, el teatro

their, su, sus

theirs, el suyo, la suya, los suyos, las suyas, el (la, los, las) de ellos, -as; (a friend) of theirs, (un amigo) suyo, (una amiga) suya

them: for them, para ellos, -as; I know them, los (las) conozco; I speak to them, les hablo

then, entonces

there, allí; there is (are), hay; there was (were), había

therefore, por eso, por consiguiente

these (adj.), estos, -as; (pron.), éstos, -as

they, ellos, -as

thief, el ladrón

thin, delgado, -a, flaco, -a

thing, la cosa

think, pensar (ie), creer; to think of (direct one's thoughts to), pensar en; (have an opinion about), pensar de; I think so, creo que sí; I think not, creo que no

thinker, el pensador

third, tercero, -a (tercer)

thirsty: to be thirsty, tener (ie, g) sed

thirteen(th), trece

thirty, treinta

this (adj.), este, esta; this (one) (pron.), éste, ésta, esto

Thomas, Tomás

those (adj.), esos, -as, aquellos, -as; (pron.), ésos, -as, aquéllos, -as

thought, el pensamiento

thousand, mil

three, tres; three hundred, trescientos, -as

through, por

throw, echar, arrojar, lanzar (c), tirar

Thursday, el jueves

ticket, el billete, el boleto; round-trip ticket, billete de ida y vuelta

time, el tiempo; (hour), la hora; (in a series), la vez; a long time, mucho tiempo; at the same time, a la vez, al mismo tiempo; at times, a veces; at what time?, ¿a qué hora?; from time to

time, de vez en cuando, de cuando en cuando; to have a good time, divertirse (ie, i); on time, a tiempo; several times, varias veces; What time is it?, ¿Qué hora es?

tip, la propina

tired, cansado, -a

to, a, hasta

today, hoy

together, juntos, -as

tomato, el tomate; tomato soup, la sopa de tomates

tomorrow, mañana; tomorrow morning, mañana por la mañana

tonight, esta noche

touch, tocar (qu)

toward(s), hacia

town, el pueblo

toy, el juguete

train, el tren

translate, traducir (zc)

travel, viajar

traveler, el viajero

treasurer, el tesorero

tree, el árbol

trip, el viaje; round-trip ticket, el billete de ida y vuelta; to take a trip, hacer (g) un viaje

trunk, el baúl; to pack one's trunk, hacer (g) el baúl

true: it is true, es verdad

truth, la verdad

try to, tratar de + inf.

Tuesday, el martes

turn, volver (ue); to be one's turn, tocarle (qu) a alguien

twelve (twelfth), doce

twenty (twentieth), veinte

twice, dos veces

two, dos; two hundred, doscientos, -as; two weeks, quince días

umbrella, el paraguas

uncle, el tío

understand, entender (ie), comprender

understanding, el entendimiento

United States (the), los Estados Unidos

unity, la unidad

university, la universidad

unless, a menos que

until, hasta, hasta que

unwillingly, de mala gana

up: to get up, levantarse

upon: upon reading, al leer

upstairs: to go upstairs, subir la escalera

Uruguay, el Uruguay

us: for us, para nosotros; he sees us, nos ve; he speaks to us, nos habla

use, usar, emplear, servirse (i) de

useful, útil

usually, generalmente por lo, general

vacation, las vacaciones

vain: in vain, en vano

vanilla, la vainilla

vegetable, la legumbre

very, muy, -ísimo, -a; very much, muchísimo, -a; it is very warm, hace mucho calor

violin, el violín

visit, visitar; to pay a visit, hacer (g) una visita

voice, la voz; in a loud (low) voice, en voz alta (baja)

volume, el tomo

wait (for), esperar, aguardar

waiter, el mozo

wake up, despertarse (ie)

walk, andar, caminar; to take a walk, dar un paseo

want, querer (ie), desear

war, la guerra

warm: it is warm (weather), hace calor

warrior, el guerrero

wash, lavar; to wash oneself, lavarse

watch, el reloj; to watch, mirar; watchmaker's shop, la relojería

water, el agua (f.)

way, el modo, la manera; in this way, de este modo, de esta manera; in that way, de ese modo, de esa manera

we, nosotros, -as

weak, débil

wealth, la riqueza

weather, el tiempo; How is the weather?, ¿Qué tiempo hace?; the weather is good (fine), hace buen tiempo; the weather is bad, hace mal tiempo

Wednesday, el miércoles

week, la semana, ocho días; every week, todas las semanas, cada semana; last week, la semana pasada; next week, la semana que viene; two weeks, quince días

welcome: you're welcome, no hay de qué, de nada

well, bien

what, lo que; what?, ¿qué?, ¿cuál?; what a . . . !, ¡qué . . . !; at what time?, ¿a qué hora?; What time is it?, ¿Qué hora es?; What's the matter with you?, ¿Qué tiene Vd.?

whatever, cualquier, cualquiera

when, cuando; when?, ¿cuándo?

where?, ¿dónde?; (to) where?, ¿a dónde?

wherever, (a)dondequiera

which, que; which? (before noun), ¿qué?; which (one)?, ¿cuál?; which (ones)?, ¿cuáles?

while, mientras (que)

who, que; who?, ¿quién?, ¿quiénes?

whoever, quienquiera

whom, que; (after prep.), quien(es); (to) whom?, ¿a quién(es)?; with whom?, ¿con quién(es)?

whose, cuyo, -a; whose?, ¿de quién(es)?

why?, ¿por qué?

wife, la esposa, la mujer

willingly, de buena gana

wind: to wind, dar cuerda (a)

window, la ventana

windy: it is windy, hace viento

wine, el vino

winter, el invierno

wish, desear, querer (ie)

with, con; with me, conmigo; with whom?, ¿con quién (es)?

without, sin, sin que

woman, la mujer

won't they?, ¿(no es) verdad?

wooden, de madera

wool, la lana

word, la palabra

work, el trabajo; to work, trabajar

worker, el trabajador, el obrero

worse, peor; worst, el (la) peor

worth: to be worth, valer (g)

wound, la herida; to wound, herir (ie, i)

wrap, envolver (ue)

write, escribir

wrong: to be wrong, no tener (ie, g) razón

year, el año; to be . . . years old, tener (ie, g) . . . años; every year, todos los años; last year, el año pasado; next year, el año que viene

yellow, amarillo, -a

yesterday, ayer

yet, todavía; not yet, todavía no

you, usted, ustedes (Vd., Vds.); tú, vosotros, -as; I know you, le (lo, la, los, las, te, os) conozco; I speak to you, le (les, te, os) hablo

young, joven

younger, menor

youngest, el (la) menor

your, su, sus, tu, tus, vuestro (-a, -os, -as)

yours, el suyo, la suya, los suyos, las suyas, el (la, los, las) de Vd. (Vds.); (a friend) of yours, (un amigo) suyo, (una amiga) suya